Sleeping WITH THE DEVIL

A SHOCKING TRUE STORY OF EROTIC DEPENDENCE, OBSESSIVE LOVE AND MURDER-FOR-HIRE

SUZANNE FINSTAD

AVON BOOKS ◆ NEW YORK

With gratitude to
W.A.J.

AVON BOOKS
A division of
The Hearst Corporation
1350 Avenue of the Americas
New York, New York 10019

Copyright © 1991 by Suzanne Finstad
Published by arrangement with William Morrow and Company, Inc.
Library of Congress Catalog Card Number: 90-22837
ISBN: 0-380-71932-0

The William Morrow and Company edition contains the following Library of Congress Cataloging in Publication Data:

Finstad, Suzanne, 1955-
    Sleeping with the devil/ by Suzanne Finstad
    p.cm.
    1. Rape—United States—Case studies. 2. Piotrowski, Barbara, 1953— . 3. Rape Victims—United States—Biography. I. Title.
HV6561.F57   1991   90-22837 CIP
364.1'532'092—dc20

First Avon Books Printing: November 1992

AVON TRADEMARK REG. U.S. PAT. OFF. AND IN OTHER COUNTRIES, MARCA REGISTRADA, HECHO EN CANADA.

Printed in Canada

UNV 10 9 8 7 6 5 4

ACKNOWLEDGMENTS

I wish to thank all those whose lives intertwined with Richard Minns and Barbra Piotrowski, and who opened their memories to me. Each provided pieces of the puzzle without which this book could not have been written.

Special thanks to Dick DeGuerin. There are others whose assistance extended beyond the ordinary, to whom I am equally grateful: Doug O'Brien; Victor Martinez; Bobby Newman; Irving and Janice Weissman; Mimi Minns Erwin; and Ken Williamson, whose dedication to solving Barbra Piotrowski's murder-for-hire is matched only by his generous spirit.

Thanks to my agent, Michael Carlisle, for trusting my instincts and helping make them a reality, and to my editor, Douglas Stumpf, my great supporter, for his grace and skill and wisdom.

I would also like to acknowledge my in-house "editors," Debbie Balise, Bruce Finstad, Elaine Finstad; and my dear friend, Lesley Ann Mullen, whose encouragement and support exceeded the bounds of friendship. My gratitude to Mark and Anita Kittridge, for the unflagging enthusiasm, and the ride to prison. Thanks also to my two honorary godmothers, Mary Smith Fay and Clara Simon Eisenman, and to Terri Diehl of the *Houston Post* library. To my friends and rescuers Elaine Lipon, Diane McGrath, and Melinda Allen, my sincere appreciation.

Finally, I wish to thank Barbra Piotrowski, now Janni Smith. Many authors have approached her over many years and she has remained silent. I salute her for her courage in talking to me. What I have conveyed on these pages is not "her" story, per se. It is, to the best of my knowledge, after more than three years of research and investigation, the truth.

v

The brain may take advice, but not the heart, and love, having no geography, knows no boundaries.

Truman Capote
Other Voices, Other Rooms

Part One

PROLOGUE

Although it was well into October, the Houston heat had not lifted after one of the most scorching summers on record. The humidity hung in the air. Without a blue norther, the summer torpor filled the city with a sense of restlessness, danger.

Barbra Piotrowski rose around five A.M. this Monday morning, as was her custom. She threw her long, honey-colored hair into a ponytail with barely a glance in the mirror. But then, Barbra was one of those fortunate women who didn't need to put any effort into looking good. When she had modeled, people used to tell her she looked like Lindsay Wagner, television's *Bionic Woman,* or Elizabeth Montgomery, the actress who played Samantha on *Bewitched.* She had pretty, delicate features with large hazel eyes and a pert nose—the kind of face Hollywood producers associate with the "girl next door"—(if the girl next door happens to be a beauty queen).

She put on her leotard and began stretching what press photographers once voted "million-dollar legs" in a beauty pageant ten years earlier. Her legs were the stuff of male fantasies: long and slender, yet curvaceous, so perfectly pro-portioned they seemed to have been sculpted by an artist's hand. A swimsuit photographer who occasionally worked with her in Los Angeles pronounced them the most incredible legs he'd ever seen. As a model, Barbra Piotrowski's nearly flawless legs were her fortune; as a competitive athlete, she considered them indispensable to life.

She planned to join a friend later in the day for a "long slow distance run"—a ten- or twelve-mile run at a relatively slow pace. Since she had taken up running three years earlier, it had become almost a religion for her. Her toned, taut body was testimony to her devotion. Racing out the door to meet her friend, late as usual, Barbra ran to her red Firebird. For the first time in many months, Barbra was feeling good about herself. Her premed classes were going well, and she was getting a lot of satisfaction out of her job as a burn nurse at Hermann Hospital, Houston's venerable institution in the famed Texas Medical Center. She was even planning to start a small business teaching aerobic dance classes.

Just as quickly, her good mood was replaced by a more familiar feeling: loneliness. *If only Richard were here, everything would be perfect,* she thought, then she immediately hated herself for thinking about him. For the past four of her twenty-seven years, Barbra had loved Richard Minns with a ferocity that sometimes frightened her. Since they broke up seven months earlier, she could not make the flame die.

Merely thinking of Richard brought tears to her eyes. Barbra tried to hold them back but couldn't. After backing out of the parking lot, she headed for a familiar location—a doughnut shop a few blocks from her apartment. Somehow the gooey, sugary doughnuts helped fill the empty space where Richard had been. That's what she needed now, she decided. A doughnut and a good cry. Then she'd take her run and be back to her old self again.

She emerged from the store with a bag containing an apple fritter and a glazed doughnut. When she returned to the car and put the key in the ignition, Barbra noticed a shadow over the steering wheel. She looked up and saw out of the corner of her eye a black man wearing a ski hat and fumbling with a brown paper bag.

Instantly Barbra ducked. Although she had never seen him before in her life, she knew he had been sent to kill her and she knew who sent him and why. In fact, she'd been waiting for him.

In the din of rush-hour traffic, few heard the four gunshots, one right after the other; gunshots everyone in the city would be talking about for months and years to come, long after that Monday afternoon in October.

Ten minutes after she purchased her apple fritter, Barbra was being wheeled into the emergency room at Hermann Hospital. She was losing blood faster than the medics could replace it. Doctors and nurses, Barbra's coworkers, stared down at her with anguished expressions. A few weeks earlier, Barbra had discussed serious injuries with them. "I wouldn't want to live if I were paralyzed," she had said flatly. "If that ever happens to me, just let me die."

Now, with four bullet wounds in her back and her spinal cord shattered, her words came back to haunt them. They wondered whether Barbra Piotrowski was going to make it through the night; if she did, there was no question she would be paralyzed for the rest of her life.

She had warned all of them this was going to happen. Until now, no one had believed her.

1

A friend of Barbra Piotrowski's once remarked that he could never quite figure her out. No one who looked like she did, he reasoned, could be that innocent.

That was the enigma of Barbra.

A photographer who had shot a good number of *Playboy* and *Penthouse* centerfolds and who had worked with Barbra Piotrowski early in her modeling career called hers the sexiest body he ever photographed. For their photo session, the photographer would meet her after she got off work. In her nurse's uniform, Barbra seemed the "virgin in white," as he put it. The two would scarcely exchange a word on the way to the shoot—Barbra was too shy for small talk. She would change into her bathing suit, pose for the camera, and a different person would emerge, one who radiated an extraordinary eroticism in front of a camera.

In truth, there was no figuring out Barbra Piotrowski. She was the most disciplined student in her class. Then, on the weekend, she'd put on a slinky gown and compete for such titles as "Miss Wahini Bikini" or "Miss Marina Del Rey." Barbra would be the first to say that she had a history of blending in, but in a lineup of golden girls, Barbra Piotrowski would be the one to remember.

Without giving a thought to food or makeup, she would devote days to helping someone. Then, under different circumstances, she would fret because someone might see her with her hair uncombed. And, for all her apparent timidity, Barbra had a tenacity that could only be described as relentless. When she set her mind to something, she would stay with it until she or it were down for the count.

* * *

Barbra's father, Wieslaw Piotrowski, was a man on whom the gods alternately smiled and spat, who had prevailed through sheer strength of character. Wieslaw relates that he came from a family of wealthy landowners in Poland. He remembers a childhood of tailored suits, live-in servants, and early morning horseback rides. In the wintertime, the Piotrowski children would bundle up in velvets and fur hand muffs and go skating. As they grew older, they were taught ballroom dancing for gala evenings at neighboring estates. However, when such evenings arrived, Wieslaw would often stand alone, mesmerized by the music of his favorite composers.

Wieslaw's mother was a strong influence on him. In an era when women were often relegated to the drawing room, Stanislawa Piotrowski (or "Stasha" as she was known) obtained her teaching certificate and a master's degree in child psychology.

While still a toddler, Wieslaw would sit at his mother's knee, his eyes wide with wonder as Stasha read to him for hours. Stasha Piotrowski was also keen at math, and she found her oldest son an eager and able student.

Wieslaw was taught a strong sense of social and moral responsibility that would stay with him throughout his life. "My parents made me understand very early that possessions have obvious advantages, but one must be prepared to handle them," he would preach in later years, in his careful, heavily accented English. "One has *obligations*."

When he was twenty, Wieslaw had to interrupt his studies at Warsaw Polytechnic for mandatory duty in the army, where he began a three-year officer's training program. A year later, in 1939, World War II broke out.

With his homeland occupied by Germany, Wieslaw was denied the opportunity to continue his education and advised to work with a shovel and pick. He joined the Polish underground. For eight months he engaged in active missions to disrupt the German communication system and preserve radio contact with London and France. Later he dynamited railroad trestles and bridges.

Many decades later, Wes would point with pride to the fact that he had been shot at less than ten times. More

important to him, he resisted the urge to kill. "When will
we learn," he would often say, "that life brings enough
hardships . . . why add to that?"

In July of 1940 Wieslaw found himself in Warsaw with
a few hours to pass before his train departed. While taking a
stroll through the city, he ran into an old school friend, who
invited him back to his house. Once there, his friend said he
feared the Nazis were after him. "I must leave," Wieslaw
said immediately, and rose from his chair. Just then there
was a knock at the door. Minutes later gestapo agents were
in the apartment. Although it was his friend they were after,
Wieslaw was taken to Pawiak political prison in Warsaw.
He never saw his schoolmate again.

The next thing he knew Wieslaw was hanging by his
wrists in chains alongside sixteen other political prisoners.
German officers kicked out the stool from beneath him.
Then they went from man to man, demanding secret information, beating those who did not answer.

While he was hanging by his wrists, Wieslaw observed
his fellow prisoners. Within ten minutes several of them
were signing anything they were offered. Some confessed
to things they never did. Within fifteen to twenty minutes
even the strongest passed out from the pain.

He considered his alternatives. *There are two key things,*
he told himself. *I have to stand up to torture and live.
And I cannot betray my friends or my country.* From his
reading and from his own experiences, he believed that
if one were brave it could not help but evoke admiration.
Besides, Wieslaw pitied men who crumbled. He resolved
to be brave.

Twenty-one days later, after continuous beatings and
interrogation, Wieslaw was released from Pawiak. Of his
brutal imprisonment he would later say: "I was proud that
I survived without betraying myself or my country. I was
battered and beaten and had kidney problems for years after.
But I survived."

August 15, 1940, the day he was released from Pawiak,
Wieslaw Piotrowski was assigned #2304 and sent to
Auschwitz. Five months later he was transferred to a con-
centration camp, where he managed to stay alive, barely, five

years. When he was liberated at the end of the war in 1945, he had lost two brothers.

What can I do to get even? was the first question his fellow prisoners asked themselves upon release from captivity.

At that moment, he would later say, Wieslaw recognized some fundamental truths about himself and the nature of revenge. "I realized that if I sought revenge I would be no better than my captors, and I made the choice not to imitate what they had done to me." Instead, he stayed in Germany for four years, then headed to the United States.

Life in the United States was a far cry from Wieslaw's privileged childhood. He found himself working in a junkyard in Lynn, Massachusetts, where he put newsprint into bailing presses for seven dollars a week. His dignity, however, remained intact. While his cronies swigged beers and went bowling, Wieslaw took the train nine miles to Boston to enroll in night school.

Within a year and a half, Wieslaw, *Wes* to his adopted countrymen, was speaking fluent English, putting in full days at the junkyard, and attending Northeastern at night, where his major was engineering. Like his mother, Wes had a brilliant mind for mathematics. He appreciated the logic and discipline of engineering. Wes strove to truly *understand* the way things worked. He was a loner and an idealist, an aristocrat in a blue-collar world.

One Saturday he chanced to attend a purely social event (a rarity for the hardworking Wes)—a picnic in Lynn—and there he met the woman with whom he would spend the rest of his life. He was thirty-two; she was twenty-two. She was from Poland and her name was Stanislawa, nicknamed Stasha, like his cherished mother.

Stasha Zielonka was short, pretty, well-rounded, and spirited. She never learned to read or write and had not attended school, but oh, she dearly loved parties and dancing. Beneath her gaiety, however, lay a will of steel, for Stasha's life had not been an easy one. Her early family life was one of crushing poverty.

Years later, Barbra, in particular, marveled at the dissimilarity between her parents' backgrounds. "When she was young my mother never had a toothbrush," she would say, shaking her head in disbelief. "Her family had a cow and when it got sick they kept the cow in the house because that was their sole source of income."

Little Stasha was the second youngest child in the family and her father's favorite. Her mother died in childbirth with Stasha's younger brother. Shortly thereafter her father remarried and his new wife was cruel to the children. So cruel, in fact, that, years later, Stasha refused to discuss with Barbra that period in her life, except to say that she constantly thought of escaping.

When the war broke out, she got her wish, in a peculiarly horrible way. One day while her father was at work, some German soldiers came to the house and kidnapped Stasha. She was taken to a camp near Hannover, Germany, to be offered to German families for hard labor. While the other children around her were crying, Stasha forced herself to be cheerful and smile. The ruse paid off. A German family selected Stasha for light domestic work and to act as a nanny to their children. She never forgot the lesson. Into adulthood, Stasha's four children saw her cry only twice.

Many years after the Holocaust, Stasha learned a long-kept secret in her family. One Christmas as she was unwrapping gifts with the family, she received a phone call. For the first time in her children's memory, she took the call in the bedroom with the door closed. "What's going on?" her four children asked each other. "Who's she talking to?"

When Stasha came out of the bedroom half an hour later, she was quiet, but said nothing about the call. It was, in fact, some time before she would discuss it with her family. Even then, she told some, but not all, of her children. The caller, she explained, was her half-brother, whom she never knew existed. He had been born to her father and stepmother after she was taken from the family by the Germans. From him Stasha learned that her mother, whom she had always believed to be Catholic, was Jewish. Before Stasha was born, her half-brother told her, the family had been persecuted and moved from town to town. When her mother died and her father remarried a Catholic woman, he decided not to tell the children about their Jewish heritage.

It was thus ironic that when peace came to Poland, a Catholic priest provided Stasha with the money to go to the United States, where an immigration clerk Americanized her name to *Stella*. She would alternate that name with her real first name in the years to come.

Stasha and Wieslaw were wed on February 24, 1952, in Lynn. Stella, forever the social creature, continued to attend parties. Wes obligingly tagged along. While she danced, he sat in a corner with his books.

On Easter Sunday, March 29, 1953, Stasha gave birth to her first child, a daughter, Barbara Isabella. The deeply religious Wes and Stella would always celebrate her birthday on Easter regardless of the date on which it fell. To hear Wes Piotrowski tell it, Barbara was special from the time she drew her first breath. Even the name he selected, Barbara Isabella, was strong, proud, regal, worthy of a princess. Wes knew Barbara would live up to her name.

Barbara was baptized in a service conducted entirely in Polish. In the tradition of the old country, she was christened Barbara Isabella Piotrowska, with her surname ending in an *a,* as do the surnames of all baby girls born in Poland—though Piotrowski was the name to be used publicly. A decade and a half later, as a teenager, she would drop the second *a* in her first name to become *Barbra,* to make space for her name on school forms.

Barbara was Wes's girl. When she was still a tiny baby, he knew instinctively that she was an intellectual soul mate. Someone in whom he could invest his dreams, impart his knowledge, instill his vision of the world.

At the first sign of a sniffle, or just a sneeze, Wes would bundle up Barbara and take her to the doctor. A mild case of colic was cause for a twenty-four-hour vigil.

"Sometimes," the pediatrician would say to Wes after one of his frequent false alarms, "I think maybe you need a doctor more than *she* does!"

Wes would just shake his head and smile. Better to get there three minutes early and be reassured—that was his motto.

Besides, he told himself and others, Barbara was no ordinary child. Even as he observed her in her crib, Wes could see that Barbara had tremendous gifts. At six months,

Barbara was speaking her first word. By eleven months she was talking in complete sentences. She also had a nearly photographic memory and a knack, her parents noticed, for saying the most unusual things.

When Barbara was a year and two months old, Wes consulted a physician about her advanced development. In addition to her impressive language skills, Barbara had a trait her father found disturbing—the ability to focus on something to the point of obsession. What should I do? he wondered. Is there anything to be concerned about?

The pediatrician looked closely at Wes's anxious countenance. "Children who develop early sometimes stabilize," he said calmly. "Don't worry about it. She'll reach a certain level and stay there." Wes went home satisfied.

Never mind that her father toiled as a toolmaker. Or that her mother worked in a shoe factory. Barbara Piotrowski was brought up like a little czarina, with books spread before her on her father's lap like so many riches. She cut her teeth on *Anne of Green Gables*, just as her father had so many years before. Wes had Barbara reading Plato by the time she was nine. When she was finished, they would discuss the moral implications of what she had read.

"You must always do the right thing, Barbara," Wes would say to her. "That's the most important thing in life. Not to do what is easiest or most convenient. To do what is *right*." Barbara would look up at him solemnly and nod, "Yes, Daddy."

The Piotrowski home was filled with classical music. Barbara would request Rimsky-Korsakov's "Scheherazade" over and over, themes from which she eventually learned to play for her father on the accordion with lessons, naturally, provided by Wes. At the early age of three, she was enrolled in dance classes. Swimming lessons came a year later.

Stella gave birth to Irena in 1955, Richard in 1957, and John in 1960. Even though Wes was a tender, loving father to all his children, nothing could rival the kinship he felt with his eldest. "Barbra and her dad," a friend of hers later remarked, "that was the deal."

In 1956, the year Barbara was three, the Piotrowskis left Massachusetts for good. The bitter winters in Lynn aggravated the arthritis condition Wes had developed in

German concentration camps. Los Angeles was the place to be, he figured. He could continue his college education in night school at the University of Southern California and he had been offered a starting position as an engineer with Gilfallen (later Gilfallen-ITT) in Los Angeles.

2

The Piotrowskis settled in a modest three-bedroom white frame house at 3969 McLaughlin Avenue in the Los Angeles suburb of Mar Vista. Although it was situated in the shadow of MGM, a mere five minutes from the beach, the neighborhood's residents were mostly hardworking laborers, many of them immigrants like the Piotrowskis. The homes in Mar Vista were boxlike, on small lots that lined long, tree-bordered streets. To be sure, the Piotrowski house was not the grand manor of Wes's youth; neither was it a home to be ashamed of for a Pole who had come to the United States with no more than the shirt on his back.

Once, when the teacher in her Catholic grammar school asked who wanted to be priests and who wanted to be nuns, Barbara raised her hand along with the boys in the class to indicate that she wanted to become a priest. The sister, who thought she was being impertinent, sent Barbara to the principal and called her father. Alarmed, Wes rushed to the school. When the sister explained what had happened, Wes shrugged it off. "Oh, ja," he said to Barbara's teacher, "it is true. But what she really wants to be is a saint."

Barbara often accompanied her father to such biblical epics as *Moses, The Ten Commandments, The Bible,* and *The Story of Ruth.* After one of the pictures she and her father saw together, she wanted to become a scientist so she could "bring back voices from the past." Her hero was Charlton Heston, star of *The Ten Commandments.*

Wes was, of course, thrilled with his daughter's view of the world. When she started school, however, the other first-graders thought she was weird. Barbara, who listened to classical music, quoted from the Bible, and studied all

14

the time to make good grades, was dubbed "The Walking Encyclopedia" by her classmates. When she saw an unpopular classmate, she took him under her wing. She would let everyone else ahead of her when the class lined up for ice cream. "Strange," she would later say of herself as a child. Although she was a pretty, delicate child, in her mind's eye she was homely, perhaps because her father placed such an emphasis on academics.

As a consequence, she was something of a loner. "I felt as if I had chosen a separate path," she would reflect in years to come. "And that I was different. But it didn't really bother me, because I knew that what I was doing was what I wanted to do."

In the second grade, when Barbara was asked to write a book report, she came home from school and talked it over with her father. "Why don't you read a dialogue by Plato and write the report on that?" Wes suggested. "Then we'll discuss it."

When Barbara brought her paper to class, the teacher sent her to the principal's office and promptly called Wes, who was fast becoming a regular at St. Gerard.

"Do you really understand this?" the nuns asked Barbara, as they held up the "offensive" book.

Barbara looked up at her father, then at her teacher, and fell into a bewildered silence.

Wes immediately launched into an eloquent defense of the writings of Plato. But it was no use. Barbara's teacher and principal denounced the book as unsuitable for a second-grader.

Wes ignored the nuns' unsolicited advice and continued to push Barbara to excel. "Hey," he would say to her when they were bent over their books, studying, "you are gifted. I expect you to do not just good work but *outstanding* work."

And Barbara delivered. By her father's standards, a *B* meant she was flawed. "Leave whatever you do better than it was before you touched it, Barbara," Wes would say to her.

At the age of six, she had decided her life's ambition. She wanted to become a doctor. On her twelfth birthday Wes gave Barbara a biography of Albert Schweitzer. Barbara lingered adoringly over its pages, reading and rereading favorite passages, placing the book in a position of honor in her room. For Barbara, Schweitzer embodied the ideal human being: He had a sharp mind for science and medicine, combined with the saintly quality of a biblical character. She resolved to get her medical degree, go to Africa and help the underprivileged. Then one day, she fantasized, she would marry a scientist and the two of them would conduct medical research together. That was her goal. And, as Wes had already observed eleven years earlier, when she was still a toddler, once Barbara had an objective she was like a dog with a bone. Nothing could wrest it away from her.

Until she was in the eighth grade, Barbara never had a girlfriend—no one with whom to giggle in her room with the door closed, share secrets, plot romantic intrigues. The few friends she did have were boys in the neighborhood, with whom she played, as she would describe, "climbing up trees and over fences, exploring the canyons, adventures of the mountains" kinds of games. To them she was the shy, tomboyish girl down the street who was always up for an adventure.

Irena, her younger sister by two years, was the popular, and, in Barbara's eyes, "normal" Piotrowski. Like most sisters, Barbara and Irena were the best of friends and the worst of enemies. They shared a bedroom in the little house on McLaughlin Avenue. And, for a time, Irena was the closest thing to a girlfriend Barbara had. Although Barbara and Irena both were blonde, pretty youngsters, the two sisters had little else in common. While Barbara was alone in their room reading, Irena filled the house with friends. She joined clubs, was elected president of her class, went out with boys.

Barbara's tastes ran more to animals than boys. Friends from her childhood remember Barbara as always keeping all sorts of animals about the house—cats, turtles, collies, bunny rabbits, Siberian huskies, birds. Always birds.

When she was six years old, Wes and Stella bought Barbara a parakeet which she called Tweety Blue. Tweety Blue was soon joined by cockatoos, cockatiels, lovebirds, finches, even an Amazon parrot. Barbara's fondest dream was to acquire a penguin. She was fascinated with their quaint tuxedo coats. "Did you know," she would ask, eyes sparkling, "that their coat is really *feathers?*"

When the Piotrowskis' small house began to resemble an aviary, Wes actually built one in the backyard. Each month there seemed to be a new addition, often orphans or cripples Barbara had rescued from certain death. Once, on a trip to the beach, she stumbled upon a crippled baby duck. Another time, she found an injured owlet in the bottom of a tree. Barbara would spend hours alone with her menagerie, teaching them unusual tricks, inventing games.

Barbara's gentleness was tempered only by a competitive streak that was, on occasion, ruthless. If someone were to tell Barbara she could not do something, she was hell-bent on proving him wrong. That quality, coupled with a certain shyness, sometimes caused others to regard her as unapproachable, even cold.

Stella Piotrowski was less taken with Barbara's individuality than Wes was. She viewed it as stubbornness, pure and simple.

"Vhat? . . ." she would say to Wes, "she some kind of a princess?"

To Barbara, Stella was the house disciplinarian, who never revealed her true emotions, who used corporal punishment rather than reason to make a point. Although they did not really clash, Barbara decided when she was very young, they had little in common. Stella had no interest in books, ideas, philosophy. She was a practical woman, rooted in reality. Barbara found this exasperating.

Still, when Barbara needed her, Stella was always there for her, as she was for everyone in the family.

Sometime in the sixth grade, Barbara developed a crush on Allen Berkema, literally the boy next door. Allen was a year older, popular, and well-mannered. For three years, from the sixth through the eighth grades, she secretly pined for him. Since Allen was as timid as she, a romance never got off the ground until, ironically, the Berkemas moved to Sacramento. That summer, when Barbara was in the eighth grade, the Piotrowskis took a family vacation in northern California, where they visited the Berkemas. Allen and Barbara's mutual attraction blossomed into a full-scale infatuation. When the Piotrowskis returned to Los Angeles,

Barbara and Allen stayed in touch by telephone until the long-distance calls became too expensive and their respective parents ended the budding relationship.

More than twenty years later, when Allen Berkema recalled Barbara Piotrowski, he was still tongue-tied. "Yeah," he said sheepishly, "I probably was her first boyfriend." Barbara, Allen recollected, "took a little while to get to know" and "seemed like she was ahead of other people, like she was in control of things."

Their most daring moment, he suggested, was the time he and Barbara drank wine.

Shortly after Allen faded from her life, Barbara woke up one morning and decided she was a misfit. All brains and no personality.

What led to this epiphany is not really clear, even to Barbara. "I decided," she would later say, "that there were certain things I was very good at, primarily, I think, because I worked very hard. Because I wanted to please my father. But I had no self-confidence in terms of the social aspect and the physical aspect."

She decided to remedy the situation immediately and embarked on a radical self-improvement program. Barbara, her father would one day say, was never one to plan. She preferred to make decisions on the spot. And her latest impulse was self-enhancement.

To the fifteen-year-old Barbra (she had by now shed the second *a* in her name), the door to personal development was marked Patricia Stevens, one of a hundred or so modeling school chains throughout the United States that cater to teenage girls who fantasize about becoming the next Christie Brinkley.

Barbra persuaded Wes to finance weekend modeling classes, and from the outset she was hooked. Monday through Friday, Barbra was "The Walking Encyclopedia" of Notre Dame Academy for Girls. When Saturday morning arrived, she was transported to another world, the world of Chanel and Shalimar, where she was introduced to the arcane secrets of feminine charm. Barbra learned how to walk, what to wear, how to exercise to improve her figure, and, most important, the elusive art of makeup application. "It was," as Barbra would recall, "all very proper." As part of the program, the school arranged for professional photographers to shoot the girls, taught them basic modeling techniques, and sent them out on an occasional assignment or beauty contest.

Barbra, who had always been naturally pretty in spite of her self-doubts, was soon recognized as a beauty. Seemingly overnight, her skinny, tomboyish frame had metamorphosed into a figure, which one man would admiringly describe, "like a Coke bottle." Although she was only five feet six inches, several inches shorter than the average model, Barbra was perfectly proportioned. There was only one imperfection. Whenever she was nervous or overtired, Barbra's face would break out. To combat it, friends would remember, she heaped on nightly doses of Noxzema, a habit that became a sort of Piotrowski trademark.

In her wholesome, inadvertently sexy way, Barbra was a knockout. Still, no matter how many times her instructors at Patricia Stevens told her she was pretty, she still saw herself as skinny and bucktoothed, with thick glasses. Public exposure inspired a combination of dread and desire. She would practically push herself onstage, as if each new pageant or modeling assignment were a horse that had thrown her and that she was going to force herself to ride again. At the same time, Barbra relished the attention. Soon she was not only entering beauty contests, she was *winning* them. By the beginning of her senior year at St. Bernard, she had accumulated such titles as "Miss Santa Catalina Island Board of Tourism," "Princess of the Artists and Models Ball," and "Miss Natural," which title gave her the opportunity to represent a health food company for a year.

When she was sixteen, Barbra signed with a bona fide modeling agency, William Adrian Teen Models in Pasadena, the same agency that discovered Cheryl Tiegs. A photograph from her first day, taken by Adrian himself, shows a stereotypical California beauty, all hair and legs, propped up on seventies platform heels. In the photo, she is looking over her shoulder with a wistful smile as she opens the door to the agency, the door to tomorrow. There is also, if one studies her eyes, the barest hint of foreboding, as if she might be afraid of what lay on the other side of the door.

"I wasn't believing this," she would later reflect. "All of a sudden there were people out there who actually thought I was pretty. I would think, 'Are these people blind? What's going on?' "

Somewhat peculiarly, Barbra never suffered from stage fright once she was actually on the stage or in front of the camera. The camera, and the stage, she believed, protected her. She could become someone else. It was almost, she would say, like acting.

Work . . . that was Barbra's passion. "When I get involved in something," she would say, "my work becomes my life." At fifteen, she took a part-time job at Taco Bell; in her free time she busied herself making and selling crafts. "Barbra," a longtime friend from her childhood would say, "was always a work person."

Work provided Barbra with an identity, gave her an outlet for her prodigious energy. And it furnished a comfortable, protective shell from the social contacts that so intimidated her.

Like boys.

They had started to notice her. They even dubbed her "Canned Heat," because, one would say, she was "such a hot-lookin' girl."

Barbra paid them no mind. When she actually dated a boy her junior year, Jim Birmingham, she barely seemed to notice. He was just a friend, she would tell people. They were all "just friends" to Barbra.

Poor Jim. He was genuinely awestruck. Barbra wasn't like the other girls, he noticed. She was smart. She had goals for the future.

Saturday nights, Jim would pick up Barbra, talk to Wes for a few minutes; then he and Barbra would see a movie together and afterward maybe walk along the beach. He was always careful to have her home by midnight. Other weekends, when he wasn't with Barbra, Jim would party with his friends till all hours. The way Jim figured it, there were girls you took to wild parties and there were girls you married. Barbra was the kind you married.

There was another boy on the fringes of Barbra Piotrowski's world, a boy from around the neighborhood. He was different, this boy. To look at him, one would never put him together with Barbra. He was darkly handsome, in an ominous, street-gang sort of way. But Barbra discovered that beneath the black leather jacket was a sensitive soul. His name was Oliver de la Torre. He liked to call himself colorful, a Gemini born in the year of the tiger. When Barbra first met him at age fourteen, she paid Oliver little attention, if she noticed him at all.

When the right man came along, Wes let Barbra know, she would know it immediately. Until then, he believed, sex was something sacred, not to be shared. "Your body is a very precious thing. The most beautiful thing you can give to the man you love. It should be saved."

Barbra listened to her father. She believed that somewhere in the universe there existed the man God had chosen for her, the other half of her soul. She would save herself for him. That was what her father had taught her, and her father was always right.

Thanksgiving morning 1970 Barbra bounded out of bed, her eye catching her reflection in the bedroom mirror as she passed by. *Hmmmm,* she nodded appreciatively. *I almost look pretty.*

Certainly there were many others who told her so. That very morning, while most Americans were defrosting turkeys, Barbra was stepping into a brightly colored bikini and matching sarong, the royal raiment of her latest beauty pageant triumph, "Miss Wahini Bikini." Earlier in the month, Barbra had been selected to represent the South Sea Islands in an annual Los Angeles extravaganza known as Charlie Sea's International Pageant of Beauty.

Charlie Sea, a Los Angeles businessman of Oriental descent, had achieved an underground cult status in the pageant world as a purveyor of beauty contest spectacles. Each year on Thanksgiving, he assembled a float of beauties from, it was supposed, around the world, to ride down Hollywood Boulevard in the Santa Claus Lane Parade, shown on television to kick off the holiday season. Since Sea could not afford to fly in the actual beauty queens from every country, he would select local pageant winners, and put them in appropriate costume.

Because Barbra had already been voted by the media as the contestant with the best legs in the 1970 parade, Sea astutely chose her to represent the South Sea Islands, the better to exploit those prize-winning limbs. To the press, Barbra Piotrowski was 1970's "Miss Million-Dollar Legs."

She was seventeen years old and a senior in high school.

As the day progressed, Barbra could not believe her good fortune. Out of all the girls on Charlie Sea's float of glamour, she was the one selected for a TV interview by a local commentator covering the parade. It was, she thought to herself, *her* day. Her long blonde hair glistened in the warm California sun. She could practically feel the admiring stares of those along the parade route. She couldn't wait to get home and tell her best friend at St. Bernard that she was going to be on television that night.

Late in the afternoon, when the parade ended, she hurried to find the other girls, so she could change into her street clothes, meet up with her ride, and go home. Somehow in the mob scene, all the streets looked the same to her. She wandered up and down Hollywood Boulevard for ten minutes, looking down each side street for the designated meeting place.

Barbra scanned the thinning crowd for some sign of a familiar face. Now that evening was approaching she was beginning to feel chilly and slightly foolish in her skimpy costume. A feeling of panic passed through her. What if she couldn't find them? She began to walk more quickly, looking for a telephone. *I'll call my father,* she decided. *He'll come pick me up.*

Just then her eyes locked on a face in the crowd, a man who seemed to appear out of nowhere among the stragglers from the parade. As he moved closer, Barbra could not break his gaze. Then her eye was caught by a glint of gray under his right hand. It looked like a gun, she thought to herself. Why didn't anyone else see it? Her heart began to pound wildly.

Before she could react, the stranger's body was brushing hers and she could feel cold metal through her thin sarong. *Oh, my God, he* does *have a gun,* Barbra thought. She froze in fear. The man pushed the weapon further into her side.

"Keep walking," he said in a hoarse whisper, concealing the gun with his body.

The stranger pushed her toward a parked car. Then he shoved her in on the driver's side and got in himself. When they were both inside the car, he pointed the gun directly at Barbra's head and, without saying a word, started the engine.

Barbra felt a cold, indefinable terror, as if someone had injected ice water into her veins. This couldn't be happening to her. It was just a dream. *In a moment,* she thought, *I'll blink and be at home and this will all have been a nightmare.*

All of a sudden she felt sick to her stomach. This *was* real. And it was happening to her.

He's going to kill me, she thought suddenly, as her kidnapper turned the car onto one of the winding roads leading up to the canyons, the gun still aimed at her head.

Newspaper headlines from the past flooded Barbra's mind: GIRL RAPED AND KILLED. BODY FOUND IN COLDWATER CANYON. She saw images from her childhood mixed together like some surreal kaleidoscope.

When she was growing up, one of Barbra's favorite Bible stories was about a woman who chose to be killed rather than be subjected to the ultimate humiliation of rape. This was what she would do, Barbra had decided. She would never allow a man to do that to her. She would die instead.

Now, inside the car with this frightening stranger, all she could think of was living.

"I'll do whatever you want," she heard herself murmur in a voice that seemed to be coming out of someone else's body. "Anything."

Her captor said nothing. When they reached a remote area in the hills, far above the lights of the city, he stopped the car and turned off the engine. It was pitch-black and the silence was infinite.

This is it, Barbra thought. *He's going to kill me.*

"Get out," the man commanded as he grabbed Barbra by the arm. With the gun still pointed at her head, he led her through the brush and trees to a desolate clearing in the canyon. There, on the bare ground, lay an old, dirty mattress.

Barbra shuddered. This was not the first time he had brought a victim up to this spot, she thought, and she was filled with revulsion.

Just let me out of this alive, she repeated in her mind, as a desperate mantra. *Let me out of this alive.*

In the next five minutes, her fantasy of saving herself for the man she loved was replaced by the ugly reality of a brutal stranger ripping her hymen open with his bare hands.

She closed her eyes. As she lay motionless on the hard mattress, she felt the attacker force himself inside her vagina, which was already sore and bleeding. Barbra lay perfectly still. *Just let him do what he wants to do,* she reasoned with herself. *Don't fight him. That's the only way you're going to live through this.*

She opened her eyes and looked up at the sky. The stars and treetops spun round her, faster and faster. Her body ached inside, as the stranger on top of her continued to thrust. Barbra closed her eyes again, which somehow made her mind feel detached from her body. Her mind focused solely on survival.

When she opened her eyes she was staring at the barrel of a pistol.

"Open your mouth," her attacker barked.

He's going to put the gun in my mouth and shoot me! Barbra thought to herself. Then her inner voice returned. *Just cooperate,* it said to her.

She opened her mouth slowly. The kidnapper shoved his penis inside. Repulsed, Barbra gagged.

Suddenly the violence was over, as abruptly as it began. Barbra lay numb on the ground, afraid to move. As her captor pulled away, her eyes followed him intently. *Now he's going to kill me,* she thought. She watched as he picked up his clothes off the ground. When he bent to step into his trousers he set down the gun.

This is my chance, Barbra thought instantly. A chance, she knew instinctively, that would be her last.

She grabbed her sarong and stumbled into the darkness.

She would not even remember whether she heard gunshots, or if the man followed her. Her instincts told her to run. And she ran, naked and battered, into the black darkness of the canyon. Spotting a clump of bushes, Barbra crouched down, barely daring to breathe. An eternity passed as she waited for daylight, afraid that every sound she heard might be her attacker.

In the eerie stillness of the canyon, Barbra was consumed with one thought: Tomorrow she would get to the police and bring them back to the spot where she was raped. This man would never do to anyone else what he had done to her.

When daylight finally came, Barbra felt reborn, blessed with the gift of life. Holding up her torn sarong, she stumbled in and out of the tangle of trees in the canyon, trying to find her way back to civilization. She had lost all concept of time. Finally, when she found a road through the hills, it almost seemed like a mirage.

Barbra sat by the side of the road, waiting for a car to come along so she could get to the police station. Finally, a car appeared. The driver slowed down, then stopped.

"Please take me to the police," Barbra stammered as she opened the door on the passenger's side.

The driver took one look at her and tried to persuade her to go to the hospital. Barbra was adamant.

"No," she said firmly. "I have to go to the police."

During the long, winding drive down the hill and back to the city, Barbra closed her eyes and tried to visualize the route the kidnapper had taken the day before so she could describe it accurately to the police. When the car pulled into the station, she was ready.

Once she was inside, the sergeant who was assigned to question her cut her off in mid-sentence.

"You're going to the hospital," he said flatly. "Now."

By the time they got to the hospital, Barbra was nearly hysterical.

"I have to take you back to the canyon . . . now," she said emphatically, "or I'll forget where the mattress was. Please, somebody drive me there."

The police officer and the doctor in the emergency room exchanged looks. Then they took a long, hard gaze at Barbra's sarong and the blonde who was wearing it. As she sputtered out the story of her kidnapping to them, they continued to stare.

When she had finished, there was a long silence.

Did she ever think, they wondered aloud, that she might have *provoked* this man?

Barbra recoiled. As the doctor in the emergency room continued his examination, wearing an expression of disdain, she stopped asking to be taken back to the canyon. She stopped talking altogether. Barbra no longer cared whether the police apprehended her attacker. She didn't care about anything. She was consumed by self-loathing.

As she lay in her hospital bed, replaying in her mind the events of the previous two days, Barbra berated herself. Why hadn't she asked the man to kill her? That was what her heroine had done in the Bible story.

For the first time in her life, Barbra believed, she had not done what was right. She considered herself, she would later say, a "piece of garbage."

Instantly her thoughts turned to her father. How could she face him after what she had done? If he knew what this man had done to her body, what he made her do to him, she would never be able to look him in the eye again.

"Please," she pleaded with the doctor and the police, "whatever you do, don't tell my parents what this man did to me. You can tell them I was kidnapped, but don't say anything else. *Please* . . ."

Barbra searched their faces with desperation. It was agreed. There was no reason her parents had to know she was raped.

A few minutes later, a frantic Wes burst into Barbra's hospital room, the anguish of the previous two days etched in every line of his careworn face. He scoured the length of his daughter's body for confirmation that she was all right. Then, as he had done so many times before, he stared into her eyes to discover the truth there.

Barbra barely looked up at her father. At that moment, she hated him, too.

3

When Barbra checked out of the hospital in November of
her senior year in high school, she was a different person.
She felt dirty inside, and she did not know how to vent
her anger and bitterness. She hated herself for allowing the
rape to happen. She hated God for deserting her. And she
hated her father for spinning dreams and expectations, and
not preparing her for the real world.

For Wes and Stella, who were never told about their
daughter's brutal rape, the new Barbra was a complete
bewilderment. Suddenly, the girl who lived with her books
and her birds was rarely home. The phone would ring for
her incessantly with calls, she would tell her parents, from
friends. "Friends" whose names Wes and Stella had never
heard before. Friends she met at the beach, or at the Taco
Bell. Friends with whom she smoked marijuana, snorted
cocaine, and shot heroin.

She stopped studying altogether. Her grades dropped from
A's to C's, then to D's, even a few F's. She was insolent and
disrespectful to teachers.

In this, as in all things she pursued, Barbra was excessive.
Her drug of choice, she would tell people, was "anything
she could get her hands on." Marijuana, Seconal, heroin.
Anything but LSD. Although she took her share of hallu-
cinogenics, Barbra drew the line at LSD. She remembered
that LSD could alter her chromosomes. She might straighten
out someday and want to have children, she told herself. She
wouldn't want to harm her unborn child.

Literally overnight, Barbra was transformed into the
school druggie. "If you needed anything," Theresa Peery, a
schoolmate, remembered, "you just went to Barbra's locker."

One afternoon in late May, Barbra was called out of her home economics class to report to the vice-principal's office. When she got there, Sister Mary Dennis, the dean of discipline, was sitting with two uniformed police officers.

"Open up your purse, Barbra," Sister Mary Dennis said calmly. "We have reports from some of the other students that you've been selling drugs on campus."

The nun looked at Barbra wearily. When she had received the tip, she had not been surprised. Lately, she noticed, Barbra had a hard look about her. There were rumors that she liked to hitchhike. Like the other nuns at St. Bernard, Sister Mary Dennis knew nothing about the kidnapping and rape.

Barbra emptied her purse on the nun's desk. Along with the usual brush, wallet, and assorted odds and ends, a plastic box spilled out. When one of the police officers opened it, he found Seconal and Benzedrines.

Barbra gave him a glazed look. "I just bought them from a friend," she said casually. "I wasn't trying to sell them. I'm taking these gelatin capsules for a burn on my leg. My photographer gave them to me so my burn wouldn't leave a scar."

The officer took a look at Barbra's thin, drawn face and the circles under her eyes. Then he rolled up the sleeves of her white schoolgirl's blouse. The insides of both arms were covered with needle marks.

"I shoot up once in a while," Barbra said coolly. "Just Seconal, though. The last time was two or three weeks ago."

In June, when the other 240 students in her class celebrated commencement, "The Walking Encyclopedia" of St. Bernard High School was not permitted to participate in the ceremony. She was in a drug-induced stupor.

The arrest barely fazed Barbra. She continued to ingest Seconal, marijuana, and heroin. When her wages from Taco Bell could not support her habit, she learned that she could pay for her own cut by buying more than she needed and selling small amounts of marijuana and Seconal to her friends and acquaintances.

Wes was beside himself. He sat down with Barbra, pleaded with her, attempted to reason with her. Didn't she know she was destroying her life? That her future was going down the drain? Barbra looked back at him with empty eyes. No kind of punishment worked. Finally, in desperation, her parents tried locking her in the house. Barbra broke the windows to get out.

What was happening? His golden child was slipping away from him and Wes was powerless to do anything about it.

"I was hurting and I was crying out for help," Barbra would say years later. "And I didn't know how to ask for it."

Barbra found a kindred spirit in Oliver de la Torre.

Oliver was two years older than Barbra and the quintessential rebel without a cause. His friends, he was proud to say, were the lowriders, surfers, hotrodders—the anarchists of high school. Yet he was not *of* them. Oliver danced on the fringes of any group.

His parents, who were of wealthy French and Spanish descent, lived on the other side of town from the Piotrowskis in an exclusive community. His brother and sisters were routinely elected class officers at school. Oliver was the kind who started a petition to remove the sixth-grade teacher because he didn't like her; who was asked to choose another high school after he decided to "take a few days vacation." For the latter prank, he was deposited in Barbra's working-class neighborhood, where his father owned a small grocery store.

Barbra referred to him affectionately as the "black sheep of his family." Oliver preferred to say he was the "casual" one. "I'm not a straight arrow," he would reflect. "But I'm true to my friends, I'm straightforward with people. I'm basically really honest. I get that little twitch in my eye sometimes. I have a real warped sense of humor. But then I like to have fun."

Tales of his exploits were legend. Years later, when his long, hippie-style dark hair was short and balding and his face was puffy from too many late nights, Oliver de la Torre would deny them all. "There's always been a lot of 'alleges,' " he would say with a twinkle. "In twenty some years there've been all kinds of alleged things that I was a drug dealer. It's never been proven. I happen to know all kinds of people and if I wanted to I could probably have thirty-five kilos of cocaine here in ten minutes. It just happens I know these people. I happen to keep secrets and I look the other way. But that's not my thing. I never made my living at it. But I did get high."

After Barbra's kidnapping and rape, she and Oliver de la Torre came together like two magnets. For all their apparent differences, they had a lot in common. Besides drugs, they were both loners. And, no less important, Oliver was the first person Barbra met other than herself who had a pet duck.

To Oliver, Barbra was a female Tom Sawyer—a girl he could "do things with," who wasn't, in his words, "afraid to climb rocks," who liked the outdoors. The two of them would hitchhike up the coast to Santa Barbara or southeast to Palm Springs and camp out under the stars. Always, Oliver would point out fondly, some type of an adventure.

Once, Barbra taught Oliver how to ski. As he snowplowed down the mountain at full speed it occurred to him she never told him how to stop. Barbra was on the sidelines, laughing uproariously as he crashed into a crowd.

The absence of any sexual contact was a condition of the friendship. Oliver was one of the few people Barbra told about her rape, partly to keep him at arm's length. "She had a real block about any kind of touching," he would remember. "She was real fragile."

The rape continued to haunt Barbra. She was desperately afraid of sex and hostile toward men. "I remember specifically feeling as if I wanted to pay them back," she would say. "As if, 'OK, if they think I'm so pretty'—even though I thought I was even uglier then—but I thought, 'If that's what they think is pretty, then I'm going to just drive them crazy.' And I ran around in short skirts and bathing suits and was in beauty contests and did all sorts of things, but no one touched me."

The Barbra whose picture is with the senior class in the St. Bernard High School yearbook bears little resemblance to the fresh-faced junior of the year before. In the 1971 annual, Barbra appears with heavy eye makeup, bleached-blonde hair, and a come-hither look. Except that once the guys came hither, she sent them away.

After about a year, even Oliver began to be concerned about her self-destructiveness. His views of drugs had always been romantic: "Maybe a line of coke, smoke some weed, a little wine, or something like that. Our thing wasn't really drugs. I love the senses, that's what I love a lot. I like good food and I like chitchat."

Barbra's foray into the drug world was much darker. She was shooting heroin in back alleys with kids she picked up at the beach. "One of my friends was found O.D.'d in a trashcan. I had many friends that died. But it didn't really matter, because I thought I wanted to die, too. Except I didn't have the guts to do it, so I figured I could slowly destroy myself or accidentally overdose."

One morning after her eighteenth birthday, Barbra's darkest fantasy came true: She woke up in a hospital room overdosed on heroin and downers. As she stared at the white walls and the doctors and nurses hovering near with pained expressions, something clicked.

"My God," she thought to herself, "I almost died."

In that instant Barbra was seized by the same feeling that had overwhelmed her when she was kidnapped and raped. She wanted to live at any cost.

She looked down at her own frail, dissipated body beneath the thin covering of the white-and-blue standard-issue hospital gown, and she realized what a shambles her life had become. She was barely hanging on in her biology classes at Santa Monica City College. Her family had lost touch with her completely. She, who dreamed of being a doctor, of helping other people, was a junkie. In the hospital room, Barbra Piotrowski made a promise to herself to kick her heroin addiction and get her life back on track again.

For the second time in less than a year Barbra Piotrowski emerged from a hospital a changed person. Within a few weeks after the heroin overdose she was on what her friend Oliver referred to as "the good road"—working double shifts as a ward clerk at a hospital, making an effort with her college classes, and, with Oliver's help, slowly weaning herself from drugs. Some days were a descent into hell, when the demons of heroin threatened to repossess her. But Barbra persisted. It was a battle of wills, a showdown between the drug and her, but she was going to prevail.

When Easter and her nineteenth birthday came around, she decided to spend her spring break with some friends camping on the beach in San Blas, Mexico. The trip began inauspiciously. Her friends left early and Barbra missed her ride down. So she called Oliver, who threw a few clothes in a backpack, jumped in Barbra's car, and hit the road to Mexico with her.

When they arrived in San Blas, Oliver pitched a tent on the beach and then took off for nearby Santa Cruz in pursuit of a girl he'd met that day, leaving Barbra with her friends in San Blas. The first night she was there, a party sprang up on the beach and she danced and drank *cerveza* and mescal.

Sometime after midnight Barbra had to go to the bathroom. She stopped at the tent, picked up her shoulder bag with all her belongings, and set out to find a bush somewhere away from the group.

When she was walking back toward the party, she suddenly became aware of two Mexicans behind her, lurking in the moonlit-shadowed beach. Her heart began pounding furiously. She walked faster, and wished she could be someplace else, anyplace else. The two men behind her picked up their pace. Terrified, she dropped her shoulder bag on the sand and ran as fast as she could in the direction of the tents. Her pursuers, she figured, would be more tempted by her bag than by her. She was right.

The next morning, when she returned to the spot, the bag was gone, along with her camera and four hundred dollars, all the money she had with her on the trip.

Barbra stood on the sand in the hot sun, thinking. Suddenly an idea formed in her head. She wondered if she could survive on her own in Mexico. It would be, she decided, a great learning experience.

"I had lost all my money and had no real way of getting back," she would say later. "So I became very creative. I thought it would be a real adventure."

It would be, Oliver was later to say, an Easter vacation that lasted until Christmas for Barbra.

For the next six months, Barbra and Lee Ann Santaluce, a girl she met in San Blas, traveled together through Mexico down to Central America, living on bananas, papayas, and oranges, pitching their tents in jungles and villages, supporting themselves by buying articles of clothing at cheap prices in small villages and reselling them for a profit in border towns. Once, they stayed at an American consulate in Mexico near Central America. For a time, they lived with the Huichole Indians in Tepic, Mexico. Another time, they were dropped off by a cargo plane in the mountains of Michoacán, where they stayed with another primitive tribe. Barbra was fascinated with the Indians' life-style, which centered on religion and peyote. She and Lee Ann dabbled in their religious ceremonies, smoked peyote, and tried magic mushrooms. "But in a different sense," Barbra would say later. "Not destructive or to party. It was a real learning experience."

While she and Lee Ann were camped out in Calderitas, Mexico, near the border of British Honduras (now Belize), Lee Ann decided to go back to the States with some Americans who were passing through. Barbra stayed on. From time to time she would write to her parents and let them know where she was. Oliver, who had started an antiques business, occasionally wired her money he owed her. They were her only contact with the outside world.

At Christmastime, nine months after she and Oliver drove down to San Blas for spring break, she was ready to come home. She was nineteen years old, drugfree, with a clear mind and her goal firmly reinstated: to become a doctor.

When the Christmas holidays came to a close, Barbra reenrolled in premed classes in night school at Santa Monica City College, entered the Licensed Vocational Nurse program at Marina Mercy Hospital, and began working double and triple shifts as a nurse, living alternately with her parents, her sister Irena, and, for a time, Oliver.

Her friendship with Oliver blossomed into a romance, of sorts.

The intimacy, by both their admissions, was awkward, ill-defined, and short-lived. After so many years of being together as friends, Barbra and Oliver couldn't decide what their relationship was. Before long, they were back to being friends.

The problem was Barbra. The rape continued to haunt her. She had no confidence in her sexuality—even though, Oliver would later say, every guy wanted to go out with her. No one was permitted to come near her. She had never been a demonstrative person, even as a child; now she had an aversion to being touched.

So Barbra concentrated on her work. In typical Barbra fashion, this meant to excess. In addition to nursing school, night classes, and double shifts at the hospital, she created time to help Oliver run his antique business. With her assistance, the operation expanded, in three or four months' time, from a six-hundred-dollar inventory in Oliver's mother's garage to a storefront business boasting an eighty-thousand-dollar inventory. She and Oliver dubbed it The Ritz.

Between the antique business, her studies, nursing, and modeling, Barbra still found time to enter beauty contests. In the year 1973, she was named "Miss Aries," and placed a second-runner-up to "Miss California." For Barbra, it was as if the crown on her head somehow offset the insecurity she felt inside.

Yet, for all her lack of confidence, there was an element of prankishness about Barbra. Once, when she was living with Oliver, she entered the Miss California World contest, a televised local beauty pageant. Backstage, she and the wardrobe mistress disagreed about her costume, while the rest of the contestants were already lined up in front of the audience. Barbra crawled across the stage on all fours, trying to look inconspicuous. Oliver, who was watching the pageant on television, howled at the sight of her, sneaking onto the stage. "That was Barbra!" he remembered. "Her personality would just bubble out. You can see all these girls where it's not sincere, but she was, and it came across."

By July of that year, Barbra's hyperactivity caught up with her and she landed in Washington Hospital in Culver City with ulcerative colitis, brought on by stress. When the doctor recommended a vacation, she and Oliver drove to Ask Mr. Foster, a local travel agency. While they were hurrying the few blocks to get from Oliver's car to the travel agency, a policeman on foot patrol stopped them and wrote out a pair of tickets for jaywalking. Barbra thought nothing of it. In fact, months went by and she and Oliver neglected even to pay the fines. Years later, when memories of the day and her summer vacation were misted over with time, there would come a moment when the jaywalking ticket would reenter Barbra's life in a strange and sinister way.

That fall, when things returned to normal, her friendship with Oliver began to cool. After her purifying sabbatical in Mexico, Barbra was repelled by drugs, seldom drank, and had found a new religion: physical fitness. Oliver, on the other hand, was still the cool rebel he had been at Culver High. When Barbra would arrive at the antique store to work, after her nursing job and her classes, Oliver and his friends would be in the back, drinking and carousing. Barbra was torn. She owed Oliver her life, she believed. Now he was threatening it. Weeks went by, then months, and she couldn't get through to him. So she drifted away.

When Oliver was arrested for printing counterfeit money in the back of The Ritz—a practice Barbra knew nothing about—she threw in the towel. She had worked too hard at pulling herself out of the abyss to have Oliver drag her back down. Even so, guilt gnawed away at her soul. *He never gave up on me,* she told herself.

With Oliver in jail, Barbra continued her workaholic ways, studiously avoiding any romantic entanglements. As long as men were "buddies," it was fine. If one of them should happen to try to cross the line, however, Barbra would erupt into, in her words, "sobbing hysteria."

Of all the men who swarmed around Barbra in those years, only one was granted even the semblance of a relationship. His name was Brad Katz[1] and he was, on the outside, at least, every young girl's dream: a doctor who was tall, dark, handsome.

Brad and Barbra met on her first day as a student nurse at Brotman Memorial Hospital in Culver City, a few minutes from her parents' house in Mar Vista.

Of the thirty or more doctors on staff at Brotman eager to check out the new nurses at orientation, Brad was the only one who *didn't* come on strong with Barbra. Out of breath and dressed in gray sweats, he sat down at a table in

---

[1]Not his real name

the hospital lounge where Barbra and another student nurse named April were seated. Barbra breathed a sigh of relief when he ignored her and talked to April, mostly about athletics. By the time Brad left the lounge, Barbra had signed up for his ski club. When he asked her and April to play tennis with him a few days later, she immediately accepted.

Barbra felt comfortable with Brad, protected from the other doctors. When they thought she and Brad were a couple, she noticed, they stopped making passes at her. Within a few months of their meeting, Barbra was living in Brad's house in Malibu. By April, they were engaged.

Inside the picture-perfect relationship, Barbra was desperately unhappy. Even though she and Brad shared many of the same interests—tennis, skiing, jogging on the beach—he somehow saw to it that they pursued these activities separately. The rare times they were together, he would almost suffocate her. He was also extremely possessive. Yet, in spite of his reputation at the hospital as a playboy, Brad showed little interest in Barbra sexually. Some days, he was supportive and loving; other days he made her feel like trash.

Apart from her abortive efforts with Oliver, Barbra had never had a sexual relationship with a man. She had no idea what she was supposed to do. She felt awkward and self-conscious. And she was still afraid. Instead of taking the lead or showing understanding, Brad lost patience. "I can't deal with it," he would say to Barbra, and turn over on his side. When she asked him why, he would brush her off and say, "It's your fault."

Finally, Barbra saw a psychiatrist, who told her the problem was her. "Try to loosen up," he advised her.

Barbra went home, shaken. That afternoon, on the advice of the psychiatrist, she prepared a romantic meal and changed into her sexiest evening dress. When Brad arrived home from the hospital, she greeted him at the door with a kiss, the table set for two, with candles in the background.

Brad looked at the dress, then at Barbra, and an expression of distaste passed over his handsome features.

"Who do you think you are?" he said sarcastically. "A schoolgirl trying to be a whore?"

Barbra ran to the bedroom in tears.

She began to gain weight. Her self-image plummeted. Brad was continually telling her how worthless she was, and Barbra was beginning to believe him.

One day, when Brad was out of town at a medical conference, Barbra packed her belongings and moved out of the house in Malibu. Since her own car was in the shop, Barbra used Brad's Mercedes. They parted as friends, but Barbra's self-esteem was at an all-time low.

She stood alone in the cold Aspen air that January morning in 1977, anxiously awaiting the next ski lift to take her
up the mountain. Barbra felt invigorated by the cold air. She
loved to ski by herself, free and unfettered. The grace and
athleticism required by the sport exhilarated her, made her
feel as if she had wings.

It had been nearly a year since she removed Brad Katz
from her life and she was just beginning to heal. At twenty-
three, Barbra had both her Licensed Vocational Nurse and
Registered Nurse credentials and was in her second year of
microbiology at UCLA, where she carried a 3.8 grade-point
average. Ever since Oliver "got a wild hair up his butt" and
moved to Aspen, then took a job as a relief operator with the
ski corps, she spent every free moment at Snowmass or with
friends at other ski resorts. After early efforts at Oliver's
cabin in Utah, Barbra had become an expert skier.

On this brilliant January morning, Barbra planned to put
in a solid day of skiing, then go back to Oliver's and hit the
books, as was her routine. Since Oliver had a night job as a
cook, her time in Aspen was almost completely her own. As
she was climbing onto a lift, her eye was caught by a male
skier coming down another lift, dressed in a snowsuit so
incandescently yellow he seemed to glow. As she watched
in stunned disbelief, the object of her curiosity bounded out
of his ski lift and, before she knew what was happening,
raced over in her direction, grabbed onto the lift, and heaved
himself into the seat next to her, nearly knocking himself
over in the process.

Oh great, Barbra groaned to herself. *Now I'm going to*

have to put up with this joker all the way up the mountain. There goes my solitude.

To her surprise, at first the stranger in the neon ski suit barely said a word to her. When he did, he was polite and well-mannered. Almost a little shy, Barbra thought. She looked at him out of the corner of her eye, both curious and appalled. He was actually not bad-looking, she thought to herself. He appeared to be in his late thirties or early forties, and had a shock of yellow-blond curls. If you could get past the fluorescent snowsuit, Barbra decided, he was handsome in a flashy, movie-starrish way: He had classic Roman features, piercing blue eyes, and the winter tan of the jet set.

He had to be a tourist, Barbra imagined. Somebody who doesn't know the first thing about sports. The kind of guy who hangs out in singles bars and asks what your sign is.

His name was Richard Minns, he told Barbra, and he was from Texas.

Figures, Barbra thought to herself. She deliberately withheld her own name and kept an icy distance.

The two rode up the lift in silence.

"I saw you yesterday, down at the lodge," Richard Minns said finally, interrupting the silence between them. His voice was strong and masculine, with just enough of a Texas drawl to be charming.

Barbra's eyebrow went up immediately: *Here it comes. . . .* She braced herself.

"I don't know if you noticed me or not," he went on, "but I was standing a few feet away from you with a friend of mine, a guy named Bob Schwartz. You were polishing your skis, and you were all covered up in a ski hat and a snowsuit."

Richard Minns flashed a dazzling grin. "He and I made a bet about what you looked like under all those ski clothes. I bet you were a dog. He said you were probably a real knockout."

Minns turned and stared into Barbra's face with an intensity that made her squirm in her seat. "Obviously, Bob won that bet."

Barbra had no recollection of seeing Richard Minns or his supposed friend at the lodge the day before, and she wasn't quite sure why she was sitting next to him now. Still, she couldn't help but be amused, on the long ride up, by this colorful character who was so hell-bent on meeting her.

"You may have heard of me," he said at one point. "My name's been in all the papers. I'm the famous shark fighter from Houston."

Barbra shook her head and thought: *This guy is unreal.*

As she listened, dumbfounded, Richard Minns told her about his plan to fight a great white shark in Western Samoa in August. He always performed some feat of athletic daring on his birthday, and this year, his forty-eighth, he wanted to do something extra spectacular.

At that, Barbra's ears perked up. Whatever crazy stunts this man did or did not perform, he did *not* look forty-seven.

As they rode farther up the mountain together, Richard told Barbra what great shape he was in. So great, he told her, he had to have his trousers specially made because his calves were too muscular for ready-to-wear pants.

Barbra coughed to cover a snicker.

As if he could read her mind, Richard began to blush. "Oh," he stammered, in a charming, Jimmy Stewartish fluster, "I'm sorry. I didn't mean to sound so egotistical."

Barbra laughed in spite of herself.

When they got to the advanced slope, Barbra jumped off the lift, eager to lose her companion. She turned to say a polite goodbye, but Richard Minns showed no inclination to leave.

Barbra took off down the mountain at top speed. When she took a quick look over her shoulder, Richard Minns was still on top of the mountain, fumbling with his equipment.

Barbra laughed out loud. The great shark fighter and all-around athlete was obviously a novice skier! When she reached the base of the mountain, certain that she had lost the Texan for good, Richard Minns suddenly flew out of the sky, barreling down the mountain, headed straight for her. Whatever he lacked in style, she noticed wryly, he made up for in sheer energy and determination.

Barbra couldn't help but be charmed by somebody who went to that much trouble to keep up with her. *If he sits next to me on the next lift,* she decided, *at least I won't be rude to him.*

True to her presentiment, Richard Minns did join her on

the next ski lift. And the next and the next. By the end of the day, Barbra found that she actually enjoyed his company. After their initial ride together, Richard stopped talking about himself and began to talk about sports. He had just taken up snow skiing, he told Barbra, which explained his awkwardness. But he was a world-class water-skier, tennis player, scuba diver, and weight lifter.

The two also talked about art and literature. Richard was particularly fond of Ernest Hemingway, and recited passages from his work verbatim. In some ways, Barbra decided, this was better than skiing alone. Richard was interesting company with no pressure and a buffer from anyone else who might bother her.

When they finished skiing for the day, Richard casually asked Barbra if she would like to get together that evening. When she said a polite "No, thank you," he accepted it without question.

"Well," he asked hopefully, "do you want to ski together tomorrow?"

Barbra scrutinized the face of the world-class athlete and adventurer from Texas, looking up at her with beseeching eyes. The effect was so incongruous it made her laugh.

"Sure," she found herself saying. "If we happen to see each other, that's fine with me."

The next morning, when Barbra walked through the lodge on her way to the slopes, Richard Minns was waiting for her, standing in the very spot where he said he had seen her polishing her skis two days earlier.

Well, he's persistent, I'll say that for him, she thought to herself.

By the end of the second day, Richard and Barbra had established a pattern for the rest of their stay in Aspen. They would meet on the slopes early in the morning and ski together until sunset; then Richard would ask Barbra out and Barbra would refuse. Richard seemed content to accept Barbra's friendship for what it was, an attitude that raised him considerably in Barbra's esteem.

During their long rides on the lift, Barbra and Richard talked with the easy familiarity of old friends who hadn't seen each other in a while. Barbra was astounded at how much she had in common with Richard Minns. He loved to travel, just as she did; like her, he participated in sports with zealous determination; *and* he decried smoking and drinking. Without a doubt, he had more energy than any human she had ever encountered.

Before long, Barbra found herself looking forward to seeing Minns. By the beginning of the second week, she was confiding her deepest secrets to him: her kidnapping and rape, how badly she had been hurt by Brad, and how wary she was of another relationship. She even told him about her sister Irena, who was dating a doctor who had been through a bitter divorce. Barbra was concerned, she said, that Irena would be hurt.

"I know what you mean," Richard said sympathetically. "I've been through a divorce myself. They're hell." He had been dating for five years, Richard told Barbra, and had almost given up on finding the perfect mate. "Most of the women I go out with like to get dressed up and go to fancy restaurants for dinner," he said. "It's hard to find someone who has the same interests as I do, who likes sports and likes to hang around in blue jeans."

Barbra nodded understandingly. *My God,* she thought, *he's describing* me!

The more she got to know Minns, the more fascinated Barbra became. Not only was he interested in nutrition and sports, but he also owned a health spa back in Texas. Although he never came out and said he was rich, Barbra assumed by his life-style that Richard must have money. How much she wasn't sure.

The sole interruption in Barbra and Dick's daily ski routine was a quick lunch break at a cafeteria-style restaurant called Sam's Nob, where they ate at picnic tables. Or, *Barbra* ate, anyway. Most days, Richard would be on the phone inside the restaurant, talking business. One day when they were there, he introduced Barbra to his son, a handsome, strapping teenager named Myles. Other Texans, some of them evidently friends of Richard's, lunched at Sam's Nob from time to time. When he wasn't on the phone, Dick loved to gossip.

"She's from Houston, too," he said to Barbra one noon, pointing to a redhead at the opposite end of the picnic table.

"Oh, really?" Barbra said idly. "Who is she?"

"She works for my company." Richard made a slight snicker and motioned toward a handsome German sitting near her. "That's her ski instructor," he whispered to Barbra. "I think they're having an affair!"

Barbra giggled. She didn't know when she had felt so comfortable with another person.

"I don't know what you think I do at night," Richard said to Barbra one afternoon. "All I do is go to the Aspen Club and work out. I just thought you might like to go with me sometime."

Toward the end of her stay, Barbra finally relented. On her last day at Snowmass, she and Richard exchanged phone numbers.

"Maybe we could ski together another time," he said shyly, with Barbra's phone number in hand. "Do you have any plans to come back here?"

"Well, as a matter of fact, some of my nursing friends and I were planning to go skiing in March," Barbra stated, "at the end of the season."

"So was I!" he said exuberantly. "Let's meet, OK?"

Barbra smiled, secretly pleased. "OK," she said casually.

"I met this guy," Barbra told Oliver, as she was preparing to leave Aspen. "He's a real nut, but there's something about him. . . ."

When Barbra returned home to Mar Vista, the phone started ringing. First Richard called her at her parents' house, then at the hospital. Flowers arrived at the doctor's office where she worked. The last day in February she received an eight-by-ten-inch glossy of Richard Minns in a brief bikini suit and a muscleman's pose.

Early in March, Dick, as he now signed himself, sent Barbra a telegram:

HAVE TRIED TO REACH YOU. TIED UP IN POLITICAL CAM-
PAIGN SO HAVE TO POSTPONE ACAPULCO. I WILL DEFI-
NITELY BE AT SNOWMASS MARCH 5—MARCH 19. SNOW
IS GOOD. WANT YOU THERE WITH ME. CALL ME AT (713)
771–1391. MISS YOU. DICK

Barbra was flattered and a little amused, but she had no interest in him romantically. Dick was a friend, someone who listened and made her laugh.

The instant she laid eyes on him in Aspen on March 9, that changed.

Instead of connecting on the slopes, Dick and Barbra arranged to meet at his place in Crestwood Condominiums. The Dick Minns who answered the door bore little resemblance to the character in the incandescent ski suits Barbra remembered from the slopes. He was wearing a pair of tight blue jeans and a rugged jean jacket that emphasized his physique and set off the blue in his eyes. When she saw him, Barbra caught her breath. *Is this the same guy I skied with in January?* she asked herself. *He looks fabulous!*

When they sat down and started talking, it was as if they had never left each other's side. For the next week, Dick and Barbra were inseparable. They skied, they laughed, they worked out at the Aspen Club, they talked—about books, Barbra's dream of becoming a doctor. . . . They couldn't get over how much they had in common. They were, Dick kept saying, a perfect fit.

Not a day went by that Richard didn't tell Barbra how beautiful she was at least fifteen times. Barbra drank it all in. When she was with Dick, for the first time she *felt* beautiful.

On their third or fourth day together, Dick and Barbra spent a quiet evening at his condominium, roasting hot dogs and marshmallows in front of a fire. When they both got sleepy, Dick suggested that Barbra stay the night. She crawled into bed with her clothes on and fell asleep next to him. Sometime around four, they both awakened. The attraction between them was electric. As Barbra looked over at Dick, lying next to her in bed, she felt real passion for the first time in her life. For the rest of the night, they made love together, then fell asleep in each other's arms.

When Barbra woke up late the next morning, she got out of bed, walked over to the kitchen, and made coffee, still naked. As she looked down at her nude body, she was amazed. Normally, she was too self-conscious to allow her *mother* to see her without clothes. With Dick, it felt perfectly natural.

That day, Barbra moved her suitcase from her girlfriends' hotel room to Dick's condo. By the end of the week, he was begging her to come and live with him in Houston.

"Please," he pleaded. "I can't live without you. We were meant to be together."

He wanted her to find an apartment for the two of them in Houston, Dick said. He actually lived at Lakeway Resort in Austin, he told Barbra, because he was such a workaholic he would never relax if he lived in Houston. As far as his business was concerned, Dick stated, he could come and go as he liked. If he needed to be in Houston for business, he generally stayed at the office. Now that he was going to be with her, he told Barbra, he wanted a place in Houston for the two of them.

Barbra demurred. She had to finish her classes at UCLA. They could continue to see each other from time to time. She still had to go to medical school. It was impossible.

Dick was persistent. "This is ridiculous," he entreated. "You're looking for every excuse not to come to Houston. You're saying you have to be in California to go to medical school, because that's where you have your life, your career, your job. If you come to Houston, it would be even easier to go to medical school, because I will not only be emotionally supportive, I can support you financially."

He paused for a quick breath, then dove right back into his pitch. "Let's concentrate on doing what we do best," he continued. "I make money better than you do, so why should you spend all those hours making a little bit of money when you can be spending your time making our life together pleasant? Why be out in California struggling and working your way through medical school when you can come to Texas and we can build a life together?"

Barbra had to admit there was truth to his logic. But she still couldn't do it.

"Hey," Dick said insistently, "we love each other. We've got to find a way to make this work. I can't let you go."

His face brightened. "Look," he said suddenly. "I've got a friend who can help you get into medical school in Texas!"

Barbra eyed him skeptically. "Nobody has connections to get into medical school," she said flatly. "You have to have the grades."

Dick grinned. "Not where I come from! I know everybody there is to know in Texas."

He picked up the phone and dialed the long-distance operator. In a few seconds he was explaining Barbra's situation to a man named Bill Small. When he hung up, his face bore the triumphant look of a Roman gladiator in successful battle.

"There!" he gloated. "You're in."

Barbra could only laugh. She had never met anyone like Richard Minns before in her life. As their days in Snowmass unfolded, he showered her with declarations of love. They talked of having children someday. Dick said he wanted two boys.

She began to think seriously of his proposal. She could go to medical school *and* be with him. The only difference is she would be living in Houston. It was tempting, she had to admit. But she held her ground.

Dick continued his barrage of words. "You *have* to come live with me," he said to Barbra one day, suddenly reflective. "I've only come close to a love like this once before," he said softly. "It was five years ago. I lived with a girl named Janet Poulton for two years and I let her go. I can't let that happen again. What we have only comes along once in a lifetime."

Barbra was touched by Dick's confession. *Gee,* she thought, *if I let this go, I could be making the biggest mistake of my life. We have the perfect relationship. I may never have that again. Can I just let it go?*

That week, Barbra and Dick made arrangements to have dinner with Oliver de la Torre at the Stonebridge Inn so Barbra could introduce the new man in her life to one of her oldest friends. As Oliver observed the Texan who had won Barbra's heart, he felt twinges of misgiving. He looked at Richard Minns's fur moccasins, then at his gold-studded designer blue-jean jacket and thought, *This guy's a flasher. A label person. Barbra's no flasher. What a weird match.* All through dinner, Oliver kept stealing glances at Barbra while Dick talked nonstop. When the conversation turned to Dick's plans to fight a great white shark, Oliver tried one last time to catch Barbra's eye. She was far away, lost in a lover's reverie. "Well, I wish you good luck," he said finally. ". . . and I wish the shark good luck."

For the remainder of Dick's and Barbra's stay in Snowmass, Oliver requested to work the other side of the mountain. Barbra may have fallen for this guy, he told himself, but that didn't mean he had to watch it.

Richard Minns was a man possessed. He was head over heels in love with Barbra Piotrowski. "Let's call your parents," he said excitedly, "and tell them you met a man and you're in love and want to move to Houston."

Barbra balked, but a smile played on the corners of her mouth.

"Oh, come on," Dick persisted. "Just do it."

"Oh, all right," Barbra said gamely at last, cracking a smile.

She picked up the phone in Dick's bedroom and dialed the familiar number, then she heard her father's strong Polish accent on the other end of the line. As she talked, Dick hovered over her. When Barbra didn't get to the point fast enough, he picked up a yellow legal pad and began writing on it in huge block letters. When he finished, he held the page up to Barbra's face:

TELL HIM YOU ARE IN LOVE. TELL HIM THAT I LOVE YOU. TELL HIM THAT I BUILD YOU UP, I DO NOT TEAR YOU DOWN, I MODIVATE [sic] YOU. I WANT YOU TO BE EDUCATED AND BE AN INDEPENDENT THINKING PERSON WITH NO LOSS OF YOUR IDENTITY.

Barbra glanced at the paper and waved Dick away.

A few minutes later, Dick was back again with more instructions:

TELL HIM THAT YOU ARE READY FOR ME. THAT YOU NEED ME. THAT YOU CAN'T LIVE WITHOUT ME.

Barbra ignored him and kept on talking.
Dick wrote more furiously:

TELL HIM THAT I WANT A FAMILY AND WHEN YOU GET
READY TO GIVE HIM SOME GRANDSONS YOU WILL BE
WEARING A WEDDING BAND.

Barbra continued her conversation with her father, slowly
working her way to the matter of Richard Minns.

Dick paced back and forth across the room. Then, with
new purpose, he picked up the pen and pad and wrote
some more:

TELL HIM THAT YOU HAVE SEEN ME WITH MY SON.
TELL HIM THAT I HOLD MORE WORLD'S RECORDS THAN
ANYONE. THAT I HAVE A BODY YOU HAVE NEVER SEEN
BEFORE. TELL HIM I AM A GIVER—NOT A TAKER. I AM A
WORLD FAMOUS

1. ATHLETE   4. WRITER
2. FINANCIAL GENIUS   5. COMPOSER
3. ARTIST   6. OIL WELLS
                      7. MOVIE PRODUCER

MY PERSONAL INCOME IS IN EXCESS OF $THREE MILLION
DOLLARS! YOU CAN VISIT L.A. ANYTIME YOU LIKE!

When Barbra continued to ignore his missives, Dick took
one last stab:

TELL HIM, IN MANY WAYS RICHARD IS JUST LIKE YOU.
PERHAPS THAT'S WHY I LOVE HIM SO MUCH. HE EVEN
SOUNDS LIKE YOU. HIS ATTITUDE TOWARD LIFE AND
PEOPLE IS THE SAME AS YOURS.

Barbra proceeded with the call, doing her best to incor-
porate Dick's ideas into her conversation with her father.

When he could stand it no longer, Richard grabbed the
phone from Barbra.

"Hello, Wes!" he boomed into the receiver, and a torrent of words came out. "This is Richard Minns . . . I'm
in love with your daughter and I want her to move to
Houston to be with me . . . I know she wants to go to
medical school, and I can make sure that she gets into

the best . . . I'm well-connected . . . I'm the best thing that ever happened to Barbra . . . I can't wait to meet you. . . . As soon as we're ready to give you some grandsons, I'm going to put a wedding band on your daughter's finger. . . . What do you say?"

Barbra covered her mouth, convulsed in laughter. This man never gave in and he never gave up. She felt completely enveloped in love. There really were Prince Charmings, she thought to herself. And she had just found hers.

Dick hung up the receiver with an air of satisfaction. He had gotten what he wanted. Barbra was going to move to Houston to find a place for the two of them. They would be together forever.

In the space of a week, Barbra withdrew from her classes at UCLA, packed all her belongings and some of the furniture from the antique business, and quit her job as a nurse.

All Wes could do was shake his head. He had apprehensions: Shouldn't she give this more time? Finish out the semester? Get to know Richard better?—but they went unspoken. He knew better than to buck Barbra when she had her mind set on something. So he did what he could: He made sure her car was in good condition, he cautioned her about driving safely, and he sent her teenaged brother John along for the ride.

Within a day or two of her twenty-fourth birthday, Barbra set out for the long, barren drive across the desert from California to Texas. To her, it was the most thrilling adventure of her life. In three days, she would be reunited with the man she wanted to spend the rest of her life with; a man who promised excitement, the fulfillment of her dream, and everlasting love.

Back in Texas, Richard Minns had told few people, if any, of the impending arrival of his dream girl: not even his son Myles, who had met Barbra in Aspen the previous January. The woman he had to have at all costs was, for the moment at least, his secret.

But then, Richard Minns was a man who kept secrets easily. One of them was the redhead he had pointed out to

Barbra at Sam's Nob restaurant in Snowmass: While it was
true, as he had told Barbra, that the woman worked for his
company, what he neglected to say was that she was also his
wife of twenty-five years, Myles's mother, and the mother
of his three other children, ranging in age from fifteen to
twenty-six.

5

By the time he had become a wealthy and prominent man-about-town, Dick Minns would tell reporters that his father was a native of England, that the Minns family descended from Charles Dickens ("It's in the preface of the *Pickwick Papers*," he would tell people, betting they would never bother to check, for it was a fabrication), and that his father owned several south Texas ranches, where the family "talked of cattle and of medicine."

His father, Dick would say, had the knack for either staying in the chips or going dead broke. "It was either steak or spuds when I was growing up," he would proclaim, "feast or famine."

The truth was more prosaic. In fact, Richard Louis Minns was the son of a middle-class Jewish merchant of ladies ready-to-wear named George Minns, born and bred in Uvalde, Texas, who moved the family from one small Texas town to another.

That was "just Dick," friends would say with affectionate smiles. He was given to hyperbole. It was as natural to him as breathing.

There was a tie, albeit a slender one, to medicine in the family. Richard's mother, born Ethel Goldberg, a nervous, modest woman (her tombstone would read, SHE TRIED HER BEST), came from a family of several doctors. When she went into labor with Richard, she and George drove across the plains of Texas on a hot August day from Granger to Temple, where Ethel's uncle Louis practiced medicine, so he could deliver her firstborn child. Richard's middle name, Louis, was a tribute to that uncle. His mother hoped it would be an auspice. It was Ethel Minns's fondest desire that her

51

only son follow in what she perceived as the family tradition. But all the signs—even the astrological ones—pointed in another direction. Richard was born on August 17, 1929, and in later years he would brag about being a Leo. Astrologer Linda Goodman writes in her book *Sun Signs:* "Leos were *born* superior. The Leo gazes at his image in the mirror and makes the noble vow: 'I WILL.' " This passage could have been written with Richard Minns in mind.

In later years, he loved to tell people how, as a child, he resembled aviator Charles Lindbergh's infant son, the most famous baby of his time. "He looked like the Lindbergh baby," his wife Mimi would say, repeating the oft-told tale. "He was blond-headed and gorgeous. His parents were stopped numerous times by people thinking Dick was the Lindbergh baby." According to his younger sister, Janice, based on information from her parents, it was *Dick* who told strangers he was the Lindbergh child. Whichever version is true, Richard Minns was a beautiful child. He had the face of an angel—sweet and cherubic, with big blue eyes and a halo of blond curls.

It would come as no surprise to anyone who knew him if Dick had been born talking. From the time he first put words together he had what one relative referred to as the "salesman's gift of gab." He somehow *compelled* people to listen to him. His sister Janice was to say their mother "acted as though she thought he was Jesus." Janice, who came along the year Richard was six, spent her childhood courting attention from Dick. He was, his wife Mimi would say, the "special one."

When Richard and Janice were eight and two, George Minns opened a ladies' fashion store in Mercedes, Texas, and the family lived in McAllen, a small town on the Mexican border. In 1940, when Dick was eleven, George Minns decided to branch into real estate development and moved the family north to San Antonio, so he could manage his sister's tourist motel court.

The Minnses settled into a comfortable, well-tended house at 3026 Plum Street, across from a junior high school. There Richard acquired seemingly contradictory reputations for being both a hellraiser and a budding artist. He loved to draw and sculpt, and displayed an unmistakable creative flair. When he was thirteen, he talked his parents into paying for art classes; a year later, he held an exhibition of his work in downtown San Antonio. In one of those peculiar coincidences in life some ascribe to fate, Richard especially enjoyed painting ducks. He once bought a family of ducklings and brought them home to use as live models. When his father's tenants complained about the mess on the front lawn, Dick was indignant. "Those are golden droppings!" he proclaimed to his parents. The ducks stayed.

Both Richard and Janice had a tendency to put on weight, a trait that, combined with the diminutive stature of the Minns men (George was under five foot three inches and Richard would top out at five foot nine inches) doubtless caused Dick considerable anxiety in his teen years. As an adolescent, he was so chubby, the story goes, that his thighs rubbed together when he walked and his trousers wore out in that spot.

Around this time, Richard's behavior became an issue. When he was fourteen, George and Ethel sent him to a military school, reportedly at the suggestion of either their rabbi or the local police. "Because he was a *boy!*" his wife would later say staunchly. Richard himself once bragged to a reporter how, as a teen, he was booked for aggravated assault. He told another journalist that he had been a "wild and woolly youngster." Whether the assault story is true (no police record exists), his parents did enroll him at the Peacock Military Academy in San Antonio, where he was a full-time boarding student, even though the school was just a few miles from the Minns home.

Every Sunday morning, George Minns would check Richard out of the Peacock Academy so he could attend Sunday school. According to his sister Janice, Dick would walk them down back alleys the eight blocks to temple, so none of his friends would find out he was Jewish. Dick was Jewish, his wife would later remark, "when he wanted to be." Bob Delmonteque, who was to become one of his closest friends for more than twenty years, had no idea Richard came from a Jewish background. Dick told Delmonteque that he was Protestant.

Richard's months at Peacock were spirited, rowdy ones. One of his classmates was Dan Blocker, who grew up to play Hoss Cartwright on *Bonanza*. Eventually, more than likely for disciplinary reasons (Dick himself spoke of being "bounced in and out of a series of military schools"), Richard transferred from Peacock to Texas Military Institute, a smaller and even more austere academy in San Antonio.

One day in his junior year, Dick came across an advertisement in the back of a magazine that caught his eye. YOU, TOO, CAN BECOME A HE-MAN! the copy promised. DEVELOP YOUR MUSCLES! Richard was hooked. He tore out the ad, enclosed a few dollars, and mailed it to the address in the magazine. Before long he was the happy recipient of a Charles Atlas Bodybuilding Kit, which he put to immediate and effective use.

Dick dropped the extra weight he was carrying, developed a sort of junior Charles Atlas Bodybuilding Kit-physique, and soared through his studies with a predominance of A's. At sixteen, he dropped out of Texas Military Institute and went straight to the University of Texas in Austin, where he declared himself a premed major. Ethel Minns was overjoyed.

Her happiness was short-lived, however. By his second year at college, Dick had abruptly switched majors from premed to journalism. In later years, he would tell people he dropped out of medicine because of the failure of the family's apocryphal ranch, a colorful substitute for the true reason: Richard Minns, whatever his mother's aspirations for him, was not cut out to be a doctor in any way, shape, or form. He was not particularly skilled at science, he had no patience for the long years of training and sacrifice that were necessary to become a doctor, and he had little inclination to help other people. On top of that, he had a weak stomach. When he was thirty, his six-year-old daughter Cathy cut her chin and had to have stitches. Dick nearly passed out in the emergency room.

Dick's talent was for talking. If ever a human being *belonged* in communications, it was Richard Minns.

At the University of Texas, Richard attended classes straight through the summers, made superior grades, pledged a fraternity (Phi Sig, later to become Zeta Beta Tau), and joined the staffs of both the campus newspaper and magazine. He also tried out for the football team, but dropped out, he said later, because it was too "interdependent." Richard preferred solo sports: handball, racquetball, weight lifting and boxing, to which he directed his prodigious energy. Gone was the pudginess of his youth. Dick Minns, campus hero, was a fighting one hundred and forty pounds of lean muscle.

The change did not go unnoticed. When Dick sauntered down the tree-shaded sidewalks of the University of Texas with his chest out and his stomach muscles rippling, female hearts fluttered. Richard did his level best to go out with them all.

One night, as he stood in a pledge line with his Phi Sig fraternity brothers, Dick did a slow pan of the sorority house, casually assessing the campus belles in order to decide which one he would favor with his attention. He failed to notice a diminutive reddish-brunette, who, for her part, was busy scrutinizing every Phi Sig. She was not the prettiest girl in the room, nor the most glamorous. But she *was* cute and perky, with dark curly hair, big brown eyes, and dimples so deep you could put quarters in them. Her name was Miriam Joan Levy, but no one had called her anything except Mimi (pronounced "Mimmy" for so long no one could remember why) since she was a child. She was a former high school twirler from Nacogdoches, Texas, majoring in radio-drama and she was all of sixteen years old.

When she saw Richard Minns, Mimi Levy stopped dead in her tracks. Standing before her was the most gorgeous specimen of young manhood she had ever laid eyes on. He had sculpted features, a head of thick, naturally wavy hair, and blue eyes full of mischief. He even had a movie-star cleft in his chin.

Suddenly aware of the new pledge's interest, Richard flashed one of his 100-kilowatt grins in her direction. Mimi Levy decided, then and there, she wanted him.

"I'm going to marry that boy . . ." she whispered to the sorority sister next to her, "and he's going to make us both *rich!*"

Ever since she was a child, Mimi Levy had a sense of destiny. When she was six years old, she announced to an aunt that she was going to be a millionaire when she grew up and own the biggest ranch in Texas. For a little girl whose father was a tailor in the small Southern Baptist town of Nacogdoches, Texas, those were big dreams.

The year she was eight, Mimi Levy would tell people in later years, her grandmother studied her closely and said to a relative, "One day she will own horses and they will kneel to her." Her father's mother, Mimi would explain when she told the story, was from Russia, and the only people who owned horses in Russia were the czars and czarinas.

Mimi Levy saw Richard Minns as the means to fulfill her destiny. "I probably saw in him something that nobody else saw till much later," she would remember. "I saw the brilliance in him, I saw the capabilities in him. I fell madly in love with Dick Minns, my heart pounded every time he walked into a room—but other than that, I saw the ability I needed to get where *I* wanted to go."

When pledge night broke up, Mimi Levy left with her prize. As she and Richard Minns walked back to her dorm, they came upon a hedge that was nearly as tall as they were, blocking their path. Without hesitating, Dick picked up Mimi and, with one arm, deposited her on the other side. When he leaped over the hedge himself, Mimi stood for a second, staring. That night, alone in her bed at Littlefield Hall, she closed her eyes and thanked her lucky stars.

From pledge night on, Dick and Mimi were a couple. It was a relationship that seemed, at times, more like combat than courtship. Between Mimi's feistiness and Dick's burgeoning ego, they broke up, Mimi would later joke, every five minutes. The two had little in common. Richard was on a vitamin regimen and pushed himself to the limit in sports to test his endurance. For Mimi, twirling a baton was the acme of physical exertion. Mimi was in her element at a party, dressed to the nines. She saw nothing wrong with having a drink now and then, and she smoked cigarettes like a fiend. Dick, to her, was a "health nut," an eccentricity she indulged because it was Dick.

But there was a force more powerful than compatibility at work: Mimi's determination. Once in her sophomore year, when Richard threatened to stop seeing her, Mimi staged a highly theatrical scene in front of Littlefield Hall that would become family legend.

"You can't break up with me!" she pleaded with Dick, tears streaming down her face. "If you do, I'm going to turn into a prostitute! I'll go to bed with every guy on this campus."

Dick stood in the courtyard, speechless for once. Whatever else was going through his mind at that moment, he had to be impressed with a girl who would go to such lengths to win him.

A few days after Dick's graduation from the University of Texas, on June 24, 1950, he and Mimi were married at the country club in Mimi's hometown of Nacogdoches, Texas. Mimi dropped out of school, two and a half years shy of her degree. "I went after my MRS," she would later say proudly, ". . . and I got it!"

The bride was eighteen; the groom was twenty. Between them, they had several hundred dollars Mimi's father, Sam Levy, scraped together as a wedding gift, Richard's journalism degree, and Mimi's raw ambition to make them rich.

6

In years to come, whenever anyone spoke of Dick and Mimi—and that would be often—the word "team" or its image crept into the conversation inevitably.

"They worked well together," was one friend's assessment. "They complemented each other," offered another. Mimi herself described the marriage by saying, "We were a good team."

"What we did in a lifetime," Mimi would reflect grandiloquently, "is the great American dream."

When they returned from their honeymoon the summer of 1950, Dick and Mimi moved to Houston. Dick and Houston were a perfect match. Like Richard, the city was young, brash, wide-open and wild, a place where anyone with enterprise and ambition could break in and make it big. Everything in Houston was big: big fortunes, big personalities, big murders.

From the outset, Dick was on the hustle. Drawing on his most obvious skill, he took a job at a newspaper, the *Houston Chronicle,* in advertising.

As an advertising rep for the *Chronicle,* Dick was the very model of the rising young businessman. Three nights a week, Mimi would pick him up at the office and drive him to the "Y" to play handball. Ten months into the marriage, they produced their first "image" (as the *Chronicle* gossip referred to babies in her column): a healthy, spirited male heir named Michael Louis Minns.

Much later, when he was the subject of a magazine profile, Dick would tell the writer he became a self-made millionaire at the age of twenty-three. In reality, Dick, Mimi, and Mike lived in a two-bedroom walk-up in Montrose, a Houston neighborhood of once-grand homes whose early residents included the young Howard Hughes. With time, neglect, and Houston's lack of zoning laws, most Montrose homes had been converted to quaintly shabby duplexes and triplexes that stood next to pet-grooming salons or gypsy parlors with flashing neon palms and hand-lettered signs in the windows.

At the *Houston Chronicle,* Dick was remembered for being a go-getter, hard-working, and ambitious; still, there was little about him in those early days to distinguish him from all the other hungry young men climbing the corporate ladders, except for his and Mimi's dreams.

The following year, Richard abruptly quit his job at the *Chronicle,* where he had risen to the position of co-advertising manager of the Sunday magazine, to start his own advertising agency. The "staff" consisted of Dick, the president and founder; Mimi, vice-president and self-described "general flunkie"; and one part-time artist. With typical bravado, Dick christened the new company All-State Advertising Agency.

It was an audacious proposition for a twenty-four-year-old with a wife and son, no savings, no borrowed money, and another baby on the way.

In the beginning, All-State Advertising Agency was a seat-of-the-pants operation that consisted of a few minor accounts Dick managed to lure away from the *Chronicle.* The office was a tiny box on Hawthorne Avenue, a few blocks from the Minns's apartment. What All-State did have going for it was Dick Minns's unique brand of magic. No matter how small the client or how prosaic the product, Dick thought big and promoted bigger.

"He had all these marginal accounts," his brother-in-law Irving Weissman recalled. "The one I remember . . . he got an account called Ricchola. Little one-ounce bottles of olive oil they promoted for sunburns and burns. After Dick got ahold of the account, I saw billboards all over town and big ads in magazines. They were promoting the hell out of it— these little bottles of olive oil!"

Dick's technique for acquiring new clients was simple. Once he got his foot in the door, he'd promise the sun, moon, and stars in a never-ending stream of rhetoric. By the time he made his pitch, the prospective client had been through the business equivalent of a cult deprogramming. "He'd lock you in a room," one client recalled, "and wouldn't let you go till he had a deal. He'd wear you down." Once Dick reeled in the account, most agreed, he delivered almost everything he promised. "Nobody," one client remembered, "got the job done like Dick Minns."

From sunup to midnight Dick worked the phone. There wasn't a soul on earth who understood the value of publicity better than Dick. An hour's conversation with Marge Crumbaker or Maxine Mesinger (Houston's two rival gossip columnists) could mean a column of free publicity for one of his accounts. Besides, he began to think, it couldn't hurt to have his *own* name on people's lips.

By 1955, All-State was beginning to live up to its name, with branch offices in Los Angeles, New York, and Detroit. Somehow, Dick seemed to be in all places at all times. When he was in Hollywood, his California clients would marvel, he seemed to have more connections than the heads of studios. "He knew everybody," Bob Delmonteque, a Los Angeles client, commented. "He put me on all the shows." Dick felt at home in the schmoozy milieu of Hollywood. His brashness fit right in. Celebrities fascinated him; he was endlessly intrigued with fame. "He used to come over to the house an awful lot and talk business around the pool," a visitor of Seymour Lieberman's (Dick's corporate lawyer) remembered. "He went out to California a whole lot and oh, he thought he was a big shot! He was always bragging about all the movie stars he met."

Irving Weissman, who married Dick's sister Janice, compared his first meeting with Dick to an audience with royalty. "It was seven o'clock on a summer evening," Weissman remembered, the day Janice and her parents took him to Dick and Mimi's house in Montrose. "They led me into the bedroom. Here's a guy sitting up in bed in his pajama bottoms—seven in the evening!—and his wife is moving around, his mother's moving around, catering to him. They remind me of a queen bee with all the drones. And he's barking orders to everybody and we have a cursory salutation. And I said to myself, 'What kind of person is this, on a summer night, seven o'clock, sitting up on a bed with women running around?' And the whole time everybody was telling me, 'Oh, my son's so brilliant, he's so successful, so brilliant. . . . ' "

And Dick provided nonstop entertainment. On car trips with his family he would belt out Broadway show tunes. He loved to sing, and even compared himself with Frank Sinatra and Tony Bennett, his favorite singers. Mimi, on the other hand, would usually sit silently on such trips.

They were still an odd match, Dick and Mimi. The differences in their personalities that had surfaced in courtship grew even more exaggerated during their marriage. Dick, one relative would observe, was the feminine half of the relationship; Mimi was the masculine side. She talked like a man, direct and to the point, in a graveled, whiskey voice that reeked of cigarettes and martinis. Mimi's idea of a perfect holiday was a week in Las Vegas, where she could sit at a blackjack table. She loved to wear expensive clothes ("My clothes," she would later tell a journalist, "were *always* designer, from Isabel Gerhart"—an expensive Houston shop). Her taste ran to what the fashionable society doyennes of River Oaks, Houston's old-money neighborhood, would cattily refer to as "flashy." Not that Mimi gave a hoot. She thought her taste was the epitome of class, and she had the confidence to stick with it. She talked like a man, acted like a man, even drove a car like a man.

Dick, on the other hand, could get lost pulling out of his own driveway. He was the idea man, an artist; spontaneous, creative, emotional. Mimi's was the calm voice of reason; she was the practical, sensible one. Mimi, friends would say, was Dick's pendulum, the stabilizing force in his life. Dick, they would add ominously, would go "way the hell up." When he did, only Mimi Minns could bring him down again.

One day in 1955, Dick presented a sales pitch for an advertising campaign to two men who would change his life. The older of the two was named Ray Wilson, a one-time wrestler who had purchased a chain of exercise clubs throughout the country called American Health Studios. Wilson was thinking of hiring a new ad agency to breathe some life into the clubs. The man with Wilson was Robert Delmonteque, the production representative for American Health.

Dick was immediately fascinated with Delmonteque. Here was a Charles Atlas model come to life: six feet four, with

dark, wavy hair, a perpetual tan, and a physique straight
from Muscle Beach (where, in fact, Delmonteque was discovered)—a man who, like Dick, couldn't walk past a mirror
without glancing at himself in it. As Dick listened, clearly
impressed, Delmonteque sprinkled his conversation with
references to Clark Gable, John Wayne, Betty Grable . . .
movie stars he said he helped get into shape between films,
back in the forties. He also dropped the name of Joe Weider,
one of the pioneers in the health club industry.

By this time, the Richard Minns sales presentation had
been refined to an art form. A prospective client of the
All-State Advertising Agency could expect to be met at the
most impressive meeting room in one of Houston's most
luxurious hotels. At the appointed hour, Dick would make
a grand entrance, followed by an entourage of assistants and
models carrying a projector, movie screen, and all sorts of
papers. For the next several hours, Dick put on a multimedia
extravaganza. Veterans of this presentation proclaimed him
the world's greatest salesman. "Did you ever see the movie
The Hucksters?" one client asked, trying to explain Dick's
phenomenal appeal. "That was Dick. He was an absolute
genius—way, way ahead of his time."

As Delmonteque listened and watched Minns putting on
this show for him and Ray Wilson, he suddenly thought of
Mike Todd, the flamboyant Hollywood producer who was
married to Elizabeth Taylor.

"That's it!" he thought to himself. Delmonteque had been
trying to think who it was Richard Minns reminded him of
and kept drawing a blank. Before the rental on the room
expired, Richard Minns had a new client, and American
Health Studios got a surge of new blood. Neither would ever
be the same.

Dick threw himself into the ad campaign for his newest
and largest client. Before he put pen to paper, however, he
decided to do a little research on the health club industry and
check out the competition.

What he found was a small industry dominated by two
men, neither of whom was any stranger to self-promotion.
The first of these, Vic Tanny, was an enterprising former
schoolteacher who, in 1940, came up with the notion of
starting a commercial gym where Americans could pay to

get into shape. The Vic Tanny Gym was the first health studio in the United States, a sort of all-purpose family fitness center, with exercise equipment, bowling alleys, a skating rink, and cartoons for the kids. Before long, Vic Tanny Gyms began to spring up all over the West Coast, where a lifetime membership at Vic Tanny became a World War II-era fad.

Later in the forties, a business-savvy bodybuilder by the name of Joe Weider, sensing a good thing, burst onto the scene. Weider's claim to fame was a system of training principles for would-be bodybuilders. It would become something of a Ten Commandments of fitness, with Joe Weider the Moses of bodybuilders. By the early fifties, the "Joe Weider method" was on the lips of everyone with any connection to the health club industry.

Apart from that, Dick discovered, little had changed in the fifteen years since Vic Tanny opened his first gym. In 1955, as then, most of the existing studios were bare-bones grunt-and-sweat shops with no more than the basic equipment and a minimum of frills, or Vic Tanny-style family-oriented fitness centers.

What American Health needed, Dick decided, was a little sex appeal.

Dick understood well the appeal of American Health: vanity. And Dick knew exactly how to exploit it: "Before" and "After" pictures of studio members who had been transformed from paunchy, double-chinned fatties into slender, smiling advertisements for the American Health fitness program.

The idea was simple, but inspired. Who could resist American Health Studios' promise of a better-looking body? And the proof was right there, in the pictures. The wonder was that no one had thought of it before.

Once he had his brainstorm, Dick flooded the market with before-and-after testimonials in newspapers, magazines, and, for the first time ever, on television. Although it was just being introduced on the market, Dick was a great believer in the power of the little gray box that could beam pictures right into the living rooms of potential consumers with money in their pockets.

Many years later, Mimi would claim that Dick was the first person to put fifties' fitness icon Jack LaLanne on TV, at a small station in California—a claim LaLanne denies. The real truth is difficult to assess since, over the years, LaLanne would come to have reason to distance himself from Dick Minns.

As a symbol of their new prosperity and to mark their new position in society, Dick, Mimi, Mike, and Cathy, their second child, moved out of their Montrose walk-up to a cozy, traditional house in west Memorial. The residents of Memorial, an upper-middle-class sampling of lawyers, engineers, insurance brokers, and junior oil barons, took great pride in their community, which consisted of genteel brick homes on large wooded lots cloistered around Memorial Drive. In its early days, Memorial Drive was a winding country road that led out of downtown Houston. As the city grew, Memorial Drive became the Hallelujah Trail of the city's newly monied class.

With the house in Memorial came a maid, naturally, followed in time by a cook. Mimi's trips to Isabel Gerhart, a chic shop that specialized in designer clothes for the ladies-who-lunch set, became more frequent. Any social luncheons, however, were restricted to Saturdays. Monday through Friday, Mimi Minns was all business, as the administrator of All-State Advertising Agency. Life was good.

Then, toward the beginning of 1957, the bottom fell out. It was an old, familiar story. American Health Studios, Bob Delmonteque would later say, was the victim of a recession and poor management. It was simply opening too many clubs and spending more money than it was taking in. That year, it declared bankruptcy. Its second largest creditor was All-State Advertising Agency in Houston, Texas, which it owed a whopping $150,000.

Richard Minns was utterly frantic. This was a situation he couldn't persuade, charm, or cajole his way out of. All-State could not withstand a $150,000 loss—*would* not, if Dick Minns had anything to say about it. Day and night, he turned the situation over in his mind, planning and scheming and coming up blank.

Just when things looked bleakest, a cousin of Mimi's named David Toomim came to the rescue. Toomim lived in Houston and played golf from time to time with a savvy lawyer named Seymour Lieberman. Why didn't Dick give Seymour a call, Toomim suggested, and see what he had to say?

Not only was Seymour Lieberman one of the canniest bankruptcy lawyers around, he held two world's records in the fifty-yard dash and the fifty-yard low hurdle and was the founder of the Houston junior Olympics. He was also a health "faddist," and often lectured on the subjects of cardiovascular fitness and exercise, topics that were near to Dick's heart. From the earliest days of his marriage, Dick had forbidden Mimi to use anything but saffower oil in their home, and instructed their children to avoid white sugar, white flour, and white bread. From the age of fourteen until she was a woman of thirty-three, Cathy Minns didn't so much as touch a piece of candy. "When I was five years old I remember going to a friend's house," she related, "and her mother made us cinnamon toast. And I started crying because I thought it was poison."

When Lieberman agreed to take the American Health case, Dick called him every day, sometimes every hour on the hour, to check on his progress. Dick's obsession was getting his $150,000. After countless weekend confabs and hourly weekday progress reports to Dick, Seymour Lieberman came up with an intriguing alternative. Why not, he proposed to Dick one day, take over three American Health Studios in Houston in repayment of the debt? With Lieberman's knowledge of the health club field and his skills as a corporate lawyer, the lawyer could help Dick manage the business end of it. At least that way Dick wouldn't have to take a total loss.

Dick was still not enthralled. At the same time, he realized Seymour was probably right: Taking over a few of the studios was most likely the only way to avoid a complete loss. And if there was one thing Dick hated in the world above all else, it was losing.

So, in 1958, All-State Advertising Agency became the reluctant bridegroom in what Richard Minns would refer to as a "shotgun wedding" with three failing health studios in Houston, Texas.

*   *   *

Once the nuptials were complete, the groom did his best to avoid the bride. Dick promptly relegated the management of the studios to Mimi while he ran the advertising agency and plotted ways to dump the dubious boon of his bankruptcy case. He did, however, provide one creative contribution. Instead of calling the studios American Health, Dick decided they should sound like they were connected to a real person, someone like Jack LaLanne or Joe Weider. Someone flashy, to give the clubs a new image. The problem was, he didn't want to spend any money on new signs.

One day, as he was staring at the bold AMERICAN sign in front of one of the studios, sweet inspiration struck. What if he removed the M from AMERICAN and replaced it with a C . . . then separated the letters into two words: ACE RICAN? Dick beamed triumphantly. It was perfect. ACE RICAN conjured up images of a comic strip hero with bulging biceps and a steel-edged smile . . . just the image he had in mind for the studios. And it had cost him only a few dollars.

Mimi took over the reins on the three Ace Rican Studios with Scroogelike efficiency. She "pennied and dimed" cosmetic changes to the clubs, and kept a vigilant eye on the budget.

Dick's input was promotion and motivation. Dick loved to motivate. Once a week, he would breeze into the studios, whip the employees into a selling lather, and breeze out again. Between pep talks, he would be on the phone with Seymour Lieberman. Finally, Lieberman could take it no more.

"Dick," he said one day, wearily, "I have other clients besides you. And I don't have time to help any of them because I'm always on the phone with you!"

Lieberman recommended another lawyer for Dick, a young, dark-haired, extremely serious corporate attorney named Joe Reynolds. Reynolds was smart, tough, and soon to become one of Richard Minns's closest friends and a lifelong adviser.

A peculiar thing happened. Just when a prospective buyer appeared to take the studios off his hands and the papers were drawn up, Dick decided not to sell. His only explanation was the rather perfunctory, "If the gyms are worth a hundred and fifty thousand dollars to someone else, they ought to be worth that to me."

Mimi agreed. Although she was less than thrilled with the caliber of people associated with the health club business—bodybuilders and weight lifters did not figure into her fantasy of life among the rich and famous—a little voice kept telling her that Ace Rican Studios could be the means to a fortune.

Once he made the commitment to Ace Rican, Dick's first project was Dick. For close to three years, he had been smiling through clenched teeth at the nickname Ray Wilson and Bob Delmonteque, American Health's bodybuilding duo, had conferred on him.

"Hey, Penguin!" they would taunt, as they flexed their well-oiled biceps in Dick's face. "When are you gonna lose some weight and get in shape like the rest of us men?"

Between his long hours and constant travels for All-State, Dick's handball games at the "Y" and Mimi's sugar-free kitchen had given way to five-course dinners at four-star restaurants. When he stepped on the scales one morning, Dick was shocked to see the arrow go up to 185, 45 pounds above his college weight of 140. The next time Bob Delmonteque and Ray Wilson teasingly offered to put him on a fitness program, Dick said yes.

Wilson and Delmonteque shared a conspiratorial smirk. In the coming weeks, they cut Dick back to a spartan diet, filled him with protein powder and food supplements, and started him on a strenuous workout plan. Then they sat back and waited for him to collapse.

They didn't know Dick Minns. For all his braggadocio about his prowess in sports, Dick was not a natural athlete. He was small and not especially well-coordinated. What he lacked in innate ability, however, he compensated for in sheer will. He once told someone he considered physical pain an ally. "Pain is a friend," he remarked. "As soon as I start feeling some pain, I get accelerated because I know my opponent has got to be feeling pain and he can't take it and I can."

More than thirty years later, when Bob Delmonteque recalled Dick's tenacity, his voice still registered awe. "It was unbelievable!" he said, shaking his head. "He used to pass out, we'd hit him on the ass, he'd run to the john, throw up, and come back for more. In two or three months, he's outdoing us! *Tiger* tough . . . that's what he was.''

By the end of the regimen, Dick, by Delmonteque's assessment, "almost looked like Adonis." Every inch of his slight five-feet-nine-inch frame had been sculpted into hard-bodied, muscle-rippling perfection. His stomach, he would brag, was "as hard as the trunk lid of a 1937 Cadillac" from countless hours of sit-ups; his shoulders were strong and powerful; and his legs were like one long, hard continuous muscle.

When the makeover was complete, Dick Minns was a walking advertisement for Ace Rican Studios. Once converted, he became a fanatic in the house of fitness. With a little prompting by Bob Delmonteque and after a brief encounter with Jack LaLanne, Dick was soon swallowing from eighty to a hundred vitamins a day, prompting Delmonteque to remark that he and Dick had the "richest urine in Houston." Before long, Ace Rican was selling its own brand of vitamins in the studios, a new promotional idea of Richard's.

They were heady years for Dick and Mimi. The country had a new and glamorous young President, John F. Kennedy, who exuded vitality and pushed Americans to work on health and fitness. Dick promptly rechristened the three Ace Rican studios the "Kennedy Fitness Centers" and bestowed a free membership on President Kennedy, who actually visited the studios once. Dick, his sister Janice would observe, "was in the right place at the right time."

Dick and Mimi threw themselves into their new vocation full tilt. In 1959, after Mimi had given birth to their third child, a baby girl, she took three months off to spend at home; when their son Myles came along in 1962, she was working at the studio when she went into labor and was back at the office in ten days.

When they weren't at the fitness center, Dick and Mimi were flying around the country to other health and beauty facilities for ideas. Mimi, whose taste and interest definitely ran to the beauty side of the equation, made pilgrimages to the Golden Door and the Main Chance, two of the first luxury spas in the United States. She also, she would later point out with pride, met with Elizabeth Arden and with

Helena Rubenstein's sister, and on another occasion visited Revlon headquarters to explore the possibility of creating an exclusive line of makeup for the studios.

Dick's time was spent at athletic clubs, from Las Brisas in Acapulco, to the New York Athletic Club on Central Park South, to Mexico City, where his old colleagues Ray Wilson and Bob Delmonteque were opening a new club. Dick was particularly impressed with the posh Los Angeles Athletic Club and its equally posh general manager, David Roller.

Apart from the few luxury clubs he visited, Dick noticed, most of the health studios in the United States were like the Kennedy Fitness Centers: utilitarian workout rooms directed at the general population. Why not build a full-service, all-luxury health *club*—like the Los Angeles Athletic Club—in downtown Houston?

Dick figured out exactly how he wanted the club to look: like the ancient Greek and Roman spas. It was a stroke of genius, he told Delmonteque and Wilson. The Greeks and Romans had always been associated with baths and spas and they were known for glorifying the human form. Just look at all those statues.

Dick thought he might even be able to lure the dapper David Roller away from the Los Angeles Athletic Club to add a touch of class.

Wilson and Delmonteque didn't even think twice when Dick approached them with the idea. They were in.

In 1962, the President's Club (a continuation of Dick's John F. Kennedy theme) made its debut in downtown Houston in a glittering, gala party the likes of which the city had never seen before.

When the doors to the club swung open, a few of the guests could be heard to gasp. The interior of the club, decorated by Mimi, was like a Hollywood set designer's version of a Roman bath, with huge, stately, free-standing columns, reproductions of Greco-Roman statues, wall murals with street scenes of ancient Athens, and massive sunken tubs in gleaming white marble. The only thing missing was Charlton Heston in a toga.

Guests at the opening party (hand-selected by Dick from the upper echelons of Houston's rich and powerful) were invited to stroll amid the statues through Swedish rock mineral sauna baths, humidity-free desert-dry-heat rooms, inhalation therapy rooms, solariums with ultraviolet sun lamps, private body massage rooms, and infrared therapy rooms, all lushly carpeted and bedecked with glimmering, glistening floor-to-ceiling mirrors. Then there were card rooms, a billiard area, a swimming pool with a poolside terrace, sleeping quarters, a Ping-Pong area, a health food restaurant, and a health juice bar (dispensing President's Club all-natural vitamins).

Dick took special pride in the President's Club's patented logo: the "Discobulus," a sculpture of a male nude bent over in preparation to throw a disc. In Dick's version, the figure was slimmed down to be more in line with the ideal male of the 1960s; the model, it was said, was Dick himself. Everywhere guests at the opening looked, Dick's trademark version of the discus thrower was on display: in the reception area, on the President's Club stationery, on the walls.

Also on hand were the club's official "exercise consultants," shapely women with beehive hairdos trained to assist club members with their fitness programs. For their uniforms, Mimi had selected clinging, space-age costumes in shocking colors with matching tights.

The President's Club was an immediate and overwhelming success. On any given day at almost any time, one could stroll into the sauna room at the President's Club and glimpse the naked, sweat-drenched bodies of Houston's most prominent lawyers, oil men, and entrepreneurs, their Neiman Marcus suits and specially made snakeskin boots exchanged for President's Club signature white cotton towels.

In fact, one local magazine noted it was "a who's who of the city's most aggressive businessmen," with such prominent clients as Bill Hobby, Willie Rometsch, and Judge Elkins.

There was another member of the President's Club who, although no less eminent in his field than those mentioned above, achieved a certain notoriety as well. His name was Dudley Bell, and he was a private investigator. Bell knew everyone in town, and everyone in town who mattered knew or knew of Dudley Bell. Sooner or later, when trouble came knocking on their doors, Houston's rich and famous knocked on Dudley's.

When his time came, Richard Minns would be among them.

7

Richard Minns was a driven man on a fast track, his foot on the accelerator at all times.

The huge success of the President's Club, his old friend Bob Delmonteque observed, put "sizzle" in Dick's life.

"Time didn't really mean anything to him," his assistant, Jim LaHaye, remarked of Dick in the days after the President's Club began to soar. "He just did his thing whenever he wanted to do it." Dick would begin each day as he had ended the previous one; on the phone. Then he would prepare an ambitious, highly organized "agenda" for the day and cross off items as he completed them. "A lot of times he would wake up at six o'clock in the morning, get up and start making telephone calls," his assistant remembered. "Several times he called me at home at six because he was awake. And then we'd work until late hours at night, too."

Other President's health clubs began to spring up: eight more in Houston; four in Dallas, including a luxurious President's Club in Turtle Creek, the city's most fashionable address. Dick's strategy was to open an exclusive, all-male "hub" club in the center of a metropolitan area and then follow it up with smaller, more affordable chain clubs in suburban neighborhoods that admitted both men and women. He would fly all over the country scouting locations. A President's Club opened in Phoenix; then one in Boston; Rockford, Illinois; Oklahoma City; St. Louis. When the space program hit Houston, Dick used his contacts to ingratiate himself with NASA officials and started working with the astronauts. A NASA club soon followed.

Every time a new President's Club opened, Dick put on the razzle-dazzle. Flyers would go out, the media would be blitzed with TV and print ads, movie stars would "wing in"—everyone from Dean Martin to Frank Sinatra. If Jack and Elaine LaLanne were in Houston, they stayed with Dick and Mimi. When President Kennedy ordered the first space shots, Dick and Mimi were invited. *"Everything* was big," Mimi would later boast. "There's hardly a movie star I haven't met. I've played blackjack with half the stars. I played with Gracie [Allen] Burns one night. . . . We were always in interesting places at interesting times."

Once, on a trip to Copenhagen, Mimi noticed how the Danes submerged themselves in icy water after their steam baths to stimulate circulation and improve their overall health. When she and Dick got home, an "ice plunge" was incorporated into the President's Club facilities. Dick and Mimi were also the first in the nation to introduce the round whirlpool to club members, another of Mimi's inventions. Mimi dubbed herself forever after the "mother of the whirlpool."

Dick raced to take out a patent on Mimi's round whirlpool, and immediately designated it a trade secret. Then he took Mimi's invention a step further. He combined the round whirlpool, the sauna, and the steam room to create a so-called "wet area" in the clubs. The concept was the first of its kind, but soon became a standard in the industry.

Dick dreamed up the idea of opening a deluxe club for women, much like the President's Club, in Houston. After driving around the city, he settled on the perfect location: Post Oak Lane, a fashionable street in the heart of an area of Houston called the "Magic Circle," so named because it was adjacent to River Oaks, Tanglewood, and Memorial, the city's three most affluent neighborhoods. The club, he decided, would be called the First Lady, the female counterpart to the President's Club.

"I predict," Dick said of his latest inspiration, "women from River Oaks and Memorial will *fight* to get into the First Lady!"

Dick turned over the budget and decoration to Mimi. When she finished, it was a sight to behold. The foyer of the First Lady was a rococo fantasy of huge crystal chandeliers, tufted velvet couches in sinuous S-curves, pedestal end tables in faux marble and gold, accented by reproduction Greco-Roman statues presided over by Greek goddesses in life-size wall murals. The furniture was Louis XIV—an elegant assortment of ladies' writing desks, chairs, and armoires—framed by flowing, custom-made curtains.

The First Lady *tepidarium* (the ancient Greek word for a tepid room in their public baths) was no less lavish. A visit inside was like stepping into a scoop of spumoni. Faux marble and gilded mirrors covered the room as far as the eye could see. Stately columns stood on each corner of an immense bath filled with aquamarine-colored water. The huge, sunken bath was surrounded by thick, plush carpet the color of cotton candy. Bathing oils in gilded decanters were arranged artfully around perfumed whirlpool baths. Even the normally staid *National Geographic* was moved to purple prose in an attempt to recreate Mimi's fantasy on paper.

Dick's publicity photos of the First Lady displayed sylph-like models in brunette bouffant hairdos (all bearing a distinct resemblance to Mimi) dressed in the First Lady bathing costume: short white togas decorated with gold embroidery at the bust, tied at the waist with royal-purple sashes. Even the exercise bicycles were upholstered in mink and the bidets were 24-karat gold.

Dick's symbol for all this luxury was the Venus de Milo, the famous statue of Greek antiquity, which he had resculpted to a more slender form to represent the ideal beauty embodied in the First Lady Club. The real symbol of the First Lady, however, was Mimi. To celebrate the opening of the club, she commissioned a portrait of herself in a gown created for her by the Italian designer Travilla.

When Mimi's phantasmagorical creation opened to the public, Houston's first ladies of society began rearranging their luncheons and Junior League meetings around perfumed baths and bridge games at the Post Oak First Lady: Oveta Culp Hobby, wife of Will Hobby, twice governer and president of the *Houston Post;* Gene Tierney, the beautiful movie actress, married to Texas oilman Howard Lee . . . they all came.

You couldn't reside in Houston in the sixties or seventies and *not* know about the President's-First Lady health spas. The disc-thrower and Venus de Milo insignias were ubiquitous: on television, in newspapers, on billboards, and on storefront marquees in every new shopping center that went up in the city.

At one point, Dick and Mimi owned thirty-two separate President's-First Lady Clubs throughout the United States and had over one thousand employees. In the cities where Dick started clubs, it was said, the health club market *belonged* to him. "Nobody would open up against him," a colleague and competitor, Bob Schwartz, remarked.

In 1969, President's-First Lady (which had taken over Dick's three Ace Rican Studios) became the first health club in the country to become publicly owned and nationally underwritten. As a result of the stock sale, Dick and Mimi Minns made health club history and, in the bargain, an estimated five million dollars.

The ink was barely dry on the stock sale when Mimi went shopping for a new house. A house suitable for an empress.

The mansion Mimi selected to announce her arrival into society was in "inner" Memorial, closer to the city, to River Oaks, Memorial Park—places with true prestige.

Most of the homes there were rambling, ranch-style dwellings on capacious wooded lots down small, winding roads.

Mimi's house was startlingly contemporary, a dramatic three-story structure of glass and redwood set at a diagonal on a huge corner lot at one of the most conspicuous and prestigious intersections in Memorial, where Memorial Drive crosses San Felipe. Everyone who drove by remembered the house. The entrance, off Memorial Drive, was marked by an imposing wrought-iron gate.

The house featured a sunken living room with marble floors and a solid marble fireplace, from which one could look up twenty feet. At the top of the third level were a bar, sundeck, master suite with "his" and "hers" bathrooms, and a study. In addition, the mansion boasted an elevator, an outdoor spiral staircase to all three floors, six bedroom suites, nine bathrooms, and a heated, eighty-foot swimming pool with a glass wall through which swimmers could glide freely from indoors to out.

While Mimi gorged herself on reproduction French antiques, Richard left his own imprint on the Minns manor. One of his first purchases was a life-size sculpture of the President's Club discus thrower in solid Florentine marble, which he placed in the backyard, beside the pool. Another contribution was a custom-made, king-size circular bed for the master suite, set on a raised, revolving platform and covered, in Mimi's inimitable style, by an immense round bedspread in peacock-blue velour. There were thirty telephone jacks, one in every room, with a telephone in each jack. Wherever he might find himself in his new house, Dick would never be far from a phone.

The house at 11408 Memorial Drive soon commanded a full staff, including a live-in cook/maid and butler/chauffeur, a gardener, and assorted other servants, dressed, by their mistress's explicit instruction, in formal uniforms. Dick hired a chauffeur, whom he took along to help select a new car. The two came home with a white and red Cadillac convertible with white sidewalls and a hood ornament— "like 'Uptown Saturday Night,' " chuckled Dick's friend Bob Delmonteque.

When the Houston heat dipped below seventy, Mimi would choose from one of her eleven fur coats, among them a leopard jacket, a sable stole, and several minks. Her jewelry collection was equally impressive. For their twenty-second wedding anniversary in 1972, Dick, who was notoriously tightfisted, presented Mimi with a $51,400 sapphire necklace created exclusively for her by jeweler David Webb. Three years later, on their twenty-fifth anniversary, he gave her a $15,000 platinum ring and two $15,000 brooches with eighty-four diamonds.

Mimi's gifts to Dick were only slightly less ostentatious. For his birthday or on anniversaries, she generally presented him with jewelry which she helped design, usually in the form of a lion, since Dick loved to advertise the fact that he was a Leo.

It was easy to see what motivated Mimi: money and status. She would be the first to admit both. Dick, one could safely say, loved money every bit as much as his wife, and he was not immune to the seductions of social status. But there was another force that propelled Richard Minns: power. Mimi began to notice it when he started to earn his first big money.

Dick's role model was a man called, ironically, Melvin Lane Powers, the nephew of a flamboyant Houstonian named Candace Mossier, a Jayne Mansfield–style blonde who married an aging millionaire named Jacques Mossler. Candace became the benefactress and chief symbol of the Houston Livestock Show and Rodeo.

One couldn't drive five minutes on a Houston freeway in the seventies during Fat Stock Show month without seeing Candace's larger-than-life image on a billboard to promote the rodeo, her peroxide blond hair teased sky-high, anchored by a cowboy hat, her ample showgirl's figure decked out in brown suede with fringe—a cross between Mae West and Annie Oakley.

In the mid-sixties, Candace's husband Jacques was brutally murdered at his luxury apartment in Key Biscayne, Florida, the victim of thirty-nine stab wounds and repeated blows to the head with a blunt instrument. The chief suspects were Candy and Mel Powers, who was also her lover. Both Candy and Powers were eventually acquitted, due in no small part to the theatrical defense of their lawyer, Texas legend Percy Foreman.

When Dick met Mel Powers, Powers had become a mini real estate mogul. He was a "different breed of cat," one Houston colleague described him, known for his casual-hip style of dress and throwing lavish parties at his mansion in Houston or on his fabulous yacht in Florida. Yet Powers himself never drank at his soirees. He sat alone in a corner, observing everyone else in the room.

Minns was captivated by Powers. "From now on," he told columnist Marge Crumbaker, "I'm never going to wear a suit again. I'm going to wear casual clothes all the time, just like Mel."

Dick was true to his word. For every occasion except black tie (sometimes even then), he dressed in skintight blue jeans or western pants. He would wear them with turtlenecks or multicolored form-fitting polyester shirts unbuttoned to the chest and cinched with wide, western-style belts ("always a notch or two too tight," one local decorator sniffed), often with his initials.

Dick delighted in displaying his body. There is an old saying among bodybuilders that "your waistline is your sex line." Dick, Mimi would later note with pride, was known for having the "best 'abs' in the business." Every day, he would work out for hours to preserve his "waspish" (as one reporter described it) twenty-eight-inch waist and, in Bob Delmonteque's words, "Apollo-Belvedere" physique. Dick's pants were so tight he refused to keep a wallet in his pocket because, he told Mimi, it spoiled his physique. As a result he lost his wallet so many times that he switched to traveler's checks, which became a sort of Minns trademark.

Dick's once-golden locks turned golden again. If a long-time friend happened to comment on it, as Bob Schwartz (an American Health Studios associate) once did, Dick would say the "sun did it." But in fact Dick spent many an afternoon at a men's hair salon in Houston under a bonnet.

Among Richard Minns's many and frenzied acquisitions were an ever-growing assemblage of political cronies, many of whom he met through his shrewd young corporate lawyer, Joe Reynolds, who was fast developing a political power base in the Houston legal community himself. Politics in the state of Texas, as any old-timer will attest, have long been associated with an outstretched palm or two, and Dick Minns was a firm believer in the practice.

There were those who felt Dick was pushing too hard. Ted Kaplan, an old friend and client, was one of them. But Dick was too busy, and having far too much fun, to notice, or care. The man with the Midas touch for promotion suddenly awakened to the ultimate product for his public relations genius: himself. He devoted so much time and energy to it, he forged a friendship with Marge Crumbaker, the social columnist for the *Houston Post*, a big, earthy, dark-haired, down-home gal from Dumas, Texas, who began her career as the owner of an entertainment agency at the old Rice Hotel in downtown Houston. Dick would call up Marge and brag about his kids, his car, his house, his clubs—anything and everything he could think of that might get him in her column.

Houston in those days oozed with colorful personalities and instant millionaires, from "Silver Dollar" Jim West to wildcatter Glenn McCarthy, who built his own hotel, the legendary Shamrock, home of the famous Cork Club, as a playground for the nouveaux riches. And if, as Marge Crumbaker was later to state, "everyone was tooting their horn," Dick Minns tooted the longest and the loudest. Every month for over fifteen years, a minimum of twenty minutes at a time, he called Marge. "Dick," she used to say to him, "I'm not gonna speak to you unless you limit your calls to three minutes, and I really mean it!" Finally, in exasperation, Crumbaker installed a timing device on her telephone. At the end of three minutes, it would ring automatically. "Well," she would tell Dick, "your three minutes are up!"

But, in truth, hardly a month went by that Crumbaker didn't mention Minns in her column, sometimes several times in the same week. When Dick's parents celebrated an anniversary at the Rivoli, one of Houston's society hangouts, Marge recorded it for her column, under one of her well-known headings: SUPER PEOPLE, MOVERS AND SHAKERS, or BIG SHOTS. If Dick and Mimi went to dinner with Bob Delmonteque and his wife Madeleine, they were a "celebrity table at the Rivoli to toast Madeleine's birthday."

Crumbaker had another pet phrase for Houston's jet set. She called them the "Zum Zum [pronounced zoom zoom] Gang." Dick Minns was its undisputed king. A typical Marge Crumbaker column one January featured the day's "photo stars," country-and-western singer Rusty Weir, pictured with the owners of the Texas Steak House, where Weir was performing, all of them dressed in cowboy hats and broad Texas smiles. Next to the lead SUPER PEOPLE, Crumbaker gushed:

> Let's face it. Biz deals made among our town's Very Rich just aren't always carried out in the traditional fashion of Meetings in the Board Room. Case in point: when millionaire sportsman **Dick Minns** signed that multi-million dollar deal Tuesday with **Les Hemingway** for the movie and play rights to the life of Les' famed writer-brother **Ernest Hemingway**, it was done at the President's First Lady while Dick was working out. Standing on his head, that kind of thing. Dick's pal, super millionaire **Al Dugan** will co-produce with him. Big stars already are standing in line for the role. Dick wants **George C. Scott**, who is not in line . . .

The day of his thirty-fifth birthday, in the flush of the President Club's triumphal opening, Dick Minns gave

Marge Crumbaker a call that was unusual even by his standards.

"Hey, Marge!" he yelled into the mouthpiece. "Guess where I am and what I just did!"

Crumbaker thought for a moment. She knew Dick and his family were on vacation at Las Brisas, the luxury resort in Acapulco, so she assumed he was doing what he always did on holiday in Mexico: water-ski.

"Nope!" Dick cried gleefully. "I just swam across Acapulco Bay! It's six miles long, and I swam it in eight hours."

"Are you crazy?" she gasped.

"Maybe!" Dick said cheerfully. "I just decided I wanted to do something spectacular for my thirty-fifth birthday, and this seemed like a good idea. Now I'm not so sure. The water was so rough I lost nineteen pounds!"

The columnist was speechless. The man was a nut! But it sure made great copy. Crumbaker listened attentively, and copied down every word for her next column.

"I'm gonna do this every year until I die!" Dick bellowed into the phone. "From now on, on my birthday, I'm going to perform some incredible feat. Something nobody else has ever done."

The next day, Marge ran her column and a tradition was born. To perform a dangerous act, Dick would tell people, he would "psych" himself so he had no fear, then his instincts would take over. "I overcome it by sheer willpower, self-hypnosis, and prayer," he said. "When you've pushed yourself past total agony to the nth degree of human endurance, it's at that point that you find supernatural strength to keep going and win through." By Dick's next birthday, when he captured a giant red snapper, the wire services were printing news accounts across the United States, complete with pictures. By his forty-third birthday, in 1973, a writer for the Fort Worth *Star-Telegram* devoted an entire article to Richard Minns and his birthday feats. Based on his conversation with Richard and numerous news accounts, Jerry Flemmons printed what he referred to as an "official record" of Minns's previous nine birthday accomplishments:

—Age 35: Swam the length of Acapulco Bay, through rough water and heavy tides. Six miles in 8 hours. Lost 19 pounds.

—36: From a depth of 155 feet, speargunned and brought up a record Red Snapper. Also killed two sharks with a special underwater gun.

—37: Waterskied 8 hours, 16 minutes, nonstop.

—38: Performed 2000 consecutive sit-ups in 4 ½ hours.

—39: Became first person from United States to dive from famed cliffs of Acapulco. Height is 165 feet.

—40: Dived from the cliffs again because no one believed he had done it the previous year.

—41: From a depth of 168 feet, became first person, aside from Acapulco natives, to bring up alive a 300-pound snapping sea turtle.

—42: Off Cozumel in the Yucatan, free-dived 325 feet on a single 30-minute air tank, a claimed record.

—43: Twice waterskied 76 miles around the perimeter of Lake Tahoe on one ski at speeds up to 38 miles per hour in 1 hour 54 minutes.

"And not everything is saved for birthdays," Flemmons wrote in the *Star-Telegram*. "Minns dropped in on Acapulco a few weeks ago and scuba dived to 150 feet, returning with a 130-pound amberjack. Another record. A former Golden Gloves champion, onetime Brahman bull rider, ex-newspaperman and journalism teacher, Minns just does these things for the 'joy of living.' "

And the joy of publicity. While he was telling Jerry Flemmons he "didn't do his feats for an audience," Richard was busy preparing and sending press releases about his birthday stunts to the wire services and other reporters, and he wallpapered an entire room in his mansion with every clipping published, which he then dubbed the "Ego Room."

Between the dazzling success of President's-First Lady and his Barnum and Bailey-style self-promotion, Richard Minns became a full-blown celebrity in the state of Texas, and a national personality. *Muscle* magazine, Joe Welder's publication, featured a cover story on Dick in September 1976, headlined DICK MINNS: BUILT, DARING AND RICH. It was a gushing tribute—complete with he-man poses and shots of Dick water-skiing, posing with a giant sea turtle, presenting a check to Chris Evert at the Houston Virginia Slims Tennis Tournament, and standing next to his beloved discus thrower in his backyard—to, *Muscle* said, a "man of adventure, an artist, poet and philosopher."

"You talk about John Wayne," Mimi would say, years later. "Heck, *we* signed his name in so he could come to LaConcha Beach Club because he wasn't staying there! John Wayne stood and watched Dick eat a steak in Hawaii, because it was a thirty-two-ounce steak and he said nobody that size could eat that steak."

By this time, Dick ate only one meal a day, usually around eleven P.M. It consisted of two pounds of beef and his standard eighty-plus vitamins. Just about everyone in the city had heard about Dick's "high-protein meal," either from Marge Crumbaker's column or general gossip. Not only did he not mind his reputation as an eccentric, he cultivated it. He often signed his notes to Mimi "World's greatest nut," or "Your lunatic Leo."

But if, as some who read about his antics in the paper tittered, Dick was "crazy," he was crazy like a fox. He was, in the opinion of many, a genius.

"He has a genius IQ, I'm certain of that," Bob Schwartz once said of Dick, when asked to describe him. "And he's got a photographic memory. He never forgets anything."

By his own definition, Dick's genius was his ability for total concentration. "Just about everything he did," one President's-First Lady executive, Sonny Reser, remembered, "he just focused in totally on it. If it was work, he'd focus in totally on work. If he was telling you a story, he'd just focus in totally on the story and stay with it."

It was this quality that was the source of his charm. "He'd just turn all his attention on you," observed one associate, "and, being as successful as he was, that was flattering to most people, to have someone that big be interested in *them*."

But not everyone was completely taken in. His brother-in-law Irving Weissman would say, "Dick was the kind of man you don't want to get in an argument with because it leads nowhere. Just agree with him," Weissman, a lawyer, would advise people who had dealings with Richard. "He just keeps going on and on. He won't," Weissman would warn, "take 'no' for an answer."

There were other complaints. Dick, it was said, used his photographic memory as a "weapon." Those who worked with him spoke of how he could recall everything there was to know about another person—everything he was told, plus other things he would find out on his own, all the way back to the beginning of the person's life. "He kept an encyclopedia in his head about you," said one former employee, who became entangled in a lawsuit with Dick, "then when he needed to, he would use it against you."

His skirmishes, and there were many, always took place in the legal system. Dick, Mimi was fond of saying, was a "frustrated lawyer." More than one person who had an argument with Dick got a knock on the door the next day from a process server. The judicial system was like a giant board game to Dick. He loved to play, and he played to win. Everything about the legal process enthralled him— the stratagems, the intrigue, the showmanship, the manipulation, the intimidation, and, most of all, the thrill of victory. He kept Joe Reynolds so busy handling lawsuits for him Reynolds became his unofficial "in-house counsel."

A few years after the President's Club opened, when President's-First Lady was in the early days of its national expansion, he even found himself in court with Bob Delmonteque, the man he called his best friend. When Delmonteque, who was the executive vice-president of the President's Club, filed a motion to require Dick to allow him to examine the company books (Dick had been balking at Delmonteque's repeated requests), Dick got Joe Reynolds on the case. In his answer, Dick claimed Delmonteque's motives were "corrupt" and "improper" because he was harboring plans to "wreck" the President's health clubs.

The suit, like most of Dick's litigation, was eventually settled out of court, and both parties went their separate ways. Afterward, Delmonteque's only comment was a terse and somewhat cryptic: "Dick tried to *own* people."

Shortly after they met on the ski slopes in Aspen, Richard Minns bragged to Barbra Piotrowski that he could "make" people fall in love with him.

And indeed he could. Once, as a teen, his daughter Cathy water-skied in a rainstorm for an hour and a half, bloodying her hands and feet, just to impress her father. When she returned to shore, Dick was cheering, along with the rest of the family. A friend who had accompanied Cathy and her family to the lake later told Cathy she thought it was the "sickest thing she had ever seen."

Dick gathered around him a corps of employees with the same fanatical devotion. His personal secretary, Cathy Mosley, was among them. She was remarkably efficient. No call made it through to Dick at the President's-First Lady headquarters building without first going through Cathy Mosley, who, some said, was secretly in love with him. It was a power she took very seriously. Mosley protected Dick from the rest of the world with the wild fierceness of a lioness guarding her cub.

Other long-term employees formed an orbit around Dick and Mimi: Jimmie LaHaye, Dick's folksy personal assistant; David Roller, the David Nivenesque manager of the Houston President's Club; Bob Delmonteque, his muscle-bound fitness director (before the schism); Joe Reynolds, Dick's dour, politically connected lawyer, who was named to the President's-First Lady board; Ed Shelby, PFL's canny finance director, whose daughter married Dick and Mimi's son Mike; Charles Syptak, the corporation's boyish-looking comptroller; David Toomim, Mimi's cousin, who had recommended bankruptcy lawyer Seymour Lieberman way back when. It was a tightknit group with Dick and Mimi— but especially Dick—at the center. Wherever he went, an entourage of employees went with him. For whatever reason, Dick could not be alone.

Sometime in the early sixties, right around the opening of the President's Club, Mimi interviewed a heavyset, mannish-looking woman in her mid-thirties for a bookkeeping position; someone who, in time, she hoped to train to relieve her of some of the duties of overseeing all the clubs. The woman's name was Patsy Ruth Moore Hall, called Pat.

Mimi was impressed right away, despite the rugged interviewee's lack of solid credentials or certificate in accounting. Hall was married, with two sons, and seemed to be a good mother to her kids. She was also, Mimi could see, a smart woman, and an extremely capable one. Mimi was a woman who trusted her instincts. She hired Pat Hall on the spot.

There was something unnerving about Pat Hall. She was, at the least, an unusual-*looking* woman: barely five feet two inches, slightly cross-eyed, with dark-brown hair cropped short, topped by short fringe bangs cut straight as a ruler. But there was more to Pat Hall's disturbing persona than her appearance. As she continued with President's-First Lady, she quickly advanced, despite her lack of formal training, to office manager of one of the clubs, then, after the company went public, general manager over all the clubs.

Her rapid advancement was at the direction of Dick and Mimi, who asked Hall to keep her eye on the other employees and report back to them. "Pat," Mimi once said, "was kind of like a detective if you wanted one." Hall carried out her duties with steely efficiency. She even took to wearing men's clothes and became more brazen about her personal life. She divorced her husband and "married" a woman named Susie. She kept a framed photo of the ceremony on the walls of her office: Susie in a white gown, Pat in a tuxedo.

Because she was so good at her job and extremely dedicated, Mimi turned a blind eye to Pat's idiosyncrasies. "Pat has some strange ways," she once said, "but if I want to accept Pat Hall, I accept her ways. She's a good worker, that's all I can say."

Others in the organization considered her loyalty to Dick and Mimi fanatical. Pat Hall, one said, was the type of person who would do *anything* for someone to whom she felt an allegiance.

8

Evinia Rometsch, the young, beautiful wife of one of Houston's top restauranteurs, occasionally found herself at the same social gatherings as the Minnses. She caught herself wondering how the two of them happened to be together at all. She would have expected Richard, she thought in her cattier moments, to be with someone more attractive, or at the least, flashier than Mimi. Someone really into exhibiting her body.

It's true: Superficially Dick and Mimi *were* still an odd match. Several years of marriage had done nothing to lessen their differences. The glue that held the marriage together was money: making it, and reveling in it afterward.

So Mimi went along with Dick on the family's yearly holidays to Lake Tahoe and Las Brisas in Acapulco, where Dick skied nonstop, even though Mimi would have preferred to be at the blackjack tables in a casino in Las Vegas. And she didn't object when Dick bought a lake house in Austin for weekend waterskiing marathons. Dick, although he placed a NO SMOKING sign over the desk in his office, tolerated Mimi's smoking, drinking, and socializing, and turned a blind eye to her lavish spending, in spite of the fact that he was a man known to pinch pennies.

One small cloud hung over Dick and Mimi's marriage, something Mimi never even told her children.

In 1959, the year she was pregnant with her third baby, and shortly after Dick's advertising agency took over American Health Studios, Mimi got a call from a friend of the family. (She would later identify the caller as Ted Kaplan, Dick's friend from the *Chronicle* years. Kaplan denies it.)

"I'm concerned about Dick," the friend said to Mimi. "He's been spending a lot of time lately with Gail Ledford," a shapely brunette saleswoman at one of the clubs. "At first I ignored it," said the caller, "thinking it would play itself out, but it's obvious they're having an affair, and I think it might be getting out of hand. I thought you should know."

Mimi thanked the friend and hung up. Later, when she got up her nerve, she confronted Dick about the supposed affair.

"It's not true," he said to her. "Whoever told you that is lying. I'm not having an affair with Gail Ledford."

But it kept nagging at Mimi. One afternoon, when she knew Dick was at the office, she drove to Gail's apartment. When Ledford answered the door, Mimi's eye came to rest on a collection of stuffed animals inside the apartment. She recognized them as identical to the stuffed animals she had at home—gifts, over the years, from Dick.

"Thank God you know," Ledford blurted. "Now he'll divorce you and marry me."

Dick continued to deny that he was having an affair.

"But I saw the animals!" Mimi shouted.

"It wasn't me," Dick swore. "I'm not having an affair with Gail Ledford!"

Mimi Minns considered her options. She was twenty-seven years old, five months pregnant and thirty pounds overweight, with two children under the age of eight. What choice did she really have? She had to believe Dick. Besides, she told herself, maybe he *didn't* have an affair with Gail Ledford. Maybe he was telling the truth. She and Dick were a team. They had an empire to run.

By the mid-seventies, Dick had been in the health club business for nearly twenty years and he was getting fidgety. The federal government was beginning to take a closer look at spa advertising and membership contracts. The business, Dick decided, just wasn't as much fun as it used to be.

Or as profitable. Between December of 1969 and January of 1970, stock in President's-First Lady dropped from an all-time high of twenty-one dollars to a depressing two dollars a share. Dick began buying up shares from PFL stockholders at a price of three dollars a share. When he had acquired enough, he returned the company to private status.

Then he got on the phone. Chicago Health and Tennis, a giant conglomerate owned by the aptly named Don Wildman, a mover and shaker who traveled the same international party circuit as Dick, offered to purchase fifteen of the clubs at a price of eight to ten dollars a share. As part of the bargain, Dick was to keep the original President's Club in downtown Houston. He also agreed to sign a five-year agreement not to compete with Chicago Health and Tennis.

It was a coup of Charles Atlas proportions. Dick and Mimi made a profit of six to eight dollars a share on the stock Dick had bought back from shareholders at three dollars a share, earning them, Dick would later boast, a cool fifteen million dollars.

For a time, Dick talked of retiring. That lasted, he would later say with a smile, "about fifteen minutes." When he got a call one day out of the blue from Bob Delmonteque, whom he had not seen in the ten years since their lawsuit, it was clearly a work of fate. Dick pressed him into a tennis game, and when they met on the courts, it was as if nothing had ever interrupted their friendship.

"Hey, Bob!" Dick shouted over the net. "I've got an idea for a business that I know is gonna make millions!"

Delmonteque smiled. *Yeah*, he thought to himself. It was the same old Dick.

"I've been givin' this a lot of thought, and I wanna open a health and beauty and fitness resort for men and women that's all deluxe. Kinda like La Costa. A place where people can go for a couple weeks to take a 'health vacation.' And I wanna open it up in Conroe, at April Sound. If you get on board now you can be my executive vice-president. Are ya interested?"

Conroe was less than an hour's drive north of Houston, and it had a beautiful manmade lake in the middle of a forest of thick, lush pine trees. It was the perfect location for a health and beauty resort, right next to all that wonderful Houston money.

"All right!" Delmonteque whooped, eager to make a comeback. "Let's do it!"

Dick was filled with the intoxication of a fresh conquest. When the owner of April Sound changed his mind about leasing to Richard Minns and Bob Delmonteque (because, Delmonteque would later say, they threw a party at April Sound that got "too rowdy"), Dick simply came up with a new plan. As soon as his agreement not to compete with Chicago Health and Tennis expired, he and Bob would open a new health club chain. Except that these would not be just ordinary health clubs. This, Dick and Bob agreed, would be the health club to end all health clubs. The name, Dick decided, would be Olympia.

That spring, Dick went to see the movie *Jaws*. When he came out of the theater, he knew what he was going to do for his next birthday. It would be his most spectacular stunt ever. He was going to fight a great white shark.

By April, Marge Crumbaker was reporting that *Muscle* publisher Joe Weider offered Dick $250,000 to kill a shark off the coast of Australia, to be filmed by a movie crew.

Come September, Crumbaker's column reported Richard Minns had been to Australia and back, without having a go at the sharks, due to "pressure from ecological groups," Samoan red tape, and "foot-dragging by Hollywood promoters."

Late in 1976, Dick announced that he would battle the great white shark on closed circuit television in western Samoa on May 3, 1977.

From all indications, this was going to be the year of Richard Minns's greatest triumphs.

When President's-First Lady went into liquidation, Mimi, who once had been consumed with PFL business, spent her days playing an endless series of tennis games—so many, in fact, she began to keep a diary just to put them all in order. Without the President's Clubs to keep them together, Dick and Mimi had nothing in common except their four children, three of whom were either married or away at college. Dick's trips out of town became more and more frequent. Mimi's eyes began bothering her. She was bored. Dick was restless. It was, she could feel, the perfect recipe for disaster.

On January 16, 1977, disaster struck: Richard Minns met Barbra Piotrowski on the ski lift in Snowmass, Colorado.

The instant he cast his eyes on her sitting at the ski lodge, he was obsessed. Earlier that year, Dick had confided to a reporter that the reason he performed physical feats on his birthday was to demonstrate "there's no such thing as age." When he was with her, Barbra Piotrowski possessed a powerful aphrodisiac: She made Richard Minns feel like he was nineteen again.

Years later, when she was filled with bitterness, Mimi Minns would ask Dick what he saw in Barbra. "She loves me," Dick told her, "the way you did when you were sixteen years old."

Part Two

Part Two

9

Late in March 1977, Barbra Piotrowski and her seventeen-year-old brother, John, pulled into Houston in her blue Volkswagen camper, all her belongings and some of the furniture from her antique business with Oliver stuffed inside.

It was a glorious spring day. A slight breeze was redolent of azaleas. To Barbra, who was seeing the world through the eyes of a woman in love, Houston was paradise.

She and John drove straight to the apartment of Cathy Mosley, Dick's secretary. Dick suggested that she and her brother sleep at Cathy's for a few days because while he was entertaining businessmen from out of town, he was staying at his ex-wife Mimi's mansion in Memorial. He and Mimi were still good friends, he explained. Like brother and sister. He often stayed at her house on the nights when he didn't sleep at his office. That way he could see the children more often. He also listed the Memorial house as his legal residence for tax purposes. From time to time, he said, he *had* to stay there. "Sometimes," Dick said earnestly, "business will have to come first. You're just going to have to trust me."

Barbra nodded understandingly. She was still pinching herself to be sure what was happening was real. The next day was her twenty-fourth birthday and she was going to spend it in a new city with the man she always dreamed she would meet, the man with whom she wanted to spend the rest of her life.

The next morning, Dick had an assignment for her. While he was with his clients, he wanted Barbra to find an apartment for them. Eventually, he said, they would retire to his permanent home at Lakeway in Austin, but until then, he and

Barbra needed somewhere other than his office to live when they were in Houston.

Barbra attacked the project with a newlywed's zeal. As she drove from apartment to apartment, getting to know the city, she hummed along with the radio. She smiled as she thought of Richard back in Aspen, pleading with her to move to Texas. She was certain she had done the best thing. She really *could* have it all. After two days of intensive apartment-hunting, Barbra settled on a two-story New Orleans-style townhouse that rented for $325 a month in Westbury Square, deep in southwest Houston. After getting Dick's approval, she signed the lease and moved into the townhouse. The date on the calendar was the first of the month. April Fool's Day.

Before she had a chance to catch her breath, Barbra found herself in the middle of a whirlwind of activity, set into motion by Dick. The morning after she moved into Westbury Square, five days after she arrived in Houston, Dick told her to grab her suitcase. They were flying to Aspen to spend Easter week with his friend Don Wildman.

"Oh, and by the way," he added matter-of-factly, "my son Myles is going with us."

Barbra didn't blink an eye. If Dick wanted to bring his teenage son along to Aspen, it was fine with her. She had nothing to hide. Nor, she assumed, did Dick.

Once in Snowmass, the three of them shared one of Don Wildman's two-bedroom luxury condominiums at the Aspen Club, with Dick and Barbra in one room and Myles in another. For the next week, Dick and Barbra, joined occasionally by Myles, put in fifteen-hour days on the ski slopes and four-hour nights at the Aspen Club, working out.

Dick and Myles, Barbra decided on the trip, had an unusual relationship. They were always competing with each other, she noticed, especially in sports. Even though Myles was bigger than his father, with a football player's build, he couldn't keep up with Dick, and it seemed to bother him. They acted, Barbra thought, more like buddies than father and son. They even talked about their double dates together. It was odd, Barbra thought, but she liked Myles and he seemed to like her, and that was the important thing.

Barbra wanted to be accepted by Dick's family.

Barbra also liked Don Wildman, the thrill-seeking Chicago multimillionaire who had purchased Dick's clubs a few years earlier. His lifestyle, however, took her aback. Although he had been married for many years to a woman named Dorothy who worked in his organization in Chicago, Wildman had come to Aspen with a sweet, comely brunette named Rebecca Shutter, a former Playboy bunny.

As soon as they were alone, Barbra asked Dick about the arrangement. "Don and Rebecca?" he asked casually. "She's been his girlfriend for years. Dorothy knows all about it. They're separated. She doesn't care."

Although they became good friends, every time Barbra looked at Rebecca, she shuddered inwardly. Even though Don was rich and good-looking, Barbra thought to herself, it must be horrible to be with a man you know is somebody else's husband.

Dick Minns, who was very much somebody else's husband, did astonishingly little to conceal Barbra Piotrowski's presence from his wife, or the world at large. He was, in fact, spectacularly brazen. Although Mimi would later claim she knew where Dick was every hour of the day from the notes in her tennis diary, the fact was, once Barbra arrived in Houston, Dick was with her nearly every weekend, and sometimes for days, even weeks, at a time. He literally advertised the affair. Within a month after Barbra arrived in Houston, Dick had Barbra modeling for print ads for President's-First Lady, with her name stated prominently under a photograph of her in a tight black leotard and platform heels.

During the weeks he was in Houston, he spent two or three nights a week at the Westbury Square apartment with Barbra. The other two or three nights he would sleep at his Memorial house as if nothing had changed. He explained his absences to Mimi by saying he had out-of-town business. Barbra would later say she believed Dick stayed at the Memorial mansion from time to time so he could see his children, entertain clients, and fulfill his tax requirements.

Dick's friends and coworkers were the audience for this farce. According to "super-millionaire" Al Dugan, a

longstanding crony of Dick's, Barbra "suddenly appeared
on the scene." One morning when Dugan was meeting
Dick for their regular jog around Memorial Park, Barbra
was beside him. From that point on, Dugan recalled, when
he and his wife, Lydia, met Dick at Tony's or the Rivoli,
Houston's most chi-chi restaurants, Dick would stride in
with Barbra on his arm and look over his shoulder at the
admiring glances. Barbra was with Dick when he worked
out at the President's Club, late at night. She was with
him at his office at PFL headquarters. She was with him
on weekends at Lakeway, two or three times a month.
One weekend, Bob Delmonteque would recall wryly, he
watched Dick slip away from the family vacation house at
Lakeway to visit Barbra at the Lakeway Inn, a few miles
down the road.

Dick's employees at PFL headquarters bit their tongues
about the boss's behavior. His friends scratched their heads,
but said nothing. If asked, he made it clear that he had no
desire to get a divorce from Mimi. Their partnership was
too expensive to break up. The problem was Dick *couldn't*
give up his new love. For a man who prided himself on
discipline, Richard Minns had found an addiction: his drug
was Barbra Piotrowski.

In years to come, when people would speak of Richard
Minns and Barbra Piotrowski's love for each other, they
would use the word *illness*.

Their desire for each other, those who were around them
observed, went beyond mere physical attraction. It was an
obsession.

"They were both insanely in love with one another," Bob
Delmonteque said of the relationship. "Once in your life
you run into someone who really turns you on. For Dick
it was Barbra, and with Barbra it was Dick." Richard,
Delmonteque would later say, "had no control emotionally
when it came to Barbra."

Even Barbra was amazed at the intensity. She had
assumed it would taper off after the first few times she
and Dick made love. That had always happened with her
girlfriends, whose dates stopped calling after the novelty of
sleeping together had worn off. Since she had never really
had a sexual relationship before, Barbra kept expecting

the same thing to happen with Richard. Instead, it got hotter.

Whenever they were apart for even a few hours, Barbra would bound up to Dick, jump up on his waist, and wrap herself around him in a leg scissor. "It was embarrassing sometimes," remarked one colleague. "Here was this forty-plus guy carrying on like this."

"I remember," Barbra was to say, "times when I was driving to the health club to meet him. Just by thinking about him—just thinking that we were going to be together—was all I needed. Maybe it was because I was deprived all those years."

Perhaps that was true. Dick showered Barbra with compliments and declarations of love—hundreds of them—every day. Some of them were humorous, others touchingly poetic, some carnal. "Let's go in the other room," he would scribble on a note and pass to Barbra when she was on the telephone, "and FUCK!!!"

Dick and Barbra made love three or four times a day, every day, sometimes for as long as four or five hours at a time. Dick was in awe of his endurance. "I get ready to leave," he would say to Bob Delmonteque when he got to the President's Club, "and that goddamn thing would stand up again!"

Bob Delmonteque, who kept nude calendars on the walls of his office at the President's Club and talked openly about sex with shocked society mavens at cocktail parties, listened to Dick talk and observed him with Barbra with trepidation.

There was something about them, he decided, that wasn't quite right. Their relationship was too . . . *erotic*. It wasn't normal.

Since Dick did not eat breakfast or lunch, neither did Barbra. Meals, Dick told her, were a waste of time. And he didn't want to gain weight. Their sole meal was his famous protein feast of a sixteen-ounce steak served blood-rare with a baked potato and vegetable, at around midnight or one A.M. With his vitamins, of course.

The first thing Dick brought to the apartment, Barbra took notice, were his vitamins—boxes and boxes of them, which she was expected to separate into daily packets and take herself. Then, when they were at dinner, Dick would open a package and swallow all ninety at a sitting, sometimes without water—especially if he thought it would get attention. Richard, Barbra noticed, took a prankster's delight in shocking people, particularly those he considered stuffy or uptight.

Once when he and Barbra were dining in a tony restaurant with a priggish older woman, Dick laid out his dozens of vitamins in front of him. "What are all those?" the woman inquired, incredulous. One by one, Dick identified each vitamin and its purpose. "This one," he said finally, pointing to a large red pill and watching the woman's face with an impish grin, "is for virility." Ten minutes later, when the woman had recovered from embarrassment and the conversation had taken another turn, there was a loud bang under Dick's plate. "See?" he said exuberantly. "It works!" Barbra, who had seen Dick bang his knee under the table, had to cover her mouth to keep from laughing.

In addition to following his meal pattern, Barbra was expected to keep his insomniac hours. Dick viewed their constant togetherness with urgency. Barbra *had* to stay up with him. Once, when Barbra happened to nod off ahead of Dick after they finally retired around four in the morning, she was awakened by the sound of Dick jumping up and down on the bed and making pig noises in her face. "Come on!" he shouted gleefully, when she wearily opened her eyes. "Let's play!" Then he grabbed her by the hand and pulled her up on the bed to jump with him. Dick, Barbra once said, "couldn't stand being alone . . . ever, ever, ever."

If he chanced to wake up early in the morning when Barbra, who was a five A.M. riser, was sometimes out jogging, Dick would talk on the phone nonstop, occasionally on two lines at once. "I'm kind of a telephone addict," he once said during a legal deposition.

After a few months, Barbra had the phone company install a secret third line in a closet in the apartment because Dick was on both lines at the same time so often she wasn't able to receive incoming calls. One night, when he wasn't on either line, Dick heard a phone ringing in the distance and nearly went insane trying to figure out where it was coming from.

On the days Dick went into the office alone, he called Barbra or she called him every hour. On the unlikely chance she might forget, he left notes reminding her, scattered around the apartment like clues in a treasure hunt.

When he wasn't telling Barbra how much he loved her, Dick was writing it on slips of paper, bits of newsprint, pages of yellow legal pads, in strong, urgent prose. "I love you," he wrote one day. "I love you very much. I love you with all my heart, all my soul, all my might. Please love me as I love you. . . ."

Sometimes, when they were flying together, Dick would scribble little love notes on airplane cocktail napkins and pass them to Barbra in the next seat. Once, when Barbra was drying her hair, Dick sat a foot or so away, watching her. After a few minutes, he got up impatiently, found a pen and paper, quickly wrote a few words, and handed the page to Barbra.

She looked at the note in disbelief. Then she giggled hysterically.

"I'm so jealous," Dick had written, "of your hair dryer. Your every thought you think that isn't me."

One night, when they were lying in bed together, Dick turned and looked at Barbra. "We have something other people only dream about," he said. "Our lives make other people's lives humdrum."

Barbra nestled into his shoulder, listening contentedly.

"We have such a wonderful, exciting relationship that most people in the world are envious of it. They would do anything they could to destroy us."

Barbra looked up, puzzled.

"They would do it," he continued, "probably by telling you things about me that are untrue. If you want our relationship to last," Dick said, staring at Barbra, "you have to block out anything that anybody might tell you about me. They would only be doing it because they're jealous of what we have.

"Trust me," he kept telling her. "If you really love me, you won't question me. Just trust me."

Barbra nodded soberly. Dick, she decided, said some strange things sometimes.

Shortly after Barbra arrived in Houston, Dick went through her closet and inspected every article of clothing in her wardrobe.

"Not tight enough," he said, with a wave of his hand. "I like clothes that are *tight*. I like to see the form of the body."

For the next week, Barbra tried on all the clothes in her closet in front of Dick and his tailor, who marked them all for alterations. When they finished, her wardrobe, which consisted mainly of blue jeans and short shorts, fit like a second skin, a female version of Dick's. "I used to kid Dick," said Bob Delmonteque, "and ask him whether the tailor left his hand in his pocket!"

Dick's influence didn't end there. He encouraged Barbra to grow her shoulder-length hair even longer, and to dye it a lighter blonde than her natural sun-streaked blondish-brown. For the most part, Barbra complied. When she was with friends, she would make jokes from time to time about how she and Dick were both blonds and both "from the same bottle."

When she shopped for clothes, Dick accompanied Barbra, even into the dressing room, where she tried on everything in front of him. When the final selections were made, they were Richard's. He even designed some of Barbra's clothes, generally in leather, often with feathers. To Dick, leather and suede were pure sex. On the hottest days in Houston, when sweat drips off ten-year-olds in swimsuits, Dick would parade around in skintight leather pants and jackets, his shirt open to the mid-chest, gold chains flashing in the sunlight. Dick's own wardrobe was a Technicolor collection of form-fitting polyester pants or skintight jeans studded with rhinestones, and blue-jean vests or jackets with elaborate hand-embroidered designs. His favorite was a spectacular white cockatoo digging its talons into a brass ring, sewn onto the back of a denim jacket.

"You know," Barbra suggested tactfully after she and Dick had been together a few months, "if you want a young look, why don't you go ahead and stay with that style of shirt, but try it in a cotton or a blend, instead of polyester?"

"I like shiny clothes," Dick protested. "They get people's attention."

Barbra, by nature, was a little brown wren to Richard's majestic peacock. After a childhood and adolescence of avoiding the watchful eyes of strangers, suddenly, with Dick, she commanded the center of the spotlight. And while she would have preferred to continue wearing her blue jeans in their original, prealtered size, or the simple, classic suits that hung in her closet, untouched, but she willingly submitted herself into Richard's hands to be molded into his ideal of beauty. "If that's what it takes," Barbra would say to her sister or a girlfriend when they questioned her about the changes in her appearance, "if I can make him happy by wearing my hair a certain way or by wearing certain clothing, then why shouldn't I make him happy? It's more important to me to make the person I love happy. Those things are superficial compared to the kind of person you are."

So, when Dick suggested Barbra get her breasts enlarged, she made an appointment with a plastic surgeon, even though the extra cleavage made her uncomfortable and embarrassed.

Bob Delmonteque witnessed Barbra's submissiveness with a mixture of contempt and envy. "She couldn't pee," he was later to say, "without asking Dick."

Sometime during that first spring, Dick broke the news to Barbra that he wasn't actually divorced from Mimi.

The way Dick explained it, they were effectively divorced, anyway. "We're legally separated," he said to her. "That's the same thing as a divorce, really. The difference is just a technicality."

Barbra had no reason to disbelieve Dick. It was obvious to her that he and Mimi were not living together. Dick was almost always with her, whether it was in front of his friends, in restaurants, out of town, or at the health club. His own son, Myles, occasionally went with them on trips out of the city. What was there not to believe?

Barbra had more pressing thoughts on her mind. Dick

was talking more and more about fighting a great white shark in Western Samoa in May, and she lived in constant fear that he was going to be killed.

"Please, Dick," she pleaded. "Don't do it! I don't want to be a 'widow' at twenty-four!"

"I have to, Barbra," he said insistently. "I made a commitment. I didn't know I was going to fall in love with you when I made that commitment. I gave my word. Everyone's expecting me to do it. I can't go back on it now. People would think I was a coward."

Dick was a sports maniac, and Barbra was determined to be his equal. Sonny Reser, a young and athletic executive with the Dallas President's-First Lady clubs, had met Barbra in Antigua with Dick and was impressed with her determination from the first day. Even though Barbra had just been checked out to dive that week, Reser noticed, she went along without blinking an eye when he, his girlfriend, and Dick, all experienced divers, dove fifty feet underwater in a cove to spear a huge bass grouper.

"She was really up for anything," Reser recalled. "If someone said, 'Let's go run five miles,' Barbra would be the one to go run five miles."

The first day Dick took Barbra jogging, at Memorial Park in Houston, he took her aside before his running partners arrived. "I told all my friends that you're a female jock," he whispered in her ear, "so you're gonna have to keep up with us or you'll embarrass me, OK?" For six miles, Barbra, who had jogged only a few times in her life, ran alongside Dick and his friends. When they finally stopped, she could barely walk. Five and a half months later, when she eventually saw a doctor, he told her she had bilateral knee injuries from that day. Barbra never complained. She had pleased Dick and she had accomplished her goal. Those were the only two things that mattered.

Toward the end of that same trip to Antigua, Dick pulled Barbra over to the side of the dive boat.

"Listen," he said in a low voice. "I've been thinking. I know how much you don't want me to fight a shark in Samoa next month, and you know I have to go through with it, because I said I was going to do it. Maybe there's a way out of it. . . ."

Barbra's eyes lit up. "What is it?" she said anxiously.

"Well," he continued, "there's nobody here except us. None of the film crews are here. What I could do, just for you, is tell everyone that it looked like the waters were just right for sharks here, so I decided to just fight a shark now, instead of in Australia. That way you don't have to worry about me, and I don't have to lose face."

Barbra squealed with delight and threw her arms around Dick. "Oh, thank you!" she cried. "Thank you! I'm so grateful. Thank you, thank you, thank you!" Then she looked at him quizzically. "But how are you ever going to convince people you killed a shark when you didn't?"

"Don't worry," Dick said calmly. "I've got a plan. Just wait and see."

When they got back to their bungalow later in the day, Dick picked up the phone and dialed the long-distance operator. A few seconds later he was booming into the phone. "Hey, Marge!" he said excitedly, on the line with the *Houston Post* columnist.

Barbra stood across the room, smiling. He was actually going through with it!

"Guess what I did!" Dick teased into the phone, in his high-intensity have-I-got-an-item-for-you tone of voice. While Barbra listened, fascinated, Dick went into excited, elaborate detail with Crumbaker about how he had killed not one but two great white sharks that afternoon with nothing but a bang stick—a rod with an explosive charge on one end that fires .44-caliber bullets.

As he continued the story, a light suddenly went on in Barbra's mind. What Richard was telling Marge Crumbaker was straight out of a paperback she saw him reading on the plane to Antigua called *Jaws of Death*.

When he hung up, a huge grin covered Dick's face. "There!" he said with a flourish. "Now we don't have that to worry about anymore."

Barbra sighed with relief and hugged him. She was touched, she would later remember, by Dick's sacrifice for her.

Before they left the island of Antigua, Sonny Reser noticed, Dick made a point of buying a huge supply of shark's teeth from vendors on the beach. Souvenirs, Reser figured, to bring home.

As they were flying back to Houston, Dick casually mentioned to Barbra that his wife Mimi was going to be at the airport to meet their plane.

Barbra looked at him, astounded. "What?" she cried. "She's not picking *me* up. I don't want to meet your wife!"

Dick responded instantly and evenly. "You already did. She had lunch with us when I met you at Snowmass."

Barbra furrowed her brows and tried to picture when and how she had met Mimi Minns. She couldn't. Then she fidgeted in her seat. There was no way, she told herself, she was going to meet Richard's *wife*, even if they were legally separated. She would feel strange, like his mistress or something. Was he crazy?

"You go ahead," Barbra said to Dick. "This flight goes on to L.A. I'm just going to stay on the plane and fly back to Los Angeles for a few days and see my family. I'd like to see my parents anyway."

Dick glowered. It was not OK. Barbra's place was with him. He certainly didn't want her back in California by herself. What if she met someone else while she was there? It was too risky.

The two sat in tense silence. Finally, as the plane made its approach through the thick, lush grove of trees surrounding Houston Intercontinental, Richard passed Barbra a note. It read: "You are not my mistress, nor my concubine, nor my girl. You're my life, my dream, my companion, my woman. I am your man. If you want to go to L.A., I will not deny you."

Barbra breathed a sigh of relief and stuffed the note into her purse to save forever. The crisis was passed.

Or so she believed.

The next day, when Sonny Reser was back home in Dallas, he opened the morning paper to see a huge article about Richard Minns's death-defying battle with two 3100-pound great white sharks on a dive trip off the coast of Antigua.

When he noticed the date of the fight, he laughed out loud. Hell, he thought to himself, that's the day *he* was out diving with Dick and Barbra. The water wasn't any more than fifty feet deep! And there sure as hell weren't any great whites around.

Reser folded up the newspaper and chuckled. Dick was always laughing about how the press would write anything. Maybe Dick was working on a book about how easy it is to get things printed in the paper. He decided not to even call Dick and rib him about it. Marge Crumbaker, who had broken the story after she received Dick's phone call from Antigua, continued to perpetuate the myth with breathless follow-ups, fed to her by Dick. A day or two after Barbra got back, she reported that a local Houston jeweler had "snagged the big fat contract" from "sportsman and ad tycoon" Dick Minns to design gold mountings for "quite a lot of great white shark teeth."

"When Dick won in his recent battle with two great whites," Crumbaker wrote in her column, "he made sure he kept the teeth. In exotic bauble circles, a great white tooth in good condition is valued to $1000. Dick has 800 of them. Some of his most choice friends will receive the gold-encased teeth as gifts."

Over the coming weeks, "choice friends" such as "super-millionaire" Al Dugan, lawyer Harry Brochstein, and local TV-news personality Marvin Zindler proudly sported gold-plated shark's teeth from Richard Minns on chains round their necks. There was one friend who pointedly did *not* receive a gilded shark's tooth from Richard Minns. That was Sonny Reser.

By early summer, Dick had amassed a collection of newspaper clippings about his bogus shark fight that numbered in the hundreds—from newspapers as diverse as the Altoona, Pennsylvania, *Mirror* to the *National Enquirer* to the London *Observer*.

The newspaper accounts, which had been sent over the wires by both the Associated Press and United Press International, were filled with colorful quotes from Richard Minns, the only witness mentioned by name.

Almost all of the hundred-plus articles about the shark fight contained pictures of Dick's "kill"—provided, naturally, by Dick. If anyone had looked closely, he would have seen that one of the two photographs Dick supplied was identical to the poster from the movie *Jaws 2*. The other was an exact replica of a photo taken by Philippe Cousteau in a Jacques Cousteau book called *The Shark— Splendid Savage of the Sea*, a gift to Dick from Barbra.

A careful reading of the articles would also have revealed that the story Dick gave to AP differed in certain significant respects from the accounts he gave to UPI.

No one noticed. Or if they did, they didn't care. For weeks, Dick was kept busy cutting out articles with headlines like, DON'T MESS WITH MINNS, from the *Atlantic City Press*, to HOUSTON MILLIONAIRE GETS 2 SHARKS FOR PRICE OF 1, from the *Waco Tribune-Herald*.

Barbra was impressed beyond belief. Not only had Dick managed to fool the city of Houston, but he also had half the world believing he had fought and killed two great white sharks that existed only in his mind. And he had done it all just for her.

Barbra's happiness knew no bounds. When she signed up for the first summer session of premed classes at the University of Houston, Dick not only supported her, financially and emotionally, he even sent one of his secretaries to the college campus to stand in line and fill out forms for her, so she could go out of town with him the week of registration. When the secretary quit in disgust, Dick just shrugged it off. Dick now talked insistently about how he wanted Barbra to get pregnant and have two sons with him.

Barbra was also able to continue her modeling. Although Dick was insanely jealous of the modeling photographs of Barbra in bathing suits on California beaches, he had no problem using Barbra as a model. In one photograph to promote the opening of a new club, Dick, wearing skintight bell-bottom jeans, wide belt, gold chain, and western shirt, is crouched over a spade being pushed into the ground with a "shapely assistant," according to the caption—the "current Miss California," Barbra Piotrowski, dressed in a tight black leotard, tights, and platform heels. The two are pictured next to another shapely blonde model, and Carl Silvani, a former pro football player for the Washington Redskins who had been made a vice-president of the Houston President's-First Lady Clubs. In another photo, Dick and Barbra are arm in arm with Silvani and a brunette model, identified as "Miss Guam," who is holding a shovel to publicize the ground-breaking of a PFL club in a Houston suburb.

Barbra, of course, was not the reigning "Miss California." Nor was the brunette model posing with her "Miss Guam." She may have never even *been* to Guam for all Richard Minns knew. The point, Dick told Barbra, was that it sounded better. "And besides," he said to Barbra, "she *looks* like a 'Miss Guam'!"

When it first came up, Barbra tried to correct the misimpression about her title. Although it bothered Barbra she didn't want to nag him about it. In return, she was getting oceans of love and happiness.

On May 18, 1977, Dick and Barbra celebrated their four-month anniversary together with a candlelight dinner at the Rivoli. While they were lingering over their last few bites, gazing tenderly into each other's eyes, restaurateur Willie Rometsch approached the table with a cake that caused other diners to drop their forks and gape. On top of the cake were miniature scenes from Dick and Barbra's four months together, painted by an artist Dick had hired for the occasion.

Barbra's eyes misted with tears of joy. Earlier in the day, she had gotten not one, but four, anniversary cards from Dick, each one a testimonial to his undying love. Anyone can *buy* a gift, she thought. Especially a millionaire like Dick. His time was the greatest gift he could give her.

Days later, Mimi Minns received an anonymous envelope in the mail. In it were photographs of Dick with a cute and rather chubby teenage girl. In one photo, the two were standing in the snow with their arms around each other's waists, dressed in ski clothes and smiling. Another photo of them Mimi recognized as being taken in Acapulco.

Mimi stared at the pictures for a long time. She had found suspicious photographs of Dick another time, in his office desk drawer. In those, he was standing next to two shapely young women "with their hands over Mr. Minns in a rather obscene manner," as Mimi later described it. When Mimi showed the photographs to Dick, he told her the two women were models. "I thought it was a very strange picture for models to be taking," Mimi once said, "but that's what he told me."

There was no way, Mimi thought, looking at the pictures that arrived in the mail, that this girl was a model.

Mimi picked up the phone and started dialing. When she couldn't locate Dick after an hour of calls to his usual places, she got in her car. Three and a half hours later, she pulled into the driveway of their place at Lakeway. Dick was not there.

Late that night, Dick called Mimi at Lakeway. The following day, when she returned home, she spilled out the contents of the unmarked envelope in front of him.

Dick studied the pictures, a puzzled look on his face. "I don't know who this girl is," he said, when he put down the photographs.

Mimi searched his face for signs of guilt. There were none. Then she looked at the proof, on the table. Mimi was wearying of scenes like these. Somebody out there was getting a little cruel and ugly. And, on top of everything else, she had just been to the eye doctor, who told her she had cataracts. Dick didn't even seem to care. She sighed, picked up the photographs and walked out of the room, leaving Dick alone with his thoughts.

That Saturday, July 2, would be forever etched on Barbra's brain. It was the beginning of the long Fourth of July weekend. Barbra always looked forward to holidays. Dick was less inclined to work. She had his full and undivided attention.

This particular Saturday, she noticed, he seemed preoccupied. Distant. Late in the morning, Dick came to Barbra with a strange look on his face and a letter in his hand. A letter, he told her, from his wife Mimi.

Barbra squirmed in her seat. She felt awkward when Dick brought up his wife, even though, he kept telling her, they were "as good as" divorced. It's not that she was jealous. She knew that part of his life was over. He and Mimi were legally separated. Barbra just wished Dick wasn't married at all.

Mimi, Dick told Barbra, was having health problems. Serious health problems. It was her eyes. She had cataracts and was going to have an operation on her eyes. She might even be going blind. He was going to have to spend some time with her. She needed him.

Barbra was confused. Why did Mimi need Dick? They were essentially divorced. She was sorry Mimi had cataracts, but wasn't that *her* problem?

Dick anticipated Barbra's question before she could get the words out of her mouth.

"This is going to be really tough to explain," he said to her with a pained look. "But there's something I have to tell you. I've been dreading it for months. I can't avoid it any longer. I have to tell you."

Barbra's heart fluttered wildly. What was the matter? What was so horrible?

"Mimi and I," she heard Dick saying, "aren't really legally separated."

The words came out in gentle, supplicating tones.

"I know I lied to you," Dick said softly. "But I had to. I didn't have any other choice. I knew from the first time I saw you that you were the woman for me. And I knew, once I got to know you, that if I told you I was married you would never come and be with me. I couldn't live without you. I would have done anything to get you. I've only felt like this one other time, and that was with Janet, the woman I told you about at Snowmass. And I lost her. I couldn't let that happen again. I loved you too much. I couldn't lose you. Can you understand that?"

Barbra felt nauseated and dizzy. "So you're not getting a divorce?" she said weakly. "But what about Myles? . . . And how come you're never with her?" It didn't make sense.

"We've got an open marriage," Dick responded. "We have had for about six years. Mimi and I actually have a pretty good relationship, but it's not like a husband and wife. I told you, we're more like brother and sister. We don't have anything in common sexually. We don't have anything in common, period. Mimi likes to drink and gamble and dress up and go out. All the things I *don't* like to do. She hates working out. And she smokes! I hate people who smoke. I can't stand the smell of cigarette smoke, and it's all around her. It's even entrenched in her clothes. I can't kiss someone who smokes. You *know* that."

Barbra thought for a moment. That was true. Once, when she had ordered a hamburger with onions, Dick wouldn't go near her for hours. He threatened to never kiss her again.

"We're just really good friends," Dick continued. "We decided a long time ago that we'd stay together for the children, and for the business. It's just easier that way. All Mimi cares about is money."

Barbra glared at him. "What exactly is an 'open marriage'?" she asked. "Does that mean you and Mimi can sleep with anyone you want and nobody cares?"

Dick nodded his head vigorously. "She already knows all about you!" he cried. "You met her—I told you—at Sam's Nob at Snowmass. She knows I'm with you. I've had several relationships before you. She knows about all of them."

As Barbra sat, shocked, Dick told her about other relationships he had had in the past, while he was married to Mimi. Mimi knew about them all, he said.

One of them, Dick told Barbra, was a famous actress. He almost married her before Mimi became pregnant with their fourth child. What Richard Minns didn't say was that, like Barbra, the actress, a bubbly, well-known starlet-comedienne, believed Richard Minns was single when she started dating him. He even asked her to marry him and begged her to have his child. When she became pregnant, she discovered he was married and ended the relationship and the pregnancy. A few years later, when the actress and the man she later married were performing at the Cork Club in Houston, Richard Minns stopped backstage. He brought with him a portrait of a little girl, whom he identified as his daughter. He and his wife, he told the actress and her husband, had named their daughter after the comedienne. When Dick left the dressing room, the actress's husband stared at her, dumbfounded. How could anyone, he wondered, name his wife's child after a mistress?

Barbra was doing her best to comprehend what Dick was telling her. To try to be understanding.

"Yes," she said numbly, when Dick asked her, for the fiftieth time, if she could see why he did what he did. He had no other choice, Dick repeated. He was desperately in love with her. He couldn't risk losing her. He *had* to keep his marriage a secret. Otherwise she would never have moved to Houston. He would have lost her forever.

Then, just as quickly, Dick was gone. Out the door without a backward glance to spend some time with Mimi. For the first time since she moved to Houston, Barbra was going to be apart from Dick for more than forty-eight hours.

She looked around the apartment she had selected for the two of them, filled with photographs of her and Dick, laughing and holding each other. She glanced into the kitchen. The counters were filled with Dick's vitamins, still in boxes. Everything she looked at reminded her with a sharp pang of Dick and the life she believed they were building together.

Barbra picked up a glass figurine and smashed it to the floor, screaming and sobbing violently. How could Dick do this to her? She began grabbing glasses and plates, throwing them wildly. "I was so upset," Barbra would later write in a legal document, "I thought I would die."

After half an hour, Barbra stopped. The apartment was deathly quiet, a painful reminder of Dick's absence.

Barbra picked up the phone and dialed one of the few girlfriends she had made since she moved to Texas, a nurse named Mary Ann Batiz.

"Hello, Mary Ann?" she said, in a voice that was barely audible. "It's Barbra. Do you want to go to Padre Island with me for a few days? I've got to get out of this apartment. If I don't, I'll probably commit suicide."

Mary Ann was at Barbra's door in less than an hour. She had never heard her friend sound like that before. Her voice had been desperate. Maybe a few days camping at Padre Island would help. It certainly couldn't hurt.

When Barbra pulled her camper into a clearing on Padre Island and helped Mary Ann pitch their tent, she couldn't get Dick's conversation with her that morning out of her mind. She knew she ought to feel betrayed, but she didn't *want* to feel that way. If she did, she would have to end the relationship, and she wasn't sure she was prepared to do that. Barbra's brain started rationalizing. Yes, Dick had lied to her. But, she told herself, he did have a point. She would not have moved to Houston if she had known Dick was married. What if that had happened? She would have missed the man of her dreams. Barbra had always believed there was only one true love in a person's life. Dick was her true love. And she was his.

Barbra looked down at her arms. There were little red dots all over them. Mosquito bites, she figured. She got the calamine lotion from Mary Ann and bathed herself in it. That night, when she undressed for bed, she found itchy, red bumps all over her body. When she and Mary Ann looked at them more closely, Barbra realized she hadn't been bitten by mosquitoes. She was so upset about Dick she had broken out in hives from head to toe.

By the end of the trip, her decision was made. She was going back to Dick. She had to. To a lovesick, naive girl of twenty-four, it was the only choice imaginable.

10

Dick returned to the apartment on Arboles in Westbury Square after a week or so, blithely unaware of the torment Barbra had been going through while he was gone. For a while, Barbra managed to keep it under cover. But suspicions began to gnaw at her.

It was one thing for Dick to spend a few nights at the Memorial house to see his children or entertain clients back when she thought he and Mimi were legally separated. Now that she knew they weren't, Barbra was haunted by dangerous thoughts. What if Dick *wasn't* turned off by Mimi, as he said he was? Maybe he was lying about that, too. Maybe he and Mimi still made love together.

The thought tore at Barbra's heart. She couldn't be with a man who was making love with another woman. She got jealous when someone else even *looked* at Dick. Once, when a pretty girl eyed Dick during one of their trips out of town, Barbra walked over to her, stared at her and said, "Do you mind? He and I are very much in love. I know you wouldn't want to do anything to spoil our happiness." Barbra finally issued an ultimatum. If Dick was having sexual relations with Mimi, she was leaving. Those were her conditions. Dick assured her he was not, over and over again. No matter how many times he repeated that he and Mimi hadn't had sex in years, Barbra continued to question him.

The way in which Dick dealt with it would become, in a few short months, a point of dispute between Dick and Barbra on one side, and Mimi on the other. Barbra's version of what happened, which Dick supported and Mimi denied, would even make its way into a legal deposition.

According to Barbra, Dick came up to her one day and said, "I'm going to call Mimi and I want you to listen in on the other phone and I'll prove to you that I haven't had sex with her in years."

While Barbra secretly listened in on an extension, Dick engaged Mimi in some chitchat about their marriage and some of their problems.

"Well," Dick said after a few minutes, "we've had four kids together . . . things couldn't have been that bad, were they?"

"Yeah," Mimi said sarcastically. "That's really funny."

"Well," Dick continued slyly, "that didn't happen without sex."

"But the last one happened sixteen years ago," Mimi responded dryly.

"Are you trying to say," Dick baited, "that we haven't had sex in sixteen years?"

"No," said Mimi. "But it's been several years."

Dick hung on the line for a few perfunctory minutes. Then he threw down the receiver, raced in the other room to find Barbra, and hugged her tightly. "See?" he said ebulliently.

With her darkest fear that Dick was sleeping with Mimi dispelled, unknowingly, by Mimi, Barbra calmed down. One day, when they were riding in Dick's red Cadillac convertible on a busy Houston freeway, Dick suddenly ordered his driver, Elmo Curry, to stop the car. Dick opened the door, stepped out on the freeway and dodged between cars to the center median. He returned a few seconds later with a flower, which he handed to Barbra. "Here," he said tenderly. "This is for you." Barbra was touched, as she always was, by Dick's unexpected, often extravagant gestures. "He has a way," she said to a friend on the phone one day, "of melting your heart."

Dick was far less extravagant where money was concerned. To assuage Dick's paranoia about being used for his money, Barbra would turn down Dick's offers to buy her a fur—not that the opportunity came up that often with the tightfisted Dick. Barbra was totally under Dick's thumb when it came to finances. The week she moved to Houston, Dick put Barbra on a budget of $600 a month, out of which she was expected to pay the $325 rent on their apartment, buy food, clothes for herself, and any other necessities for the two of them. After twenty-four years of seldom giving a thought to money, Barbra spent every third week preparing an itemized account of every expenditure she made. At the end of the month, Dick sat down with her and went over each purchase, down to the last bottle of shampoo, so he could dole out her allowance for the following month, which he gave to her in traveler's checks. Most of the time, Barbra was too embarrassed to ask for things she would have bought herself if she'd been supporting herself on her nurse's salary.

Between budgets, Dick delivered lectures on the "real world." "You've got to pay your dues," he would say, time and again, over nothing in particular. One day, Barbra could stand it no more. "What dues?" she said wearily. "What are these dues you keep talking about? And who do I have to pay them to?"

Dick was undaunted. "If you want to make money in this world," he said forcefully, "you have to learn how to handle it. That's the most important lesson anyone can teach you."

When the second summer session began at the University of Houston, Dick insisted Barbra take an accounting class along with her biology courses. She hated every moment. But Dick wanted her to study business, so she did.

The first time she visited Dick's private office on Claremont in the southwest Houston suburb of Sharpstown, the home base of President's-First Lady, Barbra let out a gasp. In the center of the room was the largest desk she had ever seen in her life. It was designed in the shape of a semicircle and mounted on a giant pedestal next to an enormous lion's-skin rug sprawled on the floor. In front of it were at least a dozen small chairs dwarfed by the desk.

"Now I want you to notice how I did this," Dick said to Barbra, when they had been in the office a few minutes. "It's all been very carefully planned. You see how big my desk is?" he asked. "And how it's higher than everything else in the room?"

Barbra nodded. How could she miss it?

"Well, that's for a reason," Dick answered. "A psychologist advised me on all this." He motioned to his desk. "If you sit at a big desk like this, on a raised platform, then whoever's in your office will have to look up at you. And because the desk is so big and the chairs are so small, it gives you a position of power. See? And the more chairs you have and the smaller they are, the more anonymous whoever is sitting there will feel."

Barbra's jaw dropped. Never in her life had she met anyone so thorough, so consumed with coming out on top.

"*Winning*," Dick said earnestly. "That's what it's about. If you're gonna play the game, you have to play to win. You have to wear 'em down. That's my philosophy."

He leaned over Barbra intensely. "Say I have some guy coming to my office for a negotiation. I schedule the meeting for the middle of the afternoon, a few hours after he's had lunch. Then I keep him waiting for three or four hours before he gets in to see me. But I have my secretary keep telling him, 'It'll be five minutes' every fifteen minutes or so. That way he won't get up to go to the bathroom or get something to eat. By the time he gets into my office he's probably already hungry and has to go to the bathroom. Then I wear him down until he doesn't care anymore." Dick grinned maniacally. "I just wear 'em down. That's my philosophy. And it obviously works. I haven't lost a lawsuit yet."

Barbra was too awed to speak. A part of her was shocked and appalled at Dick's business techniques. But you had to respect someone, she thought, who had that much ingenuity and energy, all directed toward one goal: winning.

"You wouldn't believe what Bob Schwartz did!" Dick continued, referring to the man Barbra had met briefly in Aspen with Dick. After working for Dick, Schwartz had quit and opened a rival health club called Slenderbolic. Dick accused Schwartz of stealing his club space and Mimi's whirlpool and sued him. "While I was suing him, he was trying to steal my employees so he could get inside information and steal my trade secrets! So he hired this private investigator named Neil Todd, who was kicked off the police force, to go through all our office garbage. Then Todd tried to bribe the cleaning lady in the building to tie a blue ribbon around the garbage from my office so he wouldn't have to go through all the bags to find mine."

Dick's mouth turned up in a twisted smile. "But I fixed him," he sneered. "The cleaning lady called the building supervisor and the building supervisor called me. So I hired the most famous P.I. in the city of Houston, Clyde Wilson. Clyde told me to put some papers in a seven-hundred-and-fifty-dollar alligator briefcase I owned, stuff the briefcase in a garbage bag, and tie a blue ribbon around it."

Dick beamed. "When ole Neil came by to pick up the bag with the blue ribbon, the Houston police were waiting for him and arrested him for stealing my briefcase! They threw him in jail and booked him for theft."

"I won." Dick said loftily. "We settled out of court. I even paid Schwartz sixty thousand dollars to buy out one of his clubs. I told you, I've never lost a case." Dick paused dramatically, his eyes fixed on Barbra. "And I never intend to."

But a few months later, Dick's brother-in-law Irv Weissman told the story differently to Barbra. "Dick didn't win that case!" he said. "Bob Schwartz did. They settled in the middle of the trial. Dick paid *him* money."

Barbra look at Irv quizzically. "But Dick said he paid Bob Schwartz sixty thousand dollars to buy one of his clubs," she protested.

Weissman looked at her with amusement. "If you listen to Dick," he said, "he won the case. The outcome was, *he* paid Schwartz money. And to salvage his ego, he got an agreement from Schwartz—some type of noncompetition agreement—so that he could claim a victory. But he was the one who paid money. He lost." Weissman confided that Dick also tried to get him to bribe one of the jurors, who happened to be Weissman's mailman.

Barbra was silent for a moment, pondering what Dick's brother-in-law had just told her. Maybe Dick *did* lose, she thought. What was the difference anyway? Besides, Irv might be wrong. After all, he wasn't representing Dick on the case.

Irv Weissman was, in fact, right. Actually, he had only scratched the surface in what he told Barbra about the Richard Minns-Bob Schwartz feud.

According to Bob Schwartz, the problems between him and Dick arose long before Schwartz opened his first Slenderbolic in competition with Dick. The problems began when Schwartz was still an employee at Ace Rican and Dick broke his word about providing Ace Rican employees with vacation time. "I felt," Schwartz said, "when that happened, I couldn't trust him, and I couldn't work for somebody I didn't trust." So Schwartz quit his job, got his mother to mortgage her home, and borrowed enough money from her to start his own health club. He named it Slenderbolic, or "slender forever."

When Dick got wind of it, Schwartz would say later, he launched an all-consuming, obsessive campaign, legal, illegal, and extralegal, to run him out of business.

Dick, Schwartz recalled, "sued us for two-point-two million dollars for stealing the design of the whirlpool."

A week later, Slenderbolic came out with ads proclaiming it as "Houston's only 2.2 million dollar health spa chain." "We took something that was supposed to put us out of business and hurt us," Schwartz said later, "which it did for about three days, and suddenly turned it to our benefit. We weren't worth two-point-two million—I doubt if we were worth two hundred thousand dollars—but if he thought so, maybe everybody else would."

After the lawsuit came the battle of the slogans. One August, President's-First Lady began to run ads with the catch-phrase, "What do you have to lose?" Around the same time, Schwartz's Slenderbolic chain came up with the slogan, "What have you got to lose?"

Eventually, Minns sued Schwartz and Schwartz sued Minns for copyright infringement. Twenty years later, neither Schwartz nor his lawyer could remember which slogan came first, President's-First Lady's or Slenderbolic's. The irony was, neither one was original. Both Dick and Bob Schwartz had lifted the slogan from a club in California.

There was an uglier, darker side to the proceedings, injected by Dick. After he learned that Bob Schwartz had secured a lease for club space from Joseph P. Johnson, Dick rushed to Johnson's office and interrupted a meeting between Johnson and a businessman named Bill Plummer to try to persuade Johnson to break his lease with Schwartz.

When Johnson refused, Dick called Schwartz a "faggot and a queer." Word trickled back to Schwartz, and he sued Dick for slander for a total of three million dollars in damages. The following year, 1966, Schwartz added another incident to his lawsuit. That May, he alleged, Dick told a man named Robert Bender and his wife that Schwartz "allowed homosexuals and lesbians to throw wild parties in the studios at night."

Some months into the slander suit, Dick's friend and lawyer, Joe Reynolds, entered a sworn affidavit in the case from a Houston police chief named William J. Holton. Holton stated that he had received a complaint in the 1950s against Robert Schwartz from an "irate father" in his district. The father, whom Holton did not name in his affidavit, reportedly told Holton that Robert Schwartz had "solicited or attempted to perform an act of sexual perversion" on his minor son (also unnamed) at a drive-in movie. When he got the complaint, Holton stated in his affidavit, he "confronted" Robert Schwartz. Schwartz, he said, "did not deny it, but apologized."

Schwartz and his attorney were both dumbfounded and stymied by the police chief's affidavit. Since truth is an absolute defense to slander, Holton's affidavit could absolve Minns of the slander charges, and Schwartz didn't even know who had made the complaint against him to the police chief.

"Bob isn't a homosexual at all," Schwartz's lawyer, Thomas Bousquet, said, years later. "But you can prove you *are* homosexual, but not that you're not."

Bousquet demanded to know who the "irate father" was in the police chief's affidavit. Reynolds refused to divulge the information, or to produce the son who was allegedly solicited. The police chief likewise refused to name names, saying it was an "internal investigation" and therefore privileged information.

After months of deadlock, the judge, Phil Peden, ordered the police chief to meet him in his chambers and tell him who the father was. The father of the boy Schwartz solicited, Holton told the judge, was Bill Miller, a county court judge whose chambers were only about a hundred feet from Peden's.

Schwartz's lawyer, Bousquet, immediately made his way to Judge Miller's chambers to question him.

"That's a pack of lies," Miller responded, when Bousquet told him what was in Chief Holton's affidavit. "It never happened."

After talking to Judge Miller and finding out the police chief's affidavit was a sham, Bousquet pushed to bring the slander case in front of a jury. "Just before it goes to trial," he remembered, "Minns pays us sixty thousand dollars to settle."

"I think Dick makes things up first," Schwartz would say later, reflecting on the slander suit and Chief Holton's affidavit, "and then he looks for evidence to back it up."

After what she heard of Dick's lawsuit against Bob Schwartz, Barbra could scarcely believe that Bob Schwartz was the same man she had seen laughing and skiing with Dick at Snowmass the month they met. "In court and in business," Schwartz's attorney, Thomas Bousquet, said of the pair, "they hated each other. But personally, they got along pretty good."

Mimi Minns went even further. Bob Schwartz, she would say, when the lawsuits were but a distant memory, "loved" Dick.

Bob Schwartz did not disagree. "If you've ever met Dick," he would say, when an ocean separated them and their paths hadn't crossed in years, "he can be very charming and very powerful. Very charismatic." The former health club owner grew thoughtful. "I don't think anymore for me . . . I think I outgrew that." He paused for a moment, searching for words to express what attracted him to Dick all those years, through all the vitriol, and after. "There was something," he added, "about dancing close to the flame that did it for me in the old days."

Barbra was too caught up in her love for Dick to give much thought to his business tactics or some ancient lawsuit. The sheer intensity and frequency of their time together made the pain of Richard's occasional days and nights at the Memorial house easier for Barbra to bear. In addition, Barbra had her premed classes, both summer sessions, with a full load each session of biology, chemistry, English, history, and, at Dick's insistence, accounting courses. In spite of all the travel and Dick's constant demands on her time, she managed to maintain a 3.9 grade point average at the University of Houston.

Dr. Barry Kaplan, a history professor at the University of Houston with a reputation for being, in his words, a "real hard-ass teacher," gave Barbra three A's in the three classes she took from him. "To get an A with me was not a usual thing for most people," he said later. "Barbra was a damn good student. She was very diligent. The first class she took from me, half the class got D's or F's. She would put in the extra effort to get the job done."

Kaplan, who was a young, fairly new associate professor of history, was intrigued with Barbra Piotrowski. She dressed well, better than the other female students, and looked like a movie star. She seemed, he thought, older than her twenty-four years. And yet she had a vulnerability, a naivete, that mystified him. She never flirted with any of the guys in class, he noticed, nor with him. In fact, she appeared uncomfortable with her sexuality. Cool. Aloof.

"Other students were sort of put off by her," Kaplan would remember. "I guess it was sort of a jealousy thing. The male students, I think, were intimidated by her. How could a college guy even think of going out with her? She even intimidated *me!* I looked at her and said, 'My God!' The women just thought she was pretentious. Until they got to know her a little bit and they realized that what she seemed to be was what she was."

Except for occasional disagreements about an outfit he might want her to wear, the few arguments Dick and Barbra had revolved around her sporadic requests to work. She wanted to teach aerobics.

Dick was adamant. Under no circumstances could she work. When he had free time, he wanted her around. The same principle applied to girlfriends. Her time belonged to him, not to a girlfriend. Or even to her family.

One weekend at the Lakeway house, they had hardly carried their suitcases inside before Dick was in his suit, on the water, cranking up his speedboat, the name SPA painted on the back.

"I dare you to ski all the way from the Narrows to the Lakeway Marina!" he challenged, while Barbra slipped on her water ski.

She looked down at the rough, choppy water, then up at Dick with disbelief. That was over sixty miles and she had only skied a few times before in her life! Clenching her jaw, she plunged into the water. "All right!" she said fiercely, her eyes blazing. "You're on!"

Close to four hours later, when Dick turned his speedboat into the marina, Barbra was, unbelievably, still standing.

"You did it!" Dick called out gleefully, slowing the motor. As Barbra slipped off her ski and began to climb into the boat, bursting with pride, Dick accidentally tripped the gear into reverse. The rudder ripped into Barbra's leg, slicing the skin around the ankle to the tendon. Dick rushed her to the Lakeway Medical Center, where the doctor in attendance did a quick but clumsy job of sewing it up. Later, when questions came up about Barbra's injuries, Dick told people the boat driver did it. He was, he said to Barbra, too ashamed to tell the truth.

Barbra seized the opportunity. "When my classes are over next week," she said casually, "I think I'll fly home to Los Angeles and have one of my family doctors take a look at my leg. I'm afraid if I leave it the way it is now, there might be some tendon damage. I don't want to have a permanent impairment."

Her ploy to spend some time in California with her family worked. With a combination of guilt and concern over the way Barbra's leg might look, Dick reluctantly acquiesced to the trip.

On August 15, when she had taken her last final of the summer, Barbra boarded a plane for Los Angeles to see her family and consult a doctor about her leg.

Three days earlier, Dick, Mimi, and Myles took a flight to Lake Tahoe with Bob Delmonteque and his wife Madeleine. While he was there, Dick planned to stage his forty-eighth birthday feat: a new speed record on water skis around Lake Tahoe.

The week after Dick's birthday, August 24, Mimi Minns flew to Denver to enroll their youngest daughter in college. Later that day, within hours of Mimi's departure, Barbra flew in to join Dick at the Sahara Tahoe.

Bob Delmonteque raised an eyebrow as he observed the comings and goings, and smiled wryly. Dick's life, he snickered to himself, was like a goddamned merry-go-round.

11

As far into the future as thirteen years later, Mimi would insist that, from January to July of 1977, she had no inkling her husband was having an affair, in spite of Dick's prolonged absences and showy courtship of Barbra. But one day after the Fourth of July (the exact date would become a point of contention), Mimi came across an address and phone number on a scrap of paper among Dick's belongings. The instant she picked it up, she would later say, she "knew there was something about it." Something wives just know.

With paper in hand, Mimi got in her car and began driving around southwest Houston, in and out of one sprawling apartment complex after another, in search of the address. Late in the afternoon, she pulled up to a French Quarter-style two-story townhouse in Westbury Square. She got out of the car and walked in front of the apartment, then behind it, carefully examining everything in the vicinity. There was a stack of newspapers piled up by the front door, Mimi noticed. Then she got back into her car and started the ignition.

When Mimi returned home, she picked up the phone and calmly dialed Dick's office. "What are your plans for tonight?" she asked her husband, affecting a casual tone.

Dick's response was immediate and familiar. "Well," he drawled, "I think I'm gonna stick around here for a while and then go work out at the President's Club later on. I might be late, so don't wait up for me."

Mimi hung up the phone, satisfied. *Don't worry, honey*, she thought to herself, *I don't intend to.*

Later that evening, she got back into her car and drove

124

downtown to the President's Club parking lot, where she pulled up to Dick's parking space. It was empty. Then she drove straight to the address on Arboles. Dick's red Cadillac convertible was parked, conspicuously, in a space behind 5327-M.

Mimi parked her car and ran over to her husband's Cadillac and opened the door with her set of keys, then she lifted the hood. She peered under the car, searching for the battery. *Damn*, she thought. *I don't know which part is what*. She found a metal piece she thought was the battery and cursed herself for not bringing pliers. She looked for a piece she could easily take apart (it would prove to be the air filter) and disengaged it, smiling wickedly. *Try to get away now*, she thought to herself.

A few seconds later, Dick Minns and Barbra Piotrowski heard a loud pounding on the front door of Barbra's apartment as they lay in bed. A woman's voice yelled "Help!" several times.

Barbra started to get up. Dick pulled her back in bed. "Don't answer it," he said gruffly.

Barbra lay in bed, perplexed.

"You shouldn't answer your door to a stranger," Dick repeated. The woman called out "Help!" several more times.

Barbra got up suddenly. "I have to," she responded, as she moved toward the door and began running down the stairs.

The pounding continued, more insistently.

When Barbra opened the front door, she was surprised to see a red-haired woman standing in front of her, quite calm. For a moment, Barbra thought she recognized her, but she wasn't sure. Years later, she would say she might have remembered her as the redhead from the picnic tables at Sam's Nob restaurant in Aspen, but it was doubtful. The moment was too confusing. Too bizarre.

"My husband is in your house," Mimi Minns said icily, "and I want to see him. Now."

Barbra stood in the doorway awkwardly, trying to figure out what was going on.

"I want to see my husband," Mimi repeated curtly. "I know he's here. I saw his car. Tell him to come here right away."

Barbra stammered. "I'll have to go upstairs and get him—"

"He's probably naked," Mimi interrupted sarcastically. "You don't have to worry if he is. I've seen him naked before."

Barbra closed the door—Mimi would later say "slammed"—and went upstairs to fetch Dick.

The banging continued. "You'd better hurry up and get down here," Mimi yelled to Dick, through the door. "Don't leave me down here screaming or Barbie will think I'm a real shrew. And don't go out the back door because I fixed your car so it won't work!"

A long five minutes later Dick Minns opened the front door, slowly, clad only in blue jeans, barefoot.

Mimi stared into his eyes, then at his bare chest. "I had to know if what I thought is true," she said dramatically. Then she turned on her heels and ran to her car.

Dick Minns stood frozen in place for a few seconds, as if pondering what to do. Then he followed Mimi, slowly, toward her automobile. When he got to the car, the front door was locked and she was starting the engine.

"I have to talk to you," he said, through the closed window.

Mimi began to pull away, with Dick hanging onto the side of the car. "I don't want to talk to you!" she screamed, as she screeched out of the parking lot.

Dick returned to the apartment. Barbra was inside, waiting, full of questions. What was the matter? Was something wrong? Why did Mimi come over? Barbra was confused. If Mimi knew about her, what was the problem?

Dick led Barbra to his car and they drove around for a while, minus the air filter Mimi had removed. Mimi was really depressed and irrational, Dick said heavily. So many things were going wrong in her life. She felt everyone had deserted her. He had to go find her right away. Surely Barbra understood. Of course, Barbra nodded. Of course she understood.

When Dick got to the Memorial house, Mimi wasn't home, so he left.

Mimi was too upset to go home. She, too, was driving around Houston.

Late that night, Mimi returned to the big, quiet house

on Memorial Drive. Myles and one of the maids were there sleeping soundly. Mimi went upstairs to the master bedroom, feeling, suddenly, very old and very weary.

A few minutes later, Dick walked through the door, looking as though nothing had happened.

Before Mimi could open her mouth, he blurted, "I wasn't there."

Mimi Minns stared at him, disbelieving. "I heard that story once before," she said sardonically, "but this time I saw you with my own eyes."

Later, when she talked about that night, Mimi would say she told Dick she wanted a divorce and that he told her he didn't want one. Dick would say there was no talk of divorce at all. "He got ready for bed like nothing had happened," Mimi would say of the incident. "Got in bed. I went into my dressing room, my bathroom, and I spent the night on my chaise longue."

Late in the night, Mimi Minns asked the question that had been burning inside her since she found the address. "Are you going to give her up?" she said to Dick, her voice piercing the dark silence of the master bedroom suite.

Dick Minns, alone in their king-size circular bed, didn't answer.

Near the end of July, Dick played in a celebrity tennis tournament at the Westside Country Club. Sitting on one bench were Mimi and her younger daughter. On another bench, a few feet away, were Barbra and Barbara Fox, a "friend" of Dick's celebrity opponent and good friend Marvin Zindler.

If ever there was such a thing as a bona fide Houston phenomenon, Marvin Zindler was it. In 1973, Zindler was hired by Channel 13, Houston's ABC affiliate, as its consumer reporter. Twenty years earlier, he had been rejected for TV as too ugly. Since then, Marvin Zindler had had extensive plastic surgery, much of which he shared with Channel 13 viewers with "Before" and "After" pictures. The results were, in a word, astonishing. His own cameraman has said that when he first laid eyes on Marvin Zindler, his reaction was "What in the hell is that?" Atop a face heavily covered with pancake makeup, Zindler wore a pouffed

and pompadoured cotton-white wig over enormous Roy
Orbison-style glasses with tinted lenses. While the other
anchormen faced the cameras in banker gray, Zindler strut-
ted into the studio like some finger-snapping pimp in wide,
sixties-style ties, flashy gold jewelry, and ice-cream-white
suits. When he finished his consumer report every night, he
would stare into the camera, pause dramatically, then twist
his mouth and bellow at the top of his lungs, "M-A-A-
A-A-A-A-R-V-I-N Zindler, E-Y-Y-Y-Y-Y-Y-Y-E-witness
News!"

The irony was that Marvin Zindler was a star. He was
better known than the mayor of Houston. A movie (*The Best
Little Whorehouse in Texas*) was even made about his bust-
up of Texas's oldest "chicken ranch," with Dom DeLuise
playing Zindler. But Marvin preferred to talk about himself
as a folk hero, the champion of the little guy, still married
to Gertrude, his wife of many years, father of five.

When Barbra Piotrowski met Zindler, he was tucked
away in Dick's lakehouse with Barbara Fox, paranoid about
being seen. That same weekend Barbra was stopped for
speeding in LaGrange, the small town where the chicken
ranch once stood. When the local cop came to the driver's
window, Zindler and Fox, who were in the car with Barbra,
ducked their heads and hid.

Barbra was on closer terms with another of Dick's friends,
a corporate lawyer by the name of Harry Brochstein—pudgy,
rosy-cheeked, sixty-plus, with a spray of silver-gray hair.
Dick and Barbra spent many an evening with Harry and his
"friend," a fortyish blonde named Wylene Lapinski.

Oddly, considering how frequently she and Dick made
love, Barbra did not take birth control pills. Not that she
wished to get pregnant. That was Dick's fantasy. "I want us
to have two boys," he kept telling her. Barbra resisted. She
had her own agenda. She wanted to get her medical degree.

One afternoon on an occasion she would later refer to as
"spur of the moment," Dick suddenly grabbed Barbra and
threw her on the bed. Barbra tried to break away to find
some means of contraception, but Dick kept her on the bed.
"Forget about it," he whispered hoarsely. "There's nothing
to worry about." Barbra relented.

While they were making love, her body felt peculiar. "He's making me pregnant right now," she thought to herself. "I can feel it." Afterward, when they were lying in bed together, Barbra confided her feelings to Dick. He just laughed.

The next morning, Barbra forgot all about it. Later in the day, as she walked across the University of Houston campus to one of her classes, she started daydreaming about having children and raising a family. When she realized what she was doing, she shook herself like a wet animal. "What's the matter with me?" she thought to herself. "Where is this coming from?" Then she remembered the day before, and making love with Dick. That afternoon, when she got home, she pulled him aside. "Dick," she said somberly, "I know this sounds crazy, but I feel like I'm pregnant."

Dick raised an eyebrow. "Oh?" he said, with an expression of amused tolerance. "Why do you say that?"

"I just *know*," Barbra said firmly. "Remember I told you yesterday that I felt different? I just knew. I could feel it."

Dick beamed. "Well," he said exuberantly, wrapping his arms around her. "I hope you are. That'd be great!"

Barbra called a gynecologist the next day. In a few weeks the blood test confirmed it. She was pregnant.

Dick Minns was ecstatic. Within minutes, he was calling his friends to spread the news. When Don Wildman and his girlfriend Rebecca flew into town from Chicago, the two couples toasted the pregnancy.

Barbra, to her great surprise, shared Dick's joy. She felt radiant, glowing, healthy. One morning in the third or fourth month of her pregnancy, she was getting dressed for a President's Club photo shoot with Arnold Schwarzenegger, one of the spokespersons for the club. As she stood in front of the mirror, adjusting her leotard, her eye moved admiringly down the form of her body. She looked beautiful! Her waist, which had always been abnormally tiny, was still small, but the rest of her body was curvy, voluptuous, womanly. The next time she went jogging, she took out her tightest leotard, instead of her usual shorts and T-shirt. When the men she passed whistled at her, she smiled back. For the first time in her life, she didn't feel threatened by male attention. She was safe now. Protected. She was going to have a baby.

Her fears about managing both a career and motherhood simply vanished. She and Dick could conquer anything. They would find a way.

Early in November 1977, Dick invited his friend and attorney Harry Brochstein to dinner at Barbra's apartment. Harry, Barbra noticed, was in an unusually philosophical mood. "You know, Barbra," he said at dinner, "you've really changed Dick. He's a different person now. More loving, calmer, happier. And it's all because of you. We've got to make some financial provisions for your child."

Barbra studied Dick, then Harry. *That's why Dick invited him here tonight*, she thought to herself, *so he can make financial arrangements for our child.*

The thought was immediately comforting. She had tried not to think about it, but when she did, Barbra realized that she had no financial protection in her relationship with Dick. She had given up her home and her job in California and she had nothing to show for it. For weeks she had been pestering Dick about it. She didn't understand what an "open marriage" was. She had never heard of such a thing. Dick tried to assuage her. "Trust me," he told her.

When one of their discussions escalated into an argument, Dick wooed her back with a love letter and a promise. "In any event," he wrote at the end of his note, "I won't leave you out on a limb economically, since that has been a concern to you." Barbra read and reread Dick's words.

A few weeks after Barbra discovered she was pregnant, Dick instructed her to find a house for the two of them. He was tired of the apartment in Westbury. It was too cramped, especially with a baby on the way. Besides, he said to Barbra, he had never really liked Westbury. The neighborhood was too seedy. He wanted to live in Memorial. Find three houses, he told Barbra, and then show them to me.

For days, Barbra combed the Memorial area for houses. Dick didn't like any of them. When she was about to give up, he settled on two. One was a townhouse in Ethan's Glen, an upscale development in west Memorial. The other was a resale on Sugarberry Creek in Hudson on Memorial, an exclusive community near the Sandalwood lakes in the Memorial villages. After a spate of negotiations Dick agreed to pay the owner of the Sugarberry property, a divorcee who planned to move to Dallas, $151,000 for the house, with $23,000 in cash as a down payment.

Barbra was ecstatic. Sarah Hamilton, the realtor who assisted her, would still remember, many years later, how lovely and sweet she appeared, how utterly devoted to Richard Minns. All she could talk about was how she and Dick were going to be married some day. When the three got together at the President's Club one night to discuss the Sugarberry house and Hamilton met Dick Minns for the first time, she could understand why Barbra was so smitten. The man was a charmer!

A few days later, Hamilton got a call from Dick Minns. Could she come over to his house in Memorial? he wondered. When Hamilton got there, Dick introduced her to his wife Mimi and announced that they wanted to sell their home. Would she take the listing? Mimi, Hamilton would later remember, barely said a word and showed little emotion. As Dick showed her out the door, he whispered in the realtor's ear, "I'm planning on getting a divorce. My wife may be needing another house later on." Hamilton thought little of it. It was all, she assumed, part of Dick Minns's plan to marry Barbra Piotrowski. But Barbra Piotrowski had no idea Dick and Mimi Minns had put their home on the market.

There were, in fact, a number of things of which Barbra was not aware. She didn't know, for example, that Mimi had been threatening to file for a divorce. On November 11, Mimi and Dick actually met with Harry Brochstein at the lawyer's office to discuss it. Dick was adamant. He didn't want a divorce. If Mimi insisted, couldn't she at least wait until January so she wouldn't spoil the family's annual Christmas trip to Las Brisas? Besides, he pointed out, it would be financially disastrous for them if she filed for a divorce before their house was sold.

Mimi surveyed her husband, sitting on the edge of his seat, pleading with her, then Harry, who was nodding vigorously in agreement. Oh, all right, she said finally, acquiescing. She supposed she could wait until after Christmas. But she was going to start looking for another house. She wanted Dick to know that. Dick shook his head up and down. That was fine, he said cordially. Go ahead and look.

Within a few days after Sarah Hamilton took the listing on the Memorial Drive property, Mimi got in her car and started house hunting. She still wasn't sure whether she was looking for just herself, or for herself and Dick, but she found just what she wanted. The house was smaller than the Memorial Drive house, but just as elegant, close to where they already lived. Her mind was made up, she told Dick. She was going to buy a house in Hudson Oaks. It was, she had no way of knowing, the very neighborhood where Barbra Piotrowski had selected a home for herself and Dick not two weeks earlier.

If Dick Minns was aware of the coincidence, he didn't say a word.

Strange calls started coming into Barbra's apartment. Calls from friends of Dick's, wanting to speak to her. Rebecca Shutter, Don Wildman's girlfriend, was one of the first.

"Are you really sure you want to have this baby?" Rebecca quizzed Barbra, when she had her on the phone one day. "I know Dick is excited about having a baby *now*, but what about twelve months from now? Aren't you afraid that having a child is going to ruin your relationship?"

Barbra stammered a few words and hung up in confusion. Don and Rebecca had just been in Houston and toasted her pregnancy.

As the autumn unfolded, similar calls followed from a succession of Dick's friends, all urging Barbra to consider having an abortion.

Barbra was in a quandary. Dick was the one who kept urging her to have a baby. He was thrilled when she told him she was pregnant. It didn't make sense that he would be having second thoughts now. But then why were all his friends calling her and suggesting she have an abortion? Don Wildman was hardly the sort of man to interfere in her life. She hardly knew him. Why would he call her and discourage her from having a baby—unless Dick put him up to it?

Not surprisingly Barbra entered into a deep depression. Dick's friends were continuing their telephone abortion campaign, and while Dick denied any involvement, he was increasingly aloof. He was also spending more time with Mimi—consoling her, he said, because she was upset about her eye surgery. When Sarah Hamilton met with her to discuss the Sugarberry house, she was shocked at the difference in Barbra. She seemed overwhelmingly sad, the realtor observed. Lonely.

In truth, Barbra's nerves were frayed. "Are you sure you want to have this baby?" she confronted Dick one day when they were together. Dick looked at her impatiently. "I just don't understand why your friends keep calling me and telling me what a bad idea it is. I feel like something's wrong. Please tell me."

Dick's expression suddenly changed. "All right!" he snapped. "You're right. I *don't* want to have this baby. I changed my mind. I want you to have an abortion."

Barbra sat very still, hearing the words but not comprehending them completely. Dick knew how she felt about abortions. They had discussed it many times. She told him she could never do that. Whether it was some vestige of her Catholic upbringing or something else, she could never bring herself to abort a child. She cast no judgment on anyone else's decision to terminate a pregnancy; she just knew she couldn't. Dick *knew* that. Dick had always known that, way back in Aspen. How could he ask her to have an abortion? And why had he changed his mind about having a baby?

Barbra's mind reeled with the possibilities. Maybe Dick didn't love her anymore. Or maybe what his friends were telling her was how Dick really felt—maybe he *was* afraid that having a child would tie him down, change their relationship somehow. Maybe that's what happened to him and Mimi. Maybe, maybe, maybe. All she had were maybes.

A few days later, Barbra felt excruciating abdominal cramps. She immediately called Dick. She knew he hated her to see doctors. He wanted her healthy, ready and available at all times. "Just lie still," he directed. "I'll be right over."

Barbra lay down, doubled over with pain. Blood began to

flow out of her. "Oh, my God," she thought to herself, filled with terror. Her doctor had told her the main danger from a miscarriage is that a woman could hemorrhage and die if she didn't get medical help. *Where is Dick*? she thought frantically.

An hour passed and Dick still hadn't arrived. Barbra felt panicky. She had already saturated several large towels with blood. If she didn't get to the doctor soon, she thought, she was afraid she might die. She felt, suddenly, very alone and very depressed.

Bending over from the pain, she fumbled for her car keys and staggered out to her camper. She started the engine and pulled out of the parking lot, jerking the camper back and forth as she tried to steady herself. By the time she merged onto the freeway, the pain was overwhelming. She pulled the camper over to the shoulder and shut off the engine. Blood was everywhere. She sat behind the wheel with cars whizzing by her, hunched over in agony, wondering whether she was going to live or die. Then, in an instant, the pain completely disappeared.

Barbra raced to the emergency room of Women's Hospital. It was too late. She had miscarried.

When Dick arrived at the hospital later, Barbra was in a room resting from a D and C ordered by the emergency room doctor to prevent further hemorrhaging or an infection. Dick kissed her tenderly on the mouth. Then he sat down next to her and held her hand all night.

The next morning, when Dr. Peter Thompson, who had performed the procedure, came into the room to check on Barbra, Dick assaulted him with questions. "Do you think she might have caused the miscarriage," he asked, "by pushing herself too much? And jogging?"

Thompson shook his head.

"I want to try to have another child as soon as possible," Dick said, more urgently. "You don't think she'll have this same problem again, do you?"

Dr. Thompson shook his head again. "No, there's no reason she can't have another child," he said pleasantly. Then he added, more somberly, "But she can't have intercourse for two weeks so she can heal."

Barbra stared at Dick, stupefied. A week earlier he was

asking her to have an abortion. Now he was telling the doctor he wanted to have another baby right away. What was going on?

Two days later, Dick booked the two of them on a flight to Vail, Colorado, to spend a vacation with Don Wildman and Rebecca. Dr. Thompson's two-week moratorium on sex went unheeded. Dick, Barbra later noted ruefully, couldn't even wait two days. The day after she was released from the hospital, they were making love. "Let's make another baby right now," Dick murmured under his breath. Barbra didn't know how to respond.

In the following days, Barbra alternated between confusion and depression. She didn't know what to expect anymore; what was real and what wasn't. When they returned from Vail, Barbra told Dick she didn't want to move into the Sugarberry house. She needed some time to think.

Dick laughed it off. "Oh, come on!" he teased. "I know you do!" When December 7, the day they were due to close on the house, came around and Barbra was still insisting she didn't want to move into the house, Dick sprang into action.

"I've decided I don't want the house," he announced to Sarah Hamilton over the phone. "I don't think it's worth that kind of money." Hamilton was floored. "But the owner moved her furniture out," she protested. "She's already moved to Dallas and bought another house. You gave me your earnest money. We have a deal."

That's what you think, Dick thought to himself. What he had given Hamilton wasn't actually a check for twenty-three thousand dollars in earnest money; it was a *copy* of the check. The original was still safely in his possession.

When Hamilton discovered she only had a copy, her hands were tied. The contract fell through. The owner of the house collapsed in shock when she heard the news. Reports were that she had to be rushed to the hospital in an ambulance.

A few days later, when Hamilton met Dick and Barbra to go over some paperwork, the realtor took a long last look at the couple. *Why is it*, she wondered, *that the right people always fall in love with the wrong people?*

12

As the month of December approached, Mimi Minns decided she was not going to Acapulco for Christmas. She informed Dick she was going to file for divorce when he returned.

Outwardly, Richard Minns showed little signs of being affected by the news. In her stead, he made arrangements for Barbra to accompany him to Las Brisas to meet Bob and Madeleine Delmonteque. On December 10, three days after the day they were to have closed on the Sugarberry house, Dick and Barbra flew to Las Brisas, the site of Minns family Christmases for over ten years.

Any doubts Barbra may have fostered about her relationship with Dick toward the end of her pregnancy slowly melted into the Acapulco sunsets. As she gazed out at the cliffs overlooking the deep, mysterious blue of Acapulco Bay—the same cliffs from which Dick had dived on birthdays past—Barbra closed her eyes and mouthed the words, *Thank you.* It was almost surreal, she thought, like some impossible, perfect dream. In the daylight hours, when the hot tropical sun beat down on the beaches, she would lie on top of Dick for hours on a chaise by the sea, clad only in their bikinis. Passersby would stop and stare when they saw them: two beautiful bronzed bodies melded together, blond hair shimmering in the sunlight. The golden couple.

As they were dressing for dinner one night, toward the end of their vacation, Dick glanced over at Barbra disapprovingly. "I don't like that," he said flatly, motioning to the white dress she was wearing. "It's not tight enough. Put on something tighter."

Barbra sighed with frustration. Normally, she was happy to oblige Dick in his choice of clothes, even if they weren't to her taste, which was generally the case. Tonight, for some reason, she wasn't in the mood. She liked what she was wearing. It was comfortable. She didn't want to put on something tighter.

"You're just doing this because you don't really love me," Dick said spitefully. "If you loved me, you'd change clothes."

"Oh, come on!" Barbra said impatiently, zipping up her dress. "Let's go."

As she moved toward the door, she felt something smash against her face, so hard it nearly knocked her to the ground. When she struggled to regain her balance, wincing with pain, she was hit with another blow. Terrified, she looked up. Dick was looming over her, his face contorted into some strange, demented mask. Barbra barely recognized him. It was as if there were a stranger standing in front of her. Then, in an instant, it was over.

"What did you do that for?" she sobbed convulsively, in a heap on the floor.

"Do what?" Dick asked blankly.

Barbra stared at Dick. His face was vacant, expressionless. "What do you mean, *do what?*" she screamed. "You *hit* me!"

As she watched, hypnotized, Dick's expression rearranged itself again: The eyes welled with tears; his face filled with remorse. "No!" he blurted, choking out the words. "I didn't do it! That wasn't me! Something came over me."

Barbra ran out of the room, frightened and confused. When Dick found her several hours later, checked into a different room in the hotel, she was still shaking.

Dick was all tenderness. "Please, Barbra," he pleaded, in supplicating tones. "I promise it won't happen again. I don't know what came over me. It's like I was possessed."

There were tears in his eyes. Barbra almost felt sorry for him, he looked so pathetic. Then she stopped herself, remembering that he had beaten her up earlier that night. "Get out of here!" she screamed. "You hit me!"

Dick was frantic. All night, he knocked on her door. The next day, he appeared at her room with a piece of paper and a pen. "Here," he said, when Barbra opened the door. "I want you to make a list of all the good things about our relationship, and all the bad things. Then you can decide whether you really want to leave. Go ahead," he urged. "Do it."

Barbra eyed him skeptically. Then she picked up the paper and started to write down Dick's bad traits: uncontrollable jealousy and possessiveness, lack of respect for her as a human being. When she finished the list, she examined the paper with some surprise. Dick was right, she thought to herself. The positives outnumber the negatives. A feeling of warmth came over her. She picked up the pen again, adding a final paragraph to her list of positives to give to Dick: "You've opened my life to love, healed many wounds and come so close to being ideal. I have faith that my 'dream world' is possible. Thanks to you I'm not afraid to love anymore."

As she finished, a feeling of wariness gnawed at her. Dick was *always* in control, always cool. Yesterday, when he hit her, he lost total control. He was like a different person. How could she trust him not to hit her again?

Before she had time to think about it, Dick grabbed her hand. "Come on!" he said impulsively. "Let's go get married! I know a justice of the peace, right down the road. We can do it right now!"

"You're crazy!" Barbra laughed affectionately. "We can't get married! You're still married to Mimi!"

By the end of the day, Barbra was back in Dick's room. Anyone can make a mistake, she told herself. It wasn't like he hit her all the time. It was just a fluke. An aberration. Why should she throw her life away because of one mistake? She would only be hurting herself.

That night in bed, Barbra Piotrowski tossed and turned. Her mind kept coming back to one thought. If she could go back to Dick after what he did to her, she knew she would love him to the grave.

It was a frightening thought.

When Dick and Barbra returned to Houston from Acapulco the first week in January 1978, Barbra started looking for an apartment of her own. She loved Dick as much as ever, but she just didn't know what to think anymore. She wanted the security of her own place.

She found a townhouse in Ethan's Glen, one of the communities she had looked at for her and Dick. The condominiums were sort of rustic contemporary, with tennis courts and several small manmade lakes on the woodsy grounds. Barbra was enchanted. There was just one problem: She couldn't afford it. The townhomes in Ethan's Glen started at around eighty-five thousand dollars. That was out of her league. But she mentioned it to Dick, anyway, just so he would know she was seriously looking.

Dick had other things on his mind.

Six months earlier, in the middle of the summer, his oldest son, Mike, a twenty-six-year-old Houston attorney, had filed a lawsuit that was ripping the Minns family apart.

Its centerpiece was a trust fund Dick and Mimi had established for their four children in 1968, comprised of forty-eight thousand shares of stock in President's-First Lady. Each child was to receive a third of his or her share at the age of twenty-five; the other two thirds at thirty.

When Mike Minns did not get his first third on his twenty-fifth birthday, he sued the four trustees—Sam Levy (Mimi's father), David Toomim (Mimi's cousin), Irving Weissman (Dick's brother-in-law), and Joe Reynolds (Dick's lawyer)—for a million dollars in exemplary damages and $108,000 in actual damages and charged them with converting the funds in the trust as part of a conspiracy engineered by Richard Minns. His father, Mike claimed in the suit, was actually controlling the trust; the four trustees were mere puppets doing his bidding.

Dick never really discussed the lawsuit with Barbra, except to complain from time to time that his own son was "against" him. It was a classic piece of understatement. If she had known the details, Barbra would have been shocked.

Mike Minns's lawsuit was a symptom of a father-son relationship gone desperately awry. In his legal papers, Mike stated for posterity that he had "never" gotten along with his father. That his father was an "outrageous liar." That his father had bribed the trustees of the trust to sell the forty-eight thousand shares of PFL stock in the trust back to the corporation for three dollars a share, six dollars a share less than book value, without consulting Mike or his sisters and brother, so his father could "swindle" the public into doing the same thing. As a result, Mike charged in his petition, his mother and father made several million dollars in 1975, when President's-First Lady went from public back to private.

Mike's problems with his father, Mimi would later say, went through "almost a lifetime. Mike was never a player," she once stated. Nobody seemed to know, or say, when the schism started, or why. Mike's sister Cathy thought the rift began when Mike refused to sit for a family picture, and that the strain intensified. Friends of the family pointed to a classic father-son conflict: Dick wanted Mike to emulate him, and Mike, in family friend Jim LaHaye's words, "couldn't strike a match with a candle."

None of the explanations offered seemed to explain the sheer intensity of Mike's enmity, or Dick's response.

For years, Mike wouldn't even speak to his father. When Dick showed up at the hospital after the birth of Mike's first child in the beginning of 1975, Mike refused even to shake hands with him. A few months later, when Dick asked Mike to sign an amendment to the trust agreement but would not allow him to see it, Mike flatly refused. Mike's grandfather, Sam Levy (Mimi's father), sat down with Mike in the office of the Memorial house and tried to talk him into signing.

"Well," Levy said a few years later, when he recounted the conversation for a legal deposition, "it got more and more heated when I told him, 'Maybe your dad has done some funny things, but he is your father. And, Mike, you haven't been right about everything all your life, so why don't you just get together with him, be in the family?' "

Mike, according to his grandfather, exploded. "He says he doesn't want anything to do with him, and if he would get in an argument with him, he would beat him up and might even kill him."

Dick began making phone calls, scheduling urgent conversations with family relations to "pressure" them, Mimi's brother-in-law, Sam Levin, recalled, to "boycott" Mike and his family.

On June 1, 1977, around the time he filed the trust conversion suit, Mike sent an "open letter," made an exhibit in his lawsuit, to the members of his family, including both sets of grandparents, aunts, and uncles. The subject was his father, Dick Minns:

June 1, 1977

AN OPEN LETTER

. . . An old maxim my father is fond of goes as follows: "If you tell a lie long enough it becomes the truth." In other words, the truth is a lie. This is simply not true. A lie is a lie. Telling it a million times may make more people believe it, but it will never move one iota closer to being the truth.

These last three years when I struggled to support my family and earn my law degree the most difficult obstacle in my way was not academic or financial; it was the emotional stress intentionally inflicted on me by my parents. . . .

Communications from this family of the glass house were filled with Hitlerian demands. Sign this or else. Take this side or else. Be in our picture or else. A man who sells his will has nothing left. This is the step I would not take, the step I will never take to appease a "Hitler."

For over twenty years I have never had a significant dispute with any grandparent or uncle or aunt or cousin. There have been few times when my father was not in open hostilities with all of them. Overnight I was converted into the villain, he the good guy.

When I refused to obey orders I was called the provoker. When I refused to substantiate a number of lies everyone in the family knows are lies I was called a provoker. When my parents initiated a boycott to protest honoring my father-in-law by naming my son after him, I was called a provoker. When my mother cursed his name I was called a provoker. . . .

Do I feel anger and resentment toward my parents? Yes. . . .

Michael Louis Minns

Within a week, Dick had fired off letters and phone calls in response to Mike's open letter. When his father, George Minns, wrote him to request some love and understanding toward Mike, who was a favorite grandchild of his, Dick responded with a four-page, typewritten letter:

Dear Mother and Dad:
. . . There are too many letters expressing "love," "hurt," and what everyone has done for everyone during the last 20 or 30 years. I think all of those letters are a bunch of crap. I want concrete action and evidence NOW.

For best reference, I refer you to my letter of May 18, 1977. . . . My next to last paragraph on page 2 summarizes it totally:

"Notwithstanding the foregoing, if you want to retain, in addition to my love, my mental support, business support, legal support, financial support, etc., . . . then I expect you to support me 100% and to take my side 100% in any involvement or in any confrontation with any human being that walks on this earth, regardless of who that human being is, unless it is your wife and my Mother."

. . . Since then, we have received other "hate" letters from Mike, and I am now informed that you were aware of these letters before they even went out. First of all, you should have told Mike that just for writing them, he should be barred from your door.

Secondly, you should have told him that if he sent those letters out, he would be forever barred from your door. You did not comply in either event.

But I do not see any logic in sending you and Mother additional money and other compensations each month, only for you to drain them out to someone who has sworn to be the "hated enemy" of your son. . . .

Think about it.

Think about it real good, and use that excellent mind of yours.

This is the last letter you will receive from me in this regard. Either you take a FIRM STAND, NOW,

or you'll have to look to Mike for 100% on everything you need. Enough is enough for me. Things are
getting from bad to worse, <u>NOW</u> and <u>you</u> still want
to look the other way and talk about 20 to 30 years
ago.

Love, your son,

Dick

Around the time Dick and Barbra were celebrating her
pregnancy, Mike gave a legal deposition in his trust case.
The day it was scheduled, Dick showed up, unannounced,
to attend.

Mike refused to give the court reporter his business
address, standard procedure in a deposition. "I don't want
my dad to have that address," he said curtly, "because I
don't want to be harassed." For the next several hours, as
Richard Minns sat a few feet away, smiling sardonically,
Mike unleashed a lifetime of complaints about his father.
The accusations were cold and bitter: that Richard Minns
didn't care whom he hurt or used, that he was a habitual
liar, that he would lose control of his emotions and his logic
if his commands were not obeyed, that he was dishonest
and unethical, and that his lawyer, Joe Reynolds, was the
"governor's attorney," did "underhanded things," and was
"led around by the nose" by him.

"I just wonder how you smile, Dad," Mike said toward
the end of his deposition, looking with disgust at Dick.
"You're smiling, Dad, and I wonder how you can live
with yourself. Do you think what you're doing is clever
or smart or in any way particularly redeeming? I'm quite
serious, Dad. What do you think of yourself?"

Dick Minns's reply was quick and brutal. "First of all, I
don't think of you," he said flatly. "You are just an enemy
in the camp."

Mike Minns turned to his lawyer. "I hope I will never
see him again after this," he said, "except at trial."

A number of years later Cathy Minns would sum up her
brother's problems with her father in one sentence. "They
were both," she would say, "real proud . . . and nobody
would back down."

That sentence was the story of Richard Minns's life.

*   *   *

Early in January 1978, Barbra found an apartment, not nearly as luxurious as the townhouse she had discovered in Ethan's Glen, but it was right down Memorial Drive in a complex called The Pines, and she could afford it. On the fourteenth of January, she scraped together a thousand dollars for a down payment so she could move in on the twenty-first.

Four days later, she shared a romantic dinner with Dick to celebrate their one-year anniversary.

Never in her life had Barbra been so confused.

If there was a turning point that set in motion the tragedy that would wreak havoc on so many lives, it occurred that January. With everything that was going on in his life, Dick Minns had to have been a desperate man. His wife was threatening to divorce him, his son was suing him, and his lover was preparing to move into her own apartment. Mimi, he could deal with—he had been contending with her for twenty-eight years. Mike was either going to drop his lawsuit or he would be excommunicated; it was that simple. But Barbra leaving . . . that was the one thing Dick Minns could not tolerate. She was *his*. On the other hand, he didn't want to get a divorce. He had worked too hard to build up an empire only to split it with Mimi. That money belonged to *him*. Something had to be done.

On January 20, the day before Barbra was due to move into her townhouse, Dick picked up a checkbook with a special bank account in his name only. With the checkbook in his pocket, he drove straight to the office of a local realtor, where he made out a check for the down payment on the same townhouse Barbra had wanted to buy in Ethan's Glen, at 312 Litchfield Lane.

As he handed the application to the real estate broker, Dick must have congratulated himself on his brainstorm. Now Barbra would never move into her own apartment. It was a stroke of genius. It would, in fact, prove to be his undoing.

The next day, Barbra recruited one of the employees from President's-First Lady to move her belongings into her apartment at the Pines. She couldn't live with him anymore, she told Dick. Even at Ethan's Glen. She needed some security, and he wasn't willing to provide her with any.

The last week in January, Dick called his friend and lawyer Harry Brochstein, to discuss his marriage to Mimi. Then he got on the line with Mimi. "OK," he said resignedly. "If you really want a divorce, go ahead and get one. But call Harry first."

Mimi did as she was told. When Harry suggested the two of them get together with Dick, she immediately made an appointment. "I've got the perfect solution," Dick said, when the three were in Harry's office. "It will solve all our problems." He handed Mimi a list of items from the Memorial house. "These are the things I want," he said. Then he proposed they put two hundred thousand dollars in an account, from which each of them would have access to one hundred thousand. The idea was that they would live separate lives, but remain married. "That way, we don't have to mess up our finances," he explained earnestly. "But we can each do whatever we want. It's just like being divorced—only better!"

Mimi glanced over at Harry for guidance. "Dick's right," he chimed in. "I think it's the best thing the two of you could do."

"Here," said Dick, handing Mimi some papers. She took a look at the first page. At the top, in bold capital letters, were the words, OPEN MARRIAGE AGREEMENT.

Mimi barely scanned the contract. Then, with a deep breath, she signed her name on the dotted line.

"I was scared," she would say years later, explaining her decision. "Hell, I'd been married since I was eighteen years old! I didn't know where I'd be or what I'd do or who I was except Mrs. Richard L. Minns. It was a frightening experience. And then I had Harry and Dick both convincing me I didn't want a divorce, that things would be OK."

Dick tucked a copy of the open marriage agreement under his arm and went straight to Barbra's. "Oh, here," he said casually, passing the document to Barbra. "You wanted to see some proof of my open marriage? Here it is."

Dick Minns went to bed that night a happy man. In one fell swoop, he had successfully deterred Mimi from filing for a divorce, enabled himself to live freely with Barbra, and produced evidence for Barbra that he had had an open marriage all along.

Barbra, however, was still not convinced she wanted to move back in with Dick. She wanted some security. The open marriage contract was fine as far as it went, but she needed more. She needed some protection for her future, and living with Dick at Ethan's Glen in some vague, ill-defined relationship wasn't enough.

Dick refused to believe her and went ahead with his plans anyway, calling in a society decorator, Don Bolen, and Bolen's associate, restaurateur Willie Rometsch's socialite wife, Evinia, to help furnish the townhouse. For all his efforts, the most he could persuade Barbra to do was stay at the condominium for a few weeks to be certain everything was in good repair.

Meanwhile, Dick increased his pressure on Bolen, thinking, perhaps, that he could steamroll Barbra into submission. "We're going to Aspen for fifteen days," he told the decorator. "When we get back I want the townhouse to be completely finished. Glasses in the cabinets, clothes hanging in the closets. Everything."

The results were, in Evinia Rometsch's words, "disastrous." "Richard gave me a photo he had cut out of a magazine," she would later recall, "and said that was the feel that he wanted: fur throws on the bed, very man-about-town macho. And a lot of rust. He said he liked earth tones. Rusts and browns." Don Bolen, on the other hand, was a decorator accustomed to advising the ladies of River Oaks on the placement of settees in their sitting rooms. While Dick pushed for a pad Hugh Hefner might have featured in the pages of *Playboy*, Bolen was giving him pale blues.

Both Evinia Rometsch and Don Bolen felt sorry for Dick's girlfriend. Barbra, Bolen thought, seemed very young and very vulnerable and a bit insecure. Evinia Rometsch, who was one of the more stylish women in Houston, considered her quiet, rather on the mousy side. When the two shopped for accessories for the townhouse together, the decorator was appalled at Barbra's clothes. She had no wardrobe, Rometsch observed critically. Rometsch also felt Barbra was deeply unhappy. Dick, she noticed, had a habit of ordering her about. Once, when the three were at Dick's office discussing the decorating, Dick suddenly scrutinized Barbra's face, which was slightly broken out, a problem she carried with her from her teenage years. "Look at your face!" he said caustically. "I keep telling her not to eat certain foods," he said, directing his comment to Evinia as if Barbra were not even in the room. "Then her face would clear up. But no, she won't. She just eats whatever she wants, and look at her skin!" The poor girl, Rometsch thought. She was completely at Richard's mercy.

As the two women spent more time together, Barbra began to confide in Evinia, haltingly: how Dick had promised he was going to get a divorce and marry her, but somehow, the promise kept getting put off. Rometsch had been traveling in sophisticated circles for too long to believe that line. Besides, she *knew* Dick Minns; she had been at parties with him and Mimi. He had just hosted a big fundraiser at his house for Mark White, a local politician who was running for governor. It was her opinion that Dick had his eye on a political career himself. If he had his sights set on politics, he was *never* going to get a divorce.

Rometsch arched a perfectly penciled eyebrow in Barbra's direction. "Quite frankly," she said, "I don't think he's *ever* going to get married again. Number one, because he's too tight. Texas law would require that he give half of everything he owns to his wife. And I just can't see that happening. Besides," she added confidentially, "I think he's climbing the ladder socially. He's not going to get a divorce."

Barbra nodded. "I'm afraid of the same thing," she said glumly. "But he has talked about getting a Mexican divorce and a Mexican marriage. . . ."

Evinia Rometsch heaved a world-weary sigh. "That's not what I hear in the gossip mill, dear," she said bluntly. To herself, she thought: *This poor girl is so naïve. I hope she's not headed for a big fall.*

When Dick and Barbra returned home from Aspen and Dick saw the Ethan's Glen townhouse and Don Bolen's bill, he had a fit. He immediately got Bolen on the line. "You overcharged me!" he fumed on the phone. "I want everything out of here. Now!"

Bolen was flabbergasted. He had written down every item and gotten Dick's approval before he left for Colorado, and his bill was exactly what he'd said it would be. Why was Minns so furious? Suddenly a light went off in his head as he realized Dick's motive. "He thought I'd tell him he could have it for less," Bolen said later. The decorator decided to call his bluff. Within an hour, a moving truck was in front of 312 Litchfield Lane. A few minutes later, Bolen pulled up. As the movers loaded the truck, Dick hemmed and hawed. "Well," he drawled, watching each piece of furniture as it passed in front of him, "I'm not sure I want it *all* to go." Bolen held his ground. "He didn't have the guts to say he changed his mind or he didn't like it," he would later recall with contempt. "He blamed it all on Barbra."

Before the decorator could leave, Dick pressured him into signing a release. By the time the fiasco was over, Bolen didn't get a penny.

As winter eased into early spring, Evinia Rometsch took over the decorating of the townhouse. Dick continued to live at the big house on Memorial Drive, and Barbra continued to divide her time between her apartment at the Pines and the Ethan's Glen place. No amount of persuasion, charm, or cajoling could convince her to move in full-time.

Sometime that spring, Dick approached Barbra with an offer. "All right," he said suddenly. "The Ethan's Glen place is yours. You can have it. If you really want an apartment of your own that badly, you can have the Ethan's Glen townhouse. You don't even have to have *me* there if you don't want to. You can even keep it after we get our real house if it's a good investment." He paused, studying Barbra for her reaction. "Then will you give up your townhouse at the Pines?"

Negotiations continued for several days. When Barbra was still hesitating, Dick sweetened the deal. In addition to the townhouse, Barbra could have whatever furniture they bought for it. But her apartment at the Pines had to go. Dick scratched out a few lines on a small piece of notebook paper and handed it to her. It read:

. . . If we split up, you get the home and furniture, plus responsibility of payments . . . $50,000 for every year we live together until it reaches 10 years, or $500,000 in the aggregate.

A few days later, he presented her with a more formal agreement. After Barbra read it, Dick took it back and asked her for the notes he had made earlier. "I'll keep them for you," he said, putting the document in his pocket. "You've got to trust me, Barbi."

Barbra found the piece of notebook paper and gave it back to Dick. What she didn't tell him was that she had already made a copy and put it in a safe-deposit box. Dick had a habit of taking papers he had given her and then pretending not to know what happened to them. This one was too important, she had thought to herself. She wasn't taking any chances. She was going to keep a copy for herself. Just in case.

Once she was ensconced in Ethan's Glen, Barbra set about furnishing it in earnest, a task she found both challenging and frustrating on the budget Dick provided. The readers of Marge Crumbaker's gossip column who read weekly about Dick's splashy comings and goings would have been more than a little shocked to discover that the city's most famous "millionaire-adventurer" was furnishing his townhouse with furniture from Sears Roebuck and accessories from Pier One Imports. "Listen," Dick whispered in Evinia Rometsch's car one day, "don't spend a lot of money on furniture, because if Barbra and I break up, the townhouse and the furniture are hers. I don't want to put a lot of cash into something I might not even keep."

The decorator also had her doubts about the townhouse. One day, when she happened to look at the deed, her eye was caught by the name of the owner of record. It was Richard L. Minns.

On April 8, Barbra moved into the Ethan's Glen townhouse full-time.

"Be careful," Oscar Wilde once wrote, "what you wish for, because you may get it."

Richard Minns had just had his fondest wish come true.

13

The first weekend in May, Dick and Barbra flew to Dallas for the grand opening of a new President's-First Lady. Don Wildman, who now owned the clubs, had planned a three-day extravaganza, inviting local media stars, the city's movers and shakers, and Lynda Carter, the actress who played "Wonder Woman" on television, celebrity spokesperson for President's-First Lady.

Dick was in his element. Barbra was on his arm, and his face was once more glistening in the glare of flashbulbs. In the middle of the excitement, he received an urgent phone call from Mimi, who had tracked him down at his hotel. "Sorry to interrupt your fun," she said sarcastically, "but our daughter Cathy just tried to commit suicide."

"What happened?" Dick said with alarm.

"She took an overdose of sleeping pills. I think you should get here right away."

Dick paused for a moment, then said, "Is she OK?"

Mimi's voice was flat and cold. "Yeah. But you'd better get yourself on the next plane. Our daughter tried to *kill* herself!"

Dick hung up. Then he grabbed Barbra's arm and headed back to the party. There was nothing he could do about it now, he thought to himself. Cathy was fine. Why miss the entire weekend over something that had already happened? The crisis had passed.

Early on Sunday, after a function at the home of one of the Dallas President's-First Lady executives, Dick pulled Barbra aside. "We'd better go home a little early," he whispered, "so I can check on Cathy."

150

When Dick arrived at the house on Memorial later in the day, Mimi was waiting for him with a stack of papers, her eyes blazing.

"So," she said, in a voice as abrasive as sandpaper, "I understand we own a townhouse in Ethan's Glen."

Dick stood in the doorway, stunned. Mimi picked up the papers and walked in his direction. "I see you opened a checking account in the name of Richard L. Minns, Trustee," she said, with the smirky confidence of a prosecutor who has just caught the defendant in a bald-faced lie on the witness stand. "What the hell is that all about?"

Dick's mind raced. He kept the bankbook for the Richard L. Minns, Trustee account in a locked drawer in his desk at the office. Obviously, Mimi had been snooping through his papers at the office while he was in Dallas with Barbra. Then it clicked. *That's* what the phone call at the hotel was all about! Cathy hadn't tried to kill herself. Mimi had found the checking account and she wanted to get him back home as soon as possible so she could confront him.

"Fifty percent of that townhouse belongs to me," his wife said icily. "And I want to see it. *Now.*"

"I can't do that," Dick said slowly.

Mimi's eyes narrowed to tiny slits. "Who's living there?"

Dick fidgeted under his wife's piercing glare.

"I own half of a townhouse on Litchfield Lane and I want to see it, *right now*," Mimi repeated.

"You can't," Dick responded. "I can't do that."

"Fine," snapped Mimi. "Then I'm filing for a divorce, tomorrow morning."

This time, Mimi wasted no time. As soon as Dick left the room, she picked up the phone and dialed Harry Brochstein's home number, interrupting the lawyer in the middle of his Sunday afternoon. "I want a divorce," she said flatly. "No more of this open marriage crap. I want you to file for a divorce for me tomorrow morning as soon as you get to the office, OK?"

The following Friday, Brochstein filed a petition for divorce on behalf of Mimi Minns. Dick, Mimi would later say, "persuaded" Harry to delay five days before filing the papers—thinking, no doubt, that he could talk his wife out of it in the interim.

But Mimi was not to be persuaded. Not this time. Dick had committed the cardinal sin. He spent half of *her* money without her permission. When Dick saw Barbra's name on the pleadings as a correspondent, he scoffed. "This divorce has nothing to do with adultery," he later testified. "It has to do with the purchase of a townhouse in Ethan's Glen. It's economics, and not a matter of morals or anything else concerned. It's money. *Money.* It's not sex, it's money. Mrs. Minns doesn't care how many times I had sex with Barbra, but she cares how many Coca-Colas I may have bought her, because she wants half of the Coke."

Years later, Mimi would admit it. "That townhouse was the last straw," she acknowledged. "I'd wanted to [divorce Dick] for a long time, OK? But the townhouse was the straw. He used *our* money to purchase something for the first time in my life that I didn't know about. . . . That's why they say I'm mercenary. I *am* mercenary. I like what I earned. But I earned it."

On May 12, 1978, Harry Brochstein filed a petition for divorce in the case of *Miriam Joan Minns* v. *Richard Louis Minns*.

It was a declaration of war.

Once she made her decision to divorce Dick, Mimi was relentless. The instant she discovered Harry had waited five days to file the papers, she realized she had made a mistake in calling one of her husband's best friends to represent her in the divorce.

When Dick heard she was thinking of replacing Harry, he immediately got Mimi on the phone. "Come on!" he entreated. "Harry's the best. He's your friend, too. You know he'll be fair with both of us. You don't want all our money to go to a bunch of lawyers, do you?"

Mimi stood firm.

"All right," Dick said, when he realized she was beyond convincing. "If you're going to hire another lawyer, at least let me give you a list of names. You don't have any idea who's good and who's not."

A few days later, Mimi received a letter from Dick with the names of ten prominent Houston divorce attorneys. After looking over the list, she called one of the lawyers Dick had recommended. When she presented her case to him, he told her he was sorry, but he wouldn't be able to handle it. He had a conflict of interest. By the end of the week, Mimi had contacted all of the divorce attorneys on Dick's list. All ten of them told her they had conflicts of interest.

Within a week, Houston's legal community was buzzing. Dick Minns had gone to ten of the best divorce lawyers in town and given each of them a ten-thousand-dollar retainer to represent him in his divorce. Then he gave the list of names to his wife. When she called them, each attorney had to turn down her case because of a conflict: He was already representing Richard Minns. When he repeated the story to Barbra, Dick was somber.

But Mimi was used to Dick Minns's tricks. She decided to try to beat him at his own game. Tossing aside the list, she quietly contacted a lawyer whose name had *not* appeared: Ralph Balasco.

When Dick saw Balasco's name on the next set of pleadings he received, he panicked. Unlike Harry Brochstein, who was one of his closest friends, Ralph Balasco was a complete stranger, with a reputation as an aggressive divorce lawyer. The next weekend, when he was at Lakeway with Barbra, he paid a visit to the state capitol to see John Hill, the Texas attorney general, whose campaign he had helped finance. Dick wasted little time in getting to the point: It was Ralph Balasco. "I want that bastard disbarred," he told Hill. "Yesterday!" Hill made a few placating remarks in his thick Texas twang, tried to calm Dick down, and sent him out the door with a promise to "look into it."

Then a curious thing happened. Just when her most cherished wish was coming true—Dick was getting a divorce—Barbra started having second thoughts about the relationship. Perhaps, she would later hypothesize, it was some vestige of her religious upbringing, some Catholic guilt. Whatever the reason, less than a month after Mimi filed for divorce, Barbra told Dick one day that she thought it would be better if he went back to Mimi. See if he could work things out. Be certain he was doing the right thing.

"I probably was just realizing what I wouldn't allow myself to realize before," she said later. "Maybe I felt that what I did was wrong: that when I found out he was married I didn't put an end to it. Maybe I felt that in this small way I could make up for that, I'm not sure. I didn't want to be the cause, the reason, for a divorce." Even though she believed Dick—that his marriage, as such, didn't really exist—on a subconscious level, Barbra felt responsible.

She was also still consumed with the idea of achieving financial security. All Dick ever talked about was Barbra "paying her dues." If they were apart, she reasoned, at least she would have a steady job, a steady income. The way it was now, she had nothing. She was totally dependent on Dick. The uncertainty was gnawing at her.

One month to the day after Mimi filed for divorce, June 12, Barbra moved out of Ethan's Glen and back into her small apartment at the Pines. It was the only way, she decided, Dick would ever go back and try to work it out with Mimi. The only way she could ever stand on her own two feet.

Richard was shell-shocked. He drove back to the house on Memorial Drive and passed the news on to Mimi, who could hardly keep from cackling. Later in the day, she made a gleeful entry on her tennis calendar: "RLM at home. Barbara [sic] moving. Ha! Ha!"

"Why did you leave?" Dick wrote, on note after note to Barbra. "I'm in the middle of World War II right now. Please love me and forgive me for anything I might have done in the past. . . ."

After a few days of silence Barbra responded to Dick's letters with a letter of her own:

Dear Richard,

I want you to know that I love you with all my heart and all my soul. But I can't come back. Maybe someday—if you still want me and if you've resolved your situation with Mimi—but not now. I believe that you love me, but you don't respect me. I'm always trying to prove myself to you—by skiing until my hands bleed, by running until I feel like I'm going to collapse, by trying to make you proud of me. But those things don't count. I'll never earn your respect until I've "paid my dues," until I've shown endurance in the one thing you place above all else: the ability to make money.

If I come back now, I will just have thrown an emotional tantrum with no forethought; my credibility will be destroyed, and our situation will be the same if not worse. . . .

God, I'm so immature! I don't understand people and I don't understand life. Two people meet, fall in love, and develop a relationship that's so precious, so rare. But even if they are a "perfect fit," if their values don't match, a serious flaw in that relationship will develop and grow. You place a great value on the ability to make money. I don't. . . .

Please work things out with Mimi so that you're happy. Do what you have to do to resolve your life. I will try to remove my things as soon as possible so that you can sell this place. I won't take the things you gave me— I can't start a new life with pain and memories. You used to joke about me leaving behind the things you got me for your next girlfriend—here they are, nice— convenient. . . .

I don't even want any written communication, because even that puts a fresh new stab of pain into a wound that's all too new and all too open. Those stabs weaken me and right now I need all the strength I can muster up.

I wish you well   Barbra

P.S. I hope you don't miss me as much as I miss you. It hurts so badly I could die.

Dick's tone became ever more urgent. "I've told you," he wrote, "that you have been, are and always will be the *only woman for me* . . . I will never go back to Mimi, no matter what. So we can either live separate lives and be miserable, or we can be together and be happy."

After three days, when Barbra still hadn't returned to Ethan's Glen, Dick wrote by hand a two-page letter to Mimi, marked "Personal":

Mimi:

For whatever it means—and at this stage probably nothing to you—I love you, respect you . . . and I do not want either a separation (physical or economic), and I certainly do not want a Divorce. . . .

Many of your accusations (sp.) of me are correct. Many are not correct. I am far from perfect, and I am wrong. . . .

I would never leave you for another woman. And I will never marry another woman. And I don't intend to live with another woman, either. I have no place to go.

I am sorry if I have caused you any pain. And I will cooperate with you to do everything to work things out to your satisfaction. Please don't be bitter with me. (We'll drive to Harry's together Wed.)

I love you and need you, but you don't believe me.

Dick

When Mimi read Dick's letter, she snickered. "Forget it, Dick," she said coldly, when he called to plead with her to take him back. "It's all over. I want a divorce. You blew it."

At the same time, Barbra Piotrowski was reading a letter of her own from Dick, the fifteenth or twentieth he had written her since she moved out, begging her to move back into Ethan's Glen. "I'm a businessman and such a cynic by nature," he wrote. "We are the exact opposite by nature. That is the *only* opposite in our nature. We belong together . . . I want to hold you so badly. I'm torn up, but will restrain . . . I place your love above all material and personal things. . . ."

After six days, Barbra couldn't take it anymore. On June 16, she moved back into Ethan's Glen. She couldn't live without Dick. To celebrate their reunion, she and Dick drove to Lakeway for the weekend. While they were there, Dick proposed.

For the first time in a week, Barbra slept like a baby.

Shortly after Mimi Minns filed for divorce, Harry Brochstein received a package in the mail from Dick Minns. When he opened it, the lawyer let out a chuckle. Inside was a recording of Frank Sinatra singing "My Way." Dick's theme song, he laughed. He always was a frustrated Frank Sinatra.

As he tucked the 45 in a drawer, Brochstein grew thoughtful for a moment. The record, he knew, was more than one of Dick's silly pranks. It was a symbol. A symbol of Dick's divorce. Dick was telling him that he wanted to win, whatever the cost. If Harry's way didn't work, it would be Dick's. Whatever it took to win.

Dick's longtime friend and business rival Bob Schwartz was shocked when he found out Dick and Mimi were getting a divorce. The last thing Dick wanted, Schwartz knew, was to share his millions with anyone, even Mimi. Especially Mimi. Schwartz let out a low whistle. This time Dick's gonna have a real fight on his hands. Mimi knows all his tricks.

By the eleventh of July 1978, when the judge who was assigned the Minns divorce scheduled the first hearing in the case, Dick and Mimi's vitriol had already preceded them into court. Before listening to a word either of them had to say, the judge issued a restraining order to keep them from "engaging in any act calculated to embarrass, harass, humiliate, molest or injure" each other, and to make a "reasonable effort" to speak well of each other in public and in private. Then he warned them not to deplete any of the community assets before the divorce was final.

The first chance he had to speak, Dick downplayed any animosity between him and Mimi. "We're going to work out a property settlement ourselves, Your Honor," he said politely. "In fact, we should have one ready by the end of the month."

The judge looked up hopefully, peering over the bench at Dick and Mimi, standing respectfully in front of him like a civilized couple who had come to an amicable parting of the ways. Perhaps impressed by that, he announced a decision. Since both Mr. Minns and Mrs. Minns wanted to use the house on Memorial during the divorce, he stated, he was going to sign a temporary order for them to share it. It was a big house, he commented. They could come and go without interfering in each other's lives.

The next week, Dick, flanked by Harry Brochstein and Mimi, represented by Ralph Balasco, pored over reams of papers trying to work out a division of property. When they hadn't reached a compromise by midweek, Mimi announced that she was flying to New York the next day with the children and her parents to board the *Queen Elizabeth II* for a two-week cruise to Europe.

Dick was livid. How could she take off on a trip in the middle of their negotiations? he sputtered to Barbra over the phone, pacing back and forth in his office in Sharpstown. That's *my* money she's spending! She's blowing *my* money on that trip!

He hung up and quickly dialed the house on Memorial. "Get your ass over to the office," he hissed into the receiver, when Mimi answered. "We've got some tax problems to work on."

Mimi blithely disregarded him. Like the scores of other women before her who had gone through divorces and felt rejected by their soon to be ex-husbands, she was indulging herself, seeking to be reassured of her desirability as a woman. Two weeks after she filed for divorce, she had plastic surgery to have her breasts enlarged ("It was something I always wanted to do," she later explained in court). Now she wanted to take a cruise. That was the least Dick could do for her. He *owed* her.

Dick could hardly contain his anger. When Mimi returned from her cruise the end of July, he was waiting at the house, purple with rage. At the end of the day, Mimi recorded the conversation on her tennis calendar for July 28:

Talks about my trip but he spent 6 weeks in Aspen— Barbara [sic]—3 weeks in Acapulco—Barbara [sic]— Leaves the house without telling anyone. . . . Has contro. of all our money and will not let me know if I can even have money to buy groceries. Wants me to crawl. Wants to prolong divorce as long as possible. Told him all I could say to him from now on was hello & goodbye because he is very nasty & threatening. Says Charles Syptak [their accountant] will lie for him and swear he has heard conversations he has not heard. Tells me all judges are dumb and he can handle them all. . . .

Three days after she returned from Europe, Mimi signed an earnest money contract for a $115,000 townhouse at

Hudson on the Bayou, an exclusive enclave of townhomes in inner Memorial. Then she called Dick and asked him for $10,000 for a down payment. "She told me if I didn't do it," he later told the court, "she would ruin me publicly, emotionally, and financially." He didn't do it.

The next day, Dick sat down and pounded out a letter to Mimi in his familiar, emphatic script:

Mimi:

I've been told that Divorce Proceedings are often as emotion-charged as murder trials—even though it is a Domestic Court Procedure.

Divorce is positive proof of failure. So now your wish is granted. You are in court. And, once we get started, we will probably be in court for several years (Only the attorneys and CPA's will win). . . .

But, if we can look at this like a business, as Ralph originally suggested (before emotions took over), we could settle our differences and resolve everything in not 2 to 3 months—but in one to TWO WEEKS.

. . . I refuse to sit back and let you and Ralph take me off a bite at a time. It just is not right and it is not fair. . . .

I would like to leave for Tahoe on Saturday, August 12, with both of us Divorced. Or I can stay and devote 100% of my energy and 100% of my drive in what could end up being a very historical divorce case. If I don't leave I'll spend 24 Hours a Day working on just this for the next year. . . .

Regards,
Dick

Mimi ignored the letter.

Dick began hounding Harry Brochstein day and night for the names of the most vicious divorce attorneys in Houston. If he was going to pulverize Mimi in court, he needed an expert. Harry was great as far as he went, but Harry was primarily a corporate lawyer. He needed a specialist in the art of war. Divorce War.

The name that Harry came up with was Huey O'Toole. To look at him, one would not suspect that Huey O'Toole

was a courtroom warrior. Slender, with horn-rimmed glasses, his appearance suggested more of the legal scholar than
a hired gun. But appearances can be misleading. As a poker
player, O'Toole was, in the view of one of his card-playing
buddies, "dangerous." The kind of player who wasn't afraid
to bluff. Dick snickered with delight at the thought of Huey
skewering Mimi and Ralph Balasco in court. It occupied his
dreams, his fantasies, his every moment.

Old friends, like oil operator Al Dugan, began to notice
a change in Dick. Whenever they got together, Dugan
noticed, all Dick could talk about was the divorce. He
even insisted that Barbra not take any summer classes at
the University of Houston so she would be available at all
times to help him with the divorce. Dick had always used
the legal system as a way to solve his problems, Dugan
knew that. Even his personal ones—look at his lawsuit
with his son Mike! But this time, the oil man pondered,
he had gone a step further.

On August 3, Mimi's lawyer, Ralph Balasco, filed a
Motion for Contempt against Dick. Dick, Balasco alleged,
had threatened to "maim" him for life; called him a "shyster"
and a "son-of-a-bitch." According to Mimi, Balasco's
motion went on to say, he had also threatened to break
their daughter Cathy's jaw if she sided with Mimi during
the divorce, and told Mimi he would "do anything" to hurt or
ruin her if Myles turned against him. How much of this was
true is difficult to assess. In later years, Cathy Minns would
deny her father ever threatened her, but by that time she had
reason to deny many things.

A few weeks later, Balasco asked the court to order
Richard Minns to submit to a mental examination. His
motion was filled with accusations about Dick, culled from
Mimi and from his own experience:

> . . . given to episodes of harsh, vicious, sadistic and
> ungovernable fits of anger and temper . . . continually
> harassing, embarrassing, and humiliating [Mimi Minns]
> by threats of violence, obscene and vulgar language . . .
> threats of bodily harm or injury to herself and her attorney
> and to two or more of their children . . . has fantasized and
> hallucinated that one of his daughters is a spy of [Mimi

Minns] . . . that his tyrannical, dictatorial, sadistic, malicious and vicious treatment of [Mimi Minns] would enable him to intimidate her into doing anything he wished.

In addition, Balasco charged, his client feared that Richard Minns's "extreme and abnormal conduct" indicated a "psychopathic propensity to destroy himself and all others close to him in a financial way so that his paranoid propensities can be satisfied. . . ."

When Dick saw Mimi and Ralph Balasco's motion, he went into a tirade. "That son-of-a-bitch!" he exploded, in front of Barbra. "I'm gonna barbecue him!"

Over the coming weeks, Barbra saw reports from private investigators on Mimi's comings and goings: background checks on Ralph Balasco and the judge. Anyone and everyone who had anything to do with the divorce, Dick was having investigated. "That's the way ya do it," he said to Barbra one day. "Find out everything you can about a person. Everything. Once you know what their quirks are, you can use it against them. Everybody has something . . . and every man has a price." He looked at her, then repeated emphatically: *"Everyone."*

Barbra listened and watched, horrified. She had never met a human being in her life who could manipulate so effectively as Dick. He always knew the right button to push to elicit the exact reaction he wanted from somebody.

Once, when their car broke down in the hill country outside Austin, a local farmer stopped to pick them up in his truck. "Watch!" Dick whispered to Barbra, when they slid into the front seat. "See how I get this guy goin'!" As they headed down the road, he eased into a country twang so thick Barbra did a double-take. "You don't have many niggers up in this area, do ya?" he said to the farmer.

"Niggers?" the farmer responded, launching into what was clearly one of his favorite topics. Within ten minutes, the two were swapping stories like a pair of good ole boys from way back.

Another time, when a business crony of his wouldn't do what he wanted, Barbra witnessed Dick threaten to tell the man's wife about his mistress, whose existence one of his investigations had uncovered. "Please!" the man begged. "Our wives play tennis together!" Dick flashed a twisted smile and pushed further. "You've got to kick 'em while they're down," he said to Barbra later.

Barbra had already seen Dick threaten to expose embarrassing things about Harry Brochstein during the divorce trial. Barbra was disturbed by Dick's behavior and by what she believed the divorce was doing to him. He needed her now, she believed, more than ever. Earlier, when she had watched Dick in action, if she excepted herself from what he was doing, she had been entertained by the ways he could manipulate people. He was a genius at it. But this was different.

In the midst of Dick and Mimi's legal thrusts and parries, Dick got permission from the judge to use the mansion on Memorial to host a fundraising party for Mark White, a Houston lawyer and Democrat he was supporting in the race for governor of Texas. More than ten years later, when guests who attended the party remembered it, they would still be shaking their heads in disbelief at the sparks that flew that night. As Mimi mingled among Houston's rich and powerful amid the statues of Venus di Milo and the discus thrower, her deep, scratchy voice could be heard above the low buzz of the cocktail party political talk, piercing the air with pointed darts about Dick.

Dick's post-party spirits were exuberantly high. He had managed to pull Mark White away from the crush long enough to pocket the politician into an urgent tête-à-tête, which he repeated later to Barbra. "I told Mark White I wanted him to get that fuckin' Ralph Balasco disbarred. Now some heads are gonna roll!" He leaned closer to Barbra. "With my connections to Mark White and John Hill," he said cockily, "I could get away with murder in the state of Texas!"

Barbra looked at him oddly. White, she imagined, had probably laughed in Dick's face. Dick had a way of telling stories so that he always came out on top.

A day or so later, Dick approached Barbra with a question. "You know that eye surgery Mimi has comin' up?" he began. Barbra nodded.

"I was just wonderin'," Dick said slowly, choosing his words with the utmost care, "when you have that kind of eye operation, do they cover your eyes afterward?"

Barbra looked at Dick oddly. His face was a study in concentration. "Why?" she asked curiously.

"Well, I was just thinking. You could put on one of your nurse's uniforms and sneak into her room after the operation and pretend to be one of the nurses." His eyes glistened menacingly. "Then you could inject Mimi with insulin. I've got it all figured out."

Barbra was aghast. This was madness! Dick had talked about hiring someone to kill Mimi after Ralph Balasco filed his motion for the mental exam, but Barbra had dismissed it as a temper tantrum. Now this! "Are you out of your mind?" she cried.

Dick was staring at her, earnest as a preacher on Sunday morning.

A few days later, Dick brought the subject up again. "Please!" he pleaded. His face was twisted with anxiety. "If you really loved me, you'd do this for me."

Barbra was seething. How could Mimi do this to the man she married? she thought to herself. She and Ralph Balasco were driving Dick crazy! Look at what they had him saying and thinking! It was insanity. She was going to stay with him, no matter what, she decided. It was up to her to keep him stable. He needed her.

Dick's despondency deepened. Harry wasn't doing anything. Huey wasn't doing anything. Nobody was doing anything to help him with this divorce. Balasco had just submitted Mimi's request for household expenses. She wanted $17,856 a month!

One Sunday afternoon, Barbra and Dick were driving home from Lakeway. While they were in the car, Dick announced that he was going to kill Mimi himself. "If you're not going to do it," he said resignedly, "then I'm gonna have to do it myself." Barbra looked over at him, horrified. "I just can't take this anymore!" he screamed. "This divorce is driving me crazy! It's ruining my life! She's destroying me!"

Barbra pulled the car into a 7-Eleven, went to a pay phone and called Harry Brochstein and Huey O'Toole.

"Meet Dick and me back at the townhouse," she whispered urgently into the phone. She wanted Harry and Huey there when they got back, she decided, in case Dick tried to do something crazy. To her relief, he did not.

Richard, Barbra would insist, did not stop there. He also threatened to blow up an airplane Mimi and several of their children were boarding to San Antonio. For the most part, she did not take him seriously. It was just the divorce talking. He was berserk. A madman. And it was all Mimi and Ralph Balasco's fault.

14

Dick refused to let Mimi or her lawyer spoil his forty-ninth birthday on August 17, 1978. Settlement or no settlement, he was going to fly to Lake Tahoe and carry out his latest birthday feat: to water-ski five times around the circumference of the lake. Plans had already been announced. The media were waiting for him. He had an *audience* to impress.

Dick arrived in the woodsy California resort with all the fanfare of visiting royalty. In addition to Barbra and the ubiquitous Delmonteques, his entourage included Wes and Stella Piotrowski, who drove up from Los Angeles; Myles; the inimitable television consumer crusader Marvin Zindler and his "friend" Barbara Fox; and Marge Crumbaker, the *Houston Post* gossip columnist. Even Bob Schwartz, Dick's nemesis from the ten-year legal battle between President's-First Lady and Slenderbolic, turned up for the event.

Barbra was almost more excited than Dick. The only one of his physical feats she had "witnessed" so far was his bogus shark fight in Antigua. Last year on his birthday, when he skied around Lake Tahoe *four* times, she was in Los Angeles tending to the leg Dick had accidentally caught in the rudder of his boat. This year, she didn't plan to miss a thing.

Dick, she noticed with pride, was something of a celebrity in Tahoe. Everyone in town seemed to be buzzing about his birthday stunt. The morning of the seventeenth, reporters from all the local TV stations and the *Tahoe Daily Tribune* lined up on the shores of the lake for a firsthand account of the "crazy Texan's" attempt to set another record.

Dick played to the audience. As he got on his skis, flashing one of his electric smiles, he announced that he was going to ski the first lap of the lake with his sixteen-year-old son Myles, then continue alone four more laps. That way, he shouted to the crowd, he could set *two* new records: the first father-son team to ski around the lake, and the first person to ski the circumference of the lake five times.

Marge Crumbaker devoted an entire column of gush to Dick's continuing "battle with Lake Tahoe" for her readers back in Houston.

When Barbra read Marge Crumbaker's column, she got a sick feeling in her stomach. If only Marge knew, she thought ruefully. Dick and Myles hadn't made it all the way around the lake together. She was there. The real story, however, would never hit the papers. Dick would see to that.

The truth was that Myles had faltered some time after the boat cruised out of the sight of the crowd on the shore. As she watched him fall, again and again, Barbra's heart went out to him. Myles, she observed, was always trying to impress his father, especially in athletics. No matter what he did, it wasn't enough. Lately, Myles had even begun confiding in her. He hated his dad, he told Barbra. He felt trapped by his money. Barbra listened sympathetically. Myles was just suffering from low self-esteem, she thought to herself. How could he compete with a father like Dick?

As Dick and Myles climbed onto the boat from the freezing water, Dick told his son not to worry about it. "We'll just hide out somewhere for a while and then go back and say we did it," he said offhandedly, as he dried himself off with a towel. Barbra shot him a disapproving look. "You can't do that!" she said, frowning. "Sure we can!" Dick said breezily. "Just watch!"

When they returned to shore a few hours later, with Dick and Myles skiing behind the boat, grinning triumphantly, Barbra bit her tongue. "We did it!" Dick roared. "I told you we would!"

Later in the day, when they were alone, Barbra expressed her displeasure to Dick. A look of impatience crossed his face. "I did it for Myles!" he protested. "You know how we don't get along whenever he can't beat me at sports. I didn't want to have to blame *him* for not making it. Think what that would do to his ego! Maybe this'll help patch things up. Now everybody will think Myles did the same thing I did."

For once, Barbra did not back down. "I don't agree," she said firmly. "If you really care about your son, you should be teaching him that it's more important to be honest, and teaching him integrity, instead of trying to stroke his ego."

Dick didn't answer. He was already in another room.

For the rest of the week, and into the next, Dick spent every waking moment in the water, trying to fulfill his goal of skiing five times around the lake. By August 25, he was desperate. "This is it," he said to Barbra, as they climbed into their wetsuits in the predawn darkness. "This is the day. I've gotta do it."

As Barbra watched from the boat, purely amazed, Dick willed himself to stay up on his skis as they lapped the seventy-six-mile circumference of the lake through violent, whipping winds one time, then two, then three. At the end of the third lap, the waves overpowered him. As Dick swam toward the boat, Barbra stood up and cheered. "It was remarkable!" she said later. "Here Dick was, and he's in his late forties, and he was able to go around three times, when these young guys who were legitimate competitive skiers and had won medals could not stay up long enough to make a switch-off. I was ecstatic."

Dick was bitterly disappointed. He was supposed to ski *five* times around the lake, not three. That was his goal. He told Marge Crumbaker he wouldn't go home until he accomplished it. "Just tell them you had boat difficulties," Barbra urged. "Tell them you did it three times. That's a record."

Dick shook his head. Dick Minns never gave up and never gave in. "Nope," he said flatly. "Can't do that."

A few hours later, Richard Minns skied to shore with a grin that flashed success to the reporters and the curious who had waited around for his return. It was official, he announced ebulliently. A new record. Five times around the lake.

Barbra's face was a mask of self-control. The past two hours, she and the world-record-breaking skier had been hiding out in a cove eating Kentucky Fried Chicken.

Two days later, Barbra found her own picture on the front page of the *Tahoe Daily Tribune*,, smiling radiantly, her long hair blowing in the wind. The headline said it all: FIRST WOMAN TO LAP TAHOE: GUINNESS RECORD EXPECTED FOR MINNS'S FIANCEE.

After Dick's triumph of will, Barbra put on her skies and skied around the circumference of the lake without falling in two hours and nine minutes. It was, she told the *Tribune* reporter, "sheer determination."

Barbra's comments for the paper had the familiar ring of Richard Minns's hype. To concentrate while she was skiing, she told the reporter for the *Tribune*, "I sing songs like 'Let Me Have Everything' and 'I Am Woman.' " On Dick's next birthday, she said, she wanted to double-ski the lake with him for another record.

"Minns," the *Tribune* stated in closing, "has already set goals for his future wife, and if she is anything like him, she will do almost anything to achieve those goals."

As she packed to go back to Houston, Barbra's excitement at setting a new woman's world record for endurance skiing was tempered by a vague, discomfiting feeling. Perhaps, she found herself thinking for the first time, she and Dick had some real differences in their characters. Fundamental differences.

Besides his divorce from Mimi, Dick Minns had one other obsession in the year 1978: Olympia Fitness & Racquetball Club.

Since he and Bob Delmonteque first began weaving their dream of the perfect health club in 1974, when Delmonteque passed through Houston on his way to Atlanta, the club had remained just that: a dream. The problem was Dick's contract with Don Wildman. When he sold the President's-First Lady clubs to Wildman in 1975, Dick had signed a noncompetition agreement guaranteeing Wildman that he would not open a health club to compete with PFL for five years.

One weekend in July, Dick chatted up Mel Powers, his idol, about leasing space in some of Powers's buildings for the clubs. Then he got on the phone, putting out feelers to former PFL employees, tantalizing them with fervid descriptions of the ultimate health club he and Bob envisioned and enticing them with offers to come onboard.

That was off the record. On the record, in his divorce proceedings with Mimi, Dick was denying he had anything to do with Olympia other than to act as an occasional "consultant" to his old friend Bob Delmonteque. Delmonteque, he said under oath, was the owner.

Mimi gnashed her teeth in frustration. *She* had drawn up the original plans for the Olympia with Dick and Bob four years earlier. Dick hadn't even bothered to change the name! The reason for the ruse was simple, and purely fiscal. If Dick owned Olympia, Mimi owned half of it. If it belonged to Bob Delmonteque, she was shut out.

Thus began an elaborate charade. In court, Dick swore under oath that he was not an officer or shareholder of Olympia and did not plan to be in the future; Mimi had no way to prove otherwise. Privately, Barbra would later recount, Dick was in constant agony at the thought of trusting the whole setup to Bob. Ten years later, when the divorce was a page from the past, Delmonteque would still insist, when asked, that he owned Olympia "lock, stock and barrel."

Mimi Minns began to grow increasingly disenchanted with her supposedly vicious divorce lawyer, Ralph Balasco. While Barbra would later say that Dick was panic-stricken by Balasco, Mimi herself thought the high-priced litigator wasn't tough enough. Dick knew exactly how to intimidate Ralph, she would complain to friends.

In February 1979, Mimi found the person she considered ideal for the job. When Dick got his first glimpse of Mimi's new lawyer, he snorted with laughter. Roberta Rayborn, who went by the nickname "Burta," Mimi's choice, was the epitome of all the characteristics Dick found least formidable in an adversary. She was overweight, and she was a woman. When he was alone with Barbra, he cackled at his good fortune.

In later years, those who played a part in the Minns divorce would come to describe the injection of Burta Rayborn into the proceedings as the addition of a chemical in an experiment that causes the mixture to explode.

One of Burta's first acts as Mimi's lawyer was to attempt to oust Dick from the big house on Memorial. It was sheer lunacy, she counseled Mimi, to be sharing a house with the man you're divorcing! How could she have even considered it? It was also, she advised, an important strategic move. That house was a base of power. Whoever lived in it had an enormous tactical and psychological advantage in the divorce. And don't forget, Rayborn said slyly, it's worth a helluva lot of money. Mimi nodded with satisfaction.

Dick's original glee at Mimi's selection of Burta Rayborn was soon eclipsed by a raw thought: Somehow he had to turn the divorce around. To get something—anything—on Mimi. When the private investigators he hired failed to turn up any dirt on his wife, he started to manufacture some of his own. "I'm going to prove you're a whore," he hissed at Mimi.

"Are you *sure*," Burta Rayborn would grill her client, when the two women got together for strategy sessions, "that you're not hiding anything? Some boyfriend? An affair?" Rayborn stared her down. "Come on, Mimi," she coaxed suspiciously, "tell me the truth. You have to have seen *some*body. You'd better tell me now, or they're going to crucify us with it in court." Mimi laughed hoarsely. "There's no one," she said, in her sandpaper voice. "Dick Minns is the only man I've ever been with in my whole life!"

Beneath the laughter was the cutting edge of self-derision. "I am so stupid," she would later say, "that there was never another man in my life. Never! I didn't even look at men! I didn't even know that you have to use your eyes to make men look at you."

During one of his long weekends at Lakeway with Barbra, Dick arranged for the two of them to have dinner with John Cosgrove, an old friend and business colleague, who lived with his wife and family at Lago Vista, an Austin resort not far from Dick's lakehouse. Dick asked Cosgrove if he would do him a favor. Cosgrove listened sympathetically. "Sure, Dick," he said genially. "What do you want me to do?" Dick's eyes burned brightly. "I want you to testify at my divorce trial," he said slowly, pausing between the words, "that you had an affair with Mimi." Cosgrove did his best to conceal his astonishment. Then he shook his head. "Sorry, Dick," he said. "I'd like to help you, but I can't do that." In the car, on the drive back to Houston, Barbra glanced over at Dick, deep in concentration. If only I could do something to help him, she thought to herself. This divorce is eating him alive.

This year on Valentine's Day, Dick marked the occasion by sending Mimi a Motion for Contempt. It was filled with the vilest of accusations, including his familiar cry that Mimi was destroying his relationship with Myles and poisoning the minds of the servants. But it also contained two new charges that were unusual even in the mudslinging annals of divorce law: Dick contended that Mimi was threatening to call a press conference "for the purpose of causing him such embarrassment and humiliation that he would never again be able to make a living in the state of Texas"; and of hiring a "professional 'hit man' " to kill or injure him, his attorneys, and Barbra if the case was not "satisfactorily settled" in thirty to sixty days. The previous month, it was stated in the motion, Dick had received six telephone death threats from Mimi, all in the middle of the night, and a "similar threat" was made to Harry Brochstein's wife on January 2 at three-thirty A.M.

The charges were somewhat mysterious. A number of years later, Dick's regular divorce attorney, Huey O'Toole, would claim to know nothing about any threats on Mimi's part to hire a hit man. Nor would Harry Brochstein. Barbra, who was with Dick almost twenty-four hours a day every day, could not recall Dick ever receiving a telephone threat in her presence. Mimi scoffed at the very idea.

Mimi would later swear in a legal document that Dick tried to strangle her five days after Joe Reynolds filed the motion for contempt. According to the papers Burta Rayborn prepared for Mimi, Dick "physically attacked" Mimi in the bedroom of their Memorial mansion because she refused to show the house to a prospective buyer.

"It all got *crazy* after a while," Dick's lawyer Huey O'Toole would later say. "I mean, there were accusations back and forth. Crazy! At some point, things got out of hand."

On April 6, 1979, the judge assigned to the divorce, a retired Dallas jurist named Claude Williams, signed an order stating that Mimi Minns would get the exclusive use of the house on Memorial Drive. Neither party was to harm the other, and a receiver would be appointed to control their liquid assets. Until the final settlement, Judge Williams ruled Dick would receive $1,750 a month for food, travel, and miscellaneous expenses.

Richard Minns was not a happy man.

Sometime that spring, Barbra dropped out of her classes at the University of Houston. Dick had been complaining for months about the time she spent studying or at school. Finally, with the divorce trial around the corner, she chose the path of least resistance: incompletes in all her classes. If Dick wanted her by his side during the divorce, she would be there.

Dick was thrilled. Now Barbra could not only help him disentangle himself from Mimi, she could work with him side-by-side on the Olympia Fitness & Racquetball Club. At first, Barbra approached the notion of running a health club with great trepidation. She wanted to be a doctor. But suddenly, to her surprise, she began to enjoy herself at Olympia. She immersed herself in medical books and studied the inner workings of other health facilities to design the perfect workout uniforms for Olympia employees. She busied herself with plans for a boutique in the club, to sell the clothes she was designing to members. She already had a name—Sports Connection—and she planned to run it herself.

In early April, Barbra was given the title "Miss Olympia," the symbol of the club. When Mimi found out, legal papers flew back and forth between Burta Rayborn and Huey O'Toole with a new set of pointed questions about the ownership of the Olympia. Dick denied them all. It was Bob Delmonteque's club, he repeated, in sworn answers to Mimi's interrogatories. It was Delmonteque's idea to name Barbra "Miss Olympia."

Privately, Barbra was receiving five thousand dollars a month as a "consultant" to the Olympia, which she deposited in her personal checking account. When the total reached twenty thousand dollars, she withdrew the money and gave it to Dick. Those were his instructions.

Sometime in the middle of March, Dick received a pair of letters from his sister Janice. Janice lived only twenty minutes away from his townhouse in Ethan's Glen, but the two of them had not seen or communicated with each other in almost two years. Until that spring, Barbra had only heard Dick mention his sister's name a few times in passing, to say that they had had their "ups and downs" over the years. She knew from general conversation that Janice was married to a lawyer who once performed some legal services for Dick. When Dick mentioned Janice had invited them to a party at her house the following Saturday night, Barbra was intrigued.

"What's she like?" she queried.

"Janice is crazy!" Dick responded. "She'll like me one day, and then the next day she'll decide she doesn't want to talk to me for a few years."

Barbra looked at him expectantly, waiting for some further elaboration, but there was none. "I told her you'd call her and get directions to her house," he said casually, changing the subject. "Here's the number."

This was just the opportunity Barbra had been waiting for. She'd never even met Richard's two daughters. At times she felt like an outsider in an important part of her lover's life. She wanted Dick to be close with his family, and she wanted his family to like her. Maybe Janice's invitation was her opening.

She picked up the phone and dialed Janice Weissman's number. She immediately liked what she heard. Dick's sister's voice was friendly and effervescent. When the two hung up ten minutes later, they were giggling like old friends.

Barbra continued to be impressed when she and Dick arrived at the Weissman house, an hour late, for the party.

Like Dick, Janice was diminutive, with delicate features she accented with heavy makeup. Her husband, Irv, with his sparse, fuzzy hair, resembled an overstuffed teddy bear. His gentle eyes would twinkle when he squinted out of his spectacles. Dick and Barbra were the talk of the party that night—Janice Weissman's flashy older brother and his beautiful blonde girlfriend.

As Dick and Barbra headed toward the door at the end of the evening, Irv Weissman stopped to shake Dick's hand. "I know you're in the middle of a divorce," Weissman said commiseratively. "If you ever need any help, just let me know."

Dick paused for a moment. "Well," he said to his brother-in-law. "You can do one thing for me."

"What's that?" Weissman queried.

Dick flashed a mischievous grin. "Kill my wife!"

Weissman laughed and went back in the house. *Same old Dick,* he thought to himself.

In the weeks that followed, Barbra did her best to include Janice and Irv Weissman in whatever socializing she and Dick squeezed in between Dick's twin obsessions: the divorce and Olympia. When he complained about the amount of time she was spending with his sister, she ignored him. Barbra liked Janice. She felt comfortable around her. For the first time since she moved to Houston, she felt she had a friend.

"I'm gonna marry Dick," Barbra chirped to Janice one day when the two women were off by themselves.

Janice's expression suddenly contorted. "Barbra," she said queerly, "if you know what's really good for you, you will not." Barbra looked at Dick's sister curiously. "Really," she repeated, her eyes growing exaggeratedly wide. "He's bad news. You're not gonna want him." Barbra laughed merrily. "Oh, I really want him!" she said giddily. "And I want you to be in my wedding!" Janice forced a smile. "OK," she said, taking Barbra's hand. "But do me a favor. Don't set the date anywhere near Irv's and *my* anniversary, OK?"

Barbra nodded, perplexed. Janice *was* an odd one. In the month or so she'd known her, Janice had been telling her all sorts of bizarre stories about Dick as a child. How mean he was. That he was a behavior problem. Violent. How their parents couldn't control him. The stories bordered on the ghoulish. When she was a year and a half and Dick was eight, Janice said, he put a penny in her mouth and tickled her so he could see what happened when she swallowed it. When it went down her stomach, their mother had to take her to the emergency room for X-rays. Another time,

Janice told Barbra, Dick set her on top of a chair next to an open window when she was just learning how to crawl. She fell out the window and Dick laughed. While she was still a toddler, Dick put her finger on a movie projector light because he wanted to find out what skin smelled like when it burned.

Barbra brushed the stories off. Janice *was* a bit flighty. Scattered. Perhaps, Barbra thought, Dick was right. Maybe she was a little crazy.

15

On May 2, 1979 Dick and Bob Delmonteque hosted a black-tie grand opening celebration to launch the beginning of Olympia. Half of Houston filed through the doors in their tuxedos and flashiest gowns to ogle the club Bob Delmonteque claimed, in his newspaper ads, to have spent three million dollars to create. The Olympia was immense, boasting an outdoor jogging track, Olympic-size indoor swimming pool, racquetball courts, a carpeted, mirrored gym for men and a corresponding "contouring salon" for women, Nautilus, Paramount, Universal, and Modern Dynamics exercise equipment, desert dry heat rooms, Swedish mineral rock saunas, eucalyptus inhalation rooms, hot hydrotherapy whirlpool baths, Finnish ice plunge "wake-up," and a billiard and table tennis room. The similarities between the Olympia and President's-First Lady were, Mimi Minns would say dryly, "uncanny."

At the center of all the activity was Dick Minns, bobbing in and out of the crowd, white teeth gleaming, hand pumping furiously, like a rich and doting father marrying off his only daughter. He had even made what was, for him, the ultimate concession: He was wearing a tuxedo. When Barbra saw him dressed for the gala, her heart skipped a beat, just as it had the first time she saw him in blue jeans. Never before had Dick looked so handsome. And he was all hers. She felt a rush of excitement.

As "Miss Olympia" and Dick's partner, Barbra was the official hostess at the grand opening. The Olympia was the first project she and Dick had worked on together. It was as much her dream as his. For weeks, she had been haunting

Houston's better boutiques in search of the perfect gown. She wanted him to be proud.

She finally selected a gown designed by Halston, in the style of a Greek toga, floor-length, of a shimmering gold lamé that draped her body, crosswise, emphasizing every curve. When Barbra tried it on, she felt like a goddess. Dick even failed to let out his usual grunt of displeasure when he counted out six hundred dollars in traveler's checks.

On June 2, shortly before Dick and Mimi's divorce trial, Barbra was subpoenaed to give a legal deposition by Burta Rayborn, Mimi's lawyer.

"Our stories," Barbra said later, "were rehearsed over and over and over and over again [by Dick] until they seemed like the truth."

In her deposition, Barbra testified under oath that she already knew Dick Minns was married when she moved to Houston in March of 1977. That he told her from the very beginning that he had an open marriage. That *Dick* found the townhouse at Ethan's Glen; that he owned it and everything it it. She would say later, "Dick said that it would stir up more emotions and worsen the situation for him if Mimi knew that everything in the townhouse was mine. He told me that after the divorce everything would be mine again." "Don't worry about a thing," Barbra said Dick reassured her. "I'll be sitting right next to you at the deposition. If I want you to answer no to a question, I'll step on your foot once under the table. If it's a yes, I'll step twice."

Barbra went along with Dick's requests. He needed her. Besides, she and Dick were in the middle of a war. Mimi was the enemy.

When Barbra's deposition was out of the way, she and Dick escaped to Cozumel for a few days. One evening as they lay in bed together in their hotel suite, Dick suddenly turned to Barbra and blurted, "I want us to get married. Right now."

A look of surprise came over Barbra's face. "We can't get married now," she said, slightly amused. "You're still married to Mimi. It wouldn't be legal."

"Yes, it would!" Dick said urgently. "It *would* be legal. Not only that, but I'd be committing bigamy. You wouldn't be breaking any laws, but I could be put in jail. I'm willing to put myself in that danger for you. That's how much I love you and want to be married to you."

Barbra eyed him with skepticism. "If you don't believe me, call Huey," Dick said emphatically. "I've already discussed this with him. Don't you trust me?"

Barbra looked at Dick's imploring eyes, not knowing whether she should laugh or be touched. This was truly ludicrous, she thought, even for Dick. Then her heart began to soften. There was something terribly flattering about someone wanting to marry you that badly. "All right," she said with a sigh, afraid she might offend Dick.

Dick jumped up excitedly. "OK!" he said. "First we have to write our vows." He got up from the bed and returned a few seconds later with a pen and paper. He immediately started writing. When he finished, he handed the paper to Barbra.

Years later, when she looked back on that night, Barbra would not even remember the vows Richard wrote. The only thing she could recall, she would say, was that they fought over the word *obey*. She couldn't remember who won.

With their vows in hand, Dick led Barbra out to the balcony. Dick recited the words he had written. When he whispered to Barbra what she was supposed to say, she began to giggle. "This is serious!" Dick said angrily, his eyes flashing. "This is more sacred than a regular ceremony. This is in the eyes of *God!*"

When the ceremony was over Dick kissed Barbra. "You are my wife," he said, "and you are to consider yourself my wife."

Barbra turned to the sea. Part of her was moved to tears. Another was flushed with embarrassment.

The month of July 1979 was a period of nonstop activity. On the morning of the fifth, Dick sat down for a deposition of his own, taken by Burta Rayborn. For weeks, Rayborn had been listening to Dick's witnesses testify about Mimi Minns's "rumored" affairs. She had little doubt who had put them up to it. Now, at last, she had just the person she wanted in the hot seat. She was ready and waiting for him.

Wieslaw Piotrowski: Barbara's father remembers a childhood in Poland of tailored suits, live-in servants, and early-morning horseback rides. Later, he would be tortured at Auschwitz.

(Courtesy of Wes Piotrowski)

Stella and Barbara Piotrowski: Barbara's mother was short, pretty, well-rounded, and spirited. Beneath her gaiety, however, lay a will of steel, for her life had not been an easy one.

(Courtesy of Wes Piotrowski)

Wes and Barbara Piotrowski: Barbara was Wes's girl. When she was still a tiny baby, he knew instinctively she was his intellectual soul mate.

(Courtesy of Wes Piotrowski)

Irena, Stella, and Barbara Piotrowski: Irena, her younger sister by two years, was the popular and, in Barbara's eyes, "normal" Piotrowski. Irena filled the house with friends; Barbara spent all her time alone, reading.

(Courtesy of Wes Piotrowski)

Barbara Piotrowski: When the teacher in her Catholic grammar school asked who wanted to be priests and who wanted to be nuns, Barbara raised her hand along with the boys to indicate that she wanted to become a priest. But what she really wanted was to become a saint.

(Courtesy of Wes Piotrowski)

Barbara Piotrowski: Her first day modeling: a stereotypical California beauty, all hair and legs, propped up on seventies platform heels. Behind her eyes is the barest hint of foreboding, as if she might be afraid of what lies on the other side of the door.

(Victor Martinez photo library)

Barbra Piotrowski as Miss Wahini Bikini, Thanksgiving, 1970. Voted by the press "Miss Million-Dollar Legs," she was the contestant with the best legs in the 1970 Santa Claus Lane Parade.

(Victor Martinez photo library)

Oliver De La Torre: After Barbra's kidnapping and rape, she and Oliver came together like two magnets. She referred to him affectionately as the "black sheep of his family." He liked to call himself colorful, a Gemini born in the year of the tiger.

(Courtesy of Wes Piotrowski)

Each year on Thanksgiving, Charlie Sea assembled a float of beauties to ride down Hollywood Boulevard in the Santa Claus Lane Parade. Barbra (*walking next to the float, on right*) could not believe her good fortune. A few hours later, she would be abducted and brutally raped.

(Victor Martinez photo library)

Janice and Richard Minns: Richard's sister, Janice, said their mother "acted as though she thought he was Jesus." He was, his wife, Mimi, would say, the "special one."

(Courtesy of Janice Weissman)

Janice Minns Weissman and Mimi Minns: A rare happy moment between Richard's sister and his wife. Janice would later claim her parents forced her to include Mimi in her wedding party.

(Courtesy of Janice Weissman)

Richard Minns: Richard prepared and sent press releases to the wire services about his birthday stunts, and wallpapered a room in his mansion with his publicity clippings, which he dubbed the "Ego Room."

(Victor Martinez photo library)

Richard Minns and Barbara Piotrowski: Shortly after they met on a ski lift in Snowmass, Colorado, Richard Minns bragged to Barbra Piotrowski that he could "make" people fall in love with him.

(Victor Martinez photo library)

Barbra Piotrowski: Dick literally advertised his affair. Within a month after Barbra moved to Houston, he had her modeling for print advertisements for President's-First Lady.
(Victor Martinez photo library)

Barbra Piotrowski Modeling Before She Met Dick, and After, in the Same Dress: Barbra willingly submitted herself to Dick's hands to be molded into his ideal of beauty, including dying her hair blonder and having breast implants.

(Victor Martinez photo library)

Dick and Barbra: Passersby would stop and stare when they saw them: two beautiful bronzed bodies melded together, blond hair shimmering. The golden couple.

(Victor Martinez photo library)

Barbra and Dick After Scuba Diving: Barbra was determined to be Dick's equal. When he dove fifty feet underwater in a cove in Antigua to spear a huge bass grouper, she went along without blinking an eye.

(Victor Martinez photo library)

Bob Delmonteque, Richard Minns, and Barbra Piotrowski: Dick was immediately fascinated with Delmonteque. Here was a Charles Atlas model come to life—a man who, like Dick, couldn't walk past a mirror without glancing at himself in it.

(Victor Martinez photo library)

Arnold Schwarzenegger, Carl Silvani, and Barbra Piotrowski: In the third or fourth month of her pregnancy, Barbra posed for a President's Club photo shoot with spokesperson Arnold Schwarzenegger. Never before had she felt more radiant, glowing, healthy.

(Victor Martinez photo library)

Richard Minns, Marvin Zindler, and Bob Delmonteque: If ever there was a bona fide Houston phenomenon, Channel 13's consumer reporter Marvin Zindler, Dick's good friend, was it. Later, he would use his influence to get Barbra arrested for theft.

(Victor Martinez photo library)

Barbra and Dick: Whenever they were apart for even a few hours, Barbra would bound up to Dick, jump up on his waist, and wrap herself around him in a leg scissor.

(Victor Martinez photo library)

Myles Minns, Marge Crumbaker (center) **and Friend Betty** (second from left), **Richard Minns, and Barbra Piotrowski at the Sahara Tahoe:** Richard devoted so much time and energy to self-promotion, he forged a friendship with Marge Crumbaker, the gossip columnist for the *Houston Post*, a big, earthy, dark haired, down-home gal from Dumas, Texas.

(Victor Martinez photo library)

Dick and Barbra: Dick's wardrobe was a technicolor collection of form-fitting polyester pants and studded jeans. His pants were so tight he refused to carry a wallet in his pocket because it would "spoil his physique." (Victor Martinez photo library)

Barbra and Dick at Las Brisas: As she gazed out at the cliffs of Acapulco Bay, Barbra closed her eyes and mouthed the words *Thank you.* It was almost surreal, she thought, like some impossible, perfect dream. (Victor Martinez photo library)

Barbra and Dick: In the daylight hours, when the top tropical sun beat down on the beaches, Barbra would lie on top of Dick for hours on a chaise by the sea, clad only in their bikinis.

(Victor Martinez photo library)

Dick and Barbra's Christmas Card: Taken by Bob Delmonteque in Acapulco. Barbra had always believed there was only one true love in a person's life. Dick was her true love. And she was his.

(Victor Martinez photo library)

Barbra Piotrowski: For weeks, Barbra haunted Houston's better boutiques in search of the perfect gown for the Olympia opening. She finally selected a Halston in a shimmering gold lamé that draped her body. When Barbra tried it on, she felt like a goddess. (Photograph by Jack Morgan, courtesy of Victor Martinez photo library)

Dick and Barbra: In years to come, when people spoke of Dick and Barbra's love for each other, they would use the word *illness*. Their desire went beyond mere physical attraction. It was an *obsession*. (Victor Martinez photo library)

Barbra Piotrowski and Her Mother, Stella: At Ethan's Glen. Readers of Marge Crumbaker's column would have been shocked to discover that the city's most famous "millionaire-adventurer" furnished his townhouse with furniture and accessories from Sears Roebuck and Pier 1 Imports.

(Courtesy of Wes Piotrowski)

Barbra Piotrowski, Dick Minns, Janice Minns Weissman, and Irv Weissman: One night in Jamaica, Dick and Barbra unexpectedly ran into Dick's sister and her husband at the hotel bar. When Dick began to flick matches around the table, Janice became hysterical. (Victor Martinez photo library)

Barbra and Dick at Las Brisas: This time Barbra couldn't ignore Dick's actions. After a long day of lovemaking in their cabaña, he attacked her, fracturing her nose and spraining her index finger. (Victor Martinez photo library)

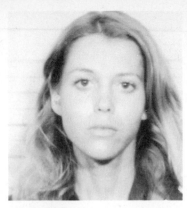

Barbra Piotrowski: At the Houston police station being booked for theft, set up by Richard. "He might as well have taken a knife and ripped my heart right open," she said later. (Courtesy of Ken Williamson, Houston Police Department)

The Device Found Under the Hood of Barbra Piotrowski's Car. Later, Adrian Franks would confess he planted a remote control "kill switch" so he could stop Barbra's Firebird and assassinate her. (Courtesy of Ken Williamson, Houston Police Department)

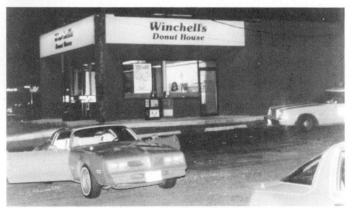

Barbra Piotrowski's Car: A few minutes after she was shot by Nathaniel Ivery. If the shooting at Winchell's had seemed routine to Houston homicide that night, by breakfast time it was beginning to dawn on them they were dealing with a hot case.

(Courtesy of Ken Williamson, Houston Police Department)

Nathaniel Ivery: Although she had never seen him before in her life, Barbra knew he had been sent to kill her and she knew who had sent him and why.
(Courtesy of Ken Williamson, Houston Police Department)

Robert Jess Anderson: Words flowed from Anderson like compliments from a gigolo. Yeah, the California trucker told police, Dudley Bell hired him to put the hit on Barbra Piotrowski. (Courtesy of Ken Williamson, Houston Police Department)

Patrick Steen: The driver of the white-over-red Cadillac was skittish with police. He spoke of being asked to "shoot a broad who was blackmailing a dude." (Courtesy of Ken Williamson, Houston Police Department)

Adrian Franks: Just shy of his twenty-first birthday, Adrian Franks woke up one morning and decided he needed to do something about his life. He was facing a prison sentence for credit-card abuse, and he had been hired once to assassinate Barbra Piotrowski for Dudley Bell. (Courtesy of Ken Williamson, Houston Police Department)

Dudley Bell: Everyone in town who mattered knew private investigator Dudley Bell. When trouble came knocking on their doors, Houston's rich and famous knocked on Dudley's.
(Courtesy of Ken Williamson, Houston Police Department)

Sergeant Ken Williamson, Dudley Bell, and Sergeant Dan McAnulty: It was somehow appropriate that the P.I. who made a living snapping surreptitious pictures of others *in flagrante delicto* should have his arrest captured by a police photographer.
(Courtesy of Ken Williamson, Houston Police Department)

Barbra Piotrowski with Her Attorney, Dick Deguerin: Her first public appearance since the shooting, at a hearing on her theft case. Symbolically, her presence was explosive. Her "million-dollar legs" dangled limply and her toes pointed inward. (Courtesy of the *Houston Chronicle*)

Dr. Jerrold Petrofsky, Stella Piotrowski, and Jennifer Smith (formerly Barbra Piotrowski): As cameras for *P.M. Magazine* and *People* recorded the event for history, Jennifer Smith walked 6.8 miles in the Honolulu Marathon on December 12, 1985, using Dr. Petrofsky's walking system...the goal Barbra set for herself from her hospital bed five years earlier. (Photograph by Nancy Scharff, courtesy of Victor Martinez photo library)

In 1984, Jennifer Smith (Barbra Piotrowski's new name) was selected to carry the torch in the Summer Olympics in Los Angeles in recognition for her accomplishments in wheelchair athletics. (Victor Martinez photo library)

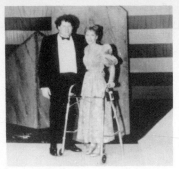

Dr. Jerrold Petrofsky and Janni Smith: In March 1990, Janni (formerly Jennifer) Smith, using another new name as a further security precaution, was named one of the Ten Outstanding Young Americans by the United States Jaycees in a nationally televised ceremony in Oklahoma City.
(Victor Martinez photo library)

Dr. Jerrold Petrofsky and Janni Smith Today: The little girl who dreamed she would grow up and marry a scientist and they would do research together is partners with Dr. Jerrold Petrofsky, conducting research to make walking and movement of paralyzed muscles a reality for others who are paralyzed. (Victor Martinez photo library)

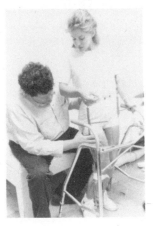

Janni Smith: Today, wearing her walking equipment. (Photograph by Dr. Jerrold Petrofsky, courtesy of Dr. Jerrold Petrofsky)

Dick Minns told Burta Rayborn, under penalty of perjury, that he thought divorce was "wrong," that he considered that he and Mimi had had an open marriage for the past eight years, and that he had "never denied or disguised" the fact that he was married from anyone—including Barbra Piotrowski—at any time. He also swore, under oath, that Mimi had "always" known that he "did his thing" with other women, and he could "line up witnesses a mile long."

Then Burta zeroed in on Mimi's alleged affairs. Was it true, she queried, that he had hired detectives to find out whether his wife had ever had an affair? Dick responded with an indignant *no*. "You're talking about my wife there. I would prefer to believe that she has never had anything to do with another person."

"Well, I can understand your preferring to want to believe that," Burta Rayborn said with icy sarcasm, "but I want to know everything I may hear from your lips about Mrs. Minns's misconduct during your marriage."

Dick acted offended. "But if you want to keep pushing . . ." he said with a shrug, offering up the names of four men, "Marty Cable, Bob Schwartz, Jimmie LaHaye, and John Cosgrove," the Austin friend Barbra watched him try to persuade to testify to an affair with Mimi. Cable, Schwartz, and LaHaye, he told Rayborn, he had "heard stuff about. John Cosgrove told me about John Cosgrove," Dick testified. "He told me that he had had sex on several occasions with Mimi."

Dick's other line of attack in his deposition centered on Mimi's involvement in the clubs. His wife, to hear him tell it, merely "counted the dollar-and-cents thing," and "couldn't run a health club if her life depended on it." To support this position, Dick had already filed in the divorce proceedings a letter he received from Bob Delmonteque (written, coincidentally, shortly after Mimi filed for divorce) in which Delmonteque lambasted Mimi as a businesswoman, saying she "never liked the health club business" and "probably thinks" health club people are "socially beneath her."

Before the court reporter turned off his machine, Dick got in one other dig. While he and Mimi were dating, he told Burta Rayborn with a flourish, Mimi "confessed" to him that she had been a "tramp" but she was "going to reform."

He had threatened Mimi that if she went through with the divorce, he was going to prove she was a whore. And Richard Minns never forgot a threat.

Two weeks later, Mimi had her turn.

Mimi's answers to Huey O'Toole in her deposition, also under oath, were the mirror opposite of Dick's. Mimi Minns denied that she and Dick had ever had an open marriage, other than the brief period before she filed for divorce. She also denied that she knew about any of Dick's affairs prior to Barbra Piotrowski—except for her suspicions about Gail Ledford, which she said Dick denied. When Huey O'Toole pointed out that Pat Hall testified in a deposition that she was one of Mimi's closest friends and that Mimi told her she'd known about Dick's affairs for "years," and that both Pat Hall and Madeleine Delmonteque testified that Mimi told both of them she and Dick had an open marriage, Mimi responded curtly that she "disagreed" with them.

Barbra was not present at Mimi's deposition, so she did not hear Mimi testify that she had been married to Dick for twenty-seven years and that "when you do anything he does not want you to do, you become Public Enemy Number One. He will go to any extreme to hurt anyone, including, but not limited to, in his words, his children." But Barbra had been around Dick long enough to know that when you sued him, you became more than an adversary, you were an *enemy*.

On the twenty-third of July, 1979, after fourteen months of slugging it out on paper, Dick and Mimi met in the courtroom to try their divorce case.

During the trial, Dick Minns was lucky if he averaged an hour of sleep a night. By day, he was a fidgety figure in the 245th Judicial Family District Court of Harris County, sitting at the counsel table between Huey O'Toole and Harry Brochstein. Every few minutes or so, he would pass a frantic note to Huey or Harry, to offer a piece of legal advice, or some off-color remark about a witness. Huey O'Toole just rolled his eyes. For more than a year, the divorce lawyer had been trying to rein Dick in. At times, the two lawyers felt like they were spending as much of their energy dissuading Dick as deflecting Burta. "He sort of enjoyed those kinds of things," recalled O'Toole. "Trying to incite Mimi, and turn her against her lawyers. And the long and short of it, to do all this, he's gonna end up spending more money on us and more money on them to run through the routines, and nothing's there. But that was that devilish streak in Dick."

Between witnesses, Dick drew cartoons of Mimi and Burta and Burta's junior colleague, Patricia Wicoff, depicting them as lesbians. When Huey O'Toole saw the caricatures he laughed and stuffed them in his pocket. Whenever Richard Minns wanted to attack someone, the lawyer had noticed, he would accuse the person of being homosexual. For months, he'd been after Huey to prove that his wife was having a lesbian affair with Burta Rayborn. "Course," O'Toole would later say wryly, "when you hear it from Dick, everybody's a butch dyke."

Throughout the five long weeks of the trial, Dick had Barbra working at Huey O'Toole's office downtown—categorizing checks, making spread sheets, formulating possible questions for potential witnesses, spot-checking depositions, photocopying, preparing inventories, gathering information. Working with Richard Minns, so the saying went, was not a one-person job. In addition to Huey O'Toole, Harry Brochstein, and Joe Reynolds, his three divorce lawyers, Dick, in O'Toole's words, "consumed" the staff of Boswell, O'Toole, Davis and Pickering. Many was the time Dick called Huey at four or five in the morning to ask him a routine legal question—forgetting, Barbra would say, that other people slept at night. O'Toole's secretary of ten years, a diligent, sensible woman, who liked to put in eight or nine hours and go home, nearly quit before the Minns divorce went to trial.

To assist Barbra at Huey's office, Dick recruited Pat Hall, his former general manager at President's-First Lady, whom he had brought back to help run the Olympia. Barbra had run into Hall several times while she was at the Olympia in the previous few months, but she had only a fleeting impression of her as a rather brusque, manly woman. One day when they were working together, Hall confided in Barbra that she was once in a mental institution and received multiple electric shock therapy.

As it dragged into its fifth week, the trial, O'Toole noticed, was taking a heavy toll on Dick. "I was picking this guy up in the mornings," the lawyer would later say, "staying with him day in, day out. This was a guy that was in control who all of a sudden was not in control of anything. He just had to sit there and everybody else told him what to do, how to spend money. . . ." On August 17, for the first time in fifteen years, Dick Minns did not perform a birthday feat. He spent his fiftieth birthday at a counsel table in the 245th Judicial Family District Court of Harris County, Texas. The year before, he had given a press conference to announce that he was going to celebrate his fiftieth birthday by skiing down Mount Fuji.

On September 27, after five weeks of testimony and a year and five months of litigation, Judge Claude Williams issued his final decree of divorce in the matter of the marriage of M. J. and R. L. Minns. Judge Williams awarded the divorce, along with a "disproportionate division" of the community estate, to Mimi Minns. Mimi Minns was also named the managing conservator of Myles Minns, for which she was to be paid five hundred dollars a month. Richard Minns was ordered to pay the costs of court. By the estimates of both sides, the split was roughly sixty to forty in favor of Mimi.

A number of years after the divorce, Huey O'Toole would say valiantly that he thought Dick "felt like he did real well" against Mimi. Harry Brochstein seconded that opinion. The sixty-to-forty cut, he would comment, was "agreeable" to Dick.

Anyone who knew Dick knew otherwise. To Mimi Minns, Judge Williams's final decree of divorce was a total victory. Years later, when she spoke of it, her voice still crackled with delight. "The problem with Huey's statement," she chuckled wickedly, "is that they *didn't* do real well, because I got more. I won the divorce! I got what the judge *thought* was more than half—what I asked for and exactly what I wanted. That makes them lose and me win."

"It was easy," Mimi claims. "It cost me some weight and some nerves, but it was easy. Their problem was that I could prove anything I said. No one else could prove *anything* they said." She leaned in a little closer, like a retired prize fighter analyzing the biggest match of his career. "You know when Dick learned the way I took my coffee? After the divorce! That's why I won. I knew Dick better than Dick. And he doesn't know me. That's true of a lot of men."

Exactly how much Mimi Minns received as a result of the divorce was a matter of speculation. Burta Rayborn's appraiser valued Mimi and Dick's community property at $10,020,740. Dick and Huey O'Toole's inventory came in at $7,046,554.78. With half the proceeds from the sale of the house on Memorial Drive, a number of bank accounts, insurance policies, and artworks, plus treasury bills and 281,037.5 shares of stock in President's-First Lady, Mimi likely walked away with between five and six million dollars.

It was more than the money that was eating at Richard Minns's soul. It was the fact that he *lost.* The divorce, Bob Delmonteque would speculate, was Dick's Waterloo.

16

Mimi, the person who professed to know Dick better than anybody in the world, sensed he was a changed man from the moment she filed her divorce papers. He was depressed, she would say later. Extremely upset. Old friends like Al Dugan and Bob Delmonteque noticed it also. They had never seen Dick so shaken.

A few months after the final decree of divorce, Dick wrote a thank-you letter to Barbra's younger brother, John, who had stayed at Ethan's Glen for a few months to help out during the Olympia grand opening. "Dear John," he wrote in the note. "This letter is long overdue and I apologize for not writing sooner. When you were in Houston and worked at the Olympia and helped Barbra and me at the townhouse, I was going through the most devastating ordeal I have ever encountered and I was probably at a record low, both emotionally, physically and financially. So you saw me at my very worst."

No one was more aware of the devastation of the divorce on Dick than Barbra. Before and during the trial, she would later say, he was "totally freaking out." For days afterward, she kept getting little notes from him thanking her for "sticking in there" with him, when everybody else let him down. Gradually, as September ended and October began, she noticed a slight lift in his spirits. One day, as she was getting dressed, she found a note from him in the bedroom. "GOOD MORNING!" it began cheerily. "I have not put a pencil to this to see how I came out, but at least I feel like 'Lincoln just freed the slaves,' so now I want the handcuffs taken off! CALL ME!"

Barbra put the note down and smiled. Dick was on his way back.

With the divorce proceedings out of the way, Barbra reenrolled at the University of Houston for the fall semester, with a full load of premed courses. Whenever she wasn't in class, she was at the Olympia, teaching her dance classes or helping Dick. By fall, she had her own office and Dick was talking about making her a vice-president.

Barbra was determined to work alongside Dick at the Olympia. Whenever she felt the urge to pull back or spend more time studying, she remembered Dick's comments about Mimi, and how she ended up on the sidelines while he was working and traveling. Besides, she found it rather exciting to be in on the ground floor of a chain of health clubs in the making. She had never felt any real attachment to President's-First Lady. That was Dick and Mimi's baby. She felt *connected* to the Olympia.

Early Autumn of 1979 was a happy time for Barbra Piotrowski. She and Richard, she observed, seemed to grow closer the more time they spent together. *Their* relationship showed the most strain when they were separated. Then jealousy would raise its ugly head, and they would question and accuse each other.

The only gray cloud on the horizon was Bob Delmonteque. Since she had started working longer hours at the Olympia, Barbra perceived, Bob had been acting resentful toward her. This came as a surprise to her. She had always gotten along extremely well with Bob; in fact, she prided herself on that fact.

Then one day she figured it out. Now that Mimi was out of the picture and she was getting more involved with the Olympia, her relationship with Bob had changed. Suddenly, she was a threat. The Olympia was Bob Delmonteque's dream come true. "It was so silly," Barbra said later, "because I was never after his position. A lot of the things that Bob did would have been a perfect role for me. He dealt with people on a more medical level, on the exercise physiology level, and those were the types of things that I guess he could assume somebody with a real medical background could easily step into. But I had no ambition to do that. I still wanted to be a doctor, and to help people who were sick. The only reason I was there was because I wanted to be a part of Dick's life."

The tension escalated until one day Bob Delmonteque confronted Barbra. "You shouldn't be here," he said hotly, no longer trying to conceal his irritation. Barbra immediately countered, "Yes, I should. I do work here and I do belong." When she repeated the conversation to Dick, later, he supported her. "That's right," he said staunchly. "You stand up to him. Because this is your place and I want you here."

Bob Delmonteque could not have been pleased about the turn of events. For years, he had engaged in a public battle with Mimi Minns over how to run the President's Club. Now that she was out of the way and he had a shot at the big time with the Olympia, in bounced Barbra Piotrowski. If she was just at the Olympia as an image, Delmonteque once said, that was fine. "But Barbra had an ego and that was my problem with Barbra. She wanted to do her little thing."

Dick ignored the tension and moved forward with his plans to expand the clubs. Now that his divorce was final, he could come out of the closet with the Olympia and make up for lost time. And wherever Richard Minns went, so went Barbra Piotrowski. By October, everyone at the Olympia was tittering about Dick and Barbra's wedding. Dick had it all planned. He and Barbra were going to be married on waterskis at Lake Tahoe on August 17, his fifty-first birthday.

Bob Delmonteque hovered in the background, frowning. "You two are too close as it is," he said somberly to Dick and Barbra. "You spend way too much time together. Working together is gonna make it even worse. This is going to end up blowing up like dynamite and the debris will be incredible."

Within a few months after the divorce, Dick plunged back into his activities. One morning, around the middle of November, he issued a proclamation to Barbra. Now that he was strong and healthy, he announced, he was going to "pay everyone back" who had taken advantage of him during his divorce and his illness. Barbra was stunned. Does that include me? she inquired. Dick's face was an impenetrable mask. Barbra ran out of the room. A few minutes later, Dick found her. "I'm sorry," he said gently, putting his arm around her. "You're the only one who stood by me. You'll never regret it. I'm going to make you happy."

Barbra didn't know how to respond. It confused her that Dick could turn on her so abruptly, with no provocation. His sudden mood swing reminded her of other changes she'd been noticing lately, changes she'd been trying to ignore or suppress. Since the Olympia's grand opening, the staff had been giving what seemed to her like an excessive number of parties. Barbra had never cared much for the parties at President's-First Lady, but they were so infrequent, and she had felt so insulated by Dick's presence, that they hardly made a ripple in her life. She liked to tell people that she and Dick were in a cocoon. "Even when we're around other people," she would say, "we sort of isolate ourselves, and somehow or other it ends up just the two of us in our own little world."

The Olympia parties were different. Barbra would later claim that there was a lot of talk of sex orgies, marijuana and cocaine, none of which she felt comfortable around. When she tried to pull Dick away, Bob Delmonteque and the rest of the staff started calling her "Little Miss Prim" and Dick "pussywhipped."

Dick Minns was in a quandary, trying to please Barbra, and, at the same time, trying to save face with his coworkers and employees. He could not bear to have his machismo questioned. Suddenly, Barbra's conservatism bound him like a too-tight suit. When the rest of the staff laughed at her for being a "stick-in-the-mud," he laughed with them.

Barbra fell into despair. She blamed Bob Delmonteque for the change. Bob didn't want her working at the Olympia, she felt. She was also convinced he was inciting the rest of the staff to taunt her and Dick. "I don't think these people who barely knew me would have just for no reason said, 'Wow, she's not a swinger. Let's get rid of her,' " she said later.

Bob Delmonteque certainly made no secret of his contempt for Barbra's prudishness. When he was with Dick, he joked that Barbra was "101 percent straightlaced" and a "professional student." In private, he mocked Dick's masculinity. "Dick was a pussy," he would say, years later.

"We'd wheel girls in and he'd watch. He wouldn't participate or perform. He needed a 'relationship.' " In Bob Delmonteque's view of the world, this made Richard Minns a "romanticist."

There were other signs of strain in the Dick and Barbra relationship that fall. Barbra was appalled at the idea of getting married on waterskis at Lake Tahoe and she voiced her complaints to Dick loudly and often. It was like a circus stunt, she sniped. A publicity gambit.

After weeks of listening to Barbra's nagging, Dick came up with the idea of having a traditional wedding in Houston, for Barbra, then flying to Tahoe to get married on skis. Barbra threw herself into planning the perfect private ceremony. The wedding would be performed in a garden outside Vargo's, a well-known Houston restaurant located on several acres of rolling hills in the Memorial area, complete with babbling brooks, quaint foot bridges, and pink swans wandering the property. She made arrangements to hold the ceremony in a gazebo there, a popular site for Houston weddings.

Yet, even with the Vargo's wedding set for August, Barbra was still upset about the ceremony on skis. This wasn't the same as lightening her hair or tightening her clothes. This was their *wedding*. It was sacred. Dick began to grumble to his friends about Barbra's nagging. She was beginning, he complained, to sound like Mimi.

That same month, November of 1979, Dick got a call from his son Mike, their first communication since his lawsuit two years earlier. It was also, Barbra would later say, the first time Mike had contacted his father in almost seven years. After a few minutes of intense conversation, Dick hung up the phone. "I have to go see Mike," he said tersely to Barbra as he headed for the door. "He's in the middle of a divorce and custody battle." Before he left, Barbra would say later, Dick also told her Mike had beaten his wife Lou Anne. "He needs my help," Dick called out the door.

Late that evening, Dick came home from Mike's apartment overflowing with conversation, especially praise for the woman Mike had hired as a nanny for his two children. Her name was Victoria Spillers, he said, and she

had answered an ad Mike placed in the newspaper for a
"mature governess." They had spent two hours talking in
the parking lot, he told Barbra. He was impressed. Barbra
smiled and nodded absently. She was just pleased that Dick
and Mike were speaking.

A few weeks later, when Barbra was home preparing
for a party for Dick's parents, the phone rang. It was
Dick, calling from the office. Victoria Spillers had just
telephoned him, he said to Barbra. She and Mike had a
big blowup. He wanted to hire her as a chauffeur and to
help Barbra with household tasks. Could she come over that
evening for Barbra to interview her?

Barbra was annoyed. She was giving a big anniversary
party for Dick's parents the following afternoon. The last
thing she needed was some ex-nanny of Mike's hanging
around the house, getting in the way. She told Dick no.
About an hour later, the doorbell rang. Victoria Spillers
was at the door. Dick sent her over, she said. He wanted
her 'to help around the house.

From the outset, Barbra would later say, there was something strange about Victoria Spillers. She seemed, in retro-
spect, to have materialized in her and Dick's lives as if by
magic. Barbra needed a new blouse for the party. Not to
worry, Victoria clucked. She would sew one for her. Did
she have any special dish she wanted prepared? Victoria
was a gourmet cook. She knew how to address anyone
from any walk of life with the studied gentility of a British
butler, and she could reach people by telephone anywhere
in the world at the snap of a finger. She was good with
children, and equally adept with old people. There was
nothing, Barbra marveled, Victoria couldn't do.

To look at her, Victoria Spillers had all the panache
of a bag lady. She ported around sixty pounds of excess
flesh and had the rumpled, unkempt look of someone who
had slept in her clothes the night before. Her hair was
a faded shade of blonde and hung in uncombed strands
nearly to her shoulders. She was thirty-one, five years older
than Barbra chronologically, light years more experienced.
Victoria cursed like a soldier (which she claimed to have
been), and administered medical aid with the competence
of a nurse, which she also claimed to be. When Barbra

mentioned some of the hospitals she had worked at in Los
Angeles, Victoria said she had worked as a nurse in those
places, too. As Barbra listened, mouth agape, Victoria volunteered the names of several of the more handsome doctors
on staff, with whom she boasted she had been romantically
involved. Barbra's ears perked up at the name of one, which
she recognized, because her sister Irena had once been
engaged to marry him. What a coincidence, she thought,
that Victoria would have worked for Irena's fiancé!

By the end of the evening, Barbra was impressed, in
spite of herself. When Victoria offered to pick up the cake
for Dick's parents' anniversary party the next day, she
jumped at it.

The following afternoon, Barbra arrived at George and
Ethel Minns's cozy house in West University bursting with
expectations for the fifty-second anniversary party she had
planned for them. This was her first performance as hostess
since the divorce and she wanted to prove herself worthy
of her new status in Dick's life in the eyes of his family
and friends. For days, when she wasn't on the phone with
caterers, she had been calling everyone she could think of
to invite to make the party a success.

The turnout was a testament to her dedication. The house
was overflowing with an odd mix of characters, from stoop-
backed elderly cronies of George and Ethel Minns from the
neighborhood to hard-bodied, muscle-bound staffers from
the Olympia. But the big coup of the evening was Mike
Minns. Dick's son had actually consented to show up at
her party! Barbra was thrilled. Mike was still acting strained
around her, but that would improve with time. Dick's parents loved her. She already felt like a member of the family.

But Irv Weissman, who was on the other side of the room
talking to Dick and Bob Delmonteque and a few of the other
Olympia employees, sensed trouble in paradise. The hot
gossip in the Olympia clique was Barbra, and the problems
Dick was having with her. Bob Delmonteque and the rest
of the Olympia gang were asking Dick when he was going
to get rid of her. His impression, Weissman would say later,
was that Dick was under a lot of pressure to dump Barbra.

By the middle of the party Barbra's good mood was
evaporating with the champagne bubbles. Dick had hardly

said a word to her since he arrived at his parents' house. He had spent the entire evening parading around the house with his arm around Mike, and for that she was happy; but he acted as if she weren't even there or as if he were ashamed of her. When the party began to wind down, she hunted down Janice Weissman. "I can't stay here anymore," she whispered agitatedly to Dick's sister. "If Dick asks you where I am, don't tell him I left." Janice Weissman frowned. "But I didn't even want to come in the first place," she whined. "I only came because you asked me."

Barbra quietly said her good-byes to Dick's parents and stopped in the kitchen to make arrangements for the help to clean up after the party. Then she walked to the front door with her purse in hand. She was certain Dick saw her leave, she would say later. And he didn't say a word.

Janice Weissman would later insist that Barbra was mistaken about that. Dick *didn't* see Barbra leave the party, she would recall. When he found out she was gone, Dick's sister maintained, Dick was furious with her for not telling him.

Dick Minns got a ride back to the Ethan's Glen townhouse from his son Mike and Mike's girlfriend. Late that night, when everyone else at George and Ethel Minns's anniversary party was long asleep, he filled the night air with apologies and words of love. Barbra hung on every syllable.

The morning after the party, Dick informed Barbra that he had officially hired Victoria Spillers. His hope, he would later say, was that Victoria would teach Barbra how to cook and clean, two areas, he would say with a wry grin, in which she was noticeably deficient. Barbra was still resistant. Couldn't Victoria help his parents? she asked Dick. They could really use her.

Victoria was undaunted. Between tasks for George and Ethel Minns, on her own time, Victoria squeezed in errands for Barbra, refusing afterward to accept money. When she addressed Barbra, it was always "M'lady." After a few weeks, Barbra relented and told Dick to hire Victoria full-time. She was, Barbra would say later, too good to be true.

Within a few weeks, Dick and Barbra were arguing about Victoria Spillers. Barbra was appalled at the low salary Dick was paying her. She couldn't decide which was more disturbing: that Dick would pay anyone so little, or that someone with Victoria's training and talents would accept what she considered an unconscionable salary. It didn't make sense. Perhaps, Barbra thought, Victoria wanted the job so she could meet interesting people. But the more time she spent around her, the less star-struck Victoria appeared to be. There had to be some reason, Barbra decided, that Victoria was so determined to work for her and Dick. She just couldn't figure out what it could be.

Then again, Barbra had always found Dick's choice of employees to be peculiar. Pat Hall, for instance. Barbra wasn't the only person who had noticed this pattern. Although they had never discussed it with Barbra, Dick's sister and brother-in-law had long observed the same thing. "Dick had misfits," Janice Weissman would later say bluntly.

Barbra put Victoria Spillers in that category. And the stories she told! Barbra happened to be on the phone one day with one of the doctors from Brotman Memorial Hospital with whom Victoria claimed to have had sex in the stairwell. When she asked him if he remembered a nurse who worked for him by the name of Victoria Spillers, the doctor answered without hesitation. "Never heard of her," he said blankly. "Never heard the name before in my life." Even more curious was the fact that Irena Piotrowski's former boyfriend claimed not to know her, either. How would Victoria Spillers have just plucked the name of Irena's fiancé out of the air if she hadn't worked for him? Barbra mused. And why?

In the coming years, she would ask herself that question a thousand times.

On December 19, Marge Crumbaker opened one of her last columns for the year 1979 with a juicy lead on her great and good friend Richard Minns, under the banner SUPER PEOPLE:

> Millionaire sportsman **Dick Minns** has a busy 1980 planned. . . .
> In March he'll be in Athens with our resident guru oilman **Al Dugan**, and they'll run the 26-mile marathon where the running bit started. From there, they'll wing to Africa and climb Mount Kilimanjaro.

Then, on Dick's Aug. 17 birthday, he'll be in Tahoe (here we go again) to ski the lake. But this time it'll be a lot different. Dick and his sweetheart **Barbra Piotrowski** will be married as they ski. Would I kid you? Certainly not! I'll be the maid of honor, following along in a speedboat.

Little did Crumbaker realize, when she wrote her column that December, how busy a 1980 Richard Minns would have.

When Marge Crumbaker's gossip column came out, Dick and Barbra were miles away at Las Brisas in Acapulco.

While they were there—Barbra would later fix the date at December 12—the two had a minor argument in their private cabaña after a long day of lovemaking. As Barbra would later tell the story, she and Dick had dressed for dinner when Dick suddenly grabbed her and tried to toss her into their private pool. Barbra pretended to be angry to tease Dick. She had just dried her hair and didn't want to do it again. She decided to teach Dick a lesson. "If you dunk me," she said, picking up the phone and taunting him with it, "I won't go to dinner with you." She started to dial room service with her right hand, with her left she was pushing down the receiver.

What happened next would later be recounted in several different versions. Dick either didn't notice that Barbra was just pretending, or was too enraged to care. He started toward Barbra and, Victoria Spillers would later claim, threw her up against the wall. Barbra has mentally blacked out most of the details. She would later remember only that Dick attacked her, that it was sudden, it was brutal, and it was quick. Hotel records would show that the Las Brisas house physician, Dr. Luis Alfredo Navarro, made two visits to the Minns cabaña in December to examine Barbra Piotrowski and take X-rays. His diagnosis was a fractured nose and a sprained index finger on the right hand. His written report noted that Miss Piotrowski "suffered an accident and fell down."

This time Barbra couldn't ignore Dick's actions, or pretend it hadn't happened, as he did. She would vaguely remember taking a taxi to the airport and calling her father. Wes Piotrowski was wary of getting in the middle of a lovers' quarrel. When his daughter told him she and Dick had a fight, he refused to intervene. Had Barbra mentioned that she had a broken nose and sprained finger, Wes would have been on the next plane to Acapulco, but she chose to keep that information to herself.

While she was on the phone with her father, Dick rushed to the airport, begging forgiveness. With Wes Piotrowski urging her in one ear not to do anything in haste she might regret, and Dick proclaiming his love for her in the other ear, Barbra hung up the telephone and returned to the cabaña with Richard.

She preferred to disbelieve what had happened. It was too horrible, too disruptive to her life. She loved Richard. Barbra started rationalizing. It was just an isolated incident, she told herself. It wasn't that Dick was a wife-beater. In the almost three years they were together, he had only been violent toward her twice—if she didn't include the time during the divorce when he suddenly grabbed her by the blouse as if he were going to break her neck, then, just as instantly, let her go. "Oh, my God, Barbra," he had said then, pulling away and shaking himself. "What am I doing? I thought you were Mimi." Although he hadn't actually hit her, Barbra couldn't get the incident out of her mind. It was too frightening, too bizarre.

Barbra knew she had to do something to insure that this would never happen again. But what? Somehow— she would not remember why or how—she came up with the idea of a marriage contract between her and Dick. She would make him promise never to strike her again. At least that way, she told herself, she would have it in *writing*. Dick couldn't deny it ever happened, or say it wasn't him. It was a crazy, desperate plan, Barbra would later concede. But it was the only one she had.

Dick leaped at the idea, eager for any device that would keep Barbra in Acapulco. For several hours, the two thrashed out the terms of an agreement. When they had it on paper, Richard signed the document and Barbra stuffed it into her purse to take back to Houston. Only days later, when she chanced to look for it again, would she notice that it was missing.

When Barbra returned to Houston from Las Brisas with

Dick in January 1980, it was with a heavy heart. Not only did she have grave concerns about his violent behavior, she was beginning to feel serious doubts and insecurities about the relationship. The days Barbra was in class or running errands, Victoria Spillers filled her ears with firsthand reports of what was happening at the Olympia while she was gone: Dick was goaded into flirting with one of the decorators; the staff was calling him pussywhipped again; some gorgeous new girl started working at the club and was coming on to Dick. Each report from Victoria was like a knife in Barbra's heart. When Dick got home from the club, she would be waiting for him, full of questions and suspicions.

They would spend the evenings they used to spend making love arguing back and forth. Dick's fantasy relationship was starting to play like a domestic drama.

On February 14, Barbra received a box of flowers from Dick for Valentine's Day. When she looked at the card, she winced. She could tell that somebody from the Olympia sent them, not Dick. She opened the box with a queasy feeling. Inside were a dozen long-stemmed red roses. A knot formed in Barbra's stomach. Dick knew she liked exotic, unusual flowers—tulips, daffodils, African daisies; anything but a cliché bouquet of roses. He also knew she hated to get flowers as a symbol of love because live flowers die. They had talked about it hundreds of times. In the three years they were together, this was the first time Dick had sent her flowers on Valentine's Day.

Barbra took it, she would later say, as an omen.

A curious thing happened later that month. During a trip to Jamaica, Dick and Barbra wandered down to the hotel bar around ten-thirty for a late dinner. By coincidence, Dick's sister, Janice, and her husband, Irv, were in Jamaica, having drinks at the same bar, listening to the band. Later in the trip, the two couples met for dinner. As they were talking over candlelight, Dick began tearing matches absently out of a matchbook, lighting them off the candle and flicking them around the table. When he flicked one at Janice, she screamed hysterically and burst into tears. There was an awkward silence. The next time Janice Weissman and Barbra were alone, Janice told Barbra that when she was six years old, Dick threw her on a butane gas stove so he could "see how skin would sizzle." She was rushed to the hospital for third-degree burns on her legs. Before Dick flicked the match at her during dinner, he had taunted, "How would you like to see how it burns again?" "He's sadistic," Janice hissed in her fluttery way. "You don't want to have anything to do with him."

Barbra fell silent. Before, when Janice had mentioned Dick's cruel behavior as a child, she had dismissed it. But lately, several other people had been telling her the same thing. Myles, she would say later, confided in her that Dick beat everyone in the family and once broke Mimi's nose and hip and his younger daughter's nose. Barbra would also claim later that Madeleine Delmonteque told her the same thing: that Dick broke Mimi's nose and hip. Barbra had brushed off Myles's comments as a typical father-son conflict.

Dick's words *trust me* were starting to sound hollow. All of Barbra's rational thoughts were telling her that Dick could be dangerous, that he was violent, and she was never going to have the kind of life with him she wanted. But the heart doesn't answer to the brain. Who else, she asked herself, could possibly be that exciting? Barbra was more than in love with Dick. She was, she would say later, *addicted*.

17

The events of March 1980 would be reconstructed so many times, in so many ways over the coming years that exactly what happened might never be known.

Sometime early in the month, Barbra would say later, she suspected she might be pregnant. She later confessed she might have tried to get pregnant to tighten her bond with Dick. The first days of the month, she kept waiting for the perfect, romantic setting to present the news to Dick.

By the middle of March, she was getting edgy. When Dick planned a weekend for the two of them at Lakeway, she circled the date on her calendar. Just before the weekend, Irv Weissman got a cryptic call from Barbra. If I'm pregnant, she asked the bespectacled lawyer, what are my rights and what are Richard's? Weissman retrieved what little he could recall of family law to pass on to Barbra, and told her he'd mail her a copy of the Texas family code in an unmarked envelope. Barbra thanked him, and Weissman hung up. As familiar as he was with Dick and Barbra's ups and downs, the call didn't faze him.

Barbra would remember the weekend at Lakeway as a fiasco. Dick brought guests along, so she had no time alone with him on Saturday. Saturday night, she would recall, Dick and their guests lingered over dinner and smoked marijuana. When Dick finally went to bed, he took a couple of sleeping pills. Barbra decided she couldn't wait any longer to tell him she was pregnant. "That's wonderful," Dick said woozily and dozed off. Sunday afternoon, Dick and Barbra returned to Houston early so Dick could prepare for a Monday morning phone conversation with a New York investment banker. President Carter's reforms in the health club industry had effectively precluded Dick's practice of selling health club memberships to banks and finance companies. The changes, Dick complained, were costing him a hundred thousand dollars a month at the Olympia. He wanted the New York reaction to Carter's policies.

Monday, March 17, 1980, began like any other morning for Dick Minns and Barbra Piotrowski. Dick had the newspaper spread in front of him so he could keep up with current events. On the front page was an article about President Carter's proposed new club regulations. When Dick saw it, he exploded. "Barbra, look at this!" he screamed, holding up the headline. "That idiot's putting me out of business!"

Barbra glanced at the article nonchalantly and made a comparison between Carter's actions and the response of an earlier president in a similar situation. Dick's eyes narrowed to slits. "Goddamn it!" he said, flinging the newspaper across the room. "You have no idea what goes on in the real world. I retired a champion in my business and now I've got to reconstruct what I neglected for two years during the divorce. You think that all this intellectual garbage that you learn in school has something to do with the real world. The reality of the situation is you don't know anything about economics, you don't know anything about running a business. This is going to destroy me, and you're just sitting there quoting history out of a schoolbook like some damn schoolchild!"

In her official account of what occurred that morning, Barbra would state that Richard suddenly came at her, throwing things. When he raised his hand and started to shake her, she screamed, "Please Dick! Let's talk about this. Don't get angry now—not when I'm having a baby!"

"That's right," he said queerly, twisting his face into a demonic expression. "I *thought* you told me you were pregnant!"

Barbra herself offered slightly different accounts of what happened next. In every version, she remembered that Dick became angry and threatening. "If I want to," she recalled him taunting her, "I can replace you just like that!" Her official police statement was that Dick told her he wanted her out of the townhouse. At other times, she said he demanded that she get an abortion. Then he left for the Olympia.

Barbra would tell this story a number of times over the years, occasionally under oath. Her account of her reaction was always the same. For the first time in her life, she would say, she was physically afraid of Richard, for reasons she didn't fully understand herself. There was something different about him that morning, she would try to explain. It wasn't like the two times he beat her, when he was out of control. This time he was eerily calm. She also felt a sick feeling in the pit of her stomach that Dick already had someone else to replace her. She got the sudden, nauseating sensation that it was all over. She didn't know what to do, where to go, who to talk to. In the blink of an eye, she was living a nightmare.

Her thoughts were interrupted by the shrill ring of the telephone. Richard was on the other end of the line, calling from the office. His voice was soothing, exaggeratedly cheerful. "Hey, baby," he cooed into the phone, as if nothing had happened. "Everything is going to be all right," he purred. Whatever it was, they would work it out. Barbra played along with Dick, pretending things were OK. But how could they be? How could such serious problems disappear so quickly? Before he said good-bye, Dick made a suggestion: "Meet me at the club tonight after it closes," he whispered. "We'll talk." Barbra forced herself to agree, to sound lighthearted.

When she hung up, a cold shiver ran down her spine. If she met Dick at the health club that night, she had a chilling feeling something terrible was going to happen to her.

Irv Weissman would remember getting a panicky call from Barbra sometime that morning. She mumbled something about moving out of the townhouse and said she was having a hard time finding a mover. Did Irv know anyone who could do the job for her quickly? Weissman was a bit disgruntled by the interruption. "Hell, Barbra," he said grouchily, "if I need a mover I'd have to look in the yellow pages and find one. Maybe if you offer 'em some extra money they'd get you out quicker." The lawyer hung up the phone and went back to his work. He didn't take the call seriously. He was under the impression Dick and Barbra had had other problems in the past. As a lawyer, he had witnessed couples separate hundreds of times. It was nothing catastrophic.

Within minutes, Janice Weissman's phone was jingling. Barbra was calling, confused and upset. She and Dick were having problems. She was moving out. "Do you think," she said timidly, "you could get your son Jeff to help me move?" Janice Weissman was full of advice. "I'll see what I can do," she clucked, "and call you back." As Dick's sister related Barbra's request to her son, she suddenly thought better of it. "No," she said to Jeff, in mid-message, "I don't think I want you to do that. As much as you and I like Barbra, I don't want you to get involved."

Barbra was a jangle of nerves. She had to, she decided, get out of the townhouse immediately. There was, she would say later, no basis for that fear, no evidence, no foundation. It was pure intuition.

Later, even as short a time as a few days later, Barbra would claim to remember next to nothing about what she did or thought that morning. She had a vague recollection of Irv Weissman suggesting that she stay at the townhouse and change the locks so Dick couldn't get in. Barbra dismissed that idea immediately. If she changed the locks, she thought to herself, that would be the end of the relationship. She didn't want to end it. She still loved Dick; she was just afraid to be near him. She played with the notion of flying back to Los Angeles, or staying with a friend. She decided against it. She had already left Dick twice. What good would leaving him a third time do? She wanted, she would say later, to make an impact.

Somewhere in her kaleidoscope of thoughts, she came up with the idea of moving out and taking the furniture with her. If Dick came home and everything was gone, she reasoned, it would have to get his attention. Melvin Taylor, the supervisor of Apartment Moving & Storage Company of Houston, would remember getting a phone call sometime that morning from a distraught woman requesting a truck at 312 Litchfield Lane for a small load of things. In later years, Barbra would not even recall making the phone call. When Taylor asked the woman her name, Barbra made one up. "I really didn't know what I was doing, or what to do," she said later. "I was a basket case."

The next thing Barbra Piotrowski would remember of that day, when she reconstructed it in later years, was the arrival of Victoria Spillers at the townhouse. She had no recollection of calling Spillers, although Spillers would later say that Barbra telephoned her that morning and asked for her help. Barbra's recollection was that Victoria simply appeared at her door, just as she had when she met her, as if on cue, ready, willing, and eager to take over.

Around three o'clock in the afternoon, Clifton Caldwell and Woody Conway, two young movers from Apartment Moving & Storage, pulled into the driveway of the Ethan's Glen townhomes. When they got out of their truck, they noticed Barbra Piotrowski standing in the carport making frantic arrangements with a twelve- or thirteen-year-old neighbor boy to find her some boxes. She was crying, they observed, and appeared to be extremely nervous.

The remainder of the afternoon, Victoria Spillers alternated between calming Barbra down and issuing orders to her and the movers with the military authority of the WAC she said she once was. Barbra Piotrowski—Caldwell and Conway remarked to each other—barely said a word. "She's running away from her boyfriend," Victoria whispered to Clifton Caldwell, when she had a few minutes alone with the mover. "She's scared of him."

When Melvin Taylor, Caldwell and Conway's supervisor, showed up at Ethan's Glen around six P.M. and saw the hefty housekeeper taking charge, he immediately sized up the situation as trouble. Who's the boss? was the first question out of his mouth. Victoria Spillers answered instantly and emphatically, "I am." Taylor eyed her warily. Then why did the skinny girl call him? he wondered. It was her townhouse and her stuff. Spillers brushed aside Melvin Taylor's doubts as if they were a couple of troublesome mosquitoes. "I'm the boss," she repeated. "I'm paying for it." Taylor turned his eyes to Barbra Piotrowski, carrying a box out to the truck. She seemed to be in a daze. "I want you to take everything," Spillers directed, interrupting Taylor's train of thought with a broad motion of her hand. "I don't care how much it costs." Taylor's eye swept across the townhouse. There was no way, he figured, that the small truck he sent over was going to hold everything in that apartment. He needed a larger van than what he planned from Piotrowski's phone call that morning. "Whatever it takes," Spillers said coolly. "Don't leave a thing."

Taylor placed the call for a bigger truck and hung up the phone with a mover's instinct of foreboding. There was something about the deal, he thought to himself, that didn't smell right. "See if you can hurry it up," Victoria Spillers urged, a little later in the evening. "If her boyfriend catches us here he'll probably kill Barbra. She's leaving him." Taylor's eyebrow raised. After twenty years in the moving business, the word *separation* was a red flag to him. All he needed was to get his company in the middle of some legal dispute over property. Whose furniture is this? he demanded. Barbra Piotrowski looked up from the box she was packing. "It's mine," she said casually. Taylor scratched his head. If the furniture was Piotrowski's, why was the big blonde paying for the move and acting like the boss? Spillers caught Taylor's apprehensions. "Don't worry," she said confidently. "If anything happens to her, everything belongs to me. The papers are already drawn up. Our lawyer's taken care of everything." The supervisor pulled his two movers aside. "Listen," he said confidentially, "try to notice everything you put on the truck, just in case we have to remember later." Taylor hated separations. Nothing but trouble.

Sometime during the move, Clifton Caldwell positioned a dresser from the bedroom onto a dolly. Before he could take it to the truck, Barbra noticed what he was doing and directed him to dump the clothes out on the floor. They're Richard's, she explained. As Caldwell turned over the dresser, he noticed a belt buckle fall to the floor. It caught his eye, he would say later, because it still had the price tag on it. Being the nosy sort, Caldwell snuck a peek at the price and let out a low whistle. Rich folks, he thought to himself. That belt buckle cost more than he made in a month! And that skinny chick didn't even pick it up off the floor.

As the last of the boxes were being loaded onto the truck, Victoria Spillers came down the stairs with a shotgun.

"We'd better take this with us," she announced to Barbra. Barbra nodded. She would later remember thinking that if she left the shotgun for Dick, he might use it.

When the two trucks were finally loaded around nine-thirty, Melvin Taylor got his second shock of the day. Barbra Piotrowski had no place to store the furniture. This, too, would prove significant before another week passed. The supervisor looked over at Barbra. She must weigh all of ninety-four pounds. He'd been watching her tote heavy boxes to the truck all day. Taylor's heart softened. She seemed like a nice kid. Troubled, but nice. "Well," the mover said genially, "I guess you can keep your things on the trucks overnight. Just be sure you come pick 'em up first thing in the morning." Barbra Piotrowski might be pretty, Taylor thought to himself, but he still didn't want any trouble.

Barbra Piotrowski spent the night at Victoria Spillers's cramped, dingy apartment in Bellaire. Before she went to sleep, she placed a call to her father in Los Angeles. She told him she'd moved out of the townhouse and that she was afraid of Dick. Wes Piotrowski could make no sense of the call. Barbra was crazy, irrational, incoherent. She wouldn't even tell him the phone number where she was staying—because, she said, she was afraid he would tell Dick. Wes Piotrowski hung up, confused and concerned. Half a continent away, Barbra Piotrowski closed her eyes and drifted into a restless half-sleep, comforted solely by the belief that she had done the right thing by moving out of Ethan's Glen and taking the furniture.

Time would prove it to be the worst decision of her life.

Part Three

18

Richard Minns was utterly bewildered. Barbra never showed up at the Olympia to meet him after the club closed and he couldn't find her anywhere. The phone at the townhouse rang endlessly with no answer. His parents didn't know where she was. She missed an appointment with Madeleine Delmonteque. Around eleven P.M., he tired of waiting and headed for home.

When Dick Minns unlocked the door of the Ethan's Glen townhouse and saw it stripped to the carpet, he reacted characteristically: He reached for the telephone. One of the first numbers he dialed was Wes Piotrowski's.

The Piotrowski line was busy. After two or three attempts, Dick called the operator to interrupt with an emergency. Wes Piotrowski took the call. He was just on the line with Barbra, the engineer said in a troubled voice. She wouldn't tell him where she was, just that she had moved out. Dick hung up in frustration.

One of his other calls that evening was to his daughter Cathy, who lived in an apartment complex nearby. When Mimi filed for divorce, Cathy Minns hated her father and blamed him for the breakup. After two years, the anger had dissolved. Come stay with me, Cathy Minns said to her father when she got the call.

Before he left the townhouse, Dick Minns paced every square inch making a mental inventory of what was missing. The rest of his actions that night are shrouded in mystery. When he arrived at Cathy Minns's apartment sometime later, he seemed, his daughter noticed, to be in shock. Upset. Surprised. Sad. Cathy Minns comforted her father the best she could and put him to bed on her couch.

Richard Minns didn't sleep for a second. His night was a blizzard of phone calls. The man who prided himself on power, on control, was—suddenly—helpless. Before the sun rose, he had called two Houston private detectives. The first, Bobby Newman, got a message from his service around one in the morning to call Richard Minns. It was urgent. Newman was peeved at having his sleep interrupted. Whatever it was he wasn't going to call Dick Minns back at one A.M. "Tell him I'll call him in the morning," the private investigator groused into the phone, and fell back asleep.

Another of Dick's calls was to the Stanley Smith Detective Agency, a firm that specialized in home security. One can only assume he called a guard company because he couldn't get through to a private investigator in the middle of the night. His directive to the Stanley Smith Agency was simple and concise: locate Barbra Piotrowski. *Now.*

Sometime during that long night, Dick telephoned Pat Hall. When he explained what happened, Hall leaped at the chance to assist him. Immediately, Hall had the auto-theft division of the Houston Police Department on the line to report Dick's station wagon as stolen. Ever since Dick had refused to bail Barbra's VW camper out of a repair shop because he considered the bill too exorbitant, Barbra had been using the station wagon to get around town.

By the time Bobby Newman returned Richard Minns's phone call around nine in the morning, Dick told him he had already hired another detective. Within a few hours, Dick contacted his insurance company to report the furniture in the townhouse as stolen. Meanwhile, Pat Hall was at Ethan's Glen taking pictures of the interior to send to the insurance company. Later in the day, she checked in with Dick. Hall could hardly wait to tell him she'd spotted his station wagon "abandoned" in a parking lot near the townhouse. When she hung up, Hall logged the information in a notebook.

Dick ended the morning with a call to Wes Piotrowski at Piotrowski's office at TRW Defense and Space Systems Group in Redondo Beach. He wanted the engineer to pres-

and was something of a surrogate father to Mike.

Why, exactly, Richard Minns called Mickey Brown is something of a mystery. Brown himself would later claim not to remember, or to know. As a result of the call, Brown paid a visit to the Ethan's Glen townhouse. While he was there, he claimed to have found some loose electrical wires where something—probably a chandelier, he thought (although the townhouse had no chandeliers)—had been removed, with the wires pressed together to create an "electrical sparking." He also made a report of an upstairs toilet that had been drained. The combination of the two, he told Richard Minns, were proof positive that Barbra Piotrowski set up the townhouse to kill somebody. Mickey Brown's theory was that Barbra and/or Victoria Spillers drained the upstairs commode so that sewer gas would get inside the townhouse. After forty-eight hours, the sewer gas would reach the explosive point. Then, when somebody walked into the townhouse and turned on the light, the "whole top" of the condo would blow sky-high, and it would look like an accident.

After he conducted his investigation, Brown took pictures. Then he called the Houston Police Department. By the close of the day, a pair of uniformed officers arrived at Litchfield Lane to file an investigative report. Richard Minns, Mickey Brown would later say, seemed shocked at the allegations.

Late that Wednesday night, around eleven P.M., Dick called the Piotrowskis again. He wanted, he said, to "touch base" before he left the office. Wes Piotrowski was still dazed. He didn't dare call Barbra at Victoria Spillers's apartment, he told Dick. Then she'd know he got the number from Dick. He didn't want Barbra to think they were in conspiracy.

"I haven't been back to the house at all," Dick stammered to Wes. "It just depressed me. But I have sent Pat Hall there to take the inventory for the insurance company on the property there that has been on record that was awarded me by the court in my divorce."

Wes Piotrowski fumbled for words. His concern was for his daughter and his daughter was filled with fear. And he didn't even know where Barbra was or what really happened. "Something is wrong," the Pole said, in a sad, tired voice. "I don't know what she wants to do with those things she took, and obviously I cannot control what she does now. Now obviously I will listen to what she says and I will try to put some sense into her head, but I will try to protect her from exposing herself to more danger. In the first place, I want to make sure that she would be removed from any kind of prosecution."

"Wes," Dick said casually, "just between us, and we are friends—as far as Barbra is concerned, anything that she brought with her when she came here from Los Angeles is hers. Anything that is her personal effects that I have given her—and I have given her plenty of things, including clothes and other things and jewelry—that's hers. Now, unless she has expressly purchased with her money, not with money I have given her, which is my money, a specific item, then that's a . . . it's not a subject of conversation. I am not as material as letting a material thing really stand in the way of harming someone or creating something like that, but when someone strips me of every single thing I had and doesn't even leave vitamins—you know how dependent I am on my vitamins, and I import them and everything. All those were taken!"

Dick's plan was simple. Of all the people in the world, he flattered Wes, Wes was the one who could talk some sense into Barbra.

Dick asked to speak to Stella Piotrowski next. He couldn't understand it, he told Barbra's mother. When he said good-bye to Barbra on Monday morning, she walked him to the car and kissed him good-bye. "We got along perfect," he said. "She told me it was a wonderful weekend. We didn't quarrel, we didn't discuss money. No problems." It was Victoria Spillers, Dick said. She was stirring up trouble. She was a dangerous influence.

Stella Piotrowski was confused. Perhaps, she suggested, Barbra was upset because they weren't married yet.

Dick Minns paused. The day before, when he was on the phone with Wes Piotrowski, he told Barbra's father he was worried that Barbra didn't want to marry *him*. "I told her I wanted to spend the rest of my life with her," he answered carefully, "and if we could come up with a satisfactory prenuptial agreement that would spell out how our lives would be, then, even though I had been through a divorce, I was not against marrying her. But I wanted everything to be spelled out, because I never again want to get involved with attorneys or courtrooms or anything like that!"

Two hours later, Dick hung up. What he did not tell Wes and Stella Piotrowski was that Mickey Brown of the Houston Arson Division was at that very moment running a background scan on their daughter through the National Criminal Information Center.

While Dick and her parents were burning up the phone lines wondering about her, Barbra Piotrowski was operating in a fog. The morning after the move, she showed up at Apartment Moving & Storage without a clue as to where she wanted them to transport the furniture on their two trucks. All Barbra knew was that she wanted to stay in Houston. Dick was in Houston. Even though she was afraid to see him, she was still in love with him. The paradox was bewildering even to her.

Lowell Douglas, the owner of the moving company, took pity on Barbra. Since she didn't have a car, he drove her around the city several days in a row so she could look at apartments. The idea of returning the furnishings to Dick never occurred to Barbra. That furniture was *hers*. Dick promised her that the townhouse and everything in it belonged to her, that she could have it if they ever separated. Her only concern was where to keep it until the day when, hopefully, she would move back in with Dick.

Thursday morning, the man who told Barbra he would put her above all material things was sitting downtown at the burglary and theft division of the Houston Police Department pushing to have Barbra arrested for theft. At his side, offering words of encouragement, were Pat Hall and Cathy Mosley, Dick's former personal secretary.

Sam Merrill, the lieutenant in charge of the burglary-theft division, would later claim to have a fuzzy memory of how he happened to assign what was arguably a domestic dispute to a couple of his police officers. Nor would Merrill remember how the call came in, or from whom. What was most interesting, and, perhaps, enlightening, was the detective who was assigned the case, one G. N. "Spider" Fincher. Spider Fincher, like Mickey Brown, was a well-known name in Houston boxing circles. For years, he coached a boxing team that one season included a feisty teenager named Mike Minns, in the days when Mike was being managed by none other than Mickey Brown. Mickey Brown and Spider Fincher, like Mickey Brown and Richard Minns, went way back together.

Everyone concerned with the theft case would insist, at the time and in years to come, that Spider Fincher's involvement was pure coincidence. Fincher himself would go so far as to swear that he never even knew Richard Minns, that he never met the man when his son boxed on his team. If it was a coincidence, it was a remarkable one.

Richard Minns would later make note that it was Mickey Brown who instigated the investigation in burglary and theft, that Brown called Spider Fincher and got the ball rolling, and that, on the surface, makes the most sense. Since Fincher and Lieutenant Merrill would both deny receiving the first call, one can only speculate on the sequence of events.

However it was set in motion, by Thursday afternoon Spider Fincher got a call from Mickey Brown urging him to get moving on the case, to file charges against Barbra Piotrowski. Fincher balked. Both he and his partner, an aggressive young cop named Charles Wells, considered the Minns matter "family bullshit." If Richard Minns wanted to go to the D.A. and get an arrest warrant, Fincher told Mickey Brown, that was fine, but he wasn't going to take it upon himself to file charges against Piotrowski. Brown ignored Fincher's protests and continued to push.

By that afternoon, Spider Fincher was working the case. Late in the day, with information provided by Dick Minns, Fincher drove out to Victoria Spillers's apartment in the Club Creek complex to look for Barbra Piotrowski. When no one answered the door, he peered between the curtains. All he saw was a mishmash of furniture and what looked like junk. He couldn't be sure whether any of the furniture was from Ethan's Glen or not.

That same night, Barbra got a phone call at Victoria Spillers's apartment. "Is this Barbra Piotrowski?" a twangy, countrified voice inquired. Barbra muttered a yes. "This is Detective Fincher of the Houston Police Department," the voice said curtly. "I just wanted to advise you that there is a real good possibility of felony grand theft and arson charges being filed against you. I've got a long list of items you stole from the premises at 312 Litchfield Lane. If you come down to the police station and meet with me tomorrow morning at eight and you're cooperative, I personally won't arrest you. If you don't cooperate, there's gonna be a complaint filed with the D.A., it'll probably be accepted and you'll be arrested."

Barbra's heart started pounding. The voice sounded threatening, intimidating. "Ah, yeah," she stammered, "I'll be there."

Panicked, she hung up the phone and quickly dialed Irv Weissman at home. "What should I do?" she pleaded with the avuncular attorney, after she told him about Fincher's call. She didn't want to be arrested. Dick's brother-in-law was calm and reassuring. "Don't do anything," he said matter-of-factly. "I don't know what's going on here. Let me call and find out."

Irv Weissman went to bed that night slightly perplexed. He had always considered his wife's brother to be an odd man. This latest turn of events only confirmed it. If Barbra said the furniture at Ethan's Glen was hers, Weissman believed her. Wasn't it just like Dick to try to make a criminal case out of a breakup?

Weissman's conversation with Spider Fincher the next morning served to validate his suspicions. Fincher, Weissman thought, had the air of a man performing a duty he found acutely uncomfortable. After a long discussion, the detective conceded that Richard Minns was pressuring him to file criminal charges against Barbra Piotrowski, but if she would settle with Minns, that would be the end of it. There was one other thing, Fincher mentioned: Weissman might want to talk to Officer Mickey Brown about some arson charges.

Irv Weissman was still trying to figure out how in the world arson came into the picture when the phone interrupted his thoughts. It was Mickey Brown. "I'm fixin' to file attempted arson charges against Barbra Piotrowski," the former boxer said blowsily.

"*Attempted* arson?" Weissman said, with amused sarcasm. "That's a new one on me. What for?"

Brown was bellicose. "She cut some electrical wires at the townhouse, so that when Mr. Minns would come in and flip on the light switch, the whole place would catch on fire."

The lawyer was immediately skeptical. "I find that hard to believe," he said soberly.

"Well," Mickey Brown slurred, "Richard Minns is a pretty honorable man. I did a background check on Piotrowski, and I can't say the same for her." His voice grew belligerent. "She better settle up with Minns—"

Irv Weissman hung up in disgust before Brown could finish his sentence. Within seconds, he had Barbra on the phone. When he repeated Brown's attempted arson theory to her, she laughed ironically. "That was a plant hanger! I had a plant hanging from a hook in the ceiling on a piece of wire! When I left, I took the plant with me and had to cut the wire!"

Weissman smiled a half-smile. That fit together, he thought wryly. Dick Minns didn't have a practical bone in his body. If he saw an electrical wire hanging from the ceiling, it would be just like him to assume it was a live cut wire. "I also talked to Detective Fincher this morning," the lawyer related to Barbra, passing on Fincher's comments. "I told him you'd call him back by ten."

In the next roundelay of calls that Friday morning, Barbra Piotrowski telephoned Spider Fincher at the police station. The detective was furious that she had Weissman call him instead of keeping their appointment at the police station at eight o'clock that morning. "Since you're not cooperating," he said peevishly, "I can't make any promises about what's gonna happen next." Fincher sounded wearied. "Look," he said with tired resignation. "Why don't you try to work things out with Richard Minns? I'd like to get this out of the way, because I really don't feel it's a police matter. OK?

If you don't contact Minns, you'll probably be arrested. Here's Mickey Brown's number. Call him about the arson charges."

Barbra did as she was instructed. "Hello, Mr. Brown?" she said tentatively, when a man answered the number Detective Fincher gave her. "This is Barbra Piotrowski."

"It's *Officer* Brown!" the voice snapped, turning instantly hostile. "Mr. Minns has advised me that there are some serious arson charges to be filed with you."

"On what basis?" Barbra said hotly.

Brown repeated the account of the cut wires. "I inspected those wires myself," he hissed into the phone. "They were cut and they were hot. You cut 'em so you could burn the building down, and everyone in it."

Suddenly the emotion of the last few days hit Barbra. "I didn't cut any electrical wires to kill anybody," she sobbed. "Those were plant hangers."

"I went to the house personally and examined those wires and they were hot," Brown sputtered. His voice took on a malicious, taunting tone. "There's no way you're gonna get into medical school with a criminal record. By the time you've served ten years, you're gonna be too old to go to any school. You're a beautiful girl. I've seen pictures of you in the paper and everything. I don't want to have a mug shot on my desk of you with a number across it, so get your business straight."

Barbra began rambling incoherently. "She stated what a horrible person Richard Minns was," Mickey Brown wrote in his official notes of the call. "But before she finished the conversation, she was also stating that he was a wonderful person. She was then asked to make up her mind whether he was a devil or a saint and she stated that she couldn't make up her mind whether she loved him or whether she hated him."

Barbra Piotrowski told Mickey Brown a few other things in her highly emotional state that morning, statements that made their way into the arson investigator's written report to Richard Minns. She told Mickey Brown that she was pregnant, that her period was eight days late; that when she first met Richard Minns, he told her he wasn't married, and she didn't find out he was married for some time. She also told Mickey Brown that Dick broke her nose and beat her up when they were in Mexico at Christmas.

Barbra mentioned one other thing in her emotional outburst to Mickey Brown: When she and Dick were in Cozumel in June of 1979, they got married. She knew it wasn't legal, but she went along with it because Dick wanted it. Mickey Brown didn't say a word. He was too busy making notes.

When Barbra finished her hysterical spiel, Mickey Brown was unmoved. "I've got at least fifteen witnesses who say you're a rotten person of low moral character and that you've got a shady past," he said in a voice dripping with hostility. "Friends of yours. Do you have any character references?"

Barbra thought for a moment and came up with the name Janice Weissman. Brown took down the number and hung up.

When Barbra Piotrowski put down the phone, she trembled. Suddenly, she was hit with the cold realization that if she didn't cooperate with Richard Minns, she was going to be in very serious trouble.

Later in the day, Janice Weissman telephoned Barbra to say that she had gotten an intimidating call from Mickey Brown, checking up on Barbra. "I know Mickey Brown!" she said in a contemptuous snarl. "He practically raised Mike. How stupid does Dick think we are?"

Late in the afternoon, Dick called his great and good friend Marvin Zindler, "Action 13's" consumer crusader. Zindler was quick to recognize the sound of a shattered ego. "Barbra left me, Marvin," Dick said plaintively. "What should I do?"

Marvin Zindler's answer was immediate and emphatic. "Forget it, Dick," he said in his distinctive broadcast bellow. "That's part of life. Forget it."

That weekend Dick and Barbra each moved to new residences; Dick took a suite at the Guest Quarters, a swank, suites-only hotel in the Galleria, an upscale shopping plaza with a skating rink in the center, surrounded by Neiman Marcus and three levels of statusy boutiques. Barbra rented a small apartment on Lansdale, not far from Dick's Bellaire office, or from the quaint Westbury Square apartment she lived in when she first moved to Houston to be with Dick. Her new apartment at Clarendon Court, an upstairs unit in an ugly, charmless cement complex, was dark, depressing, and dismal. It suited Barbra Piotrowski's mood perfectly.

Her first night at Lansdale, Barbra was wakened by a phone call from a man whispering threats to cut her into little pieces. When she hung up, he called back. This time, he didn't disengage the line. Barbra had no way to cut the connection. All night, she stared at the telephone in terror. When the sun rose, she left her things at Lansdale and drove over to Janice and Irv's. She decided to stay at their house for a while, until she felt safe enough to live alone.

Within days, Victoria Spillers would report a series of bizarre experiences in her own life after Barbra moved out. Her dog was stolen and found dead in the Houston bayou. Her car was painted and a window was shot out. Someone put a skull and crossbones on her front door. Her briefcase was stolen. She found a golf ball with Drano on it in her gas tank. Throughout that time, Spillers would claim, Mickey Brown was making harassing calls to her, telling her to "hand over the jewelry" and pumping her for information about Barbra.

Barbra Piotrowski was getting the distinct impression she was being warned.

Monday morning, March 24, Irv Weissman received a phone call at his office from Dick's friend and lawyer, Harry Brochstein. "You representing Barbra?" the corporate lawyer asked Irv, with a professional air.

Irv Weissman assumed a tone of detached irony. "Does she need representation?"

"Well," Brochstein said stiffly, "I see some serious charges about to be filed on her."

Dick's brother-in-law refused to take the situation as anything more than another of Richard's escapades. Irv tried to diffuse the call with casual conversation. As they were saying their good-byes, Brochstein asked Weissman if he could bring Barbra to a meeting at Brochstein's office. "I'll have Dick there," Brochstein said genially, "and we'll see if we can settle this."

Wiessman toughened his stance somewhat. "Well, first of all," he told Brochstein, "she's not my client. I'm not representing her, and I'm not going to obligate myself to take on a client. She hasn't made any commitment to pay me a fee or anything."

"Well, look," Brochstein coaxed, "if you can bring her to the office, we'll give you a hundred dollars."

Weissman shook his head disbelievingly. He wasn't about to tell Barbra that Harry Brochstein had offered him money to bring her to his office, but he did feel it was in her best interest to tell her about the call. "I'll talk to Barbra," the lawyer said, "and I'll let you know."

When Weissman called Barbra to relay Harry Brochstein's request for a meeting, Barbra accepted without hesitation. Irv Weissman hung up the phone, satisfied. Barbra's position was that she had done nothing wrong, but he read her as a woman who wanted to talk, to resolve it, perhaps even get back together with Dick. Weissman returned Harry Brochstein's call and reported that he would have Barbra at Harry's office at one o'clock that afternoon.

Barbra dressed for her meeting at Harry's office with mixed emotions, excited at the prospect of seeing Dick again, but still afraid. Before she left the Weissman's house, she stuffed a microcassette recorder into her purse. She might still be in love with Dick, but she wasn't going to just "trust him" anymore.

When Irv Weissman and Barbra Piotrowski arrived at Harry Brochstein's law offices, Dick was not alone. At his side, for no apparent reason, was Pat Hall, who had already accompanied him to the police station. Barbra didn't think much of it, if she noticed it at all. She had too many other things on her mind.

Harry Brochstein's tone was friendly, conciliatory. He wanted to see what the problem was, he announced to the assembled group, and he wanted to resolve it. "Y'all have had all the trauma you want," he said, casting his gaze toward Dick and Barbra. "Each of you at least ought to have some sabbatical. I've had one with my wife of thirty-four, thirty-five years. I find it very refreshing." He paused, as if he realized he was getting off on the wrong tangent. "What is it that we want to accomplish today?"

Irv Weissman cleared his throat. "Well," he said purposefully, "let's look at it in the proper context. As far as I'm concerned, like I told Barbra, I felt charging her, or attempting to file criminal charges against her, was somewhat inappropriate. There's no good cause for it—"

"Irv," Brochstein interjected, "I cannot understand—and we're not here to debate who's right and who's wrong, if we do we'd be here forever and not accomplish anything—but in my own mind, I can't understand taking the Browning over-and-under shotgun, taking five or six pairs of Lucchese boots. . . ."

"Well, first of all, let me say this," Weissman responded, with a nod toward Barbra. "In her moving, she had help. To the best of her ability, she tried to remove her own possessions. Now, if in fact some of Dick's possessions were taken, such as those items you mentioned, we will see to it that you get them back. No problem there."

Before the two lawyers could go much further, Dick interrupted them. "Everyone out of this room except Barbra and I," he said dramatically. "We are going to talk."

Harry Brochstein and Pat Hall got up and walked toward the door, with Irv Weissman following more slowly. The lawyer glanced back at Barbra, sitting at the conference table. She looked to him like a lost child.

When the room was cleared, Dick walked over to the woman who followed him to Texas over three years earlier. "Barbra," he said gently, putting his arm on her shoulder. Barbra looked up at Dick and felt a rush of love and tenderness. As predictably as in a movie, she got up and fell into his arms. "This is all I've wanted," she sobbed.

Dick held Barbra for a few minutes. Then he called the rest of the group back into the room. "Look," he said staunchly, with his arm around Barbra. "I am in love with this woman. I want to live my life free of any attorneys, and she is going to live her life free of any attorneys, too, if she's going to live it with me."

At that moment, Dick glanced down at Barbra's hands. In one of them was the microcassette recorder, with the tape turning. Suddenly, his entire demeanor changed. He pushed Barbra away and reached into his pocket, producing a typed paper. "All right," he said brusquely, thrusting the paper at Barbra. "This is my settlement agreement. Read it and sign it."

Barbra stared at the document numbly. Dick had obviously prepared for any contingency. She should have known. She read the contract silently, with Dick, Harry Brochstein, and Pat Hall looking on. Then she handed it to Irv.

The terms were shocking. Dick agreed to give Barbra all the furnishings she took from Ethan's Glen, plus five hundred dollars in cash. In exchange, she had to sign a document stating that she was not pregnant, that she and Dick had no relationship at the present time, and that they had never had a relationship in the past. She also had to agree to waive any future action against Richard Minns, "including divorce, breach of promise and paternity."

Barbra was hurt, insulted, and degraded. Is that what Dick considered their relationship to be worth? Five hundred dollars? It was worse than offering no money at all. At least that way, she thought with remorse, she could part with her dignity. The idea of signing a document stating that she and Dick had never had a relationship was absurd. Unconscionable. Irv Weissman agreed with her, but said little. He didn't feel Barbra needed his advice. This was her business. Besides, the lawyer assessed, it wasn't that big a deal. He was used to Dick's shenanigans. The meeting came to an unpleasant and abrupt end. Weissman promised to have someone return Dick's wetsuit, shotgun, boots and belt buckle, and he and Barbra departed.

Dick Minns was not a happy man when he walked out of Harry Brochstein's office that Monday afternoon. Things were not going as planned. Spider Fincher was balking at filing theft charges against Barbra. Barbra was refusing to sign the settlement agreement. Nothing was working. He returned to his office and immediately dialed Wes Piotrowski.

When Barbra's father heard Dick's voice, his heart sank. For seven days, Richard had been calling him at all hours to report disturbing things about Barbra, and he didn't even know where his daughter was, or what she was doing.

For the next three hours, Dick poured out his problems to the Polish engineer. "Well, I really think this, Wes," he said insistently. "I really think it's next to impossible for you to get this thing done long distance. I really think that if you could nail her down and have her meet you at the airport here, you can sit down with her and eyeball to eyeball. And if you like, I will be there."

"Dick, Dick, hold it, hold it," Wes interrupted. "I can talk to Barbra. I can talk to you. I wouldn't want to be the moderator or do some settling. You can deal with each other and you can settle the thing. I don't want to put my fingers between you and Barbra."

Dick's tone turned severe. If you don't intervene, he warned Wes, there would be numerous criminal charges filed against Barbra. He couldn't help it. It was out of his hands. "Here," he directed. "This is the number for Chief Mickey Brown in arson. He's the top man for the whole city of Houston. Why don't you give him a call right now?"

Wes Piotrowski refused to get involved. It would be pointless, he tried to explain to Dick. This was between him and Barbra.

Within five minutes after he hung up from Dick, Wes Piotrowski got a call at his office from "Chief" Mickey Brown.

Mickey Brown chuckled. "The only reason I didn't carry her to jail the other night is that I know Mr. Minns and know that he feels real strongly about Barbra."

"Well, OK, Chief," Wes Piotrowski said, near tears. "I— I sure—I am grateful for, for really—I can see that you're trying to prevent any kind of damage in this case, and I'll try to talk to Barbra. I cross my fingers and pray to God that you can stop this."

Wes Piotrowski thanked Mickey Brown and put his head in his hands. What was Barbra doing? She took Richard's things, tried to blow up the townhouse, and now she was in hiding. Was she crazy? And all he could do was sit and wait for her call. He didn't even know where or how to reach her.

That night, Barbra Piotrowski called her father. Wes pounced on the phone. Didn't she know she might go to jail? he said, near exhaustion. That she was going to be charged with felony theft and attempted arson? Please, Barbra, he pleaded. Please settle with Dick.

Barbra was aghast. Not only was Dick putting pressure on her father to intervene, now he had Mickey Brown doing it, too. The rest of the night, and into the morning, Barbra Piotrowski patiently explained to her father what happened, that the furniture belonged to her, that she didn't try to set the townhouse on fire.

That night, Wes Piotrowski slept better than he had in seven days. All the same, Dick's and Mickey Brown's conversations weighed heavily on his mind, so heavily he couldn't shake them, even in his sleep.

19

Early that week the phone rang in Vic Pecorino's office in the Harris County District Attorney's Building downtown on Fannin Street. As the assistant D.A. in charge of the intake division, where all criminal charges for the city of Houston are filed, Pecorino was accustomed to getting any number of bizarre calls. A chatty, folksy career prosecutor, Pecorino had been around long enough to know everybody in the criminal justice system, and thought he'd seen just about everything. Spend an hour or two with Pecorino and you'd get a gossipy rundown on every character in Houston, dating back to the fifties, with descriptions straight from the pages of a dime novel.

The call he received late in March was unusual, even by Pecorino's standards. The man on the other end of the line was Marvin Zindler. Pecorino had known Zindler practically forever and had fresh respect for Zindler's power of the press. He had no desire to incite Marvin into a television vendetta against *him*. The prosecutor was all ears.

"Hey, Pecorino," Zindler boomed into the phone. "I've got this good friend of mine, and this girl is stealin' him blind. Would you see what you can do for him?"

Pecorino suppressed a smile. Zindler knew the average Joe wouldn't even get his foot through the door of Pecorino's office. But, as the prosecutor would later say, when Marvin Zindler calls someone in the D.A.'s office, "It's gonna get a little different treatment." Later, when accusations and denials were flying fast, Zindler would deny making the call to Vic Pecorino. The prosecutor stood by it.

Vic Pecorino was fresh out of words at what greeted
him at his office the last week in March. He had read
about Richard Minns often enough in Marge Crumbaker's
column—it seemed like Minns was in there every other
damn day—but Crumbaker didn't begin to prepare him
for the genuine article. When Minns walked in for his
appointment, Pecorino beheld a wiry, aging beach-boy–
type in a tight polyester shirt open to the waist, dripping in
chains. For the next hour, the health club magnate talked
in circles—about his birthday exploits, his divorce, his love
affair with Barbra Piotrowski, how Barbra walked out on
him and stole him blind—"the whole Falcon Crest story,"
the prosecutor would later say wryly. Pecorino sat back and
enjoyed the show. He couldn't help but like the guy.

The prosecutor had entirely different feelings about
Richard Minns's companion that day, Pat Hall. Something
about that lady, he told his cronies at the district attorney's
office, made his blood run cold. Seemed to Pecorino that
Pat Hall was pulling the strings. She kept interrupting Minns
during the appointment, answering for him. "Oh, Dick'll
never remember," she'd say. "You'd better call me." It
was like she was Edgar Bergen, the prosecutor thought
to himself, and Minns was Charlie McCarthy. Gave him
a funny feeling down the back of his spine—a "vibration,"
Pecorino called it.

Minns, Pecorino noticed, seemed to have mixed feelings
about Piotrowski. In one sentence he'd go into a diatribe
about how she was stealing from him; then he'd start bragging on her. Minns even brought eight-by-ten glossies of
Piotrowski in a bikini for the prosecutor to admire. Pecorino
couldn't blame him.

It was weird, Pecorino thought to himself. Here Minns
was pining for the girl, but he wanted her arrested. Richard
Minns told Vic Pecorino where he could find Barbra. She
was staying with a woman named Victoria Spillers. Her
"lesbian lover."

By the end of the appointment, Richard Minns had what
he wanted: a warrant for Barbra's arrest, signed by Vic
Pecorino. In the majority of cases, it is a police officer
who signs an affidavit for the district attorney's office to
show probable cause for an arrest. In the case of *State*

of Texas v. *Barbra Piotrowski*, the affiant was Richard L. Minns. Richard Minns provided the probable cause. Barbra Piotrowski, he swore in his affidavit, "came to his property" and took his possessions. He had since talked to her, Minns's complaint stated, and she "admitted" stealing his belongings.

Based solely on the allegations of Richard Minns, a warrant was issued for the arrest of Barbra Isabella Piotrowski on March 26. She stood accused of stealing one diamond tie tack, one man's I.D. bracelet, one lapis-and-gold pendant, one shark's tooth necklace, and a Browning over-and-under shotgun. All but the tie tack had been picked up by Pat Hall by four o'clock that afternoon.

When he got home from Vic Pecorino's office that night Dick called Wes Piotrowski. He said he wanted a reconciliation, that he loved Barbra and wanted to start over. If she didn't, Dick warned Wes, things could get out of hand.

Early the next morning, Wes Piotrowski called his daughter and reported Dick's message. Barbra didn't know how to respond. A part of her longed to return to Dick, to move back in with him and pretend none of this had ever happened. Then she remembered the wild look in his eyes that last Monday morning, and the way he turned on her so quickly when he saw the tape recorder at Harry's office. Furthermore, the man was trying to have her arrested. She didn't know who to believe anymore, or why. Nothing made any sense.

All she could think about were Mickey Brown's threats to put her in prison for attempted arson. She had to take care of that before she did anything. Barbra said good-bye to Wes and drove downtown to file a complaint against Mickey Brown for harrassing her and her father.

Fire Marshal Alcus Greer was surprised and pleased to see Barbra Piotrowski. He knew all about Mickey Brown's investigation. Brown had come to see him the week before to see about starting an investigation for attempted arson, Greer told Barbra, and he threw him out of his office. There were no arson charges filed against her and never were, Greer said. Brown's theory was ludicrous. The investigation was all in his mind.

Greer had a favor to ask of Barbra before she left. It seemed there were a number of other allegations pending against Mickey Brown. Would she mind signing an official complaint?

Barbra agreed and offered her father as another witness. While Wes and Barbra Piotrowski were answering questions about Mickey Brown, Detectives Spider Fincher and Charles Wells were lurking about the parking lot of Victoria Spillers's apartment complex with a warrant for Barbra's arrest. Neither Richard Minns nor his underground network of investigators had discovered that Barbra was living in a different apartment, on Lansdale, not ten minutes from Dick's office.

Vic Pecorino was beginning to rue the day he allowed Richard Minns into his office. Every day, like clockwork, Minns was on the phone or at the intake division: What was going on? What were Fincher and Wells doing? Had they served Barbra yet? Why not? If it hadn't been for Marvin Zindler, Pecorino would have booted Minns out on his ear long ago.

The queer thing was, Pecorino noticed, Minns was never without Pat Hall. She was always in the shadows, carping about how Richard should "do something about that woman," that Barbra Piotrowski was trying to take over the Olympia. When Minns and Hall left intake, Pecorino and his colleagues sat and exchanged theories about the case and how Pat Hall caused the breakup of that relationship because she was "gettin' scooched out of her place" at the Olympia. *There are obviously people out there who do not want Richard Minns and Barbra Piotrowski back together*, thought Pecorino.

Other voices in other rooms were whispering much the same thing. The most insistent was Bob Delmonteque's.

Bob Delmonteque had never liked Pat Hall, and certainly never trusted her. Whenever Dick wanted dirty work done, Bob Delmonteque noticed, Pat Hall was the one who'd do it. She was, he would say, the "take-charge woman." It was Delmonteque who gave Hall the nickname the Spy, back in the days when she was checking up on the other employees for Mimi. Delmonteque believed Hall was poisoning Dick's mind against Barbra Piotrowski—telling Dick Barbra was a golddigger. A homebreaker. Poison-mouthing Barbra. And damned if Dick wasn't listening to her.

Delmonteque had his own reasons for concern about Dick's breakup with Barbra Piotrowski. He'd already put the Olympia plans on hold for two years during Dick's divorce from Mimi. Now Dick was obsessed with Barbra. He also seemed, to Delmonteque, dangerously depressed. One of the doctors who belonged to the President's Club had been telling Dick he was a manic-depressive for years. Lately, Delmonteque noticed, Dick's highs and lows had become even more extreme. Bob Delmonteque wanted Richard's mind solely on the Olympia, not on some failed romance. "Hey!" he pushed Dick one day, impatience in his voice. "It's real simple. Just pay her off and get her out of town."

Richard Minns refused. He wanted Barbra to come back to him.

On April 3, two and a half weeks after Barbra moved out of the Ethan's Glen townhouse, she overheard Janice Weissman talking on the phone at the Weissman house. It was obvious to Barbra from the conversation that the caller was Dick. Her heart started beating faster. On earlier calls, Janice had refused to let Barbra speak to Dick.

Suddenly, the urge to hear Dick's voice, to know what was going on, was overwhelming. When Janice wasn't watching, Barbra tiptoed into one of the bedrooms and picked up an extension phone. Dick was pleading with Janice to put Barbra on the phone. He had to talk to her, to see her. He sounded desperate. He was going to be in his suite at the Guest Quarters all night, he told his sister, and he wanted Barbra to come and see him. To get back together with him. He couldn't live without her.

Barbra gently replaced the receiver and returned to the living room, shaking. A few days earlier, just before Passover, Stella Piotrowski arrived in Houston to spend some time with her daughter. Barbra pulled her mother aside. "I'm going to see Dick at the Guest Quarters, suite sixteen oh eight," she whispered to Stella. "If you haven't heard from me or I'm not back by tomorrow morning, call the police."

Stella Piotrowski's sturdy Polish features formed a deep frown, but she said nothing. She knew better than to try to stop Barbra. It hadn't worked for twenty-seven years. Why would it start now?

Barbra stole out the door and to her car without a word to the Weissmans. She knew if she told Irv or Janice, they would try to stop her and she was so afraid she would probably listen to them. She couldn't take that chance.

When Barbra Piotrowski rang the doorbell to suite 1608 at the Guest Quarters, there was no answer. Wearily, she sat down on the floor in the hall outside the door and waited, her heart pounding wildly at the thought of seeing Dick again.

Sometime around two in the morning, Dick emerged from the elevator with his arm around a brunette. Barbra felt a sharp stab of pain. She knew in a glance that Dick would never have a serious relationship with the woman on his arm—she wasn't a blonde and she was smoking a cigarette—but the sight of him with another woman filled her with an aching loneliness. "God," she thought ruefully, "what an idiot I am!"

When Dick got to the door of his suite, Barbra hit him with her purse. "Well, it didn't take you long! I can see how much you love me!" she said, running toward the elevator.

Dick chased after her, leaving his date standing outside the door to his hotel room. "Barbra, I love you," he pleaded, as he got into the elevator with her. "Come back with me. Let's get this all worked out."

Barbra glared at him. "Well, you have a funny way of showing it," she said sarcastically, getting out of the elevator.

Dick followed Barbra to the parking lot. "This is a mistake," he said urgently. "She's not even my type. Mel Powers set us up. It doesn't mean anything. This is the first time I've ever been out with her. I barely even know her." Barbra didn't respond. Dick grabbed her car keys out of her hand. "Come back up with me," he said, pulling on her arm. "Spend the night with me. Let's work this out."

Barbra stood for a long moment, fighting with herself. She hated Dick for bringing that girl to his hotel room;

more than that, she hated herself for still wanting him. She went up the elevator with Dick.

When Dick and Barbra walked down the hall, arms entwined, the woman who came off the elevator with him was still standing at the door. As Barbra looked on foggily, Dick walked over to the brunette and whispered a few words into her ear. The young woman walked away without a backward glance.

Once she was in Dick's hotel room, Barbra's long-suppressed feelings came out in a torrent. She was interrupted by a knock on the door. When Dick opened it, his date from earlier in the evening was standing in the hallway, an impatient look on her heavily made-up face. "Somebody's coming to pick me up," she said sullenly. "I'm just gonna wait here."

Barbra's eyes ignited. "I can't talk to you with her here," she said peevishly.

Dick Minns looked perplexed. "I can't just kick her out," he said awkwardly. "Come on," he said, taking Barbra's hand. "Let's go in the bedroom. She can wait out here."

Barbra felt strangely uneasy. "No," she said firmly. "Just give me my car keys." A feeling of sudden panic came over her. She wanted to leave the suite immediately.

"No," Dick said emphatically. "Don't go. I don't want you to leave." He took Barbra by the arm and pulled her into the bedroom. When they were alone, with the door closed, he pulled her close to him and kissed her. Barbra could not stop herself from responding. For the first time since she moved out of Ethan's Glen, she felt like she was where she belonged.

A sudden pounding on the door jolted Barbra back to reality. When she looked up, two uniformed police officers burst into the bedroom.

"Here she is, officers!" Dick shouted, dropping his arms from Barbra's waist and pushing her toward them. "You've got a warrant for her arrest. Take her away!"

Barbra looked at Dick in horror.

The two patrol officers acted confused. "We don't have a warrant for her arrest," they said blankly.

Dick whipped a piece of paper out of his pocket. "Yes, you do!" he whooped. "I've got a citizen's arrest, right here.

She's an employee of mine. She stole from me."

Barbra went numb. "Why is there a warrant for my arrest?" she said weakly.

Dick ignored her and pushed his way toward the two policemen. "She stole my jewelry and my shotgun," he said belligerently. "I barely know her. She's an employee."

Barbra opened her purse and pulled out her wallet. "Look!" she said hysterically, throwing snapshots at the two police officers. "Here's a picture of the two of us in Acapulco at Christmas. Here's another one of him and me with his parents. Here's one with my parents. Does that look like I'm just an employee?"

The two patrol officers glanced at the pictures of Dick and Barbra in various locations with their arms around each other. Then they studied Richard Minns, shouting, "I barely even know her!" What was going on?

"Call Spider Fincher," Dick said insistently. "He'll tell you. Here's his home number."

One of the officers dialed the number and talked into the phone for a few seconds. Then he hung up and looked at Barbra apologetically. "I'm sorry, ma'am," he said kindly, "but we're gonna have to take you in. There is an outstanding warrant for your arrest."

Barbra picked up her purse. This couldn't really be happening. "It was a nightmare. I didn't know if I wanted to be alive knowing that things like this can happen," she said later. "He might as well have taken a knife and ripped my heart right open."

When the two policemen and Barbra were gone, Dick Minns sat in his hotel room savoring his victory. While Barbra had been waiting for him to say good-bye to his date, he had made a quick call to Pat Hall, and Hall had called the police. If Spider Fincher, Charlie Wells, and Vic Pecorino couldn't get Barbra arrested, he must have thought smugly, he damn sure could himself. There was always a way.

At two-thirty A.M. Barbra Piotrowski was driven downtown to the Houston police station and put in a holding cell. All through the night she tried in vain to tell someone her side of the story, that she'd been framed. Wait until seven, she was told. Officers Fincher and Wells came in at seven A.M. She could explain everything to them.

Barbra shuddered. "Fincher and Wells set me up!" she sobbed, to anyone who came within shouting distance. "Can't I talk to somebody else? Please! Anybody."

Barbra's pleas fell on deaf ears. The arresting officers were in charge, she was told in a monotone. She couldn't make a phone call; she couldn't talk to anyone else about it.

Barbra stared at the cement walls of the cell around her. Surely, she decided, she must be in hell.

When Charlie Wells and Spider Fincher arrived at the police station for their seven A.M. shift, Barbra Piotrowski was a different person than she had been eight hours earlier. The idea of seeing Fincher and Wells no longer intimidated her. It was as if there was no pain left, no hurt.

"Hey!" Spider Fincher called out, breaking the silence of the holding cell with his good-old-boy accent. "Why don't you just settle up with Minns and we'll forget about the whole deal, just wipe the slate clean?"

Barbra shook her head mechanically. "No way," she responded. She had to show Dick that she could stand up to him and she had to do what she felt was right.

Barbra would later have vivid recollections of what happened next. Spider Fincher reached into his pocket and pulled out a copy of Dick's typed settlement agreement offering her five hundred dollars and the furniture if she would drop any claims against him. "Sign this, girl," he goaded. "If you do, we can let you go. We don't want to do any of this to you. Just sign the papers and get it over with. You don't want your life ruined."

Spider Fincher would later deny showing Barbra a copy of the agreement. He never even saw it, he claimed. What he remembered was how stubborn Barbra Piotrowski was, how hardheaded. She refused to settle with Minns.

"No way," Barbra repeated petulantly. "There's no way I'm gonna sign that agreement."

Fincher shifted his big frame from one foot to another. "OK," he said, his country twang taking on a sinister tone. "We're gonna have to throw you in jail with all the criminals. Who knows what's gonna happen to you in there. You know what women in jail are like."

Barbra snickered. "After being around *you?* And *Minns?* Go ahead. I'm not really afraid."

Fincher called for a matron to escort Barbra to a jail cell.

When Barbra got to the cell, she studied the faces of the women in jail. Their countenances surprised her. They wore expressions more of sickness than of evil; of fear rather than violence. She had, she felt, less to fear from them than from Fincher and Wells.

A few hours later, the two detectives from the burglary and theft division pulled her out of the cell. *"Now* how are you feeling?" Wells asked her. "You feeling any more like settling up with Minns?"

Barbra shook her head. Charlie Wells leaned in closer. Wells, a lean, thin-lipped former narcotics officer, didn't like playing games, especially on what he called a "shit case" like Minns and Piotrowski. "You better think about this real good," he cautioned. "Minns has the best attorneys in the world. You're gonna end up in jail. You're never gonna be able to get into medical school. You hear what I'm saying? Just give the shit back if you got it and all this bullshit will be over with."

Spider Fincher interrupted his partner. "Oh, come on now," he said in a cajoling, East Texas twang. "Sign the papers, girl, and get it over with."

Barbra sat on her chair in stony silence, observing sardonically Fincher and Wells playing the roles of good cop/bad cop. The process continued into the afternoon. Eventually, Barbra convinced a matron to let her make a phone call to Irv Weissman. Before Weissman could get downtown, Fincher and Wells had had enough.

Sometime after noon on Good Friday, April 4, Barbra stood in front of a police camera, was booked on one count of grand theft, one count of attempted arson, and a charge of aggravated assault (for hitting Richard Minns with her purse).

It was three years, almost to the day, since she pulled into Houston in her blue VW camper to spend the rest of her life with the man she loved.

In the middle of the afternoon, Stella Piotrowski rode to the Houston police station with Irv Weissman. In her purse was five thousand dollars, almost all the money she had in the world, to bail her daughter out of jail.

That Sunday, Easter day, Stella Piotrowski took Barbra to a McDonald's for dinner. Ever since Barbra was born, she and Wes had celebrated Barbra's birthday on Easter. This year, even though it was just her and Barbra, Stella had hoped to take her daughter someplace special. Instead she had only enough money for a fast-food chain.

Stella Piotrowski, the woman who never showed her emotions, stared across the McDonald's booth at Barbra and wept.

A day or so after she was released from jail Barbra returned, alone, to the apartment on Lansdale, deeply depressed. She couldn't seem to *make* herself forget Dick, even after what he did to her at the Guest Quarters. She spent the day crying, sick with self-pity.

Toward the middle of the evening, she felt a severe pain in her stomach. Since she was a girl, Barbra had occasional gallbladder attacks, some so severe she had to go to the emergency room. Groggily, she reached for a couple of Tylenol Codeine 4, swallowed them, and closed her eyes. She felt better. The pain was lessening. If she could just escape and take a break from being Barbra for a while. The room started spinning around her.

Barbra woke up the next morning in a pool of fresh blood. The pain from the night before was completely gone. She realized in an instant what had happened: She had had a miscarriage. Barbra lay on her bed and wept hot tears of self-loathing, of longing, and loss. In the month since she and Richard had been apart, her only hold on her sanity was the baby she was carrying. That child was the one thing she had that was *his*, a part of Dick that no one could take away from her. She hadn't given a thought to how she was going to raise a baby alone. She was simply going to find a way. Now that, along with everything else, was gone.

Barbra curled up in a fetal position, thinking. She wasn't going to tell anybody about the miscarriage. If Dick didn't know, she could hold on a little bit longer.

Deep in her subconscious, she knew she was only fooling herself. Nothing was ever going to be the same.

20

Richard Minns could find no peace that spring, prosecutor Vic Pecorino observed. The deputy district attorney had tried to point out that getting Barbra Piotrowski arrested wasn't necessarily going to get Minns what he was after: his furniture.

In the middle of April, a few weeks after Barbra was arrested, Dick made an appointment with John Holmes, the district attorney for Harris County. Johnny Holmes, as he was popularly known, a burly, mustachioed lawyer who looked as though he belonged in a barbershop quartet, prided himself on being a man's man, a D.A. you wouldn't find in anyone's pocket.

When he observed Richard Minns in his office, going on and on about how he had been put upon by Barbra Piotrowski, holding up pinup pictures of Piotrowski and asking if he could win his case with the grand jury because of her "appearance," Holmes barely suppressed a snicker. "Isn't it amazing," the district attorney said in mock seriousness, "how most men's brains are residing in another part of their anatomy?"

Minns, Holmes analyzed, after a long career of evaluating human beings at the peak of their emotions, struck him as a man who had had one put over on him and was out for retribution. When Holmes refused to go along with his program, Minns, in the district attorney's words, "didn't take it well."

Barbra Piotrowski was not in the least surprised by Richard's behavior. After she moved out of Ethan's Glen, she knew Dick would be expecting her to sue him for everything he had, either in a divorce or maybe a "palimony"

236

case. Irv Weissman had already mentioned the possibility of a breach of promise action to her in addition to false imprisonment and false arrest as a defense to the theft charges, but Barbra resisted. She still entertained the hope, dim as it was becoming, that she and Dick would get back together again. That would never happen if she sued him. Once you sued Richard Minns, you were an *enemy*.

The irony was, Barbra thought in idle moments, it really didn't matter. Dick was always preparing for an attack. How many times had she listened to him lecture about how he survived by staying a step ahead of his competition? By doing something on the offensive as a legal defense?

Four days after Dick's debacle with John Holmes, Irv Weissman got a call from Harry Brochstein. Brochstein's tone was jocular, but his message had a faintly ominous ring. "Talk Barbra into settling with Dick," the corporate attorney advised Minns's brother-in-law, or there would be "serious consequences."

Later that same day, Wes Piotrowski got a phone call at his home in Los Angeles from Bob Delmonteque. "Look," Delmonteque said insistently, "I'll give Barbra twenty thousand dollars if you'll get her out of town." The bodybuilder paused dramatically. "Anything could happen, those two are so goddamned intense."

Wes Piotrowski slammed down the receiver. He had barely met Bob Delmonteque; probably couldn't pick him out of a lineup of men. What was he doing, calling with offers to pay off Barbra?

On the seventeenth of April, Barbra accepted an invitation to Janice Weissman's birthday party, and, reluctantly, a blind date for the evening with a client of Irv's. "You need to get out, honey," Janice had been fussing at her for weeks. "Let me fix you up with somebody nice. Forget about Dick. He's no good!"

The birthday dinner with the Weissmans turned out to be a pleasant diversion. Irv's client, Joe Kalmick, was a nice enough guy, although Barbra had no interest in him romantically. Romance was an all-or-nothing proposition for Barbra. At the end of the evening, they chatted amiably on the short ride from the Weissmans' house in Sharpstown to Barbra's apartment on Lansdale.

As Kalmick turned the corner in her parking lot, Barbra noticed a couple of men in suits congregated near her apartment. Suspicious, she asked Kalmick to drive around the block. When they came back around the corner in Joe's black jeep, Barbra got a closer look at the group. The two men in suits were Spider Fincher and Charlie Wells, standing with Dick and Pat Hall. There was a fourth man lurking in the shadows, between cars. Barbra thought it might be Bob Delmonteque, but she wasn't sure.

At that moment, someone in the group noticed Barbra. "Get out of here as fast as you can," she directed Kalmick.

Joe Kalmick put his foot all the way down on the gas pedal. Fincher and Wells jumped in their car and followed. Barbra got a queasy feeling in her stomach. As soon as she saw a U-Totem, she asked Kalmick to pull in. At least, if they were in a public place, there would be witnesses.

When Kalmick's jeep came to a stop, Barbra jumped out and ran to the pay phone inside the U-Totem. As she was pushing the buttons of Irv Weissman's home phone number, a hand pushed down the receiver. She looked up at Charlie Wells's eyes squinting at her. "You got to come back with us to your apartment and let us in so we can look around. Now."

Barbra started to scream. "Do you have an arrest warrant?"

Wells shook his head. "Nope. Got a search warrant. Same thing. That means you got to go with us. If your name's on the search warrant, you're automatically under arrest."

Barbra became hysterical. "What are you going to do? Put me in the bottom of Buffalo Bayou?"

"You're resisting," Wells said agitatedly. "You can either come with us, or we can take you downtown to jail and lock you up."

Joe Kalmick looked on helplessly, demanding to see the two men's badges or identification. Fincher and Wells refused.

After what Wells would later refer to as some "convincing," Barbra got in the car with the two detectives. Kalmick followed in his jeep, with instructions from Barbra to call Irv Weissman if they didn't drive to her place.

When Fincher and Wells pulled into the parking space next to Barbra's apartment, Dick and Pat Hall were waiting there beside two huge moving vans.

"He's not coming into my apartment!" Barbra shrieked.

Fincher and Wells pushed her toward her apartment. "Just open the door," they said irritably.

Barbra hesitated and asked to see the search warrant. "We'll show you one once we get inside," Wells grunted. Barbra opened the door charily and headed straight for the phone to call Irv Weissman. Wells tried to stop her, but Fincher interceded. When she had Irv on the phone, Barbra spilled out what happened and begged him to get over to her apartment right away. As she hung up, Fincher and Wells announced they were going to bring Minns up to identify the items she stole from him.

A silent scream formed in Barbra's throat. "He can't come in here!" she said shrilly. "This is my home. He has no right to come in my home!"

Fincher and Wells tried to calm her down. Maybe it would be better, they said soothingly, if she waited outside while Richard was in her apartment. It might be less traumatic.

Barbra looked at them, wild-eyed. "No! He's not coming in here. These are *my* things!" She ran around the apartment, frantically pulling receipts out of drawers to show to the two detectives. "Look! These are all in my name. This furniture belongs to me!" She felt violated, stripped of her basic rights as a human being. The laws that were supposed to protect her were, suddenly, meaningless.

Fincher and Wells stood in the doorway, motionless, like a pair of cigar-store wooden Indians.

Outside, Irv and Janice Weissman parked their Cadillac in an available space and made their way through the dark parking lot toward Barbra's apartment. In Irv's hand was a camera, in case he needed to record any of the night's activities for future reference.

Janice Weissman walked tipsily, her eyes darting left and right for any sign of mischief. In the parking lot, she saw the figure of a large man, standing off to himself between two parked cars, watching. She peered at him in the darkness, trying to make out his face, but couldn't identify him.

When she reached the stairwell to Barbra's apartment, Janice caught a glimpse of her brother standing in the shadows. The wine from her birthday celebration loosened her already free tongue. "You son-of-a-*bitch*!" she hissed into the night air. A thousand memories of Dick currying her parents' favor, of Dick tormenting her, of Dick always at the center of attention, came at her. "To think you had to do this on *my* birthday, when we took Barbra out with one of Irv's clients. You son-of-a-bitch!"

"Watch what you're saying," Dick fired back, in a belligerent voice, "or I'll have you arrested."

Janice shouted a few more epithets and followed her husband up the stairs to Barbra's second-floor apartment. When they walked through the door, a wave of relief passed over Barbra's panic-stricken face. "Irv!" she cried. "Thank God you're here! They're trying to take all my possessions. I showed them the receipts for everything and they don't care!"

Fincher and Wells walked past Weissman and called down to the two movers to start loading. Then they signaled Minns to come up.

Irv Weissman laughed ironically. "Let 'em take the stuff," he said to Barbra. "Show them all the receipts. This is so great. What they're doing is blatantly illegal."

Barbra looked at him doubtfully.

"This is the best thing that could happen to you," Irv insisted. "This is so blatant, there's no way we don't have a case now."

Janice Weissman barely heard her husband. She had just remembered the identity of the man she saw between the cars in the parking lot. She recognized him from a few of Dick and Mimi's parties. It was Dudley Bell, possibly the most famous private detective in Texas.

What Janice Weissman didn't realize, as she was peering at Dudley Bell in the moonlight, was that Dudley Bell was responsible, at least indirectly, for setting in motion the chain of events that night.

But then, Dudley Clifford Bell, Jr., had a long and vivid history at the eye of the storm. Bell was known as "colorful": big as an ox, with thick, wavy hair, a beefy, jowly face, and brown eyes with the twinkle of the devil's disciple. A man's man with an eye for the ladies—usually a flashy blonde. "He's got that aura of danger about him," one famous Texas criminal lawyer said of Bell, "that seems to attract women."

The son of a golf pro at a Houston country club and the nephew of a famous Texas lawyer, Joe Tonahill (who, along with Melvin Belli, represented Jack Ruby), Dudley was a born athlete and a born charmer. He was also a hellion, the leader of a gang of rough-and-tumble boys from Reagan High School. After a stint in the army, he hooked up with an old-time Houston private investigator and quickly developed a reputation as a "gadget freak." Bell took delight in pens that functioned as radio receivers, miniature microphones hidden in tiny holes in the ceiling of his office, subminiature cameras, a hidden tape recorder in his desk drawer—anything that had to do with surreptitious recording. The only way you could be sure Dudley Bell *wasn't* taping you, the saying went, is if you both stripped naked and you had your finger up his ass.

By the late sixties, Bell had a luxurious office and a lineup of big-name clients who appreciated his finesse with electronic surveillance and his liberal interpretation of the law. As his client list swelled, so did charges of Bell's alleged criminal activities: bribing a handwriting analyst with the Houston Police Department, conspiring to transport illegal aliens, wiretapping. Dudley, his boyhood pal Bobby Newman recalled, always lived on the edge. "Danced on that line," one journalist put it. None of the charges ever stuck—Dudley hired the best lawyers in town and grinned his way through a string of acquittals. The criminal allegations only enhanced his mystique. After one acquittal Bell was elected vice president of the Texas Association of Licensed Investigators and named to their ethics committee. In 1972, *Texas Monthly* magazine published a long, complimentary profile of him called "The Best Private Eye in Texas." In 1975, Bell ran, unsuccessfully, for the Houston City Council.

A few years later, Dudley Bell was behind one of
the juiciest scandals in Houston politics: photographing a
young, socially connected Democratic mayoral candidate in
flagrante delicto with a prostitute, and, on another occasion,
a man. His employers, Bell would later claim, were a legendary clutch of political power brokers who met for breakfast
every morning at the Lamar Hotel in downtown Houston to
shape the city's destiny. A few weeks later, the candidate
quietly pulled out of the race and disappeared from public
life. The case, and the modus operandi, were pure Dudley
Bell. By 1980, Bell was making half a million dollars a
year and driving a black Cadillac.

Sometime the week after Barbra moved out—the exact
date, like most transactions involving Dudley Bell, is mired
in mystery—Dick and Dudley Bell got together for a chat.
Or rather, Richard Minns chatted. Dudley Bell listened—
for hours and hours, as Richard Minns rambled on about
Barbra, about his ex-wife Mimi, about the Olympia, and
anything else he could think of. He wanted to find Barbra,
Dick told Dudley Bell, he wanted to find his furniture, and
he wanted it done *now*. He couldn't count on the Houston
police. They were too slow. He was going to have to take
matters into his own hands. Dudley Bell smiled. That was
what he did best.

On the morning of Janice Weissman's birthday, a Friday,
Bell called Richard Minns. He had found Barbra Piotrowski,
the detective told the millionaire. And he was pretty sure he
found his stuff, too.

That afternoon, Spider Fincher's phone in the burglary
and theft division was ringing off the wall. It was Richard
Minns, demanding that Fincher prepare a search warrant.
He found Barbra, Dick crowed. He wanted his stuff back.
Immediately.

Spider Fincher hemmed and hawed. He didn't like the
Piotrowski case. Never did. Still didn't. Nope, he told Minns.
He wasn't gonna sign a search warrant. If Minns could get
one from the D.A., he'd make a run for the property. Until
then, he wasn't budging.

Late that afternoon, Vic Pecorino had two unexpected
visitors in the intake division of the district attorney's office:
Richard Minns and Dudley Bell. When he saw Minns, the

prosecutor rolled his eyes. What now? he groaned.

The prosecutor looked at his watch. It was almost five o'clock. Why did these things always have to come up on a Friday afternoon?

Dick marched straight to Pecorino's office and looked the prosecutor directly in the eye. He located his stolen furniture, he announced triumphantly. Now he needed a search warrant so he could get it back. He wanted Pecorino to draw one up for him. He already had two moving vans waiting in the parking lot of Barbra's apartment complex.

Pecorino pondered his options for a moment. It was, to say the least, *unusual* for a citizen to swear to a complaint for a search warrant in front of an assistant D.A. Nine times out of ten, it was a police officer who brought in the information for a warrant. The prosecutor studied the millionaire's face. Minns looked like he could explode at any moment. If he didn't go along with him, Pecorino thought warily, Minns was gonna harangue him until eternity, just like he'd been haranguing him since day one, when he came in for the arrest warrant on Piotrowski.

Pecorino picked up the phone and dialed Gordon Dees, a young prosecutor in the court where the arrest warrant was filed. "Gordo," the assistant district attorney said genially. "I'm sorry to bother you so late on a Friday, buddy, but I got a favor to ask of you. Richard Minns is standing here, and he needs some help drawing up a search warrant. Can I send him over to you?"

Pecorino hung up and directed Dick and Dudley Bell to the 177th District Court in the old Criminal Courts Building just down the block. Gordon Dees, he said, would write up a search warrant for them. Then he heaved a long, tortured sigh. Ordinarily, he wouldn't have given a citizen in Minns's circumstances the time of day. But most citizens didn't have Marvin Zindler hovering in the background. Pecorino's head throbbed just thinking about it. Marvin's the kind of guy, he would say later, that, if you're in public office and he comes to you with something and you don't do it, he'll turn around and just *burn* you. And Pecorino didn't want to get burned.

Gordon Dees graciously welcomed Richard Minns and Dudley Bell to an office in the back of the 177th District

Court. Based solely on Dick Minns's story, Dees prepared a search warrant authorizing any peace officer in the state of Texas to search and seize Barbra Piotrowski's apartment for three chrome dining room chairs with burnt-orange upholstery, one six-sided glass-topped dining room table with rattan base, one Thayer-Coggin tub chair of mixed colors of blue, rust, brown, and beige, and one Thayer-Coggin navy-blue sofa with satin finish, plus "any other stolen property located on said place and premises."

Under ordinary circumstances, Dees would have been listening to a police officer list the items to be named in a search warrant. Then, as an assistant district attorney, he would submit the officer's request to a two-prong test: Is the person providing the information credible, and can he independently verify it to some extent? Those were the protections afforded every citizen against unreasonable searches and seizures as set forth in the United States Constitution.

In the case in front of Dees, Richard Minns was supplying the information for the warrant, Richard Minns was swearing to the information as being true, and Richard Minns was providing whatever "independent" verification Dees might have. One wonders if it occurred to Dees that there might be some reason the detectives from burglary and theft were reluctant to swear to a complaint for a search warrant for Richard Minns. But Vic Pecorino was his boss and Vic Pecorino gave him the go-ahead. Anyway, Dees reasoned, there was already an outstanding arrest warrant on Barbra Piotrowski, so she had to at least be suspected of something. Besides, Richard Minns was a responsible businessman. If he was willing to swear that he owned the property and Piotrowski stole it from him, why should Dees not believe him? Later on, when the case took on what Dees referred to as its "uglier aspects," he would compare his position to that of the blind man and the elephant. When you're just touching a part of it, he reasoned, you don't know about the whole.

At nine-eighteen P.M., Richard Minns knocked on the door of a quiet house in West University not far from his parents' home. A few seconds later, Miron Love, the judge from the 155th District Court, met him in the foyer and signed the search warrant. Then he went back to his bridge game.

Dudley Bell, Spider Fincher, Charlie Wells, and Pat Hall were outside waiting. When Wells saw Minns emerge from the house with a signed search warrant, he whistled under his breath. In all his years on the police force, Wells had never seen a private citizen swear to his own search warrant. Minns must have pulled some heavy-duty strings, the detective thought to himself.

At that moment, however, Wells's mind was focused on Dudley Bell. Until then, he would later claim, he had no idea Bell was involved with the case. Charlie Wells attended junior high school and Reagan High School with Bell. Known him for years. If Dudley was working the case, Wells thought, it was a whole other ball game.

At three in the morning, Dick and his coterie were gone. Barbra stood in her empty apartment, clutching the invoices to the furniture, and crying. Even her plants, she would later lament, were seized. Trinkets she brought with her from California. Gifts from her father she had had since she was a little girl. It wasn't the *things* that bothered her so much; it was her helplessness against Dick's power, his ability to subvert the system.

She walked out to the parking lot with Irv. Janice was already home with their boys. Joe Kalmick had taken Janice home in his Jeep. Barbra leaned on Irv Weissman's shoulder. There was no way she could stay in the apartment that night. She was going to have to sleep at the Weissmans'.

As the two approached Irv's Cadillac, they noticed a sticky substance on the windows that felt like hair spray. They glanced down. All four tires were slashed; the antenna was broken; the gas cap was missing. Barbra looked over at the red Firebird she was renting, parked in her space. The tires on the Firebird were slit, too.

At four in the morning, Irv Weissman and Barbra Piotrowski rode in silence (in a taxi) to the Weissmans' house. For the first time since Barbra moved out, Irv was truly concerned. Dick had always been a little crazy, he knew, but now things were getting out of hand. He was afraid his brother-in-law was going over the edge.

21

The last day of April, Stella Piotrowski was bent over her garden, pulling weeds, when she noticed two men hovering over her. One of them, a big, hulking man, began peppering her with questions about an old boyfriend of Barbra's. "We're with the IRS," he said, in an official-sounding voice. The young man handed her a consent-to-search warrant. "We need you to sign this please, ma'am," he said, offering her a pen.

Stella Piotrowski peered at the two strangers from behind her wire-rimmed glasses. It was not for nothing she had been spirited away from her home by Nazis when she was a girl. Stella Piotrowski trusted no one. "No, I won't sign that," she said huffily and headed for the house, muttering under her breath in Polish.

The next afternoon, there was a knock on the Piotrowski door. Stella excused herself from a living room full of chattering neighbor ladies gathered for a coffee klatch to answer it. The same two men from the previous day were standing on the front steps, accompanied by two Los Angeles police officers. One of the policemen flashed a search warrant and demanded she let them in. They had reason to believe, he said tersely, there was stolen property inside.

Stella glared at the police officer. This was her home. She was in America. They had no right to come inside her house. "I'm gonna call my husband," she said stiffly, leaving the three men standing in the doorway.

Wes Piotrowski was unperturbed. "Let them in, Stella," he said in his singsong accent. "Let 'em look around. We got nothing to hide."

Stella grudgingly followed her husband's instructions and

246

opened the door. The younger man in a suit walked up to her and demanded the necklace she was wearing. Stella Piotrowski nearly spit in his face. "I'm not giving you this," she said gruffly. "I got this from my daughter. It was a gift."

"Yeah, right," the man in the suit snapped. "We know it's from your daughter. She stole it from Richard Minns." He took the necklace off Stella's neck and handed it to the policeman.

While Stella Piotrowski and her guests looked on in outrage, the three men wandered through the house, opening drawers, rifling through closets, and emptying Stella's jewelry box. Half an hour or so later, they left, taking with them the necklace Stella had been wearing and several other pieces of jewelry Dick and Barbra had given Barbra's mother in the previous few years.

That night, Wes and Stella Piotrowski called Barbra, upset and enraged. Barbra listened closely as her mother described the two IRS agents to her. One of them, Barbra was sure, was Charlie Wells. The other man she couldn't place.

Only later would she find out it was Dudley Bell.

To take her mind off Dick and her problems, Barbra ran every morning, and sometimes in the evenings. One day when she was jogging around the trail at Memorial Park, she bumped into Willie Rometsch, the German restaurateur who owned the Rivoli, Dick's hangout. Like Barbra, Rometsch was recently unattached, in the process of divorcing Evinia, the interior designer who helped Barbra decorate Ethan's Glen.

Rometsch barely recognized Barbra. He was so accustomed to seeing her with Dick she was almost like his appendage. She seemed, he sensed, very frightened and very alone.

The two jogged the trail together and Barbra revealed bits and pieces of what had been happening with Dick—the lawsuit, her slashed tires. She didn't have any friends in Houston, she told Willie. All of her friends were Dick's friends. His sister Janice was her closest acquaintance in Houston. She didn't know what to do.

Willie Rometsch took pity on Barbra. "Why don't you

come over to my place for coffee?" he asked, in his thick Arnold Schwarzenegger accent.

When they were together at his apartment, Rometsch suggested Barbra call a lawyer. "If you ever feel like you need to talk to somebody," he said kindly, "call me."

The next day, Barbra's phone on Lansdale was ringing. Dick was on the other end of the line. Her heart started pounding. "I hear you jogged twenty-two miles the other day," he said casually, in an exaggeratedly friendly voice.

Barbra was taken aback. Actually, it was twenty-six. "How'd you know that?" she asked.

"You don't think you can get by with something without me knowing, do you?" Dick said playfully. He paused for a moment and began reading into the phone. Barbra froze. It was the exact conversation she had had with Willie Rometsch the night before. "Let's forget about all this and go to Antigua," Dick cooed. "Come on, baby. I love you. I still want to marry you. It'll be like a second honeymoon."

Barbra hesitated. Her mind floated back to their first trip to Antigua, right after she moved to Houston, when she met Don Wildman and Rebecca at the Curtain Bluff. Now she had the eerie feeling that if she went to Antigua with Dick, it would be a second honeymoon for him, and a funeral for her.

When Barbra didn't answer, Dick reminded her of the theft case. "You know the grand jury's gonna indict you," he said coldly, and hung up.

Barbra sat staring at the telephone for a long time, filled with a strange mixture of desire and fear.

A day or so later, Dick stormed into the Rivoli. "What are you doing, dating Barbra?" he yelled at Willie Rometsch, wild-eyed.

Rometsch looked at him blankly. "What are you," the restaurateur said astonishingly, "crazy?"

"I know you went running with her," Dick shot back. "I know you two talked. I had the guys following you."

Rometsch stared at Dick incredulously. It was obvious to him the man was crazy in love with Barbra. Richard Minns was not a man Rometsch cared to tangle with. He didn't even like him. "Number one," Rometsch said hotly,

"I have no interest in dating Barbra. I had no interest before, I have no interest now. It just happened, a fluke, that she approached me and we talked and that was the end." The restaurateur scrutinized Richard. He got the impression that if Dick couldn't have Barbra, then she should leave town. Rometsch shook his head. *Those two are obsessed*, he thought to himself. *Sick. If they can't be with each other*, he thought ominously, *they'll tear each other up.*

That spring Barbra had other, equally strange indications Dick was having her followed and that he was tapping her phone. One of the sources was Victoria Spillers.

Immediately after they executed the search warrant against Barbra, Fincher and Wells drove to Victoria's apartment at three A.M. with a warrant for her arrest. When Victoria was released from jail, she told Barbra she was certain Barbra was being followed and that her phone was being tapped by a man named Dudley Bell.

Barbra still had a hard time believing that anybody was following her. She'd been watching closely, and she hadn't noticed anybody behind her; no strangers lurking in the shadows, no cars trailing her.

Janice Weissman disagreed. Ever since the night of the search warrant, she observed from time to time a gray-on-black Cadillac in her rearview mirror, the same make and model of the car Dudley Bell drove. Conversations she and Irv had on their home and office phones were coming back to them, verbatim. Something strange was definitely going on, they told Barbra. When Barbra visited them at the house, the Weissmans insisted they go outside to talk. Early in May, Barbra reported a suspected tap on her line to the phone company.

One afternoon in May, Irv introduced Barbra to a friend of his, an unlicensed private investigator named Michel Font. Font, a lumbering country giant one client described as "Gomer Pyle in the body of Lurch"—the least likely man in the world to be named "Michel"—believed in the open display of weaponry, that forearmed was forewarned.

After observing her for a few days, Font offered some professional observations to Barbra Piotrowski. First, she was definitely being followed; and number two, she was the perfect target. She needed to change her schedule around a little bit: Jog at night instead of in the morning; get up late one morning and early the next; park in different spaces in the apartment parking lot. Do whatever she could to throw whoever was following her off the track.

Barbra demurred. She had to be in certain classes at the University of Houston at specific times and she was working several days a week as a nurse in the burn unit at Hermann Hospital. How could she change that around? Font decided, ultimately, to move into Barbra's apartment so he could be her full-time bodyguard as a favor to Irv. Barbra leaped at the offer. She hadn't slept a full night since she moved into the apartment on Lansdale. With Michel Font around at night, she would feel significantly safer.

Later on, Richard Minns would claim that he was being harassed, too. Someone, he complained to Charlie Wells, "jimmied" the door to his suite at the Guest Quarters. Around the same time Irv brought Michel Font into the case, Dick hired a bodyguard of his own, a sometime employee of Dudley Bell's with a black belt in karate named Rick Waring.

Dick's other piece of evidence that he was in danger was a sworn affidavit from Woody Conway, one of the movers who helped Barbra get out of Ethan's Glen, part of Dick's legal package in his upcoming theft case against Barbra. Conway claimed in his affidavit that Victoria Spillers asked him during the move if he knew anybody who would assassinate Richard Minns, that she would pay anything.

Barbra Piotrowski didn't see or know about Conway's affidavit when it was executed, but the contents probably wouldn't have surprised her. It was the same modus operandi Richard used in his divorce, when he swore he received seven phone calls in the middle of the night from people set up by Mimi who threatened to hire hit men to shoot him.

The first weekend in May, Dudley Bell boarded a plane for Los Angeles and checked into the Beverly Hilton, in the heart of Beverly Hills. Then he got in his rental car and headed east on Route 5 to Fullerton, to a small detective agency owned by A. William Rosenfield.

Bell shot the breeze with Rosenfield for a few minutes. Then he got down to business. "I'm workin' on a case out of Houston," he said, in a low voice. "Big case. Millionaire named Richard Minns. His girlfriend, a little whore named Barbra Piotrowski, ran out on him and ripped him off for more than three hundred thousand dollars' worth of furniture and jewelry. Minns thinks she might have done the same thing to an old boyfriend of hers out here. Some doctor named Brad Katz. Took his Mercedes and probably ripped off his jewelry, too."

Bell's mission was clear: He wanted to get whatever information he could on Katz and Piotrowski while he was in California, and he wanted Rosenfield's help.

When Dudley Bell returned to Houston a few days later, he had a full report for Richard Minns. Minns was right, the detective related. Piotrowski pulled the same deal on Katz in 1976: walked out on him, stole his Mercedes, and ripped him off of some jewelry. He also had some other stuff on Piotrowski, Bell reported. Juicy stuff. The detective grinned and muttered something about being arrested for selling drugs to kids. Vagrancy charges. A heroin overdose.

Barbra Piotrowski got a startlingly different account of Dudley Bell's trip to California. The day after Bell checked into the Beverly Hilton, Brad Katz called her from Malibu, gravely concerned. A detective named William Rosenfield and some big, dark-headed man showed up at his office and his house that afternoon, Katz told Barbra, demanding to talk to him about five thousand dollars in jewelry she stole from him when they were living together. He talked to Rosenfield at the office, Katz related, and told him that Barbra Piotrowski had never stolen anything from him in her life, that he never gave her any jewelry, and that he never *had* any jewelry. Rosenfield, Katz said to Barbra, insinuated that if he was willing to come to Houston and claim the jewelry was his, he could "have" it. Brad Katz was appalled. What was going on?

A few days after Dudley Bell returned from L.A., Dick made a phone call to Evinia Rometsch. "How would the most eligible girl in Houston like to go out with the most eligible man?" he boomed.

"Who is this?" Evinia asked blankly. Rometsch suspected the caller was Richard Minns, but she had no desire to flatter what she considered his already gargantuan ego. She was aware that Dick and Barbra Piotrowski had broken up.

Everybody in their circle was laughing and joking about
how Barbra walked out on Dick. Obviously, Rometsch
pondered, Dick was calling her to get back at Willie, who
was befriending Barbra.

Evinia humored Dick for a few minutes. She had already
heard the rumor that Barbra had left with a lesbian lover, so
when Dick mentioned it to her, she was blasé. What stayed
with her from the conversation was the pain and hurt and
anger she heard in his voice. It was the voice of a man
whose ego was raw.

Barbra's preoccupation that spring was her theft case.
The idea of having a criminal record for a crime she didn't
believe she had committed haunted her night and day. With
Dick's connections, she might go to jail.

She discussed with Irv Weissman the possibility of testifying in front of a grand jury. The soft-spoken corporate
attorney was leery. Grand juries can do anything, he cautioned Barbra. They're like a legal wild card.

Barbra decided to take the risk. What did she have to
lose? she pointed out to Irv. Surely no grand jury would
ever indict her if they knew what really happened.

The first grand jury hearing, on April 7, was postponed.
Afterward, Irv Weissman called and met with the prosecutor in charge, Don McCormick, to let him know that Barbra
wanted to appear. McCormick, Weissman would remember,
was agreeable. When the grand jury hearing on Barbra's
case was postponed two or three times in the next six
weeks, McCormick called Weissman each time. Dick must
be running scared, Weissman and Barbra figured, afraid he
wouldn't get an indictment.

In the middle of May, Irv and Janice Weissman made plans
to spend a five-day weekend—Friday through Wednesday—
in Acapulco. As a safety precaution, Weissman called Don
McCormick, the grand jury prosecutor, to let him know,
and to tell him that Barbra still wanted to testify. Dick's
brother-in-law didn't expect the grand jury to meet during
the few days he was out of town; they'd been putting off
Barbra's case for almost two months and it wasn't scheduled
for the following week. Why should they hear it now?

The Friday Irv and Janice left, May 16, Barbra called
the district attorney's office, just to be sure. Her case, she

was told, was scheduled for the following Monday. Don McCormick would later claim the timing was a coincidence, but Irv Weissman has his own ideas. He was convinced Dick was tapping his phone and purposely arranged for the hearing while he was out of the country.

Whatever the machinations, on Monday morning at eight-thirty, Barbra Piotrowski was sitting on a wooden bench outside the grand jury room, dressed in her favorite color, white, nervously clutching a book in her hands. She glanced down the hall and saw Mimi Minns sitting on another bench, waiting. Barbra bit her lip. She wished Irv were there. She had so much riding on this. If she could convince the grand jury she was framed, the whole thing would be thrown out.

She opened her book and tried to read but her nerves were too jangled. Sometime in the middle of the morning, she thought she noticed Dick's back slipping into one of the side doors. Then Mimi disappeared. Barbra waited anxiously for minutes, then hours. Finally, she got up wearily and looked for the bailiff. "When are they going to call me to testify?" she queried. The bailiff barely looked up. "We'll have to see," he said perfunctorily. "It's up to the jury."

Barbra returned to her bench and forced herself to look at her book. Sometime after one-thirty, the bailiff walked up to her. "They're breaking for lunch now," he said matter-of-factly, "and they don't want to hear from you. They're all finished."

"What?" Barbra said, shocked. "Why not? I'm willing to tell them anything. Anything!"

The bailiff shrugged his shoulders. "I don't know. That's what they said."

Barbra pushed past him toward the door to the grand jury room and started pounding, tears streaming down her cheeks. She forced open the door. Inside, some of the grand jurors were getting up from their chairs. Others were in the kitchen area, pouring coffee. "Please!" she screamed, "I'm innocent! Please listen to my side of the story. You've got to hear my side. I was framed!" She started to sob.

Ed Thompson, a stern-faced high school teacher who had been elected sergeant at arms, stared at her through slit eyes as the rest of the grand jury looked on, bemused. "Bailiff!"

Thompson called out. "Get her out of here."

Mrs. W. T. Melton, one of the senior members sitting on the grand jury that day, had a hard time getting to sleep that night. The old woman kept seeing Barbra Piotrowski in her white dress, crying to be heard. It preyed on her conscience all through the night. There was something strange about that case, she agonized. Mrs. Melton felt it from the beginning. She hadn't thought much about it that morning when the bailiff told them one of the defendants wanted to testify. It was Mrs. Melton's first time to serve on a grand jury. This was all new to her. Before she had a chance to ponder the request, one of the other grand jurors, a well-to-do housewife named Joyce Hruzek, blurted out, "Oh, don't let her come in here because she would recognize me." Said she was a neighbor of Richard Minns's in Memorial. "Well, what difference does that make?" Mrs. Melton thought irritatedly. Seemed rather odd to her. Weren't you supposed to disqualify yourself if you knew one of the parties? But, no one else on the grand jury seemed to care one way or the other, so she didn't say anything. Then it all seemed to happen so quickly: The prosecutor presented Richard Minns's case in the time it took the assistant foreman, Mary Burke, to go to the bathroom. "What a mess," Mrs. Melton thought to herself, as she listened to Don McCormick. "Surely two grown people can do a better job than this." She was appalled. She didn't approve of Barbra Piotrowski living with a man—that simply wasn't done in her day—but she didn't understand where the criminal element came in at all. Then, when Barbra burst in, it was mass confusion. They were all breaking for lunch. Mrs. Melton was disoriented. If they'd been sitting in their regular seats, at the table, she might have been able to think more clearly, but they were all moving about. It was so confusing. . . .

All night, Mrs. Melton tossed and turned. She felt so sorry for that poor girl. She'd seen her on the bench outside the grand jury room that morning, sitting in her white dress, but she didn't know who she was. Why hadn't she stood up to Joyce Hruzek and said, "Look, I don't give a hoot if you know Richard Minns, Joyce! I want to hear what she has to say." She could have told her that. She could have said something when they got back from their break. All it took was one grand juror to speak up. Mrs. Melton hadn't spoken up and it was eating at her very soul.

The next morning, Mrs. Melton looked in the phone book for Victoria Spillers's number. She remembered the name from McCormick's presentation. Spillers was supposed to be a friend of Barbra Piotrowski's. Mrs. Melton picked up the phone and dialed the number. A woman answered. "Hello?" Mrs. Melton said haltingly. "Miss Spillers? I can't tell you my name, but I'm on the grand jury that heard Barbra Piotrowski's case yesterday. I'm breaking a rule by calling you, but I had to tell you how much I regret not going to bat for Barbra, not demanding to hear her. Please tell her that for me, would you?" Mrs. Melton hung up, trembling. She didn't know what they could do to her if they found out she'd called a witness—grand jurors are sworn to secrecy—and she was so ashamed for breaking the rule she didn't even tell her husband of fifty-odd years, who was sitting twenty feet from her. But Mrs. Melton didn't care. She had to absolve her conscience. She couldn't get the image of Barbra Piotrowski and her white dress out of her mind.

Exactly what went on with Barbra Piotrowski's case in the grand jury room, and before, is forever blurred. Don McCormick, the prosecutor who handled the case, would insist after the fact that it was the foreman of the grand jury who made the decision not to hear Barbra Piotrowski. All he did, McCormick would say defensively, was present the case. The foreman, James Lykes, a retired businessman, said it was up to the district attorney's office; that he would never have made a decision like that. Mary Burke, the assistant foreman, a housewife, was in the bathroom when the case was presented. All she remembered was coming out of the bathroom and seeing Barbra Piotrowski crying. The whole case upset her. It was weird. Joyce Hruzek, Richard Minns's neighbor, denied making a request not to hear Barbra Piotrowski. What struck Hruzek about the case was the cost of the furniture. All that fuss over some furniture from Sears!

Years later, Johnny Holmes, the district attorney for Harris County, would find what happened "hard to believe." If an

accused wanted to testify in front of a grand jury, Holmes
would say, he instructed his prosecutors not only to let the
person do so, but to encourage the grand jury to listen to
him. It was even in the D.A.'s operations manual.

Don McCormick, by his own admission, neither encouraged nor discouraged the grand jury to hear Barbra
Piotrowski's testimony and was hostile, years later, when
the subject was raised.

"To not encourage the grand jury," the district attorney
would say, "is not in keeping with office policy, and if I'd
known about it at the time, I'd have raised some hell."

If McCormick had encouraged them, Mrs. W. T. Melton
would say, that would have been all she needed to stand up
to Joyce Hruzek, to speak up for Barbra Piotrowski, to insist
that she be heard.

The day of the grand jury hearing, Irv Weissman's law
office was vandalized. The only items missing were three
files: the files of Barbra Piotrowski, Victoria Spillers, and
Richard Minns. When Weissman returned from Acapulco
and surveyed the damage from the break-in, he laughed
ironically. Shortly after the night of the search warrant,
he transferred all of Barbra Piotrowski's personal files to
a locked safe in the dental office next door. He hadn't
even told Barbra about the switch. The only things in the
remaining files were some inconsequential documents and
papers.

That night, Barbra was chatting on the phone with a
friend and mentioned how Irv had outsmarted a burglar
by moving her files from his office to the dental office in
his strip center on Westheimer.

The next morning, when Weissman arrived at his law
office, the dentist in the office next door was waiting to
see him. Someone broke into his office the night before.
The place was ransacked. Nothing was taken.

Irv Weissman shook his head. When he returned from
Acapulco, he had moved Barbra's files to a secret third
location.

The lawyer picked up the phone and made an appointment to see the prosecutor assigned to Richard Minns's
theft case. This had gone on long enough.

The following morning, Irv Weissman glanced through

the Minns file at the district attorney's office. Among the papers was a copy of a letter Weissman had written to Richard the day after the search warrant was executed, when all four of Weissman's tires were slashed. Irv was so angry he had dictated a letter to his brother-in-law suggesting if he was going to pull any more stunts like that, they should meet on a street corner and fight it out like men.

As Irv stared at the letter in the D.A.'s file, it dawned on him: Dick was trying to make it look like *they* were threatening *him*!

When he got home from the district attorney's office, Irv Weissman called Barbra over to his house. He was sorry, the avuncular attorney said solemnly, but he was going to have to pull himself off the case. It was obvious Dick wasn't going to settle, and his presence as her lawyer was only fanning the flames.

Barbra Piotrowski went home, consumed with gloom. She couldn't blame Irv for bowing out—he'd only been helping her as a favor. Still, things had never looked more discouraging. The internal affairs division of the police department was doing nothing with her complaint about Fincher and Wells. She hadn't heard back from the arson department about Mickey Brown in weeks. Her father had even gone to the FBI to complain about Charlie Wells's tactics in seizing the jewelry she gave to her mother. They regretted it, the FBI officials said solicitously, but there was nothing they could do. Wieslaw Piotrowski was comparing the situation to Nazi Germany.

But Barbra refused to leave Houston. Try as she might, she couldn't *make* herself stop loving Dick. Sometimes the urge to see him was so overwhelming she'd call the office just to hear his voice and hang up after he said hello. She could go on that, she would tell her friends wistfully, for weeks.

22

There was a kind of craziness about Richard Minns that summer, a wildness; he seemed irrational. The situation with Barbra, his friends and colleagues noticed, consumed him. He thought about it, talked about it, dreamed about it, schemed about it, twenty-four hours a day.

Matt Leeper was beginning to have his own moments when he thought Richard Minns was insane. At first the idea of prosecuting a theft case for a celebrity millionaire like Dick Minns had to have been exciting for a low-level assistant district attorney like Leeper, with stacks and stacks of garden-variety petty criminal cases overflowing his cramped office; but by early to midsummer, the glamour was wearing thin.

To prepare for trial, Leeper was obliged to meet with Richard Minns to go over the facts and evidence in the case. The problem, the young prosecutor discovered, was that, with Richard Minns, it was a never-ending process. The millionaire called him or stopped by his office nearly every other day, sometimes more than once in the same day, to review the same material, again and again, until Leeper could recite the sentences in his sleep.

Minns, Leeper determined, was possessed. He was also, the prosecutor concluded, still in love with Barbra Piotrowski, and said so. *Crazy* in love.

As the scorching months of Houston summer inched along, the situation grew more bizarre. Pages and pages of material about Barbra Piotrowski flooded into Leeper's office, all of it generated by Richard Minns. Peculiar, highly detailed information.

Among other things, Dick provided the prosecutor with

a "Schedule of Events," or chronology of what he perceived to be the significant incidents in his relationship with Barbra. He also sent Leeper a six-page typewritten dossier on Barbra. It was, by all accounts, a curious document. The first part featured an almost clinical description of Barbra with attached photographs for identification. The next section stated statistical data on her bank accounts, credit cards, driver's and nursing licenses, as well as her "arrest record": indictment for second-degree felony theft, "possession of dangerous drugs," and a "vagrancy charge" on December 10, 1973, in Los Angeles (the day Barbra and Oliver de la Torre were actually given tickets for jaywalking).

The second page listed her "Criminal Accomplices," Mary Victoria Spillers and Oliver Frederick de la Torre, with résumés, and "boyfriends" Joe Kalmick and Willie Rometsch, with brief descriptions of each man. One full page was devoted to "HABITS": "Does not wear make-up," "Bad (or careless) driver," "Frequents Baskin Robbins ice cream parlors, favorite flavor is 'Pralines & Cream' "; and another page to "PERSONALITY TRAITS": "Wants to be treated like a QUEEN," "Good 'con' artist," "Uses her body and sex," "Capable of extreme violence (Example: Tried to force her way into the Grand Jury room, in hysterics and screaming, and had to be forcibly removed)."

Perhaps the most unusual aspect of the dossier was a specific, almost minute-by-minute account of Barbra Piotrowski's typical day. Attached to the dossier was a detailed sketch of Barbra's apartment, within the apartment complex, and in the surrounding neighborhood.

Matt Leeper tried to ignore the barrage of propaganda filtering through his office courtesy of Richard Minns. It was almost as if he had invited the devil into his living room and now he couldn't get him to leave. The Minns case was fast becoming the hottest topic of summer gossip in the District Attorney's Building. Many an afternoon, Matt Leeper, Vic Pecorino, and Don McCormick sat around in bull sessions, analyzing and psychoanalyzing the players. Leeper shared his boss's theory of the case. Every time Minns came to his office to talk about the trial, the assistant district attorney noticed, Pat Hall was with him, saying how Barbra Piotrowski had used him. The whole case, Leeper would later say with distaste, was like a circus. Yet, had Richard Minns been a fireman instead of a fitness magnate, the district attorney's office probably wouldn't have been pursuing the case in the first place. Were it not for Dick Minns's powerful friends and millions of dollars, Matt Leeper wouldn't have given him the attention of a gnat.

When Irv Weissman pulled himself off the case, he recommended Marion Rosen, a well-known Houston trial attorney whose blonde, matronly appearance belied a singular and gritty determination. Barbra liked her immediately.

During their first meeting at Rosen's office, Barbra was filled with questions. In the past few months, the case had expanded beyond Irv's limited criminal experience. Now that she had an experienced trial lawyer in front of her, Barbra pommeled her with queries and suggestions. Might she have a case against Dick for false imprisonment? she wondered. How about false arrest? Or breach of promise?

Marion Rosen listened to Barbra's story and responded without hesitation. What she was describing, Rosen said emphatically, wasn't breach of promise, or even palimony. It was clearly a marriage according to Texas law.

Barbra looked at her quizzically. She had almost been embarrassed to bring up the ceremony Dick performed on their hotel balcony in Cozumel. *That* was a valid marriage?

Rosen nodded vigorously. The state of Texas, she explained, recognized an animal called a *common law* marriage. If the man and woman lived together and held themselves out as husband and wife, the state of Texas would recognize their union as a valid, legal marriage, even without a license. If Barbra wanted to, she could sue Richard Minns for divorce.

Barbra shifted uncomfortably in her chair, nodding without talking. She was lonely and confused. She knew that Dick's greatest paranoia was that people were after his money. If she sued him for divorce, it would put him over the edge.

Rosen nodded and agreed to concentrate on the criminal charges, which, she said, were ludicrous. Within a few days, on June 6, the blonde trial lawyer filed a motion to quash the search warrant Dick executed. In her legal document,

Rosen referred to Richard Minns and Barbra Piotrowski as married, and to the furniture Barbra allegedly appropriated as "community property."

If Dick didn't suspect that Barbra was considering a divorce action before then, Rosen's motion left no doubt.

Al Dugan was growing increasingly concerned about Dick. The oilman could only engage him in conversation if it centered on the theft case against Barbra. It was worse, far worse, than during his divorce from Mimi. He was acting, Dugan observed, *irrational*.

Without telling Dick, Al Dugan telephoned Barbra Piotrowski and asked if he could talk to her in person. When they got together, Dugan was brief. This wasn't really any of his business, the oilman said uncomfortably, but he felt the time had come for him to step in and act as peacemaker, to negotiate a "treaty." What would it take, Dugan asked Barbra, for her to drop her litigation?

Barbra was instantly receptive. When Dugan made an offer of seventy-five thousand dollars plus the Ethan's Glen townhouse, she agreed, on one condition. Her main concern, she told the oilman, were the theft charges against her. She was scared to death of having a criminal record. If she was going to settle with Dick, he had to agree to drop all the criminal charges against her.

Dugan nodded and promised to negotiate with Dick. The oil operator felt sorry for Barbra. Everyone around Dick was calling her a gold digger, but hell! What gold had she dug? Dick Minns was the cheapest man he knew. What kind of a gold digger went after some cheap furniture from Sears and Pier One Imports? It was ridiculous.

The instant he and Barbra parted company, Dugan got in touch with Dick. "I'm sick of your garbage," the oilman said irritatedly, when he had explained his conversation with Barbra. "I want a resolution to this."

Dick Minns agreed.

That night, Al Dugan went to bed a much relieved man. Perhaps now, he thought, everyone could get on with their lives.

Two days later, Dick called Al Dugan back. He couldn't go through with the deal, he said, citing some minor technicality. He had talked it over with his lawyers.

Dugan couldn't believe what he was hearing. "Dick," he said exasperatedly, "you can settle this, and you're a fool if you don't."

Dick refused to budge an inch.

"All right," Dugan said frostily. "Never speak to me again."

The oilman telephoned Barbra Piotrowski with a voice heavy with disappointment. "He backed out," he said simply. "I'm sorry." Dugan's tone changed suddenly. "Barbra," he said firmly, "I think you should leave Houston and go back to California. This whole situation is explosive." He paused ominously. "If you don't, somebody could get hurt."

But Barbra felt she couldn't leave Houston. She couldn't afford to fly back and forth for the hearings in the theft case. Besides, she reasoned, if she went back to California or somewhere else and something happened to her, the police would have a harder time connecting it to Dick. And she didn't *want* to leave Houston. Outwardly, she was succeeding in putting her life back together, bit by bit: teaching a few aerobics dance classes at churches and the YWCA (something Dick would never allow her to do); nursing in the burn unit at Hermann Hospital part-time; taking premed classes at the University of Houston; training with the Houston Herriers, a team of competitive runners, to run in the Honolulu Marathon in December. She even had a breast reduction to return her figure to its pre-Richard shape.

Dr. James Moore, a handsome young plastic surgeon who ran with the Herriers that summer, would remember Barbra as the most beautiful girl he had ever seen, fresh and wholesome and alive. But it was all a facade. The separation was literally consuming her. That summer, she took to stopping for a dozen glazed doughnuts whenever she felt a pang for Dick.

Every week, that spring and summer, something new and bizarre occurred. Not a fortnight passed that Barbra's tires weren't slashed. She changed her phone number regularly because of strange noises on the line.

In the middle of July, Marion Rosen regretfully backed out as Barbra's criminal lawyer. Her law partner was in a car accident and she was doing double duty. Every time she tried to reach Barbra, Barbra's number was disconnected or there was no answer. She could never find her when she needed her.

Barbra understood and sympathized with Rosen. Her own life was a living hell. She existed in a state of perpetual fear, forever looking over her shoulder to see if she was being followed. As if that weren't enough, Houston was experiencing its hottest summer ever. The city seemed to be on fire.

Barbra launched an exhaustive search to find the ideal attorney. If she had a skillful lawyer representing her at her theft trial, maybe she could defend herself against Richard, his power and his money. It was, she concluded, her only hope.

The last day in July, she made an appointment to see a young criminal defense attorney Willie Rometsch recommended, Dick DeGuerin, the sixth or seventh lawyer she had interviewed in as many days. On her way to the appointment, on the seedy fringes of downtown Houston, Barbra's car stalled. She glanced at her watch anxiously. She was already running late. She locked the door, grabbed her purse and walked the remaining blocks to DeGuerin's office.

Although he was still in his thirties, Dick DeGuerin had already achieved star status in Houston as a criminal defense attorney by representing Lilla Paulus, the sinister schoolmarm-looking widow accused of hiring the hit men who killed Houston plastic surgeon John Hill, who was himself under investigation for causing the mysterious death of his heiress-wife, Joan Robinson Hill. The case, and DeGuerin's legal exploits, were devoured by millions in the best-selling true crime thriller *Blood and Money*. Before the Paulus case, DeGuerin had been handpicked by the "king of the courtroom" Percy Foreman to be his crown prince. Foreman's trademarks were his almost mystical oratory and grand, theatrical courtroom gestures. Foreman could quote from the scripture, recite poetry, or tell a ribald tale from his rustic East Texas youth with equal facility.

The moment she took a seat in Dick DeGuerin's law office, Barbra Piotrowski felt safe, protected. There was never a question, she would later say, whether DeGuerin would represent her. The instant they shook hands, he somehow communicated that he was taking care of her. She wasn't interviewing him to be her attorney; he *was* her attorney. That was Dick DeGuerin's special gift. He had that rare ability to listen to another human being's problems and make him feel they were his problems. Of course it didn't hurt that he was a good-looking man with modish long blond hair, a disarming grin, and a penchant for wearing cowboy boots with his three-piece suits.

DeGuerin got straight to the heart of the matter with Barbra. Yes, she might have cause for a divorce suit, he told her. Maybe even a palimony case—Foreman and DeGuerin had a national reputation in divorce law—but that was down the road somewhere. Right now, the priority was the criminal case. Dick's charges, DeGuerin pointed out to Barbra, were a very serious matter. They needed to concentrate on the theft case. He was, he added, intrigued by something Barbra mentioned during their meeting: that at least some of Richard Minns's famous birthday stunts were bogus. Dick DeGuerin was a master at trying a case in the press. That information, he thought excitedly, could be devastating.

Barbra walked out of DeGuerin's office with a huge sigh of relief. She had found her Protector.

When she got a ride to the spot where her car had stalled, her heart jumped. The red Firebird rental car was nowhere to be seen. A few frantic telephone calls later, she located the Firebird in a police storage lot. Muttering under her breath, she arranged for a ride to the impounding lot. Once there, she paid the fine and asked the attendant if he would help her jump-start her car. Under the hood was a mysterious black metal box with two wires leading to the inside of the car.

A few minutes later, two uniformed police officers pulled into the impounding lot. When they saw the device under the hood of the Firebird, they refused to touch it. Several hours later, an officer from the Bomb Squad and another from Special Operations arrived at the storage lot to examine Barbra's car. They traced the two black wires on the metal box to the electric ignition. Then they cut the wires and took the device to the police lab for further study.

The next day, a pair of FBI agents visited Barbra at her apartment. After an inspection, they informed Barbra her apartment was bugged. There was nothing, they said apologetically, they could do about it without more evidence. Richard Minns was too powerful.

Shortly thereafter, the report from the Bomb Squad was released. The device on Barbra Piotrowski's car, they determined, probably wasn't a bomb. The problem was, they weren't exactly sure what it was.

Sometimes, when she walked up to her apartment at the end of the day and unlocked the door, Barbra imagined herself being shot in the back of the head. She whispered her fears to Tanya McCary, a pretty blonde from her aerobics class and to her old professor, Barry Kaplan. They thought Barbra was being absurd.

Barbra channeled her nervous energy into training for the Honolulu Marathon in December. Barbra always had to have a goal, some kind of focus. With Dick out of her life, running became her obsession. She jogged every day—sometimes with Barry Kaplan, or Dick DeGuerin. Like Barbra, the criminal lawyer was an inveterate runner with limitless energy. As they were cooling off in his backyard one afternoon following a run through Memorial Park, the attorney mentioned to Barbra that she needed to be extra careful. A few years back, he had represented a private detective named Dudley Bell on some wiretapping charges. Bell had shown up at his office the other day, DeGuerin said, with some unflattering photographs of Barbra going in and out of her apartment.

Barbra's mind started clicking. She had heard Dick mention the name Dudley Bell several times while they were living together, but she couldn't remember when or why. Only that she knew the name.

"He's obviously following you and tapping your phone," DeGuerin commented, interrupting her thoughts. The lawyer laughed ironically. "Bell also told me you had herpes and warned me to stay away from you."

A look of disgust played on Barbra's features. That was

Dick's m.o.—to attack his opponent with a bunch of lies. He did the same thing to Mimi!

Dick DeGuerin laughed it off. It didn't take a genius, he mused, to figure out that Dick Minns was behind that message. Minns was obviously jealous as hell. Afraid that DeGuerin was doin' it with Barbra. The criminal lawyer grew thoughtful. "I think you'd better take extra precautions," he advised. "Park your car in a locked garage. That kind of thing."

On August 14, the internal affairs division of the Houston Police Department sent a letter to Barbra Piotrowski informing her that they had completed their investigation of Detective Charles Wells and G. N. Fincher. Their actions, they concluded, were lawful and proper.

When Barbra opened the envelope she didn't know whether to scream or cry. Where else could she turn for help? Barbra asked her bodyguard, Michel Font, who had a connection to the governor, Bill Clements, to arrange an appointment. She had to tell someone about what Richard Minns was doing to her. Clements communicated back that, unless something happened, there was nothing he could do.

Toward the end of the month of August, Barbra wrote a letter to her father. Wes Piotrowski was still attempting to open an investigation of official misconduct. "Dear Dad," she wrote. "Enclosed are some things that you may want to include in your letter. You might also pose the question, 'Are we going to be facing another famous Texas murder trial before anyone is willing to pay attention?' Love, Barbra"

More than once, Barbra thought back on Dick's words to her during his divorce from Mimi: "With my connections, I could get away with murder in the State of Texas." But Barbra could not bring herself to leave. It had become, for her, a fight of good versus evil. She had to know the legal system would protect her. She had always had that streak of stubbornness. She didn't know when, or how, to give up. It was, she would say later, her greatest flaw.

Come September, Barbra picked up a few more classes at the University of Houston. She was determined to get in as many courses as she could, in spite of the constant interruptions and distractions. Twice in October, her car was broken into at the University of Houston campus and voodoo dolls left inside.

She tried to ignore the bizarre goings on. She was working on a plan to form a corporation out of the aerobics classes she was teaching, to open a quasi-fitness center. Dick had asked her to sign a ten-year noncompetition agreement when she started modeling for the clubs, so she couldn't form the corporation in her name. But, Barbra figured, if she used her friend Tanya McCary's name on the papers, she wouldn't violate the agreement. She had even pocketed enough money from her two jobs to make a down payment on a tiny townhouse in the River Oaks Condominiums complex. Barbra truly liked Houston. She felt at home there.

Barbra forced herself not to dwell on her upcoming theft trial, which had been postponed several times over the summer and early fall. It looked like the case was finally going to trial the week of October 20. She preferred to leave the details to Dick DeGuerin and concentrate on the positive things that were happening in her life.

The second weekend in October, her car started acting up again. Barbra called a friend to come over and fix the rented red Firebird. Then she borrowed another friend's blue sports car to use over the weekend. She jogged with friends, worked on her dance plans, laughed. Life was better, much better, than it had been in months.

The tall man with the wavy hair was getting impatient. "Damn-it-all," *he cursed to the man from California with the long muttonchop sideburns and the thick, Pancho Villa mustache.* "It's got to be done NOW." "I can't help it," *the California man shrugged.* "My men were staked out in the parking lot all weekend. The red Firebird didn't move for two days. Are you sure that's the chick's car?" *The big man looked at him with supreme irritation.* "Yes!" *he snapped,* that was Barbra Piotrowski's car. *He gave the man from California a steely look.* "You've got until Monday," *he harked.* "October twenty. Otherwise the deal's off."

Barbra got up earlier than usual on Monday morning. Michel Font was gone, so she was alone in the apartment for the first time since the night of the search warrant. The thought barely occurred to her. At five-thirty A.M., she was in her leotards, choreographing new dance routines for her aerobics class. Monday was usually Barbra's housecleaning day—the day she set aside to take out the trash, do the laundry, meet a friend to run. But this Monday she had too many other things on her mind. The aerobics dance business was beginning to take shape. She had already drawn up the papers for Tanya McCary and herself, and she had some institutions on line who would let them use their facilities to teach the classes.

While Barbra was walking through the steps of a new routine, the phone rang. She picked it up and said hello. There was silence, then a click. Barbra muttered under her breath. She wouldn't even answer the door anymore. She was too afraid. The night before, when she was getting out of the shower, someone rang her doorbell and pounded furiously. Barbra peered through the peephole and saw two black men standing outside. One of them asked for "Lucy." Barbra shouted through the door, "Try next door." She barely even went outside to empty her trash anymore. She wasn't about to open her door to two strangers.

The hang-up call jolted Barbra back to reality. She glanced at her watch. My God! she thought, startled. It was already five forty-five. She was supposed to meet her friend Jerry Hernandez to go running and she hadn't even gotten to the cleaning. Where did the day go? She wiped the sweat off her forehead—was the summer heat ever going to end? she wondered—and dialed Jerry's number. Barbra apologized for being late. Jerry was unruffled. He suggested they go for one of their long slow distance runs. Barbra could meet him at his place at River Oaks Townhouses, then they could run up through Memorial along the park and then jog back— about twelve miles altogether. Barbra needed to push herself for the Honolulu Marathon. She quickly threw on a pair of jogging shorts and a T-shirt, tied a bandana around her forehead, over her ponytail, and picked up a sweatband for her wrist.

When she stepped outside from her air-conditioned apartment, the heat hit her like a wall. Visitors to Houston in the summer and early fall can't fathom how the natives survive in this perpetual sauna. This fall was worse than ever. The sweltering summer heat refused to lift. Barbra minded it less than most.

As she got in her car and started the ignition, Barbra reminded herself that her life seemed to be improving. But her stomach clenched as she thought of Dick. Tears trickled down her face, first slowly, then in heaving sobs. She cursed Dick Minns. She could will herself to do anything she ever tried to do; why couldn't she *will* herself to stop loving Dick?

Barbra swung her red Firebird into the Winchell's parking lot. A doughnut would make her feel better. It always did.

The two black men in the long red Cadillac careened around the corner through the rush-hour traffic. "Hey man!" *the one in the passenger seat shouted, pointing toward Beechnut.* "I think that's her car!"

Barbra pulled into a parking space at Winchell's and reached in her wallet for two dollar bills. Then she tossed the wallet on the passenger's seat next to her purse and ran in. She was so upset she didn't even notice she had left the car running and the door open.

She stood at the counter and hurriedly ordered an apple fritter and a glazed doughnut, turning away with embarrassment at her tear-streaked face. *How much longer*, Barbra wondered, *can I go on like this?*

She carried the white Winchell's bag to the car and jumped in, closing the door behind her. As she turned to put her wallet back in her purse, Barbra noticed a figure approaching the car to her left. She put the Winchell's bag between the two bucket seats and looked up. A young black man wearing a green ski hat was hovering over her door, holding a paper bag level with her head. His whole body was shaking, like a leaf fluttering in the wind.

Barbra knew she was staring into the face of her assassin. It was the scene she'd been imagining for months. How many times had she thought about what she would do, how she would react, when it happened? She immediately threw the car into reverse and pushed on the accelerator.

From the corner of her eye Barbra caught a glimpse of the man fumbling with the paper bag. Then she saw the silver glimmer of a pistol pointed at her head.

She ducked instantly. The red Firebird lurched backward, then it died. Barbra went cold. It was the same thing the car had been doing since that device was installed. Her heart beat wildly. *Why,* she thought, *aren't I dead?*

She heard a loud blast, like an explosion. After a pause, her insides began to burn, as if she were being torched. *So this is what it's like to be shot*, Barbra thought to herself. She was amazed she was so aware. The bullets kept coming—one, two, three, four in a row, like bombs going off in her ear. She felt the first bullet enter her body, and she could sense it now, piercing her lung. Barbra ducked down farther, as if she could make herself small enough to disappear.

The whole thing was over in a few seconds. To Barbra, it seemed like an eternity. She felt her lungs collapse inside her. She started gurgling, struggling desperately to breathe. Suddenly, every part of her body went numb except her hands. Her vision disappeared. Instinctively, she reached down to touch her legs. She couldn't find them. She groped with her hands. What she felt seemed flabby and loose, like jello. Barbra's heart seemed to be pounding out of her chest. As a nurse, she had heard that when a person dies, the flesh becomes flaccid.

Suddenly, it was eerily quiet. Barbra tried to move, but she was too weak. Flashes of images appeared before her, then disappeared. The inside of her body felt as though it were on fire. She gasped for breath, but she couldn't seem to get any air.

Don't let me die, she thought to herself. She tried to speak, but all that came out was a gurgle. *Maybe*, she thought desperately, *if I conserve my energy I'll have a chance of getting through this alive*. She raised her hands and fumbled for the horn. She heard voices surrounding her and saw brief outlines of people staring into the car. It was surreal, like a scene from a movie played in slow motion.

As she lay in her blood, pain shooting through her body, Barbra felt a strange sense of relief. She had been afraid of this for months. Now, at last, it was over.

She heard a man's voice call out, "Who did this to you?"

Barbra opened her mouth to answer, but choked on the bubbles. She struggled to draw breath, to force herself to speak. Finally a few words came out. They were but a faint whisper.

"My husband. Dick Minns."

23

Barbra Piotrowski wasn't the only one who believed she was going to be killed that fall. A month before the shooting, John Liles, a detective with the criminal intelligence division of the Houston Police Department, picked up a tip that there was a contract floating around on Barbra Piotrowski; that the girl was going to get "hit." Liles, so he would claim, wrote up the tip in a criminal activities report and turned it over to homicide where it languished, he said, untouched and unseen.

When word of the shooting leaked out, everybody in Houston had something to say. The hairs on the back of Vic Pecorino's neck stood on end. "Great God Almighty!" the assistant district attorney shuddered. He knew Pat Hall was spooky. Thought that she wanted Barbra Piotrowski *out of the way.* "I'll bet," he speculated, "she hired someone to do it. Or else she pushed old Dick into it."

In a tidy house across town, Mrs. W. T. Melton saw Barbra Piotrowski's picture flash on the TV news and heard the report of the shooting. The old woman shook violently. "Oh, why?" she cried out. "Why didn't I speak up, force the grand jury to listen to her? All this could have been avoided." The old woman hung her head in shame.

Irv Weissman silently berated himself. All those years, the graying lawyer pondered, he knew that his brother-in-law was eccentric, a tyrant; but he never thought he would go so far as to have someone killed. Yet he knew with every ounce of his being that Dick was behind the shooting. Absolutely. The lawyer's heart went out to Barbra. He had misjudged Dick Minns.

Houston's café society was buzzing. The only individuals in Houston *without* an opinion about the Piotrowski shooting were, ironically, the members of the police department.

At six-fifteen P.M. on October 20, Officers William Hanby and Don Pannell were in their patrol car, working their way through the last of the Monday rush-hour traffic on Beechnut at the end of a routine day. As Pannell approached the intersection of Beechnut and Gessner, he heard a loud popping noise. His partner jerked his head in the direction of the pop. Both men recognized the sound of a gunshot.

William Hanby glanced over to the Winchell's doughnut shop on the corner of Beechnut and Gessner. A black man with both arms extended was firing a pistol through the window of the driver's side of a red Firebird. Hanby threw open his door, grabbed a shotgun out of the back seat, and ran through the traffic to the Winchell's parking lot.

As he loped toward the scene of the shooting, Hanby noticed a white-over-red Cadillac with a black man sitting behind the wheel. By the time he got to the Firebird, the shooting had stopped and the man with the gun was nowhere to be seen. Hanby ran around to the other side of the Winchell's building. Something told him the red Cadillac was the getaway car.

As he rounded the building, Hanby saw the black man get into the Cadillac. "Halt!" he commanded, leveling his shotgun at the car. "Police officer!" The black man turned for an instant and paused, locking eyes with Hanby. The policeman froze, debating whether it was safe to shoot. The Cadillac squealed out of the parking lot. Inside, the two black men turned around and stared, wild-eyed, at William Hanby.

Seconds later, Don Pannell swung the patrol car into the parking lot. Hanby jumped in and the two officers took off. Once he was inside the car, Hanby radioed for an ambulance to pick up the woman in the red Firebird. He didn't get a good look at her, but he figured if she wasn't dead, she was close to it.

The two policemen followed the red Cadillac behind the shopping center and onto the entrance ramp to the Southwest Freeway, dodging and weaving through the evening traffic. Suddenly, as they approached the Texas Instruments Building, the Cadillac darted across the lanes of the freeway to the exit ramp. Hanby and Pannell were right behind it. As they watched, the red Cadillac screeched into a U-turn and lurched out of control toward a pole, then crashed into another car. The two blacks hopped out and ran into a nearby field. Pannell and Hanby drove up to the Cadillac, jumped out and followed on foot. In the middle of the field, Barbra Piotrowski's would-be assassins lay down, crouched, waiting to be arrested.

Seldom before had a case fallen so literally in the laps of the Houston police.

As Barbra Piotrowski's attempted killers were being handcuffed and taken to jail, a pair of patrol officers on the evening shift were standing in the parking lot of Winchell's writing up a routine report. Unless there was an actual death, the Houston police didn't bother to send a homicide detective to the scene. There were too many killings in the city of Houston for homicide to handle. And, so far at least, Barbra Piotrowski wasn't dead.

In her dreams, Barbra was running. Her patient's respirator alarm was ringing. She had to get to him, to find out what was wrong. As she reached the respirator, she opened her eyes and saw the clock in the emergency room. She glanced down at her body and realized, in a sick flash, that she was the patient. The respirator was hers.

Barbra choked on the tube in her throat. Her nurse's instinct, as she lay bent over the driver's seat of her Firebird, was correct: both her lungs had collapsed, crushing her heart. Three large tubes penetrated her chest, sucking the blood from her lungs. Another tube traveled through her nose to her stomach, emptying its contents. A catheter controlled her urine and I.V. tubes poked into her arm and neck veins. Three of her ribs had been shattered into fragments, several vertebrae were broken and metal wires were holding her chest together. Her entire body ached with pain. All except her legs. Barbra's heart stopped. Her legs! Where were they? She reached down to feel them but her hands were tied to the side of the bed. Barbra fell into a morphine stupor, unaware that her spinal cord had been severed by direct hits from two of the bullets. All feeling, movement and bodily function had been cut off from the chest down.

Twenty-four hours later, after emergency surgery that saved her life, Barbra looked up and saw her father's kind, sad eyes, tears flowing from them. He didn't say a word, but she could read Wes Piotrowski's eyes. "Don't cry for me, Dad," she said in a hoarse whisper. "I will walk again." They were her first words since the shooting.

At eight-thirty on Tuesday morning, Captain Bobby Adams in Homicide got a phone call. The voice on the other end of the line belonged to John Liles, an undercover cop with the criminal intelligence division. About a month before, Liles told Adams, one of his sources tipped him off that Dudley Bell had offered ten thousand dollars for him to kill the Piotrowski girl.

If the shooting at Winchell's had seemed routine to the homicide division of the Houston Police Department the night before, by breakfast time it was beginning to dawn on them they were dealing with a hot case.

Adams called one of his young homicide detectives, Ken Williamson, into his office to tell him about Liles's call. Maybe Williamson could get some more information out of him, Adams thought in passing.

Homicide was like a three-ring circus. By mid-morning, six detectives were working different angles of the Piotrowski case, with no one in charge and scant coordination.

If a leader emerged, it was Ken Williamson. Kenny Williamson was the personification of the all-American boy: a handsome ex-jock who addressed all ladies as "ma'am"; soft-spoken, polite, easygoing. Williamson's very presence on the force was something of a fluke. After a freshman year on the "party plan" at the University of Houston, his best friend decided to join the police academy and asked Kenny to go with him. The friend was rejected; Ken became a cop. In ten years, he worked patrol, switched to narcotics, married a judge's daughter, and advanced to a detective in homicide. But it wasn't just his charm and clean-cut good looks that promoted Kenny Williamson in the ranks; beneath his affability, there was a dogged determination, a Southern Baptist compulsion to see good triumph over evil.

After his briefing with Adams, Ken Williamson marched straight to John Liles's door to question Liles about his mysterious "tip" about a contract on Barbra Piotrowski. Liles was cautious. He couldn't name his source, he told Williamson. He had to protect him. Ken Williamson tried to contain his frustration. The two cops thought along very different lines. With Kenny, everything was black and white. John Liles, by virtue of his job in criminal intelligence, spent more time in a sea of gray. He was constantly among informants, snitches, contacts he cultivated in the shadows of the night. Where Kenny Williamson was direct and modest, John Liles was, by nature, quiet, mysterious—"the Dudley Bell of the police department," Kenny once dubbed him, in less than admiring terms. And, in fact, John Liles's path had crossed more than once with Dudley Bell's over the years.

Williamson had no patience for Liles's concerns. A woman's life was at stake. "Look," Williamson finally said impatiently, showing Liles a list of names of people close to Dudley Bell and Richard Minns. "You're either gonna let me talk to your source yourself, or I'm gonna subpoena everybody on this list."

Ulimately, Liles agreed. The man who gave him the tip was Rick Waring, a black belt in karate who sometimes worked for Dudley Bell. It was, Ken Williamson would soon find out, the same karate expert Dudley Bell hired in May to act as a bodyguard for Richard Minns.

Kenny Williamson picked up the phone and dialed Dick DeGuerin's number. DeGuerin had represented Dudley Bell a couple of times over the years. He knew the private investigator personally. Maybe, Williamson thought, DeGuerin could clear this up.

Williamson was evasive. "You know Dudley Bell," he said to DeGuerin suggestively, "right?" The lawyer agreed. "Do you think," the homicide detective asked tentatively, "it's possible Dudley could be involved in this thing?"

Dick DeGuerin paused. "No," he said thoughtfully, after a second. "I don't think so. Dudley's not that sort of fellow."

Williamson hung up. *I wonder*, he thought darkly.

Fifteen minutes away, at Hermann Hospital, two other detectives from homicide, Gil Schultz and Mike Kardatzke, were in the intensive care unit taking a statement from a patient identified as Susan Smith. The first thing Wes Piotrowski did was change his daughter's name on hospital records. Who was to say that someone might not come and finish the job?

Barbra could hardly breathe, much less talk. She wondered, at times, how a person could feel so much pain and still be alive. Her doctors advised her not to meet with the police, to wait until she was stronger, but Barbra Piotrowski was determined to speak, to tell her story. Perhaps now someone would believe her.

She was certain, she told the two homicide sergeants, that her "husband," Dick Minns, was responsible for the shootings. "I had gotten warnings," she said weakly, "that I was going to be hurt, and I knew right then and there that Dick had sent someone to kill me."

Detectives Schultz and Kardatzke looked dubious.

Barbra forced herself to talk, passing out several times: how Dick was afraid she was going to divorce him, how he had her thrown in jail on false charges when she was pregnant, his threats and harassment of her and her family.

As she laid out her story, Barbra was surprised to find that she felt no vengeance. She was filled, instead, with a sense of relief, release. Her worst fear had been realized, and she had survived. For the first time in many months, she was not consumed by a longing, a yearning, for Richard. She was no longer tormented.

Before they left, Sergeants Schultz and Kardatzke showed Barbra a picture of a tall, hulking man with salt-and-pepper hair and a full, pasty face. Did she recognize him?

Barbra stared at the photograph closely. The man did look familiar. But why? Then she remembered. She had seen him before: once, when she was coming out of Dick DeGuerin's office. Another time, he was out walking a dog. And a third time, somewhere else. Who was he?

Schultz and Kardatzke answered in unison: Dudley Bell.

Barbra shivered. All those weeks, she'd been looking in her rearview mirror for someone who was following her. Dudley Bell was there all the time. She just didn't know it.

Late that day, Kenny Williamson, John Liles, and Rick Waring met in a darkened car in the parking lot near the Woodhollow Apartments, a singles complex in southwest Houston.

Rick Waring spoke in hushed whispers. Around April, the karate instructor said nervously, Dudley Bell called him and told him he'd pay him a hundred dollars a day to bodyguard a rich guy named Richard Minns, who had a big hassle. Waring had known Bell for twenty years and sometimes worked for him as an investigator, sometimes as a bodyguard. Bell wanted him to carry a gun and stay close to Minns, in case anyone tried to jump him. He guarded Minns for a couple of weeks, Waring told Williamson, then gave up. Minns was too careless, any amateur could get him; he came and went at odd hours to odd places, fumbled with his keys, parked and moved in dark locations. Waring couldn't bodyguard someone like that. Around May, Waring said, Bell changed his assignment. He wanted him to follow Barbra Piotrowski instead: to trail her when she jogged in Memorial Park, listen to her conversations, pick up anything he could.

Waring pulled out a form with the title FIELD REPORT and handed it to Ken Williamson. In the upper-left corner was the letterhead DUDLEY BELL INTERNATIONAL. Next to it was Bell's logo: a representation of the globe, with the scales of justice superimposed. The form had been filled out in Waring's handwriting, for Sunday, May 18, 1980. On it was a minute-by-minute account of Barbra Piotrowski's activities that day as she jogged with Willie Rometsch.

Kenny Williamson studied the report. The country boy with the "old-timey values" could feel his blood pressure rising.

Sometime that summer, Rick Waring told Ken Williamson as they sat huddled in the parked car, he began hearing things about Piotrowski—in the park and around Dudley Bell's office. Intimations that she was going to be made to disappear. Bell eventually approached him, Waring said, and talked in cloaked terms about a hit, and mentioned a figure of ten thousand dollars. Waring refused, but the talk continued all through the summer and fall. Everyone around Dudley knew about the contract, and everyone knew Dudley was working for Richard Minns. A few times, Waring heard Bell on the phone with Minns, discussing Barbra Piotrowski. By September, Waring told Williamson, he decided to tell John Liles about it. He and Liles were old drinking buddies. Liles knew Dudley from way back. Waring was beginning to think Dudley may have pulled him in to take the fall when Piotrowski was killed. Waring was looking for a way out. He told Liles somebody was going to make a run on Barbra Piotrowski, that it was going to be traced back to Dudley, and he didn't want to get blamed.

Ken Williamson listened and observed. Waring, a black belt in karate who stood over six feet four inches, a man who had no reason to fear anybody or anything, was quivering.

The meeting broke up before midnight. Kenny Williamson drove home, replaying what he had heard in his mind. Did Liles ever write a criminal activities report? Williamson wondered. If so, where was it? Or was Liles too close to Dudley, too close to all the players? Perhaps he wanted to distance himself from a nasty situation.

Williamson patted a small object on the seat next to him and grinned. Liles and Waring didn't know it, but they had just been tape-recorded.

The next day, homicide received official notification of the ownership of the 1979 white-over-red Cadillac driven by Barbra Piotrowski's attempted assassins. The car was traced to Transport Leasing Specialists in Rialto, California.

Ken Williamson immediately placed a call to the owner of the company, Walt Helms. Helms was friendly, cooperative. The Cadillac, Helms told the detective, actually belonged to a man named Robert Jess Anderson, from whom he had bought the company in February. Anderson had just been divorced and was awarded the car; the title hadn't been switched over to his name yet. Did he have a picture of Anderson? Williamson inquired. The answer was yes.

The following morning, Wednesday, Kenny Williamson opened a Federal Express envelope from Walt Helms with a snapshot of Robert Jess Anderson. Anderson was wearing a plaid shirt and appeared to be stocky, maybe in his late forties, with long muttonchop sideburns and a thick, Pancho Villa mustache.

Three days after Barbra Piotrowski was shot, her two attempted assassins started talking. Their names were Patrick Tony Steen and Nathaniel Ivery, they were both in their twenties, from Riverside, California, and they were each on intimate terms with trouble. Steen sometimes worked as a waiter at a café in Riverside called Rocco's; Ivery described himself as a "self-employed gardener." More often than not, they could be found on the streets.

Steen, the driver of the white-over-red Cadillac and the younger of the two at twenty-one, was skittish with Ken Williamson, guardedly cooperative. He told of meeting someone at Rocco's—identified only as "the man"—who asked him and Nathan to go to Houston to pick up a Cadillac and drive it back to California. When they got to Houston, "the man" asked them if they wanted to shoot a broad who was blackmailing a dude. He gave them her address and license plate number and said she jogged in Memorial Park all the time and that she went to the University of Houston. He told them she drove a red Firebird and had blonde hair and that she would be very nervous and "hanky" because she thought someone might be after her.

He and Nathan cruised the black neighborhoods in Houston, Steen told Ken Williamson, scored some drugs, and stole a gun. "Then we started going by her apartment where she was living. We drove out to her apartment three different times." Once, Steen said, Nathan rang her bell "and wanted to shoot her through the door, but I talked him out of it and we left." The next day, Steen confessed, he and Ivery saw her drive up to Winchell's. Nathan asked him to pull into the parking lot. "I am volunteering this information," Patrick Steen said in his statement, "because I have a conscience and because I know it was wrong for Nathan to shoot the girl."

Nathaniel Ivery, the man who plugged four bullets into Barbra Piotrowski on Monday, who wore a ski hat to cover his unruly Afro, was, by Thursday, ready to reveal anything and everything he knew.

A few months back, he told Detective Tom Ladd, he and Patrick sold some tires to a man named Bob Anderson, whom Patrick knew from Rocco's restaurant. Anderson later hired them for a hundred bucks apiece to set fire to some trucks in Colton, California. Sometime afterward, Anderson brought up a "deal" to kidnap a girl.

"He told us that he did not know the reason that the girl was supposed to be kidnapped," Ivery told Ladd, "but it had something to do with her possibly being pregnant and that she might cause trouble for this guy and his family. He did not tell us the man's name, but did say, 'Would you believe this, it is a judge?' He said that it would be better if she was dead, but that the kidnapping would be all right. He told us that we could come down [to Houston] and pick up a Cadillac, kidnap her and take her back to California, where we could hold her."

A while later, Ivery said in his statement, Anderson asked him and Steen to drive a trailerful of goods to Houston in a caravan with Anderson and a few other people. When they got to Houston, Anderson checked them into a motel and gave them a .44. They met him later, at his farm north of Houston, and from there went to a house nearby, where they picked up the Cadillac.

When they got to Houston, Ivery told Sergeant Ladd, the plans changed. Anderson met him and Patrick in Memorial Park and said he wanted them to kill the girl, not kidnap her. The price was ten thousand dollars: two thousand for Anderson, and four thousand each for him and Pat. Anderson showed them a piece of paper with the girl's name, address, license number, type of car, and description written on it. He said the man who wanted the hit was "Judge Dudley Smith." The judge needed her killed because she was turning state's evidence against him.

Anderson tried to drive them to the girl's apartment, Ivery said, but he got lost, so he called Judge Dudley Smith. Dudley Smith told Anderson to meet him at a Denny's. The judge never showed. Anderson called him again, Ivery told Detective Ladd, and this time they drove to either a Sheraton or a Marriott. Before Anderson went inside the hotel to meet the judge, he told them Dudley Smith was a "big man," six feet three inches or six feet four. He pointed to a black-over-gray Cadillac in the hotel parking lot. "That's his car," he said. When Anderson returned from the hotel, he drove them to the girl's apartment off Beechnut.

"We then began setting up on the girl's apartment so that we could get the job," Ivery confessed. "We started this the next day. We watched the apartment but nothing happened. We went to the U of H and tried to get some information on her classes but we were unable to do it. We went back and set on the apartment. We knew that she jogged so we got up one morning very early and got over there around four A.M. and found that she was already gone. On another occasion we got to her apartment around six P.M. and her car was there. We stayed there watching the car from that time till one P.M. the next day. All this time her car did not move. On another occasion we went and knocked on her door, trying to get her to open it. She would not open the door so we left."

Bob Anderson was staying with a guy named "Jerry," Nathan Ivery told the police. He didn't know if Jerry was involved in the hit or not. "After we tried several times to get the girl and failed, we went out to Jerry's to talk to Bob. He kept pressuring us to finish the girl and told us that the job had to be done by Monday."

He and Steen went back to the apartment and stayed in their car all Sunday night and part of Monday, Ivery confessed. The Firebird never moved. Then they returned to the University of Houston. On their way back to the girl's apartment, they saw her red Firebird and followed her to a doughnut shop. Anderson had told him to wrap the .44 in a cushion when he shot her, Ivery said, so he put it inside a seat cushion and stuffed it in a paper bag. When he tried to fire it, the .44 jammed, so he took out another gun he and Patrick had stolen the week before and shot the chick.

"I knew that I had hit her," Nathan Ivery said, "because on the last shot I heard her go *UGH*."

Later that day, Ken Williamson and Tom Ladd showed Patrick Steen a photograph of a beefy man standing on a balcony in front of palm trees with his back to the ocean.

He was wearing a plaid shirt and a gold medallion and had long, muttonchop sideburns and a thick Pancho Villa mustache.

The man in the picture, Steen told the two detectives, was the person he knew as Bob Anderson. "The same Bob Anderson that approached me to kill Barbra Piotrowski."

Within hours after Patrick Steen and Nathan Ivery made their confessions, a criminal lawyer appeared to represent them. Not just any criminal lawyer; a criminal lawyer with a major reputation in Houston. His name was James Eddie Tatum, known to all as Jim. Often referred to as "the cowboy of the legal profession," he wore cowboy boots to court—with blazers and shirt boldly unbuttoned to reveal a muscled, machismo chest. Jim Tatum preferred to think of himself as a sportsman first and a lawyer a humble second. And his occasional crony in athletic adventure was Richard Minns.

Tatum owned an office building on the corner of Main Street and Caroline, near the criminal courthouse, where he was known to occasionally offer space to private investigators. In October 1980, when he offered his legal services to Nathaniel Ivery and Patrick Steen, Tatum was providing office space for one Dudley Clifford Bell, Jr. Earlier in the year, one of Bell's scrapes with the legal system stuck and his private investigator's license was taken away. Jim Tatum came to the rescue.

Jim Tatum and Dudley Bell had met on opposite sides of a lawsuit in the early seventies. Each man recognized, admired, and appreciated the peculiar attributes of the other. Steen and Ivery did not know Jim Tatum from Job. Whoever sent him to their aid, and why, was, to them, an utter mystery.

To Dick DeGuerin, Barbra's criminal defense lawyer, it was an ominous sign.

On Saturday, five days after the fact, the *Houston Chronicle* printed a front-page story with the lurid headline: TWO CHARGED IN TRY TO KILL 'MISTRESS' IN TYCOON'S DIVORCE CASE. Houston homicide had been trying to keep the Piotrowski case a secret so the detectives working the investigation could snuff out whoever was responsible, pick up valuable leads. Someone, Kenny Williamson would later say, "leaked."

While Houstonians were reading about Barbra Piotrowski's shooting, Kenny Williamson was spending his Saturday trying to solve it. His unlikely companion in the quest was Nathaniel Ivery. Early in the morning, Ivery led the young detective to the trailer house in Spring, north of Houston, where Bob Anderson said he owned a farm. Then he directed Williamson through a maze of streets in a nearby residential area of upper-middle-class homes in search of the house where Anderson was staying with the man named "Jerry." The rest of the afternoon, the two combed the city of Houston looking for a Sheraton or a Marriott next door to a Radio Shack. That was the way Ivery remembered the hotel where Bob Anderson met "Judge Dudley Smith" to get directions to Barbra Piotrowski's apartment.

At day's end, Nathaniel Ivery made a positive identification of the hotel where Anderson and Dudley Smith rendezvoused: the Sheraton Town & Country, a white high-rise hotel in Town & Country Village, an upscale shopping center in the Memorial area, a few miles from the Ethan's Glen townhouse.

When the two men returned to the jailhouse, Ken Williamson wired Nathaniel Ivery to make a phone call. The night he and Patrick were arrested, Ivery told Williamson, he telephoned Bob Anderson at Jerry's house. Anderson, he told the detective, told him to "sit tight." Kenny Williamson wondered what Bob Anderson might have to say to Ivery now, and he wanted it on tape.

The call was uneventful. Jerry answered the phone and told Ivery that Bob Anderson was out.

Sometime on the same Saturday, Ray Matthews got a phone call from his old, good friend Dudley Bell. Matthews was a P.I., just like Dudley, and once acted as chief of police in Pearland, a small Texas town between Houston and Galveston.

Dudley asked Ray to read him the newspaper article about the Piotrowski shooting in that day's *Houston Chronicle*. He couldn't read it himself, Bell told his friend Ray, because he was at Richard Minns's lakehouse in Austin with Richard and Richard's criminal lawyer, Robert Scardino.

The next morning, Monday, October 27—one week after Barbra was shot—the homicide division got another unsolicited lead. Joe Schultea, the chief of the Village Police Department in Memorial, called the Houston Police Department and asked to speak to whomever was handling the Piotrowski case. The switchboard operator routed the call to Gil Schultz.

Chief Schultea was brief. He got a phone call, he told Schultz, from a woman named Dorothy Wolfe, Dudley Bell's ex-wife. The former Mrs. Bell had some rather unflattering things to say about her ex-husband, the Village police chief related. She mentioned that he was conducting a forty-thousand-dollar investigation of Barbra Piotrowski. Schultea thought the detectives in homicide might want to know about it. She might be willing to talk.

Gil Schultz was interested. When he hung up with Schultea, he dialed Dorothy Wolfe's office number. The ex-Mrs. Dudley Bell's cheerily professional voice turned ice-cold when she heard who was calling. Yes, she said reluctantly, she would talk to the police about Dudley, but she wouldn't say anything over the phone. Why didn't they meet at a friend of hers' apartment later that night? It was safer that way.

Dorothy Wolfe was not thrilled to see the two detectives from homicide that evening. Her attractive features froze with fear at the mention of her ex-husband's name.

She told her story quickly and anxiously: She and Dudley were married and divorced between 1975 and 1979. Recently, they started dating again. Everything was going fine until a week ago. Dudley suddenly started pressuring her to marry him again. Wolfe balked. When she questioned him further, he admitted he wanted her to marry him because he thought the court would "go easier on him" if he was married and had a child. Dorothy Wolfe refused and Dudley Bell beat her.

Dorothy Wolfe was a bitter woman, and as investigators know, bitter women have loose tongues. She related how Dudley was conducting an in-depth investigation of Barbra Piotrowski for Richard Minns. Dudley and Richard Minns were good friends. They had breakfast together every morning at the Guest Quarters Hotel, where Richard was staying. Dudley told her Barbra Piotrowski had filed a "common-law marriage" lawsuit against Minns, and that he was looking into her background for information Minns could use against her. She knew her ex-husband had hired Rick Waring to follow Piotrowski. He also hired another man, she told the detectives, but she couldn't remember his name. Both men were supposed to follow Piotrowski when she ran in Memorial Park, talk to her, and try to "steer her into" hiring an attorney Richard Minns wanted her to use.

Did Dudley hire someone to make a hit on Piotrowski? Detectives Schultz and Kardatzke asked. Dorothy Wolfe didn't know, or if she did she wouldn't say. But she did know this: When she was divorcing Dudley, he told her if she went out with another man, he'd pay someone to kill him.

Before she left, the blonde divorcée showed the two detectives some papers she found in a box of cancelled checks her ex-husband was keeping for an IRS audit. She thought they might be of interest.

Schultz and Kardatzke leaned in closer and examined the papers. The first was a business card from Dudley Bell International. The other two pieces of paper were torn off a notepad from the Guest Quarters Hotel. Bell had written the name *Thompson* and the number *370–1098* on the first one. The other piece of note paper from the Guest Quarters had five lines written on it in Dudley Bell's handwriting:

Barbra Piotrowski
10103 Lansdale #310
Westwood left turn off Bissonnet
724–1040
Red 78 Firebird   TMF 45

It was the same information Nathaniel Ivery said Bob Anderson read to him and Patrick Steen when he told them about the hit.

The back of the note had the abbreviations of four different types of guns listed, written by Bell: "SW 29, SW 4″ 38, Colt 45 Auto satin," and "OMC-380."

By the way, Detectives Schultz and Kardatzke said to Dorothy Wolfe, could she tell them what type of car Dudley was driving these days? Dorothy Wolfe was happy to oblige. She herself drove a Mercedes, the stylish blonde said proudly. Dudley drove a gray-over-black Cadillac.

The two detectives exchanged looks. That was the make and color of the car Bob Anderson pointed out to Steen and Ivery at the Sheraton as belonging to "Dudley Smith," the "big man" Anderson said hired him to arrange the hit on Piotrowski.

24

When Barbra Piotrowski picked up Tuesday's *Houston Chronicle* to read from her hospital bed, she gasped. There, on the front page, was a picture of her in a black bathing suit and heels, staring beguilingly at the camera. It covered the width of a column of type and extended halfway down page one. Next to it was a bold, banner headline asking, WHO'D SHOOT GOLDEN GIRL?

She read the first three paragraphs in stunned disbelief:

> She was Goldilocks, the Golden Girl, Lolita—take your pick—5-foot 5, 95 pounds, green eyes, good legs. A 24-karat show stopper. Maybe even a Bo Derek 10.
>
> She jogged 10 miles a day, popped vitamin pills, didn't smoke or drink.
>
> That was the appearance she gave. . . .

Barbra put down the paper and winced. Then she glanced down at the network of tubes keeping her alive. Why would anyone write something like that about her? It made her sound cheap, like some sort of trollop, or prostitute. What had she ever done to that reporter?

In the last third of the article, the reporters, Zarko Franks and Jon Verboon, reported that Barbra Piotrowski was once arrested "on a complaint by two nuns that she was dealing in drugs on school grounds," that she was charged with "possession of dangerous drugs," and that the police found needle marks on both of her arms.

"The girl," they wrote, "who, as one attorney described her, 'looks like the perennial virgin,' associated with some wealthy men and some not so wealthy who had police records." The biography continued:

> There was Dr. Brad Katz, for example, of Malibu, California. On her personalized checkbook from the Bank of America, she listed 18121 Coast Line Drive as her address. That's the address of Dr. Brad Katz in Malibu.
>
> All Dr. Katz would say is: "I knew her when she was a student nurse at Brockman Hospital. A very fine girl. She was a straight A student."
>
> He refused to discuss his relationship with Barbra Piotrowski and suggested: "Why don't you do your muckraking against the people who have hurt this poor girl and maimed her and the police who gave her no protection?"
>
> How did the doctor know she had been threatened and by whom?
>
> He didn't answer these questions.
>
> And there's Frederick [sic] de la Torre, 30, of Los Angeles, a ski lift operator at Aspen when Barbra first met Minns. She had been dating de la Torre then. De la Torre, according to Los Angeles police, was a registered narcotics user and was arrested at least twice for possession of marijuana. His record includes a conviction and a three-year suspended sentence for pot possession.

Why would the *Chronicle* write such a negative story about her and where did they get their information? Barbra answered her question before the thought was fully formed. Of course! she cogitated. Suddenly it dawned on her. It was Dick! She knew *exactly* what he was doing. She had seen him employ the same technique hundreds of times on other people. The best defense is a good offense; that was Dick's modus operandi. Now that she was shot, he was going to make it look like *she* was the criminal!

There was truth in Barbra Piotrowski's imaginings. Zarko Franks, the *Chronicle* reporter who cowrote the "Golden Girl" article, was a longtime friend of Dudley Bell's. All the background information in Franks's piece came from the pages of a dossier on Barbra Piotrowski, prepared and provided by Zarko's old buddy Dudley.

The detectives downtown in homicide had little time for

newspaper accounts of the case. They were following a compelling trail that led them to Robert Jess Anderson, the mustachioed trucker from Riverside, California.

Tom Ladd, who often worked as a partner to Ken Williamson, spent Tuesday afternoon with the desk clerk of the Houstonian Motor Lodge, a low-budget motel on the North Freeway near Spring, on the road to Dallas, where Nathaniel Ivery said Bob Anderson paid for rooms for him and Patrick Steen when their caravan arrived in Houston.

The female desk clerk immediately recognized the man on the balcony in the photograph Sergeant Ladd showed her. It was definitely Bob Anderson, the man who arrived on October 11 and rented rooms 134, 135, and 136. She also recalled distinctly that he said he had two cars in his party, and that he had just driven in from California. She noticed a trailer and a boat attached to the cars when she glanced out the lobby window.

Sometime in the early part of the second week after Barbra's shooting, the six detectives on the case formulated a plan. The two triggermen were already in jail, with signed confessions implicating Robert Jess Anderson and alluding to a "Judge Dudley Smith," who hired him. Bob Anderson's arrest was easy. With everything they had from Steen and Ivery, the detectives could get a warrant for Anderson in a snap. What they really wanted was the man at the top. Although they couldn't utter his name on the record, off the record every detective working the Piotrowski attempted murder case knew in his gut that "Dudley Smith" was actually Dudley Bell. Both Steen and Ivery told them Anderson said "Dudley Smith" was a "big man, six feet three inches or six feet four"—Dudley Bell was over six feet three; that his car was a gray-over-black Cadillac—Dudley Bell drove a gray-over-black Cadillac; and his first name was "Dudley." Who else could it be?

And there was more. There was the note, on Guest Quarters stationery, with Barbra Piotrowski's name, address, directions to her apartment, phone number, car, and license number, written in Dudley Bell's handwriting—the same information Nathaniel Ivery said Bob Anderson read to him and Patrick Steen when he told them he wanted the girl killed.

Then there was Rick Waring, Bell's on-again/off-again private investigator-bodyguard. Kenny Williamson heard Waring admit, in his darkened car in the Woodhollow Apartments parking lot, that Dudley Bell tried to hire him to kill Piotrowski for ten thousand dollars, the same figure the two blacks mentioned. It all fit together.

The problem was, the district attorney's office wanted more. To get an indictment against Bell, the prosecutors in Johnny Holmes's office advised, they needed direct, solid evidence.

What if, the homicide team pondered, they were to *secretly* arrest Bob Anderson, and offer him immunity from prosecution if he would give them enough information to indict Dudley Bell? They would have to play it very cagey; not let anyone know Anderson was in custody, or they'd blow their cover. Still, it *could* work. They decided to give it a shot.

That night, Tuesday, October 28, Detective Gil Schultz staked out Bob Anderson's place, waiting for a moment when no one close to Anderson was around, so he could arrest him.

Just before midnight, Robert Jess Anderson left his house for a quick run to a nearby Stop-N-Go. When he walked out of the convenience store, Gil Schultz was waiting for him with a warrant for his arrest.

Anderson offered no resistance. The jowly trucker climbed into Schultz's unmarked car for the twenty-minute drive downtown.

When the men got to the courthouse complex, Gil Schultz parked his car and secreted Anderson through a back door to a conference room on the tenth floor of the District Attorney's Building. Inside waiting for them were two assistant D.A.s: Ted Wilson and Terry Wilson (no relation). Terry, a graduate of Texas A&M University, was a beer-bellied, outspoken, hell-raising bear of a man. Ted Wilson was his physical and temperamental opposite: tall, thin, bespectacled, and serious.

They got straight to the point. If he would cooperate, the Wilsons told Anderson, and if what he told them led to the indictments of anyone higher up on the murder-for-hire chain, the State of Texas would not prosecute him for the attempted murder of Barbra Piotrowski and none of his statements would be used against him. He could, in essence, walk.

Up in the wall, barely visibly to the eye, a tiny camera was secretly recording the conversation on videotape. That would, in time, prove highly significant to Bob Anderson's future.

The words flowed from Anderson like compliments from a gigolo. Yeah, Dudley Bell approached him to put the hit on Barbra Piotrowski.

His troubles all began, the beefy trucker told his audience, with palpable bitterness, when his wife Joan divorced him. She stole him blind, he said, took over his company (Transport Leasing) and left him high and dry. After the divorce, Anderson set out for Houston to connect with Jerry Thompson. Thompson suggested he buy his hydroponic plant farm in Spring, north of Houston.

At a Fourth of July barbecue at Jerry Thompson's house, Anderson spent the party talking to a girlfriend of Thompson's named Jeannette Liles, who told him he ought to meet a man named Dudley Bell. Bell was a high-roller, she said. He could open big doors for Bob.

A few days later, Anderson's story went, he got a call at Jerry Thompson's house, where he was staying, from Dudley Bell. The two talked about growing marijuana on the hydroponic farm Anderson was buying from Thompson. They figured they could make big money on just a few crops.

Then Anderson went back to California to pick up some gems, his intended form of payment for the farm in Spring. When he returned to Jerry Thompson's house in September, he said, there were two or three messages waiting for him from Dudley Bell. He and Bell talked on the phone and made arrangements to meet in a bar, at a Sheraton at five P.M. around September 15. The two met and talked gems and guns. He was a gun collector himself, Anderson boasted to the Wilsons, and Dudley was interested. They left, he said, and Bell stiffed him for the bill.

The next night, Bell called Anderson at Jerry Thompson's house and apologized for leaving him with the check. He suggested they meet again at a Denny's. Bob Anderson gestured broadly as he recounted the story: "Comes in, kicks back, throws his feet up. He flatly told me all about myself, from the money I owed to the problems I'm in and you name it. Then he asked me how I was gonna carry on." In the middle of the conversation, Anderson related, a friend of Dudley's named Robert Renner came over to the table and chatted for a few minutes, then left.

When they were alone again, Anderson told the prosecutors, Dudley leaned over and said, in a low voice, "I got a little job for you."

"And that's when he started the situation on the girl," the trucker blurted. "He said, 'She's giving a friend of mine a lot of trouble. I have a client. She hurt him very dearly. Blackmail.' "

Did Bell, the Wilsons wondered, actually say he wanted Anderson to kill Piotrowski?

Bob Anderson's puttylike face formed an expression of exaggerated confidentiality. "Dudley didn't tell," he said dramatically. "Dudley wrote it out. Dudley wrote everything. On a piece of paper. He had it written out before he came to the table."

Anderson's story continued. "I got something for you," he said Bell told him. "If the deal don't go through, what are you gonna do?"

"I don't know what you're talking about," Anderson said he replied.

Dudley Bell stared at him. "Hit or miss," he said flatly.

Shortly after the meeting at the Sheraton, Anderson told Ted and Terry Wilson, he returned to Riverside and casually mentioned the job to Patrick Steen and Nathaniel Ivery. Within days, they all drove across the country to Houston in a caravan.

In Houston, he met again with Dudley Bell, this time at Bell's office. While he was there, Anderson said, Dudley reached into a drawer on the left-hand side of his desk, pulled out a file on Barbra Piotrowski, and began going through all the "details." "Then he laid it on the line," said Anderson. "He wants her killed." As Bell was talking, he got a phone call—from Richard Minns, Anderson wondered? When he hung up, the detective drove Anderson by Piotrowski's apartment.

The rest of Anderson's story was jumbled and rambling. He spoke of a second meeting with Bell at the Sheraton Town & Country. A man who looked like Richard Minns— blond and tanned and wearing a polo shirt—was sitting at an adjacent table with two women, listening to Bell and Anderson's conversation. Bell, Anderson said, wrote down the information about Barbra Piotrowski for him on a piece of paper. "On one side would be jail," he said elliptically, "and on the other side is a list of my guns." The "jail side," he told the Wilsons and Williamson and Schultz, had Piotrowski's name, address, license number, and kind of car: the same information written on the Guest Quarters note Dorothy Wolfe turned over to Gil Schultz.

Bob Anderson also remembered driving Steen and Ivery by Piotrowski's apartment. But, he insisted, *he told the two blacks to go back to California.*

After the shooting, Anderson said, he got a call from a lawyer named Tatum, who told him he and Anderson had a mutual friend in Dudley Bell. Tatum was furtive, Anderson told the two assistant D.A.s. Wouldn't talk on the phone. He arranged to meet Anderson at a restaurant called the Black Angus.

That night, Gil Schultz sneaked Bob Anderson into a room at the Harley, an old hotel near the District Attorney's Building. The next day Anderson continued, for Schultz and Ted Wilson, his account of his meeting with Jim Tatum at the Black Angus.

When he got to the restaurant, Anderson said, Tatum was in the club room, drinking. He sat down to join him, Anderson related. Tatum mentioned that they had a "mutual friend," Dudley Bell, and said he thought Anderson would probably be needing his legal services.

Dudley Bell walked in a while later, Anderson told Wilson and Schultz, looking nervous and suspicious, as if he'd just returned from seeing somebody.

Tatum did most of the talking, Anderson recalled. "He said he didn't know who did what to who, but he knew these people were singing, because the word had already come down that they had written a statement." Tatum, Anderson told Wilson and Schultz, "put the skids on him" to come up with twenty thousand dollars to get Steen and Ivery out of jail. They had to get the blacks out on the streets, Tatum told him, and "make them disappear because there are too many people drawn into it."

When they'd "drunk a lot of drinks," Anderson said, the meeting broke up. Before he left, Tatum told him to come in to is law office so they could talk about how to "protect" him.

Just what happened next in the Piotrowski investigation is difficult to determine. Easier to recount is what *didn't* occur.

Although Dudley Bell's ex-wife Dorothy Wolfe had already turned over to Gil Schultz a piece of Guest Quarters stationery with information on Barbra Piotrowski's car and address on one side and a list of Bob Anderson's guns on the other, in Dudley's handwriting—the same thing Bob Anderson described in the conference room of the District Attorney's Building—neither Schultz nor anyone else in the district attorney's office or in homicide ever showed the trucker the note to ask him if it was the same one Bell passed him. Kenny Williamson would later admit he was never even briefed on what Anderson said in his statement at the Harley to Ted Wilson and Gil Schultz. With six, and sometimes more, detectives working the case at the same time and no one in charge, the right hand—as one criminal lawyer would later point out with cynicism—didn't know what the left hand was doing.

The pieces of the puzzle were starting to come together, but there was no one, it seemed, to put them all in place.

Now that the homicide team had Bob Anderson in secret custody, it took them several days to figure out what to do with him. On Wednesday night, October 29, they devised their first "mission" for the trucker: to try to smoke out Jim Tatum. Tatum, they postulated, had to be a key. He had already appeared from the ethers to represent Steen and Ivery, then he offered his legal services to Bob Anderson, and he was known to be a close friend of Dudley Bell's. If there was a common denominator in the murder-for-hire chain—other than Dudley Bell or Richard Minns—common sense, Kenny Williamson and his codetectives mused, pointed to James Eddie Tatum.

At Williamson's direction, Bob Anderson placed a call to Tatum on Wednesday afternoon. Could he, the trucker queried, meet him for drinks at the Black Angus that evening? Tatum agreed and set a time, unaware that his conversation was being monitored by the Houston Police Department.

Since Tatum didn't know Bob Anderson had ever been arrested, the detectives pondered, much less that he was cooperating with the police, perhaps the lawyer would say something incriminating to Anderson over drinks; something that might implicate Bell, or Minns, or possibly Tatum himself.

Those were the thoughts running through Kenny Williamson's head as he planted a hidden tape recorder on Bob Anderson and drove him to the Black Angus. Two undercover cops followed the Californian into the restaurant and took an adjacent table so they could observe and eavesdrop. Outside, in his police car, Ken Williamson listened, and waited.

The evening was a complete bust. As Williamson sat in his car fidgeting, Anderson talked for hours in circles, saying everything and nothing. Jim Tatum's conversation was useless. If the rugged criminal defense lawyer knew the details behind Barbra Piotrowski's attempted assassination, he wasn't letting anything slip in front of Bob Anderson.

The next day, Ken Williamson came up with another undercover operation for Anderson. The target, this time, was Jerry Thompson, the onetime Burger King franchisee through whom Anderson met Dudley Bell.

The modus operandi was basically the same as with Jim Tatum: Williamson wired a hidden microphone up Anderson's trouser leg and under his shirt, then drove him to Thompson's house north of Houston to see what might come of it.

The results were just as fruitless. Much of Anderson's conversation with Thompson was muffled, and what Williamson could hear wasn't worth a damn.

Ken Williamson cursed under his breath. Everyone around Anderson seemed to be clamming up.

That was true of no one more so than Richard Minns. Since Barbra's shooting on October 20, the man who courted the press like an ardent suitor had been completely, uncharacteristically silent.

The day after Anderson paid a visit to Jerry Thompson, there was another new and bizarre twist to the case.

The front page of the *Houston Chronicle* for Thursday, October 30, boasted an interview with Jim Tatum under a headline that covered half the paper reading: MODEL HIT CASE "TOO SPOOKY"—LAWYER.

Sometime after his meeting with Bob Anderson at the Black Angus, Tatum contacted *Chronicle* reporter Zarko Franks and started talking. His story was the stuff of black-and-white B movies on *The Late Show*.

On Tuesday night, Tatum told the *Chronicle*—sometime after eleven-thirty when he got home from a political dinner, and before six the next morning, when he got up to jog—someone, some mystery figure, delivered ten thousand dollars in cash to him through the mail slot of his front door. He presumed the money was a retainer for representing Patrick Steen and Nathaniel Ivery, he said, since "the tooth fairy doesn't leave amounts like that," but he didn't know the source.

"I don't know what's going on," Tatum told Zarko Franks. "I poked the envelope at first with a cane. I thought it might be an envelope bomb or something. There was crude writing on the envelope that said, 'Private, Mr. Tatum.' Nothing else. No message or anything else."

The night before, Tatum said in his interview, he met with a "California man" who originally hired him. The California man denied delivering the money to him or knowing anything about it, Tatum told Franks. "This whole thing smells," the lawyer stated. "I've just about made up my mind to withdraw from the case. It's all too spooky. . . . What the hell is really going on? Who has seen Barbra Piotrowski? Is she really shot?"

Asked what he was going to do with the ten thousand dollars, Tatum told the *Houston Post* he would "refund the unearned part to whomever paid us."

When Kenny Williamson read Tatum's interview in Thursday night's *Houston Chronicle*, he snorted. The detective didn't believe, for one second, that Jim Tatum got any mysterious package with ten thousand dollars in his mail slot.

He gathered, from what Tatum told the newspaper, that the "California man" Tatum was referring to who "originally hired him" was Bob Anderson, since Tatum told the *Chronicle* he met with the California man the night before—the same night Anderson met Tatum for drinks at the Black Angus. There was no way *Anderson* delivered any ten thousand dollars to Jim Tatum on Tuesday night, Williamson reasoned. Anderson was in custody at the Harley Hotel from Tuesday night on!

OK, Williamson thought to himself, *maybe now I can getcha.*

The next day, Ken Williamson sent Bob Anderson to Jim Tatum's office to pick up his "refund" from the ten thousand dollars. Let's see, the detective pondered, what would happen when he called the lawyer's bluff.

When Anderson arrived at the criminal lawyer's office, Jim Tatum was out of town elk hunting. Anderson planted himself in the reception area, demanding to get his money back. Tatum's secretary tried unsuccessfully to calm him down; then she called Jim Tatum. Tatum's directive was quick and curt: Give him the money.

Kenny Williamson's boyish features wrinkled with displeasure. *Damn*, he thought peevishly. *Thwarted again.*

That same afternoon, three and a half days after he was secreted into custody at the Harley Hotel, Robert Jess Anderson was arrested *publicly*, booked, and placed in jail.

Detective Tom Ladd of homicide called a press conference to announce the arrest. Anderson, he told reporters, had "stayed missing" from the police for three days. The police had reason to believe he was connected with the shooting of Barbra Piotrowski, Ladd said. Beyond that, the detective refused to comment—due, he told reporters, to the "complexities" of the case.

Kenny Williamson and his colleagues grinned. That, they figure, should shake some melons out of the trees.

They were right.

On November 1, the day after Ladd's press conference to announce Bob Anderson's arrest, Richard Minns broke his silence.

In the *Houston Chronicle* article reporting Anderson's capture, Dick Minns issued a statement through his criminal lawyer, Robert Scardino:

> Dick has repeatedly told me he has nothing to hide. He was shocked when he heard about Barbra's shooting. Shortly after we heard of the shooting, I personally went to homicide and told them I would bring in Mr. Minns if they wanted to talk to him. At that time they told me they had no reason to want to talk to him.
>
> My client feels his name has unfairly been exploited by innuendo. He feels terrible about what happened to Miss Piotrowski, despite the fact they no longer see each other.

That same day, Dick talked to the *Houston Post* directly. Some of the newspaper stories about the shooting, he told the *Post*, implied that he was a suspect. As a result, he said, he had been "irreparably damaged, harmed, [and] wronged." He suggested reporters look to the "criminal element" with whom Barbra Piotrowski once associated.

"I don't know anything about it," Dick said to the *Post*. "It was a complete astonishment, a complete surprise. If I knew where she was," he added, "I'd send her some flowers."

Houston private investigator Bobby Newman must have found Richard Minns's last comment particularly ironic. Just that week, Dick Minns had hired Newman to find Barbra Piotrowski and to make sure she was "really shot."

At that very moment, Newman had one of his female investigators working undercover for Richard Minns as a candystriper, washing Barbra Piotrowski's hair.

A few days later, on November 4, Ted and Terry Wilson put Bob Anderson in front of a grand jury—another ploy to keep his coconspirators guessing, and to camouflage the fact that Anderson had already talked.

The newspaper accounts the next day—which the Wilsons were hoping the other suspects would read—were deliberately misleading. Both the *Chronicle* and the *Post* reported that Anderson "refused to testify" and was freed.

"We're stuck with uncorroborated accomplice-witness testimony," Ted Wilson told the *Post*. "We're wondering where in the hell we're going to go from here. It isn't like TV. It isn't simple."

That much of Ted Wilson's statement was true.

The following week, the third week of the police investigation, the detectives in homicide were visited by another surprise.

On Monday, November 10, Captain Bobby Adams got a phone call from Ray Matthews, Dudley Bell's private investigator friend.

Matthews was fishing. Why, he probed, was Bob Anderson arrested? What did they have on him?

Captain Adams dodged the question as best he could, hung up and wrote a memo of the conversation.

When Ken Williamson and Tom Ladd learned Ray Matthews called homicide, they leaped on the information. Ladd immediately called Matthews back. Why didn't he come on down to the police station, Ladd suggested, and talk?

Ray Matthews accepted the invitation. He had, it would turn out, things of his own to tell.

Matthews's story, like everyone else's in the Barbra Piotrowski imbroglio, was convoluted. Besides being an intimate of Dudley Bell's, Ray Matthews was a good friend of Jerry Thompson's, Bob Anderson's friend. Known him for ten years. Jerry Thompson, Matthews told Ken Williamson and Tom Ladd, had a lawyer and friend named Jim Defoyd. After Bob Anderson's visit to Jerry Thompson's house the week before, Matthews said, Thompson told Jim Defoyd that Anderson took him out to the garage and put his finger to his lips, then pointed to his chest to let him know he was wired. Defoyd told *him* about it, Matthews related. That's why he was sitting downtown at the police station.

Thompson and Defoyd, Matthews added, "felt like Bob Anderson was in a lot of trouble and didn't want to get involved."

Kenny Williamson took the news as gospel. *That* explained, the detective reasoned, why Thompson didn't say anything to Anderson the day at the house. There had to be a reason.

Williamson tracked down Anderson and got him on the phone. He wanted him downtown, the detective said testily. Now.

When he arrived at the police station early in the afternoon, Bob Anderson was ushered into a room with Ken Williamson, Tom Ladd, and Gil Schultz. The three police sergeants eyed him coldly. They knew he tipped off Jerry Thompson, they said, steely-eyed. Was he gonna admit it, they pushed Anderson, or was he gonna have to take a polygraph?

Bob Anderson was all bluster and blow. No, he protested. He didn't gesture to Jerry Thompson.

Within minutes, Bob Anderson had failed a lie detector test.

Ken Williamson hustled Anderson back to his office for further questioning. Again, the trucker denied tipping off Jerry Thompson. Williamson burrowed in further.

After several minutes, Anderson broke down. Yeah, it was true. He tipped off Thompson.

Ken Williamson's frown lifted. Bob Anderson, he decided, would tell a lie if the truth would suit him better.

The remainder of the week was a flurry of secret activity on the Piotrowski case. The most compelling was a conversation, behind closed doors, between Ken Williamson and a big, strapping thirty-four-year-old black man named James Perry Dillard.

The detective team had come across Dillard's name early in the investigation as one in a constellation of part-time employees (Rick Waring being another) of Dudley Bell. Dillard worked for Bell from 1973 to 1976 as a "go-fer" and private investigator-trainee. He quit in 1976, he told Ken Williamson, to get his own license. He eventually took a job with the Veterans' Administration Hospital.

While he was working at the VA hospital the previous summer, Dillard told Williamson, he got a call from Rick Waring, whom he had met at Dudley's office. Waring wanted to know if he was interested in buying a car from Dudley. Dillard said maybe.

In June or July, his story continued, Bell started calling the VA hospital. Dillard assumed Bell was trying to get in touch with him about the car. One day, Dillard told Ken Williamson, Dudley just showed up at the office. He asked Dillard if he had a minute. He wanted to talk to him about something. Maybe they could go to the snack bar.

Dillard followed Dudley to the snack bar. When they sat down, Bell pulled out a file with papers in it. "Do you know anyone who would hit a pussy?" he asked, in a low voice.

"I knew what Dudley meant by 'hit a pussy' as meaning to kill a girl," Dillard said to Williamson, "and I told him that I did not and I also asked him who it was."

Bell wouldn't tell him. All he would say, Dillard's story went on, was that the file folder was "on" the girl and that Dillard couldn't see the information in the file until he accepted the offer. Dillard balked. He didn't want to kill anyone, he told Williamson. Matter of fact, he'd been avoiding Dudley for months because he thought he was too dangerous. Trouble.

Bell fingered the file in his hands. Then he made his offer, Dillard remembered. Said if Dillard took the job, or got someone to do the job, he would get ten thousand dollars, plus a lifetime job at a health spa.

Kenny Williamson's ears perked up. A lifetime job at a *health spa?* It didn't take a genius to figure out what, or who, that suggested.

Dudley wouldn't tell him who wanted the job done, Dillard said. He just said that "the man" was in town staying at a hotel, that he was getting a divorce from this girl, and that it had to look like the girl disappeared; that there was no body found.

Dillard told Williamson he refused. Think about it, Dudley told him. I'll get back in touch. Bell called him several times over the next weeks, Dillard told Ken Williamson nervously. He avoided him.

"Things were pretty quiet for two or three months," Dillard went on, "when Rick [Waring] called me one day and asked me if I had read the papers that day. I told him no and asked him why, at which time he told me that 'the chick had been shot.' I went out and got the paper," Dillard went on, "and read the article. I knew right then that 'Judge Dudley Smith' was going to be Dudley Bell and this was in fact the same deal that he had offered me."

Ken Williamson finished taking notes. Then he sat back in his chair and meditated. If he had ever had a doubt about whether Dudley Bell and Richard Minns set up Barbra Piotrowski's shooting, it just evaporated.

The detective glanced over at James Perry Dillard. The giant of a man—just like Rick Waring—was shaking in his shoes.

The next day, Tuesday, November 11, both Houston papers printed breathless articles about a "mystery witness" who appeared in front of the grand jury on the Piotrowski shooting the day before wearing a shopping bag over her head. "Assistant District Attorneys Ted Wilson and Terry Wilson," said the *Post*, "would not comment on why the woman was disguised or whether any threats were made against her life."

Was it Dorothy Wolfe, Dudley Bell's ex-wife? Jeannette Liles, the woman Jerry Thompson dated, whom Bob Anderson said told him he should meet Dudley Bell? Or was it some new, even more dramatic witness? Those were the questions homicide detectives and the Wilsons were counting on Bob Anderson's coconspirators asking each other when the "mystery witness" articles hit the papers.

In truth, the woman beneath the shopping bag was a female police officer working, literally, undercover. Maybe, Kenny and the two Wilsons plotted, if Dudley Bell or Richard Minns or anyone else in the murder web got nervous about who the "mystery woman" could be, it might set some tongues wagging.

If it did, the wagging didn't reach the ears of anyone in the police department or the district attorney's office.

Two days later, when the grand jury reconvened, the Wilsons called another witness to the stand. A bona fide witness this time—James Eddie Tatum: friend of Dudley Bell, Richard Minns's partner in machismo, onetime defense attorney for Patrick Steen and Nathaniel Ivery, and, briefly, Bob Anderson's lawyer.

Kenny Williamson had been waiting for this day for weeks; ever since Tatum's name came out of Bob Anderson's mouth. Tatum, the young detective mused, had to be in on the Piotrowski deal up to his bare chest. He was hoping Tatum might say something to the grand jury— some slip or misstatement.

Jim Tatum agreed to testify in front of the grand jury voluntarily—giving the appearance, at least, that he was the soul of cooperation. His answers to Ted Wilson's questions, however, went 'round and 'round and up and down, like a circle within a circle within a circle.

He refused to tell Ted Wilson who originally hired him to represent Steen and Ivery—saying it was privileged information—but he would say who it *wasn't*. It wasn't, Tatum testified, Bob Anderson, Richard Minns, Dudley Bell, Bob Delmonteque, Jerry Thompson, Charlie Wells, or Spider Fincher.

Beyond that, Jim Tatum's testimony was bewilderingly confusing.

His "initial contact" about representing the two blacks, Tatum told the grand jury, came through a phone call to someone in his office on the Thursday or Friday after Barbra Piotrowski was shot. He didn't personally talk to whomever called, he told Ted Wilson, so he couldn't say he really knew who it was. Then, in the next breath, Tatum told Wilson he *knew* the person who "purportedly" contacted his office.

Further into his testimony, Tatum said the caller was a past client, from California. Then he said his office was originally given a number to contact someone in Houston about a case, and *later* the "California people" were identified as individuals he had represented in the past. "We had follow-up calls that we know were from L.A.," Tatum testified at one point; later, he told Ted Wilson he "wasn't actually certain he had talked to anybody in L.A. about the case."

Who could tell what was real and what wasn't? Tatum's testimony was like some elaborate conundrum, and Ted Wilson's examination only added to the confusion.

Kenny Williamson sat in the back of the room holding his breath, waiting and hoping for Jim Tatum to perjure himself. If Tatum testified that he got the mysterious ten thousand dollars in his mail slot from Bob Anderson, Williamson pondered, they could impeach him, because Bob Anderson was in secret custody at the Harley Hotel at the time Tatum said he got the money.

Tatum danced around the question. He wasn't sure, he testified to the grand jury, who was originally paying him to represent Steen and Ivery. It wasn't that he was avoiding the question, he told Ted Wilson. "It's unknown in my own mind."

When Tatum got up from the witness stand after an hour or so of testimony, Kenny Williamson gritted his teeth. Anyone could figure out that Jim Tatum played some part in this mess, he fumed, and the lawyer was wriggling right off the hook.

Maybe, the detective mused, Ted Wilson was going easy on Tatum because he was a fellow attorney. Williamson knew how much *he* hated going after other cops. The homicide detective tried to shrug it off. Still, he thought to himself, if he stayed with it, he *knew* he could get Jim Tatum to impeach himself. That would at least be a start.

In a week's time, three more witnesses were called before the grand jury: Ray Matthews, Jerry Thompson, and a very reluctant Dorothy Wolfe.

There was, in the combined testimonies of Ray Matthews, Dorothy Wolfe, and Jerry Thompson, a point of considerable curiosity, and it concerned a party.

In his statements to police, Bob Anderson mentioned a barbecue party he gave at Jerry Thompson's house on July 4. It was at that party, he said, where Jeannette Liles first mentioned Dudley Bell to him. In *her* grand jury testimony, Dorothy Wolfe also remembered a Fourth of July party, which she said she attended with Dudley at "Bob Anderson's house." The house Wolfe described sounded like Jerry Thompson's, although she did not recall meeting Jerry Thompson; she remembered meeting Bob Anderson.

Both Ray Matthews and Jerry Thompson also spoke of a party at Jerry Thompson's house, but they testified that the party was on August 16, not July 4, and that Thompson and Bell were there, but not Bob Anderson. Perhaps Dorothy Wolfe was simply confused. The party itself was really important only as it established the first link between Bob Anderson and Dudley Bell.

What was peculiarly interesting about the party was another piece of information that slipped by the police and the D.A.'s office. Both Dorothy Wolfe and Ray Matthews told the grand jury they remembered talking to *Mimi* Minns at the summer party. What, one might wonder, was Mimi doing at a party at Jerry Thompson's house? Coincidentally, the very party where Dudley Bell made his connection with the man who hired Barbra Piotrowski's would-be killers?

Months later, when Mimi learned what transpired at the party, she trembled. Mimi Minns was not a woman who believed in coincidences, but *that*, she would say flatly, was a coincidence. And it scared the hell out of her.

Mimi's attendance at the party was queer in and of itself. She was invited to attend by a man named Bobby Erwin, a blind date arranged by her curtain hanger. Mimi would later recall seeing Dudley Bell at the party, and remembering him from work he had done for Dick in the past. At the party, Bell took her aside and whispered that Dick was paying him to "run a check" on her date, Bobby Erwin.

Some months hence, Mimi would marry the good-looking artist who took her to the party, Bobby Erwin. Her children thought it was a setup: Erwin had been married four times, was younger than Mimi, and had no money. Only after her marriage and her divorce from Erwin would Mimi Minns Erwin discover that Bobby Erwin once worked for Dudley Bell. In years to come, Bell would brag to his old high school chum, Charlie Wells, that he "arranged" for Erwin to meet and seduce Mimi. It was all, Bell chortled, a setup for Richard Minns.

At the end of November, after Jerry Thompson's grand jury testimony, Ted and Terry Wilson made a peculiar, if not astonishing, decision.

They decided not to even try to indict Dudley Bell.

Ted Wilson's official explanation was lawyer-pat. They *couldn't* go after Bell, he argued, because of the accomplice-witness rule. The state of Texas, like most other states, follows a law that a prosecutor can't convict someone based solely on the testimony of an accomplice. There has to be something more: some other *independent* evidence to corroborate the accomplice. Without the accomplice-witness rule, anyone suspected of a crime could lie, and name a so-called accomplice, just to save his own skin.

In Dudley Bell's case, Ted Wilson argued, all the prosecution had was Bob Anderson's testimony. There was no independent corroboration.

Or was there? The night he was brought into custody, Bob Anderson told the Wilsons, Ken Williamson, and Gil Schultz that when Dudley Bell offered him the Piotrowski job, he showed him a piece of paper with Barbra Piotrowski's name, address, directions to her apartment, phone number, type of car, and license number on one side, and then wrote a list of four of Anderson's guns on the other. The day *before*, Dudley Bell's ex-wife had turned over to Gil Schultz a note on Guest Quarters stationery in Dudley's handwriting with the same information—down to the types of guns—on both sides.

That note, some lawyers would argue, was all the "independent evidence" the prosecution needed to make a case against Dudley Bell.

"All you have to do," said one Houston criminal attorney, "is sit down and look at Bob Anderson's statements, and look at that note. That's a key piece of evidence. That Schultz never took that note and showed it to Bob Anderson . . . they hadn't put all the pieces together that they had in their hands. I guarantee you I could go over today with that evidence and prosecute Dudley Bell and convict him. It'd be a great case. I'd *love* to try it!"

And that wasn't all. In addition to the note, prosecutors also had Steen and Ivery's statements saying that the man Bob Anderson told them hired him was a "big man, six feet three or six feet four," with the first name Dudley, who drove a gray-over-black Cadillac. *And* the Wilsons had Rick Waring and James Perry Dillard's admissions to Ken Williamson that Dudley offered them ten thousand dollars to, Dillard said, "hit a pussy."

"They had more than enough information to file charges against Dudley Bell," the Houston lawyer went on. "And had they gone and filed the charges, they could have convicted him."

The Wilsons' decision not to arrest Dudley Bell was not the only controversy surrounding their handling of the Piotrowski case. On November 4, the two prosecutors released *Bob Anderson.*

Again, Ted Wilson blamed the accomplice-witness rule. The state of Texas didn't have a case against Anderson, he rationalized, because they had already agreed not to use Anderson's statement against him, and without that, all they had was Steen and Ivery's testimony, with no independent corroboration.

Interestingly, Ted Wilson's own partner disagreed with that position. Months later, in a hearing on a related matter, Terry Wilson would testify that he "felt we had a case against Bob Anderson from day one." He and Ted Wilson let Anderson go, *Terry* Wilson said, because they "didn't want it to look like he was an informant."

What was going on? Doug O'Brien, a lawyer who would later represent Bob Anderson, attributed the Wilsons' decision to "either incompetence, or someone was paid off."

This much was clear: From the day Barbra Piotrowski was shot, no one in the district attorney's office, or homicide, so much as *questioned* Richard Minns, a circumstance Barbra Piotrowski considered unbelievable. Her lawyer, Dick DeGuerin, agreed. In private, DeGuerin was heard to say that he believed the State had a case against Dick Minns.

"He knows better than that," Ted Wilson has said. "He'd probably then love to represent Minns on the criminal case, because he could beat us in a heartbeat. We couldn't get to the jury as a matter of law. We don't have enough to go after Minns."

Ted Wilson did have a point. When all the smoke was cleared, what evidence *was* there that Richard Minns set up the botched hit job on Barbra Piotrowski? Steen and Ivery said Anderson told them the man who wanted her killed was concerned because she might be pregnant and "could cause trouble for the guy and his family." Bob Anderson mentioned a man who looked like Minns sitting at a table next to him and Dudley at the Sheraton, eavesdropping, when they were talking about the hit. Anderson confessed that he was hired by Dudley Bell, and Dudley Bell was conducting an investigation on Barbra Piotrowski for Richard Minns. Rick Waring told Kenny Williamson Dudley was shopping the murder-for-hire contract on Piotrowski, and that "everyone knew" Dudley was working for Richard Minns. The note Bell showed Anderson was on Guest Quarters stationery, where Dick Minns was staying. James Perry Dillard said Bell offered him ten thousand dollars plus a lifetime job at a health spa if he wanted to "hit a pussy" for a man who was staying at a hotel and getting a divorce.

Who else but Richard Minns would hire Dudley Bell to kill Barbra Piotrowski? "Obviously," Ted Wilson agreed, "Dudley Bell would not on his own motion have done such a thing. He had nothing to gain by this at all." A *ten*-year-old, Barbra would cry, could connect it to Dick. Ted Wilson concurred. "If you gave all the facts," he said, "and we weren't talking about a courtroom and rules of evidence or anything else, you'd have an opinion Minns is guilty."

But, he pointed out, "it's one thing from the standpoint of showing it on TV and a total other thing to put it on in a courtroom. I've got cases that I could give you and you can go home and read it tonight and come back the next day and tell me who killed the guy and I can't prove it. It's just part of the way it works."

Dick DeGuerin was unconvinced. "You can corroborate an accomplice with circumstantial evidence," he would argue, his feet up on his desk, decked out in cowboy boots. "And Lord knows there's plenty of circumstantial evidence that Minns was the one who did it."

25

Just before Christmas, Barbra Piotrowski, using the name Mary Miller, was transferred from Hermann Hospital and admitted to a rehabilitation institute to learn how to adjust to life as a paraplegic.

Across town, Bob Anderson, the man who hired her killers, was packing his bags to drive back home to Riverside.

Elsewhere in Houston, Dudley Bell was going about his day-to-day business.

And somewhere in the city, Richard Minns was a free man; never arrested, never charged, never even questioned.

Kenny Williamson was an angry, frustrated man, He had a lot of respect for Ted and Terry Wilson—shoot, the detective told himself, they were *lawyers*; he was just a country-boy policeman. But for the life of him, the detective couldn't figure out why the Wilsons hadn't tried to prosecute Bob Anderson and Dudley Bell. The idea of Bell and Anderson walking away from Barbra's shooting scot-free didn't set well with a Baptist boy who spent every Sunday in church listening to a minister preach about the wages of sin.

The third week in November, Williamson stuffed pictures of Dudley Bell and Bob Anderson into his pocket and drove over to the Sheraton Town & Country to interview the waitresses who were working in the lounge the month Bob Anderson said he met Dudley Bell twice for drinks to talk about "hitting" Barbra Piotrowski.

The bartender, Kathleen Millian, not only recognized Dudley Bell, she remembered him trying to sell her cocaine. Two of the lounge waitresses recalled seeing Bell at the bar "a couple of times." A fourth barmaid, Stephenie Pyle, tentatively identified Bob Anderson.

Kenny Williamson tucked his Sheraton notes into a folder and drove back to the police station with his jaw clenched.

As long as he was still working for the Houston Police Department, Kenny Williamson decided, he didn't care what the Wilsons did; *he* wasn't going to give up until Dudley Bell, Bob Anderson, and Richard Minns were behind bars.

On November 17, Barbra made her first public appearance since she was shot.

The occasion was a hearing on the theft case Dick filed, rescheduled from the week of October 20—the date Bob Anderson said was the deadline for her assassination. She received special permission from the hospital to check out for a few hours.

From a legal standpoint, there was no real reason for Barbra to be in court; although her case was scheduled to go to trial, there were several other cases ahead of hers on the docket, meaning the theft charges would not be heard that Monday. Symbolically, however, her appearance was explosive. The girl who'd been branded by the newspapers as the "Golden Girl," Dick Minns's mistress, the vitamin-popping California blonde on whom he'd "squandered" jewels and gifts, entered the courtroom in a wheelchair pushed by Dick DeGuerin, looking frail and wan and shriveled. Her "million-dollar legs" dangled limply and her toes pointed inward. Although she would later say she tried to pull herself together, to show Dick she wasn't vanquished, Barbra looked pathetic.

When Judge Miron Love called out the case number for the theft action, Dick DeGuerin shot up and urged the court to grant his client a speedy trial, saying she had been the victim of an "assassination" attempt. "We believe," DeGuerin said indignantly, "the complainant in this case is the person that hired, through intermediaries, the assassins."

A buzz started in the back of the courtroom, where TV and newspaper reporters were taking notes, and continued throughout the day.

For the first time since Barbra was shot, Richard Minns

had been publicly accused of arranging her attempted murder.

It was also the last time Barbra Piotrowski, as such, would ever be seen in public.

Dick Minns was not pleased with Dick DeGuerin's outburst in court. The next day, when the Houston papers ran front-page stories about the hearing, with giant photographs of Dick DeGuerin beside a pitiable-looking Barbra in her wheelchair under the headline MINNS ACCUSED, the columns were filled with Dick Minns's rebuttals.

Barbra Piotrowski, he said angrily, was using the newspapers to try to frame him as a "sympathy ploy" at the expense of his family's name. By linking his name and picture to the criminals who shot her, he told the *Houston Post*, they had destroyed a reputation it took him a lifetime to build.

"I'm not a defendant," he said. "I've been told I'm not a suspect. I'm just a witness in a felony-theft case. The only crime I committed was to fall in love with a beautiful girl from California. She came to Houston to become my mistress and that's true. Then I came home the night of March 17, 1980, and everything was gone from my townhouse, including Miss Piotrowski."

"Richard Minns," the *Post* reported, "said he understands Barbra Piotrowski fell in with some criminal types that led her both to stealing from him and to getting involved in something, perhaps drugs, that culminated in the shooting. Minns said he was surprised when he heard of the shooting, but thinks Piotrowski is recovering faster than her attorneys are letting the public believe."

Dick's response to Dick DeGuerin's statements in court was to file a one-hundred-million-dollar slander suit against both DeGuerin and his senior partner, the legendary Percy Foreman. The slander suit, excerpts of which were reprinted in both Houston papers, contained some of Dick Minns's most creative, vivid prose.

First he insinuated that Dick DeGuerin had "staged" Barbra Piotrowski's shooting with "incompetent actors from California" to "muddy up the waters" of her theft case and "evoke sympathy." Then he accused DeGuerin of releasing inflammatory material about him that "spread like an inferno of sensationalism and irrational hate" from coast to coast so that Barbra (a "mere puppet dancing on DeGuerin's string") could "extort money" from the Minns family. In the last pages of his eight-page petition, Dick compared DeGuerin to the attorneys of France during the Reign of Terror, when Robespierre sentenced lawyers to death for betraying the public trust.

DeGuerin and Percy Foreman scoffed at the libel lawsuit. "I feel like Brer Rabbit when he was thrown into the brier patch," DeGuerin chuckled, when he heard about the petition. How could anyone, DeGuerin wondered, take seriously a lawsuit where Richard Minns suggested that Barbra Piotrowski's lawyer "fabricated" her shooting, or, worse yet, "conceived or directed" it to garner publicity for his law firm? It was ludicrous! Barbra had other feelings. She had noticed, during her four years with Dick, that the more outrageous his accusations against someone, the more people tended to believe them.

If one examined the language of Dick's slander suit carefully—particularly the references to Robespierre and the Reign of Terror—one could detect the unmistakable hand of another Minns at work: Dick's son Mike. Four years after he sued his father (whom he compared in his lawsuit to Hitler the Great Provoker), Mike was now representing him in the suit against Foreman and DeGuerin.

In the first week of the new year, 1981, Barbra had cause for a small, ironic celebration. On January 5, Dick DeGuerin persuaded the court to dismiss Dick's theft charges against her on a technicality: The indictment Gordon Dees wrote up so hastily on a Friday night under the watchful eyes of Dick and Dudley Bell did not make it clear, the judge ruled, who had superior ownership claims to the property. Barbra was relieved the charges had been dismissed. But she felt her name had not been cleared.

Still Dick Minns refused to give up. His mind raced feverishly, churning into the night to devise new ways to avenge himself. The day the indictment was quashed, Matt Leeper, the young assistant district attorney who was prosecuting the case, announced to newspapers that he would try to get another grand jury to reindict Barbra Piotrowski and Victoria Spillers. Dick had been boasting for months that he had Leeper "in his back pocket." And indeed a few weeks earlier, his good friend Harry Brochstein offered Leeper a position in Brochstein's law firm, which Leeper accepted. Within days, Matt Leeper was also representing Richard Minns in a private capacity.

The day after state District Judge Jimmy James quashed the theft indictments against Barbra and Victoria Spillers, Minns composed a personal letter to the Harris County grand jury.

Dear Members of the Grand Jury:

A letter has been served upon your Honorable Group by the famous and powerful criminal law firm of Percy Foreman and Dick DeGuerin. This expensive firm has been retained by Defendant Piotrowski to again "beat-the-rap" in another of the many times she has been arrested. Some of Defendant Piotrowski's previous arrests include selling narcotics to high school children. This time the charge is felony theft. Her accomplice in this theft, who sometimes hires out as a domestic, is Defendant Spillers (odd, for a college educated nurse, ex-Army technician, etc.). . . .

Both defendants were indicted by a Harris County Grand Jury on May 19, 1980. The Grand Jury did not desire to talk to any witnesses because the facts were, in their opinion, conclusive. . . .

There has been a lot of publicity regarding Defendant Piotrowski being shot. . . . I have attempted and requested to appear before any police, District Attorney or State Judge to answer questions, but no one wants to talk to me. . . . I am the injured party. My property was stolen by the defendants. . . .

The Grand Jury has the job of seeking the truth, and here is the truth, without any window-dressing: (1) I am 51, a native Texan, and have spent the majority of my working life in Houston. . . . [I] have never done anything to disgrace [my] name.

(2) . . . There is "no fool like an old fool," and from the very beginning I was (and still am) being "set up" as a mark for extortion and God knows what else.

(3) The story is as old as the Bible. I was wrong, but I moved the young lady to Houston to become my paid mistress. . . . She had previously had similar "live-in" arrangements with other men before me.

(4) Finally, this culminated in the breakup of a 30-year marriage from my college sweetheart. And, like Samson, I received a haircut because of this modern-day Delilah. . . .

(5) I left my townhouse on the morning of March 17, 1980, and when I returned that evening, everything in the townhouse including Defendant Piotrowski was gone. . . .

(6) Through peaceful means, I tried to get my property and personal belongings returned to me.

. . . I wish no harm for the Defendant Piotrowski and I hope she will quickly recover if she is ill. I would not do anything to harass or to physically harm her. I could not. That is simply not my nature. . . .

Yours very truly,

Richard L. Minns

Dick DeGuerin read Dick's letter to the grand jury with a mixture of contempt and awe. You almost had to admire, the criminal lawyer thought to himself, a guy who could twist his girlfriend's attempted assassination and make it sound like *he* was the victim.

Patrick Steen and Nathaniel Ivery went to trial on charges of attempted capital murder the end of March, five months after Barbra Piotrowski was shot. In the middle of the trial, both men accepted a plea bargain: thirty-five-year sentences in exchange for their agreement to give complete statements and to testify against "any other parties."

Although Richard Minns's name was not uttered in court, his shadowy presence could be felt in every hearing and read between the lines of each newspaper article about the trial. Everyone in Houston knew about Barbra Piotrowski's shooting at the doughnut shop. Secretaries on their coffee breaks, socialites at luncheons, executives over drinks were all talking about who shot Barbra Piotrowski—and the name that came in whispers from their lips was Richard Minns.

The month after Steen and Ivery's trial, Ted and Terry Wilson subpoenaed James Perry Dillard and Rick Waring to tell a new grand jury about Dudley Bell's offers to them of a murder-for-hire. Both men, Ted Wilson noted with some surprise, were terrified at the prospect. Dillard was the more cooperative. Once in front of the grand jury, James Perry Dillard repeated, in essence, the same story he told Kenny Williamson. Rick Waring, Dudley Bell's friend and occasional bodyguard, had second, third, and fourth thoughts about testifying in front of a grand jury. The black belt stammered, stalled, and evaded until Ken Williamson wanted to strangle him.

He *had* to, Rick Waring would say later. There were too many "repercussions. Some of the things that I said in front of that grand jury," he said later, "could have gotten me killed."

Soon after Waring and Dillard's testimonies, the Wilsons decided to bring Bob Anderson back from California to testify in front of a second grand jury.

This time, when the mustachioed trucker sat down in the district attorney's conference room with Ted and Terry Wilson, the two prosecutors announced that "all deals were off." They had an agreement, the Wilsons told him. Their agreement was that *if* Anderson's help led to an indictment, he would walk. That hadn't happened, the two prosecutors stated. So all deals were off.

Bob Anderson looked wounded. "That's quite a reversal, after all I've confided in you." He paused. "What happened to Gatum or to Tatum?—or ah—"

"Nothing," Ted Wilson said flatly.

Bob Anderson was dumbstruck. "Dudley Bell has walked away from this?" he said incredulously. "Actually walked away? I can't fathom him being able to pull that."

Suddenly Bob Anderson came to the conclusion that he needed an attorney. Badly. "I feel," he told Ted and Terry Wilson, "like I'm standing here with my pants down."

On his second encounter with a grand jury, Bob Anderson told much the same tale he had in the district attorney's conference room, at the Harley Hotel, and in front of the first grand jury the year before—except that now he was implying that Jerry Thompson was involved in the murder-for-hire, too. For the first time, however, he was represented by counsel—a young court-appointed attorney named Doug O'Brien, fresh from the D.A.'s office and now in private practice as a defense lawyer.

O'Brien was mystified by the D.A.'s treatment of Bob Anderson. Why, he wondered, hadn't Ted and Terry Wilson used Bob Anderson's statements to indict Dudley Bell back in November, when Anderson was first arrested? Once they decided against that, why did they let him go?

The young lawyer was more puzzled when he left the grand jury room. After telling Anderson the deal was off, that his testimony could be used against him now, Ted and Terry Wilson *again* released Bob Anderson. The man who brought Barbra Piotrowski's assassins to Texas was still a free man.

Shortly after he started to represent Bob Anderson, Doug O'Brien got a curious call. It was from Matt Leeper, the prosecutor on Dick's theft case, now working with Harry Brochstein. Would he, Leeper asked O'Brien, consider doing "courthouse work" for Brochstein's law firm on an hourly basis? O'Brien found the call odd. *Why me?* he wondered. Leeper's explanation was confusing. O'Brien, he said, had been an assistant district attorney and knew the ropes at the prosecutor's office. O'Brien hesitated. Leeper himself had been an assistant D.A. Why did they need him? It didn't make sense.

Later, when he learned about the connection between Leeper and Minns, and Minns and Brochstein, O'Brien speculated Leeper wanted to hire him to get inside information on Bob Anderson's case for *Minns*. O'Brien turned down the job. A short while later, Richard Minns hired Doug O'Brien's best friend to represent him on some legal matters. O'Brien couldn't believe it. Now Minns was trying to get information about Anderson through O'Brien's *friend!*

O'Brien already believed, through his examination of the records, that someone from the Houston Police Department was feeding Richard Minns information about the investigation. Kenny Williamson thought so as well. Someone from Texas Governor Mark White's office visited him one day and asked to see all the files on the Piotrowski investigation—said he was making an inquiry for the Victim's Compensation Board. Williamson hesitated—cop's instinct. Later he found out the person who made the request wasn't from the Victim's Compensation Board at all. The detective was disgusted. He knew Richard Minns helped finance Mark White's campaign for governor, that Minns and White were friends. He also knew that Joe Reynolds and Richard Minns were intimates. Joe Reynolds and Mark White were former law partners. He could put two and two together.

The end of May—the same day Bob Anderson testified before the second grand jury—Ted and Terry Wilson issued a subpoena to Dudley Bell.

The afternoon of his testimony, the private eye strolled up to the grand jury room, wearing a new pair of Gucci loafers and a cocky, lopsided grin. At his side was his friend and lawyer Jim Tatum. In the course of five months, Tatum had set some sort of legal record for representing the most defendants in a single case: first Steen and Ivery, then Bob Anderson, now Dudley Bell.

Inside the grand jury room, Dudley Clifford Bell, Jr., took the Fifth Amendment on every question asked him. Outside the grand jury room, on his way down the halls, he smiled and schmoozed with reporters as if he were running for city council again. The questions, he bellowed, were "crazy, stupid, comical, ludicrous, and ridiculous."

But the tide of public sympathy was turning against Dudley Bell and Richard Minns. In May, *Texas Monthly*, a popular, respected magazine known for its investigative journalism, ran a long piece about Barbra Piotrowski's shooting called "The Mistress and the Muscleman." The article featured cartoonish pictures of Dick Minns flexing his muscles, and sarcastic references to him as a "double-knit aristocrat" and a "bottle blond" who favored "rhinestone denim ensembles" and whose "lust for the limelight" propelled him into dubious feats of daring on his birthday.

Marge Crumbaker continued faithfully to chronicle Dick's rapidly diminishing activities in her gossip column in the *Houston Post*. In the middle of May, she reported that Dick was in Acapulco "with an eye on opening a health resort" there. It was not to be. In fact, Dick and one of his lawyers had recently made a trip to Europe together. The word was that Richard Minns was looking for a place out of the country to liquidate his assets.

On July 12, Dudley Bell was admitted to the federal penitentiary in Seagoville, Texas, for perjury charges from a prior criminal case, to run concurrent with a six-month sentence for wiretapping.

The wiretapping conviction related to one of his divorce cases, for a man down in the Valley. Seems Dudley Bell was hired by a businessman named Rance Sweeten from McAllen, Texas, who was going through a rather messy divorce. Sweeten hired Bell to conduct an investigation into his wife's activities. The two talked, Sweeten said, about possibly tapping her phone.

Bell's response, Sweeten remembered, appalled him. Why bother with a wiretap? Sweeten recalled Bell telling him. Why not just have her killed?

On a sultry Houston night, close to dawn, while Jim Tatum lay slumbering in his bed, his wife, Liz, from whom he had recently filed for divorce, picked up a .22 revolver, pointed it at him, and fired four bullets into his chest and left arm.

Jim Tatum leaped out of bed and ran to a neighbor's home, naked, screaming for help. Liz Tatum called Dick DeGuerin.

The about-to-be-ex-Mrs. Tatum's tongue had been liberated by one too many arguments. Her husband, she told Dick DeGuerin, was a dangerous man. He bragged to her several times about killing people. Barbra Piotrowski's criminal lawyer listened with rapt interest to the conversation of the nearly former Mrs. Tatum. One of her comments, in particular, captured Dick DeGuerin's attention. Did he remember, Liz Tatum asked DeGuerin, her husband's statements to the newspapers about the mysterious money delivery through their mail slot? Dick DeGuerin nodded. It was a lie, Liz Tatum told the criminal lawyer. She was with Jim all night. There was never any ten thousand dollars delivered through their front door, in an envelope or otherwise. Dick DeGuerin suppressed a smile. He never thought there was. Tatum claims his ex-wife now denies telling this to DeGuerin.

A few weeks later, Jim Tatum noticed the deposition of a game warden he suspected was dating his wife. When he and Dudley Bell walked into the deposition room together and saw Dick DeGuerin, standing beside Liz Tatum as her divorce lawyer, the two men did a double take. Later, at another deposition, Jim Tatum sidled up to DeGuerin. "You know why Barbra Piotrowski got shot?" Tatum let the question dangle a moment. "Because *you* were threatening to file a palimony case against Richard Minns." Dick DeGuerin listened but didn't answer. Truth was, he had never made such a threat. It was all in Richard Minns's mind.

As the year after Barbra's shooting drew to a close, Houston private investigator Bobby Newman got his third call from Richard Minns for a job. He wanted Newman to find Barbra Piotrowski again, the way Newman had when she was in the hospital in November. He wanted to know where she was, Dick said, and he wanted to know if she was really paralyzed.

Bobby Newman accepted Richard Minns's offer. Within a day, he had located Barbra Piotrowski. One of his connections at the phone company provided him with copies of the long-distance records of a friend of hers in Houston. From them, he determined that Barbra was in Los Angeles.

Newman assigned one of his private investigators to fly to California and put Barbra Piotrowski under surveillance. The man he chose was a former Houston police officer who had quit the force to join Newman's detective agency, Don Pannell. The patrol officer who saw Barbra Piotrowski being shot in the Winchell's parking lot was being paid by Richard Minns to follow her and make certain she was really injured.

Pannell's message to Newman was brief. Yes, he said over the phone, after five or six days in Los Angeles, Barbra Piotrowski was truly paralyzed. He saw her in her wheelchair. He had pictures. She couldn't move from the chest down.

Bobby Newman filed his report and vowed never to work for Richard Minns again. The man, he decided, was "an asshole." An arrogant, paranoid, egotistical maniac. Newman resented the way Minns stormed into his office without an appointment and demanded that everyone put out their cigarettes. He was always, Newman noticed, sniffing. Sneaking off to the bathroom. The private investigator was convinced that Minns was snorting cocaine. His biggest problem with Richard Minns, however, concerned money. Minns, Newman would say, was as tight as any human being he had ever come across. He tried to force Newman's investigators to fly the red-eye, quibbled about hours, and put off paying his bill. Newman finally made up his mind he wasn't going to deal with that "nit-picking, phony son-of-a-bitch" again.

As the $4500 invoice grew more and more delinquent, Bobby Newman was having an increasingly difficult time locating Richard Minns. He wasn't going in to his office anymore. No one would say where he was. All his calls were being routed through Pat Hall.

After five months, Bobby Newman had had enough. He called Pat Hall and told her if Dick didn't pay his bill, Newman was going to sue him and get Dick DeGuerin to represent him. The next day, Bobby Newman got a check in the mail from Richard Minns. The envelope was postmarked Marina Del Rey, California . . . a few miles from where Don Pannell located Barbra Piotrowski.

On March 8, 1982—a full two years after Richard Minns feared it would happen—Barbra filed a petition for divorce, prepared by his nemesis, Dick DeGuerin. The basis of the divorce, DeGuerin pleaded, was either the ceremony Dick performed for himself and Barbra on their hotel balcony in Cozumel, or "express and implied contracts" from the beginning of the relationship.

A few months later, Dick DeGuerin initiated another lawsuit for Barbra Piotrowski. This one was more sensational than her divorce suit. Since the criminal justice system was dragging its feet in pursuing Minns, the lawyer reasoned, why not go after him through the *civil* courts, in a personal injury case? The way the law is set up, DeGuerin explained to Barbra, a civil court judge can award a plaintiff money for "wrongful injuries" from a defendant, even if there are no criminal charges against him. If they won, DeGuerin continued, Barbra could at least get a judgment against Dick to help pay for her medical costs. Plus, the lawyer pointed out excitedly, they could take Dick's deposition—question him, under oath, about the shooting. It was, he concluded, the perfect way to nail Richard.

On June 2, 1982, Dick DeGuerin filed a $220 million personal injury suit against Patrick Steen, Nathaniel Ivery, Robert Jess Anderson, Dudley Bell, and Richard Minns, based on a "conspiracy" engineered by Richard Minns and including assault, malicious prosecution, harassment, intimidation, slander, false imprisonment, and false arrest.

No sooner had DeGuerin filed the civil suit than Dick Minns began flexing every legal muscle he could think of to wriggle out of it. His first move was to file a "special appearance" in the case to test the jurisdiction of the court. He couldn't be sued in a Texas civil court, he challenged. He was living in Europe now. Permanently, he claimed.

When that failed, he adopted a new strategy. He couldn't fly to Houston to have his deposition taken, he notified the court, because he was "actively pursuing his business interests in Europe" and it would cause him "considerable inconvenience" to be deposed.

Behind the scenes, Dick Minns was quietly detaching himself from his holdings in the United States through a series of mysterious transactions. His property at Lakeway was sold, in 1982, to a British corporation called "Kremwod," then to another named "M.O.T. Industries." The president of both Kremwod and M.O.T. was Major Robert A. Wilson, one of Richard Minns's British attorneys.

About the same time, Dick Minns sold his interest in BD International, the corporate shell for the Olympia Fitness & Racquetball Center, to the same Kremwod Corporation of Great Britain.

In August of 1982, two months after DeGuerin filed the personal injury case for Barbra, Dick Minns quietly dropped his $200 million slander suit against DeGuerin and Percy Foreman.

Dick DeGuerin was disappointed. "Hell!" he'd say, and slap his knee. "I was lookin' forward to taking Richard's deposition in that slander case. I couldn't wait to ask him about all his so-called birthday stunts!" Richard, the lawyer told those who questioned him about the case, was running scared.

By the end of 1982, Barbra Piotrowski and Richard Minns, Houston's most public couple only two years earlier, had effectively disappeared.

26

Adrian Franks woke up one morning and realized he had to do something about his life. It was October 1982, his twenty-first birthday was a few days away, and his life was an unholy mess.

He was facing a prison sentence for credit card abuse. And he was already on federal probation for wiretapping.

Adrian Franks made a hasty appointment to see his lawyer, Frank Puckett. I just may, Franks told his attorney, have some information that will pull some weight with the feds.

By the middle of October 1982, Adrian Franks was sitting in a small, closed room at the FBI headquarters in Houston with Frank Puckett, three FBI agents, and Ken Williamson of the Houston Police Department. It was not the celebration he would have envisioned for himself four months earlier.

Kenny Williamson eyeballed Adrian Franks. He was slight—five feet seven, or five feet eight inches. Lucky if he weighed a hundred forty pounds. Like a high school kid. The homicide detective peered at Franks's stringy long hair and straggly black mustache. What kind of information could this punk possibly have on the Piotrowski case?

Adrian Franks started at the beginning. His father, he told the group gathered 'round him, was an old friend of Dudley Bell's—Zarko Franks. He was a reporter.

Kenny Williamson's eyebrow shot up. Zarko Franks was the reporter who wrote the "Golden Girl" articles for the *Houston Chronicle*.

When Adrian was sixteen years old, Zarko Franks suggested that his youngest son take a summer job with Zarko's old friend Dudley Bell. Adrian had a natural aptitude for electronics. Dudley could always use a go-fer. It was a perfect match.

Adrian was entranced by Dudley Bell's operation. The gadgets, the Guccis, the glamour of it all. Dudley, he remembered, started him out on "basic office electronics." Then it was on to a little bit of surveillance work. Within six months to a year, Adrian's story continued, Dudley had him doing "everything illegal that he needed somebody to do." Tap phones, bug and debug offices. "For somebody who's seventeen years old, and somebody is giving you two hundred and fifty dollars a night to go out and do something—hey! It's pretty easy to get introduced to that lifestyle."

In the spring of 1980, Dudley assigned Adrian and one of the other private investigators at Dudley Bell International, Larry Rubenstein, to do some basic surveillance and background checks on Barbra Piotrowski. One of their assignments was to tap her phone. Larry Rubenstein rented a first-floor apartment at Clarendon Court, kitty-corner from Barbra's upper apartment, for the two of them. Adrian's contribution was to drill holes into the kitchen cabinets and rig up the wiretap. He and Rubenstein didn't sleep at the apartment, Adrian told the authorities. But they spent their days there, listening to Barbra's taped conversations, sometimes following her. At the end of every day, Adrian said, he or Larry Rubenstein delivered the tapes to Dudley and reported back. Once, Adrian remembered, he brought tapes of Barbra Piotrowski's phone conversations directly to Richard Minns at the Guest Quarters. This continued, Adrian related, until he overheard Barbra call Southwestern Bell to report a tap on the line. Then they removed it.

One day, Adrian's story went on, Dudley called him into his office. He was sitting on his couch, acting more mysterious than usual. "You wanna make ten thousand dollars?" he asked Adrian, in a low, serious tone. "What for?" Franks asked. Dudley pointed with his index finger and made a motion with his thumb, like he was shooting a gun. Then he reached under the glass coffee table in front of the couch and pulled out a manila folder stuffed with cash. "Do you know anybody who would want to hit somebody?" he asked. Adrian was barely taken aback. "No, not particularly," he said casually, "but tell me more about it." Dudley Bell, Adrian said, "indicated it was Barbra Piotrowski." Adrian said no.

A few weeks later, Adrian Franks was in "financial difficulties." A ten-thousand-dollar insurance payment he had received earlier in the year was long gone. In its place were a new stereo, a motorcycle, and a stack of bills. "All of a sudden," Adrian decided, "ten thousand dollars was looking pretty good."

Adrian went back to Dudley and asked him if the job was still available. Dudley said yes. The detective reached into his desk drawer and pulled out a several-page dossier on Barbra Piotrowski. "You have any ideas on what you're gonna do?" he asked. "Well, not really," Franks replied. "I hadn't thought about it." Bell's voice lowered. "Well," he said tersely, "you need to follow her around and get her habits identified. See where she goes and what she does. Then just pick a good place and do it, however you want to." Adrian asked if he could have half the ten thousand dollars up front, as an advance. Dudley Bell, he remembered, "laughed. Then he reached into his manila folder and pulled out four one-hundred-dollar bills and handed them to me."

Adrian started following Barbra Piotrowski on his motorcycle. She drove her Firebird too fast; he kept losing her. Adrian needed a plan. He would make a remote control device and install it on her car; then he would keep the transmitter on his motorcycle and, when she was in a spot that wasn't accessible, he'd push the button and stall her car. Once she was stopped, he would stab her with his kitchen knife. Adrian couldn't afford a gun. Dudley didn't give him enough money.

Adrian started building the remote control device in the secret workshop at Dudley Bell's office. Bell came in one day and asked him what he was making. "A kill switch," Franks replied. "He seemed," Adrian remembered, "to kind of smile at that terminology."

Late one night, Adrian crept into the parking lot at Clarendon Court and installed the remote control device underneath the hood of Barbra Piotrowski's car. Then he started following her again. One afternoon, when she was on Bissonnet, he pushed the kill switch to test it. It didn't work. A few days later, Adrian heard that Barbra Piotrowski's car stalled on the way to Dick DeGuerin's office and that the police found his remote control apparatus and thought it was a bomb.

After weeks or months (Adrian wasn't sure how long), he mentioned the job to a friend of his, Bobby Day, a scruffy, self-described former juvenile delinquent who was crashing at Adrian's apartment with his girlfriend, Sue Ellen. Try as he might, Adrian Franks just didn't have the killer instinct. Bobby Day had no such compunctions. He volunteered to kill Piotrowski for a mere fifteen hundred dollars. Adrian could keep the rest.

Bobby sent his girlfriend Sue Ellen to the Royal Jewelry Pawn Shop to buy a gun—for "protection," he told her. You couldn't, he scoffed to Adrian, kill someone with a kitchen knife! Sue Ellen returned with a small $59.95 .22-caliber revolver. Over the coming days, Bobby and Adrian sat in Adrian's kitchen and built a silencer, following a manual called *The Anarchist's Cookbook*. One night, when the silencer was installed, Bobby Day smeared mascara all over his face, tied on a bandana, and asked Adrian to drive him to Barbra Piotrowski's apartment. Day rang her doorbell and asked if he could come in and use her phone. He had car trouble. Barbra didn't answer. "We were really smart," Adrian said sheepishly to the FBI agents and Ken Williamson, "weren't we?"

Soon afterward, Dudley Bell called Adrian back into his office. He was taking too long, Dudley complained. He was going to have to get someone else to do it. He needed the four hundred dollars back. He had to return it, Adrian thought he remembered Dudley saying, to Richard Minns.

Kenny Williamson took detailed notes of Adrian Franks's statement. Finally, a break! the detective thought excitedly. He returned to his office and immediately started digging, to see if he could corroborate any of the facts.

Ken Williamson visited the Royal Jewelry Pawn Shop and found a receipt in Sue Ellen Perkins's name for the purchase of a $59.95 gun on October 7, 1980. The

Clarendon Court Apartments likewise had a record of a Larry Rubenstein renting an apartment on the first level, kitty-corner from Barbra Piotrowski, in the month of May. The kitchen cabinets in the apartment still had holes in the exact spots where Adrian said he drilled to install the wiretap on Barbra's phone. Then the detective located Bobby Day, also known as "Choppy" Farr. Choppy—or Bobby—confirmed Adrian Franks's statement. Sue Ellen Perkins remembered buying the gun, remembered Adrian and Bobby building a silencer, and remembered them spending several nights "watching a girl." The police already had a record of the mysterious device that was installed on Barbra's car. The bomb squad even had pictures. Everything in Adrian Franks's story, Ken Williamson confirmed, checked out.

The homicide detective gathered his information and brought it in to Ted and Terry Wilson, with the self-satisfied smile of a student who knew he had the right answer for a difficult-to-please teacher. The two prosecutors studied the evidence and put in a good word for Adrian Franks with the federal authorities. Then they did what they had been doing since the day Bob Anderson was brought in: nothing. *Again*, Ted Wilson cited the accomplice-witness rule. Sure, he told Kenny, there was all kinds of evidence to corroborate what Adrian Franks said, and that was great. But it still wasn't enough. Ted Wilson's concern was a hairsplitting legal question: Did the State's independent evidence have to corroborate what Adrian Franks said, or that Dudley Bell made the solicitation? If it was Bell's solicitation, Ted Wilson was afraid they might have a problem. He didn't want to run the risk of trying the case against Dudley Bell with Franks's testimony, and losing. Then they'd be shut out of ever trying Bell again because of the double jeopardy rule: A person can't be tried twice for the same crime. Better, Ted Wilson decided, to wait. See if anything else turned up. Kenny Williamson felt as though he were being slowly tortured. The trail was getting cold, he fumed. It had already been two years since Barbra Piotrowski was shot. What were Ted and Terry Wilson waiting for? A videotaped confession from Richard Minns or Dudley Bell?

Dudley Bell had no idea Adrian Franks had given a statement. Eight months earlier, in February of 1982, Bell was released from the Segoville Penitentiary on parole, with the special condition that he not work as a private investigator until February of 1986. Days later, he was an ocean away, in Europe. Richard Minns's new home.

Two years passed before there was any activity on Barbra Piotrowski's attempted murder case. Two years of frustration for Ken Williamson, for Barbra Piotrowski, and for Dick DeGuerin. In this interim, Dick DeGuerin became convinced that Richard Minns was "hiding out." Every time DeGuerin noticed Dick's deposition, Dick communicated, through his lawyers, some reason why he couldn't fly to Houston. First it was "business interests" in Europe, then it was his health. No one seemed to know exactly where Richard Minns *was*. No one, that is, except his ever-loyal assistant, Pat Hall. Overnight, Pat Hall had become Richard Minns's alter-ego. Any communication with the once Great Communicator went through Hall. Even Mimi Minns directed her correspondence for Dick to Hall, who obtained a power-of-attorney to sign his checks and "consummate substantial business transactions."

Dick Minns had become a phantom.

Perhaps it was the phase of the moon, or the position of the stars, or the planetary alignment. For whatever reason, on March 22, 1984, seventeen months after Adrian Franks came forward, Ted Wilson and Terry Wilson made the decision to seek an indictment against Dudley Bell.

Why that day, that month, that year? Nothing had changed since October of 1982, when Adrian Franks gave his statement about Bell's solicitation. No new evidence. No startling revelations.

Ted Wilson's explanation was cautious and oblique; the kind of response it takes three years in law school to perfect. "We kind of wrestled with that for a long time," he ruminated one day, sitting in his office at the District Attorney's Building, "wondering whether we would ever come up with anything else. Finally, the decision—it was a joint decision between Terry and I—we felt, when we went to the grand jury, that we would never get any more than what we have now, so let's take a run with it and see."

"The time had come," was Terry Wilson's simple pronouncement.

Kenny Williamson would say it was because he "wouldn't let 'em forget it. I just kept workin' on 'em." When the decision was made, Williamson didn't stop to question or analyze his good fortune. He grabbed his keys, called his partner, Don McAnulty, and hopped in his car to make the arrest he'd been waiting to make for four years.

Dudley Bell had no idea what was awaiting him that Thursday morning. He'd been back from France almost five months—working, he assured his parole officer, in vague terms, in "real estate." On March 22, he arose early, selected a light-tan sports jacket, beige open-neck shirt, and a pair of dark-brown trousers. Then he ran a comb through his thick, salt-and-pepper waves and stepped outside to his brown Mercedes to make an early morning appointment downtown. The meeting, appropriately, was with Jim Tatum.

When Dudley Bell strolled out of Jim Tatum's office on Prairie Street at nine-twenty, Ken Williamson and Dan McAnulty were outside the building to greet him, with a warrant for his arrest. Off to the side stood a uniformed patrol officer and a police photographer. The P.I. who specialized in snapping surreptitious pictures was about to have his arrest captured in living color.

Dudley Bell acted surprised. "What am I under arrest for?" he asked Ken Williamson. The homicide detective deepened his brow. "Solicitation of capital murder," he said solemnly, as he led Bell toward the back of his car to frisk him.

Dudley Bell was the perfect gentleman. "Why didn't you call me at home?" he asked amiably. "I'd have come down."

When Bell walked out of the booking office at the downtown jail a few hours later, a crowd of reporters was gathered, studying his body language for a clue to his state of mind. Bell erupted into a dazzling grin. "Not guilty!" he blurted, as he walked by.

The front page of the next day's *Houston Chronicle* featured a photo of a smug Dudley Bell at the police station, next to photographs of a grinning Richard Minns, and a wheelchair-seated Barbra Piotrowski. The headline read: ARRESTED IN BOTCHED MURDER PLOT.

Two inches to the left, Channel 13 consumer reporter Marvin Zindler, whom Vic Pecorino claimed pressured him into filing the theft charges against Barbra Piotrowski for Dick Minns, was photographed smiling broadly after being named Houston television's "million-dollar man" that day, having signed a "lifetime contract" with Channel 13 for over a million a year.

A year earlier, Marvin Zindler's name had appeared in the same paper, buried on the back pages, for a much different reason. In 1983, he was named as a defendant, along with Richard Minns and Bob Delmonteque, in a fifty-million-dollar conspiracy and fraud case filed by five Nautilus Training Center owners in Houston.

Minns, the Nautilus owners alleged, drove them out of business by using his "political influence" and by running a "smear campaign" through Marvin Zindler.

Dick DeGuerin made copies of the Nautilus lawsuit when it was made public and put them in his Barbra Piotrowski file. Evidence, he smiled, for the future.

Four days after Dudley Bell's arrest and the announcement of Marvin Zindler's million-dollar contract, Bell was formally arraigned. Richard Minns, the *Houston Post* stated, "is reportedly in Switzerland and could not be reached for comment." A reporter with the paper called Minns's office. Richard Minns, Pat Hall said icily, was in a hospital in Europe recovering from a car accident and couldn't speak with anyone.

Kenny Williamson's arrest of Dudley Bell yielded an unexpected bonus. While the police were searching Bell's car for evidence, they found a box of microcassette tapes in the trunk of his Mercedes, neatly tagged and labeled. The tapes were recordings of the phone conversations of a woman named Latrese Carroll, a Memorial housewife who was having an affair with a Houston drilling contractor named George Savage. Savage entertained suspicions that Ms. Carroll had taken another lover, became wildly jealous, and hired Dudley to tap her phone and find out.

The tapes in Bell's trunk proved that he had not only been acting as a private investigator in violation of his parole agreement, he was also illegally recording telephone conversations. This time, Kenny Williamson grinned, Bell was caught with his hand in the cookie jar.

In the autumn, Dudley Bell was convicted of wiretapping in the Savage case and sentenced to five years in the federal penitentiary.

The next month, Dick Minns's avoidance tactics in Barbra's civil suit took an increasingly urgent tone. In a motion to the court in November of 1984, his attorney requested that all depositions in the case be abated because Richard Minns was "physically incapable of participating." He was, his lawyer pleaded, "primarily confined to intensive home confinement."

Dick DeGuerin dismissed the document as so much hooey. DeGuerin had already discovered that Dick Minns had been in Houston the first half of 1983, the same period Dick was filing motions saying he couldn't fly to Texas for his deposition because of "business interests" in Europe. When DeGuerin pointed that out to the court, Dick Minns had an explanation ready. His "lifelong friend" Joe Reynolds was seriously ill in January of 1983, he answered in an interrogatory. He had to fly to Texas to visit Reynolds in the hospital.

While Dick Minns was in Houston, he made an appointment with Dr. Craig Pratt at the Baylor College of Medicine—a young doctor Barbra met with Dick at a party a few years earlier. Dick had been experiencing shortness of breath lately when he went jogging and wanted to know why.

Pratt diagnosed a pulmonary embolism in Dick's right calf in a spot where he had been attacked by a bill fish while water-skiing sixteen years earlier. Then Pratt discovered a clot-filled pseudoaneurysm in a vein in the calf. While he was in Houston, Dick had surgery on the vein to close the defect.

Irv Weissman referred to his brother-in-law's aneurysm as a "fancy charley horse." Dr. Craig Pratt's medical reports for the court depicted it as life threatening—or, at least, sufficiently debilitating to make it impossible for Dick to have his deposition taken.

In 1984, Pratt reported to the court that Richard Minns had been in a "near-fatal" car accident in Switzerland on December 24, 1983, although, for some reason, he wasn't admitted to a hospital until January 5. Pratt said he flew to Lausanne, which he identified as Minns's "home," to examine him. This is the letter Pratt filed with the court:

> I am sorry to report that Mr. Minns' condition has worsened. First, the rare condition in his right lower extremity has not improved. I am even more concerned about his neurological condition, post-concussion syndrome.
>
> I insist that Mr. Minns not be subjected to any stressful situations, including any travel or the stress of any interrogation, oral or written, in any legal proceeding. Total rest and isolation are imperative parts of his present therapy. . . .

Elsewhere in his answers to Barbra Piotrowski's lawsuit, Dick himself swore in November 1984 that he had not been in the United States since July 1983.

At least two people had reason to doubt that. Jimmie LaHaye, Dick Minns's personal assistant at President's-First Lady for twenty years, got a call out of the blue from Richard, sometime in 1984. He was in town, Dick said, and wanted LaHaye to look for a townhouse in Houston for him to lease.

Then there was a former neighbor of Dick and Mimi's, who lived down the street from the Memorial mansion. He was certain he saw Dick Minns at Lakeway in 1984. At the marina. In his boat.

By the spring of 1985, Kenny Williamson should have been accustomed to receiving unexpected calls on the Piotrowski case. But when Frank Price, a special agent with the FBI, called, it was a stunner. About a year before, the FBI special agent told Kenny Williamson, in March 1984, he was supervising a large-scale sting operation called Camshaft, an investigation into an interstate car theft ring. That month, he assigned one of his special FBI agents, Luis Davila, to work undercover to befriend one of the men suspected to be in the ring. The target's name was Robert Jess Anderson.

Anderson, Price told Williamson, became chummy with Davila. While Davila and Anderson were talking one day, Anderson—who had no idea his conversation was being monitored by two FBI agents in another room—boasted to Davila that he'd been hired by two men named Dudley Bell and Jerry Thompson to make a hit on a chick named Barbra Piotrowski, that he'd gone to California to hire hit men, and that they made the hit. Anderson repeated the story to Davila twelve or thirteen times, Price said. Ten or eleven of the conversations were secretly recorded on FBI audio and videotapes.

Kenny Williamson smirked. Bob Anderson, he thought to himself, would probably still be talking when he was in his grave.

There was another matter, the FBI agent said to Williamson, his voice dropping to a confidential tone. It concerned prosecutors Ted and Terry Wilson. On the tapes, Price said, Anderson bragged to Davila about having paid off "one of the Wilson boys." Then again, Price added, Anderson probably mentioned ten other people he claimed to have bribed too. How well, Frank Price asked Kenny Williamson, did he know the two Wilsons?

Kenny Williamson didn't even hesitate. There was just no way, he said somberly, that Ted or Terry Wilson could have been paid off. Bob Anderson was nothing but a bag of hot wind, he told Frank Price. Half of what he said was bullshit.

Frank Price listened intently to Ken Williamson and took him at his word. The next week, Williamson got permission to go to Ted and Terry Wilson with the FBI videotapes.

The two assistant D.A.s had just been handed Bob Anderson on a silver platter.

Later that month—June 1985—Robert Jess Anderson was officially indicted on solicitation of capital murder in the Piotrowski case.

A full year passed before Anderson's case made any progress in the courts, a year in which Dudley Bell was released from federal prison for wiretapping in the Savage case. The last half of 1986, Dudley Bell was living in

Orlando, Florida, and working at a Wash-on-Wheels at an hourly wage that was less than most teenagers make at Burger King.

When his trial date on the Piotrowski solicitation case came around in February 1987, Dudley Bell was no longer on friendly terms with Jim Tatum—a dispute, both said, over money. Two other longtime criminal lawyer buddies of Bell's, Bob Hunt and Jim Patterson, agreed to try the case.

From the moment the defense attorney uttered the last word of his closing argument, it took the jury only one hour to convict Dudley Clifford Bell, Jr., of solicitation of capital murder. When the verdict was announced, Dudley Bell's ever-present smile disappeared. It was the first time, Charlie Wells observed, Dudley Bell had ever turned his back to a camera in his life.

Five days later, on March 3, 1987, the same jury sentenced Bell to thirty-eight years in a Texas penitentiary and fined him ten thousand dollars. The judge, Mary Bacon, whom even Bell's attorney praised, was so moved by the testimony she pronounced Dudley Bell a "dangerous man."

Behind the scenes, there was perhaps as much drama going on as there was in court. The day of Dudley Bell's sentencing, Kenny Williamson would claim, one of Bell's attorneys approached him and the Wilsons and asked them a question: If Dudley could produce tapes incriminating Minns that led to Minns's indictment, would the State dismiss the charge against Bell? He and the Wilsons, Williamson would recall, said no. They'd cut a deal with Bell, the detective related, but they wouldn't let him walk. Even if it meant losing Richard Minns. They'd been waiting for Dudley too long, was the way Kenny Williamson looked at it. They couldn't just let him go. Dudley wanted all or nothing, so the deal disintegrated.

Terry Wilson would remember the same conversation in the same way. Ted Wilson remembered it differently. Dudley Bell's attorney, he insisted, never indicated he actually had tapes incriminating Richard Minns. His conversation, Ted Wilson maintained, was strictly a "What if." Kenny Williamson, Ted Wilson scoffed, "wasn't even there."

Long after the fact, Dudley Bell's two attorneys denied having had any such conversation at all.

Whether or not one of Dudley Bell's attorneys made an offer of tapes to the Wilsons and Ken Williamson, there was one point on which everyone agreed: Dudley Bell would have secretly recorded his conversations with the person who hired him to have Barbra Piotrowski killed. "Dudley is not stupid," Ken Williamson would remark. "I would bet my last dollar that he's got tapes of talking to Minns. Something that he can hold over Minns's head. I just believe that with everything I've got—that there's a large bank account somewhere that either he's already got access to, or that he'll receive or have access to when he gets out of the pen."

It would not be the first time Dudley Bell tried to make money by serving a prison term. Two years earlier, when he and oilman George Savage were indicted after police found tapes of Savage's girlfriend's phone conversations in the trunk of Bell's Mercedes, Dudley Bell arranged a tête-à-tête with Savage. He had a proposition for him, Savage said Bell told him. He would take the rap for both of them in the wiretapping case if Savage paid him a $250,000 flat fee, plus $6,000 for every month he had to spend in prison.

Bell was doing the same thing for Richard Minns. Kenny Williamson just *knew* it.

That same spring, Bob Anderson's strange case proceeded to trial. The year before, in 1986, his attorney, Doug O'Brien, argued that Anderson should not be tried at all. The Wilsons, he observed, promised Anderson immunity the night he was secretly arrested, back in October 1980. "There was no immunity discussed, period," Terry Wilson said flatly. Ted Wilson said he remembered that he and Terry told Bob Anderson that if Anderson could help put together a case to indict anyone else, he would not be prosecuted. What about the video? O'Brien asked. Wasn't Anderson's questioning in the district attorney's conference room secretly videotaped? The answer would be on that cassette. Ted and Terry Wilson stared at O'Brien blankly. They had no idea where the videotape might be. "I don't believe it was videotaped," Terry Wilson offered. The judge ruled in favor of Ted and Terry Wilson: Bob Anderson, he determined, was not given immunity from being prosecuted for Barbra Piotrowski's attempted murder.

Late in August 1986, as the case was getting close to trial, the two Wilsons disqualified themselves from prosecuting Anderson—because, they explained, they could be called as witnesses. On the very eve of the trial, a young assistant district attorney named Ruben Perez opened an envelope in the D.A.'s file room marked "Patrick Steen." Inside was the missing videotape of the Wilsons' conversation with Bob Anderson. On it, Ted and Terry Wilson promised Bob Anderson, on camera, that if he provided them with enough information, he could "walk out free." Didn't matter, the Wilsons argued. Even if Anderson was given immunity, he forfeited it by tipping off Jerry Thompson that he was wired. The judge agreed with the Wilsons.

Anderson's trial, in May 1987, was a mere technicality. Based on the many statements he made to undercover FBI agent Luis Davila that he hired Piotrowski's killers, Bob Anderson was found guilty and sentenced to thirty-eight years in prison, with a ten-thousand-dollar fine—the same sentence as Dudley Bell was given three months earlier.

Doug O'Brien, Anderson's lawyer, immediately filed an appeal. Bob Anderson might not be a Boy Scout, O'Brien argued, but he got a raw deal. Anderson, he pointed out, gave Ted and Terry Wilson all kinds of information—more than enough to indict Dudley Bell—way back in 1980. "If I were Barbra," O'Brien commented one day, musing on the case, "I'd be pissed off that they had this information back then, that they could have prosecuted Dudley Bell, and that he walked the streets for years. And had they done that, who knows what he would have done? He may have gone ahead and turned, and they may have then been able to prosecute Minns."

Barbra Piotrowski and Dick DeGuerin were just grateful Dudley Bell was finally in prison. Seven years after the fact,

four individuals in the murder-for-hire chain were behind
bars. That left, to their calculation, only one. If he couldn't
indict Richard Minns in a criminal court, Dick DeGuerin
was determined to get him in civil court.

27

Bob Anderson's conviction in May 1987 marked the five-year point in Barbra Piotrowski's civil suit against Richard Minns. In those five years, Richard Minns had never set foot in a Houston courtroom. His deposition had yet to be taken.

Dick DeGuerin was tired of Dick Minns's games. Early in 1986, the lawyer stared in disgust at the latest letter from Dr. Craig Pratt describing Minns's "life-threatening" pulmonary embolism and "post-concussion syndrome." "Under no circumstance should Richard Minns make a long trip from Switzerland to the United States," Pratt directed, "nor be subjected to any stress situation including trial or legal proceeding."

A few weeks later, DeGuerin received a phone call from a woman who was visiting Houston from the Cayman Islands. She had read something in the newspaper about Dudley Bell and Barbra Piotrowski and Richard Minns, she told DeGuerin, and she was concerned. "I just leased my condominium in Cayman to Richard Minns," she said anxiously. "What should I do?"

"Get a lawyer," DeGuerin responded immediately. "And be careful."

In the coming months, scattered reports filtered into DeGuerin of Richard Minns sightings. He was in the Cayman Islands, witnesses related, water-skiing, deep-sea fishing and having, apparently, a grand time. Other sources placed him in Israel. Pat Hall testified he called her from a London hotel. Dick himself claimed, through interrogatories, to be a resident of Switzerland. It was all, DeGuerin grumbled, a giant hoax.

Sometime in 1986, Dick DeGuerin got his hands on a
set of legal documents that proved indisputably that Dick
Minns was in the United States in 1985, when he was,
according to Craig Pratt, too ill to travel. On October 16,
1985, the legal pages showed, Richard Minns was in New
Orleans trying to get a passport for himself using the name
Robert Lender Chester. He provided the clerk with a birth
certificate in the name of Robert Lender Chester, and a
written history of the Chester family of Oklahoma. When
the clerk asked his date of birth, Minns answered July.
Robert Chester's birth date was December 25, 1923. A
United States customs special agent arrested Minns, took
him to customs, and he confessed. He was trying to leave
the country, Minns told the assistant U.S. attorney, and he
didn't want to leave under his own name because he "had
some problems with his wife" and didn't want her to know
that he was coming and going out of the country under his
own name.

Richard Minns was not alone that day in New Orleans.
His companion was Pat Hall. When the customs agent questioned Minns about the false birth certificate, Hall admitted
that Robert Lender Chester was her deceased cousin, and
that she had given Dick the birth certificate and family
history so he could get a passport under another name due
to "personal problems." She also signed an affidavit stating
that she knew "Robert Chester" (alias Richard Minns).

The afternoon of his arrest, Dick Minns posted a twenty-
five-thousand-dollar bond and was released. Eight days later, Peter Strasser, the assistant U.S. attorney, would remember, Minns and his lawyer, Irving Warshauer, "pleaded and
pleaded" with him to classify the crime as a misdemeanor.
"We finally relented," Strasser recalled. In exchange for a
guilty plea, Richard Minns was given five years probation
and fined three thousand dollars. "The past three years,"
Irving Warshauer wrote in his brief to the court, Richard
Minns "has primarily resided in either the United Kingdom
or Switzerland and has substantial business interests in
Europe that make it essential that he be permitted to travel
throughout Europe and other parts of the world." Minns, he
added, "has no prior criminal record and has never been the
subject of any arrest."

Two months after Dudley Bell's sentence, the same month Bob Anderson was imprisoned, the judge in Barbra Piotrowski's personal injury case, Family District Judge Bill Elliott, scheduled a videotaped deposition of Richard Minns, to be held in his courtroom on May 8, 1987. For the sixteenth time in five years, Richard Minns failed to appear. His attorney, John Gano, brought with him a letter from Minns's "Swiss doctor," Jean-Pierre Hungerbühler of Lausanne. Richard Minns, Dr. Hungerbühler said in his letter, was at the Clinique Cécil in Lausanne with a "severe nervous breakdown." The symptoms were familiar: post-concussion syndrome, poor memory, inability to think or concentrate, lack of vision, depression, continuous bursting headaches. So was the treatment: total rest and isolation, no stress, no travel, and no interrogatories or medical examinations for "an indefinite period of time."

Dick DeGuerin and his co-counsel, G. P. Hardy, blew up. Elsewhere in his letter, Dr. Hungerbühler had referred to Richard Minns's condition "worsening" due to an "unfortunate accident" the previous February. The accident, DeGuerin and Hardy pointed out, occurred while Minns was water-skiing!

"Seems he only gets these sudden illnesses, throbbing headaches, when the court orders his deposition," Hardy railed.

Judge Bill Elliott was evidently wearying of Richard Minns's excuses, as well. When the hearing came to a close, he fined Minns twenty-five thousand dollars for contempt of court (which Minns never paid) and set a trial date of July 8, two months hence. The rumor in Houston lawyers' circles was that Minns was heading for a default judgment if he didn't appear in Elliott's court the day of the trial setting.

Richard Minns was beginning to get exceedingly nervous. Through his lawyer, he filed a motion in Judge Elliott's court claiming he was a Swiss resident. A court order demanding his appearance, he petitioned, violated the sovereignty of Switzerland.

Behind the scenes, he was making one of his emergency calls to a Houston private investigator, from a number in Geneva. His choice this time was Clyde Wilson, a man who justifiably held the title Dudley Bell claimed as the "most famous private eye in Texas." Clyde Wilson was the P.I. to the rich and famous before he was mentioned in *Blood and Money;* afterward, he rose to the status of legend.

Dick made small talk with Wilson for a few minutes and brought him up to date on the Piotrowski case. Then he headed straight for the point. "Well," he drawled to Wilson, "I'll tell you why I'm calling. I'm calling because I've given thought to the various people that I know in Houston and in Texas and it seems like you might be the one person that can do somethin'. . . . If you think you can be of help, then you'll report to Joe Reynolds, or [former governor] Mark White or whatever, you know, and that'll preserve the privilege.

"Here's the bottom line," Dick went on, with more urgency. "Bill Elliott is about to drop somewhere between a twenty to thirty-million-dollar default judgment on me because I didn't show up for a videotaped deposition in his court, and so that's punishment." He paused. "Is there any way you can stop that? Do you have any stroke with Bill Elliott?"

Clyde Wilson listened politely while Dick rambled on about how Bill Elliott "runs his court like Judge Roy Bean, the law west of the Pecos," what a "ludicrous" and "phony" marriage claim Barbra had against him, and how he was a resident of Switzerland and Barbra was a resident of California, so "it doesn't even come under the law." Then the seasoned detective hung up, pushed a button to rewind the tape on his telephone recording device and took it out to turn over to the police. Wilson had been involved in some bizarre cases over the years, Lord knows, but he had no desire to get tangled up in this mess.

How ironic, the private investigator must have thought, when he ended the phone conversation. Richard Minn's last word to him was *Peace.*

On Wednesday, July 8, 1987, the starting date of the trial in Barbra's personal injury case, Richard Minns's prophecy came true. When he failed to show up in court—for the seventeenth time—Judge Bill Elliott entered a default judgment. Then he ordered Richard Minns to pay Barbra Piotrowski $28.6 million: $10 million for past damages,

$10 million for future damages, and $8.6 million in interest. "Mr. Minns's string," Barbra's lawyer G. P. Hardy announced afterward, "finally ran out."

While Dick DeGuerin and G. P. Hardy faced a collection problem—how to locate and seize the assets Richard Minns had been liquidating and funneling out of the country for years—the default judgment raised anew the question that had gone officially unanswered since October 20, 1980: Did Richard Minns pay Dudley Bell to have Barbra Piotrowski killed?

On a beautiful Indian summer Sunday in 1988, Dudley Bell sat behind a glass panel in the visitors' room of the Beto I prison unit in Tennessee Colony, Texas, and talked, for the first time, about the Barbra Piotrowski shooting.

Yes, he admitted, he did do a background check on Barbra Piotrowski for Richard Minns, and yes, he had Larry Rubenstein and Adrian Franks tap her phone. But he didn't know who Richard Minns was at the time. He swore it.

This, of course, was impossible. According to Mimi Minns, Dick Minns hired Dudley Bell the year before Barbra was shot to help Mike Minns with his divorce case, and Dick had used Bell for other jobs through the years. Furthermore, Dudley Bell was a longstanding member of the downtown President's Club.

Dudley Bell also professed pure and utter innocence in the Piotrowski shooting. He dropped the Piotrowski case in March, he said indignantly, after a month and a half. He and Minns, the detective said, had a "falling-out" over the bill. Bell couldn't explain why it was, then, that he showed up at Dick Minns's lakehouse in Austin with Dick Minns a few days after the shooting. Minns, he said testily, still owes him thirteen hundred dollars.

Everyone who testified against him, Bell said—everybody—lied. Adrian Franks "cut a deal" with the district attorney and lied. James Perry Dillard made up a story about being offered ten thousand dollars by him to "hit a pussy" because Dillard "wanted to get in with the D.A.'s office" so they'd send him some detective business. John Liles, Bell volunteered, reversed Rick Waring's warning the month before the shooting. Waring *really* told Liles that it was Piotrowski who was trying to put a hit on Minns. Liles switched it, Bell said, because Liles is "jealous" of him.

Dudley Bell leaned in closer to the glass partition. He conducted his own investigation after the shooting, he said eagerly. This is what really went down. Barbra Piotrowski and a girlfriend who was staying with her from Las Vegas ripped off Bob Anderson on a cocaine deal out of California. Anderson saw Piotrowski's picture in a Houston newspaper and brought the two blacks from California to Texas to kill her. The blacks screwed it up. Dick DeGuerin couldn't get any money out of Steen and Ivery, so he "put it on" Richard Minns instead.

He'd never seen Bob Anderson in his life till he met him at the county jail in 1986 or 1984, Bell insisted. Jerry Thompson had talked to him about some tomato farm, the detective admitted, but he never met Anderson. Never even saw him before.

What about Rob Renner? The man who testified to a grand jury that he met Bob Anderson sitting with Bell at a Denny's before the shooting? More lies, Bell responded. He never even met Renner until 1984, at a federal penitentiary in Big Rock.

How did Bell explain the meeting at the Black Angus five days after Piotrowski was shot? Both Jim Tatum and Bob Anderson said they met with Bell as a threesome at the Black Angus on October 25, 1980. That would prove he knew Bob Anderson before 1984.

Dudley Bell squirmed uneasily in his seat behind the glass partition, stalling for time to come up with an answer. He "forgot all about that," he said finally, wearing a sheepish grin. That was Jim Tatum's deal, he said. Tatum arranged it. Tatum paged him one night at the Back Stage bar in the Galleria and asked him to meet him at the Black Angus. Said he got a funny call from some guy who wanted his help to get two guys out of jail. He wanted Dudley to go with him.

That still didn't make sense. Why would Tatum call Bell to meet with him and Anderson at the Black Angus if Bell didn't know Bob Anderson?

Dudley Bell moved his large frame from side to side in his chair. A look of worry crept into his face. "There's gotta be a reason he'd call me and get me out of the damn club," he puzzled, thinking out loud. After a long time of quiet—long enough for Bell to come up with an explanation—the detective's face brightened. "I remember what it was!" he said, smirking. Anderson—or someone, probably a lawyer, Bell thought—used his name to call Tatum. That's why Tatum called him, Bell said excitedly. "I forgot all about that," he repeated, trying to reinforce this flimsy explanation.

The detective yammered on about how he was writing his autobiography in prison. He had, he said, eighteen yellow legal pads filled already. Gonna be a big book. Huge.

"That's Dudley," Larry Rubenstein, the private investigator who rented the apartment below Barbra's with Adrian Franks, said simply. Even Jim Tatum, Bell's friend and, for a time, criminal lawyer on the Piotrowski case, indirectly implicated him. "I cannot say," Tatum acknowledged, two years into Dudley Bell's prison sentence, "that anybody has been wrongly convicted." Tatum paused. "But there's still one main player who hasn't stepped up to the window yet."

Who was the puppeteer, the person behind Dudley Bell, pulling the strings that almost ended Barbra Piotrowski's life? Adrian Franks dared to say the name that everyone in Houston had been whispering for months, years, now, unbelievably, almost a decade. It was Richard Minns, Bell's former employee said confidently. There were no other possibilities. "Dudley'd never come out and say Minns exactly," said Adrian Franks, "but hell! What other options are there in the world? I personally—and I can swear to this on anything—I personally delivered wiretapped tapes and put them in his hand." Zarko Franks's son curled his lip. "Let's not be stupid," he said, deadpan. "You can't draw conclusions in a court of law, but in life you got to *live* by it."

Even Dudley Bell's most recent attorney, Bob Hunt, points the finger at Richard Minns. "I would assume," says Hunt, "that Minns probably had something to do with it. If he didn't, he wouldn't be gone."

"There's no doubt that Richard Minns did it," Bob Anderson's criminal lawyer, Doug O'Brien, says confidently. "In the criminal law, we always talk about flight being evidence of a person's guilt. Hey, why would he have taken off and left town and be hiding out if he didn't have anything to hide?"

Off the official record, Houston burglary and theft officer Charlie Wells, Dudley Bell's old high school classmate, will talk about how "everybody in Dudley's office" was approached by Dudley about the hit. He heard that, Wells would say in a low tone, from one of Dudley's secretaries.

Many theories were batted around Houston law offices, living rooms, and cocktails parties as to why Dudley Bell would contract with Richard Minns to kill Barbra Piotrowski, but they all came down to the same thing: money.

Rick Waring, Dudley Bell's friend and sometime P.I./bodyguard, believes Dudley is still holding out for money: that he intends to blackmail Richard Minns one day with tapes he made of Minns discussing Piotrowski's murder. "There *are* tapes," Waring insists. "And he's got 'em. I can tell you frankly that he taped everything. Now why in the world he wouldn't tape his conversations with Minns to protect himself . . . he *told* me he did!" Those tapes, Waring contends, are Dudley Bell's retirement fund. "Now you're talkin' big money. I think they're worth half a million dollars."

Bell himself has boasted, from his cell in the Beto prison unit, that he has a huge box of Richard Minns recordings— "every time I talked to the damn guy."

For a while, Rick Waring hints, Dudley kept the tapes in a safety deposit box at his bank, Lockwood National, then he switched them over to Waring's name. "I'm sure they've been moved around by now," Waring says coyly. Perhaps to an Igloo cooler, buried somewhere. That was one of Dudley's "favorite tricks," Waring reveals, because the contents would stay dry. "I honestly don't know where they are now," Waring said recently. "I'm not in that close of a deal for anyone to have that trust bestowed to me." The karate expert paused. "*Somebody* does."

Jim Tatum—whom Waring says "knew more about it than he can ever tell"—had a long conversation about the Piotrowski shooting recently, as Dudley Bell approached his second year in prison. It is, his longtime friend pondered, "extremely probable" that Dudley has tapes that would incriminate Richard Minns. The lawyer stopped to analyze it. That explains, he reasoned, why Bell hasn't turned Minns in yet. "Because the only chance that he has of making a big financial score is to keep quiet," Tatum suggested, "and since there's no statute of limitations running against Minns, Dudley can always pull the cork on him."

Jim Tatum took a breath. "Well, if you were Minns," he posed, "and Dudley could put you in the joint or maybe even fly for an attempted capital murder, and Dudley had exactly what it took to put you there—you know that and he knows that—and you have some money and you're outside the United States and you can remain free as long as you're unindicted, would you up the money or not?" Tatum didn't wait for an answer. "He's either got to up the money or kill him, one of the two."

Jim Tatum was asked if he thought Richard Minns hired Bell to have Piotrowski killed. "Certainly," the lawyer answered instantly. "Who else had any reason to do anything like that? It's self-evident as far as I'm concerned."

Richard Minns's only defenders in the tenth year after Barbra Piotrowski's shooting are his family and his lawyers, plus one or two old friends who speak guardedly, if at all.

All of them say there is "no link" between Richard Minns and Barbra Piotrowski's shooting. Nearly all claim "not to have kept up with" the investigation.

"It's just been the grossest form of witch-hunt, year after year," Earle Lilly, the lawyer representing Dick in Barbra's divorce suit, offers. "To run the man out of his home, his state, his country. It's a major, major tragedy and travesty of justice as far as I'm concerned. I think the man is a totally innocent, misunderstood human being that but for the grace of God go a lot of people."

Explaining why Richard Minns has left the country and gone underground is more difficult for his spokespersons. Both Lilly and Richard Minns's daughter Cathy say they don't know. "I only surmise," offers Lilly, "that Richard Minns left because he was in a state of agony and pain and couldn't handle it anymore." Cathy Minns suggests "when you go through a two-year divorce—I think he just didn't want to be bothered anymore. He wants to be left alone."

Ironically, one of Dick Minns's loudest champions has been his ex-wife Mimi. Richard left Texas, Mimi Minns Erwin says, in her distinctive raspy voice, seething with the fury of a woman scorned, "because he doesn't want to fool with all this crap. Everybody took Barbra's side in this thing. I don't understand why she's so important. She's a nonentity. What the hell does he have to spend the rest of his life messing around with that for?"

Who do Richard Minns's supporters think arranged Barbra Piotrowski's shooting, if it wasn't Dick? "She had been very wild," his daughter Cathy suggests, "and wild people get in trouble. The whole thing is so embarrassing. Here's my dad. He met this girl and she swept him off his feet, and then he and my mom divorced. And then perhaps he wouldn't marry her right away or whatever. She walked out on him. And he was upset, he went on with his life, and eight months later she was involved with something and got shot."

The story Dick Minns is circulating through his old friend and lawyer Joe Reynolds, through Mimi, through Earle Lilly, and in his own letter to the grand jury, is that Barbra "arranged" their meeting in Aspen and set him up as a mark, then she was shot by unsavory characters from her past.

"I believe," says Earle Lilly, "that she was a very volatile, histrionic lady that had a past that borders on golddigging. There's a *lot* of people that might have had some motive to shoot her, such as the doctor in California, one of her former lovers." Barbra Piotrowski was, in Dick's lawyer's pronouncement, "a lady in the streets."

The idea that Barbra is still afraid for her life, Cathy Minns claims, is "ridiculous. We feel fear from *her*," Dick's daughter says. "It's just been a plague on all of us. I mean, what is *she* afraid of?"

"The greatest book I ever read in college was *Les Misérables*," Earle Lilly said one afternoon, when he was feeling "philosophical," sitting in the reception area of his expensively furnished law offices in downtown Houston. "All of Jean Valjean's life he was hounded and harassed and trailed and followed—and everybody knew that he was innocent." The lawyer stopped to clear his throat—he gets, he explained, very emotional when he talks about the Minns case—". . . and there's such a similarity in Richard Minns. That's what the folks in Houston have done to Jean Valjean Minns."

Then why, a visitor wondered, doesn't Richard Minns defend himself? Speak out against his accusers?

Earle Lilly's voice dropped to a velvety near-whisper. "You can't talk to Richard," he said soothingly. "Only because of fear of misconstruction, misunderstanding, and that sort of thing." Richard Minns's manner of speaking, his lawyer suggested, "would lead some people to think he's hiding something."

Houston private investigator Bobby Newman believes, beyond a shadow of a doubt, that Richard Minns is guilty. After the shooting, a few of Dudley Bell's oldest friends—friends who grew up in Bobby Newman and Dudley Bell's neighborhood, who went to junior high and high school with Bell and Newman—confided in Newman. Dudley, they said, told them before Barbra Piotrowski was shot that Richard Minns was paying him sixty thousand dollars to have Barbra Piotrowski killed. He showed them the cash, Bell and Newman's mutual friends told Newman. Counted it in front of them.

"I know," says Bobby Newman, "—and I believe this as much as I believe anything in the world—Dudley had at one time sixty thousand dollars in cash that he claimed that's what it was for. I know Dudley, and I know the relationship between Minns and Dudley, and I know what Dudley said, and I *know* that Dudley was being paid by Richard Minns to do it."

Dudley's friends, Newman observes, would never come forward. It would be too risky, and they have too many loyalties to Dudley.

That was the problem all the way around, Kenny Williamson lamented, when he fantasized about making the final arrest on the Piotrowski case. The fear factor.

Would anybody ever dare come forward? That was the concern that kept Kenny Williamson digging on the case, long after most detectives would have given up.

Out of the courtroom, safe in his house deep in the Texas piney woods, Rick Waring had more to say about the Piotrowski shooting. Things he knew working for Dudley Bell, from bodyguarding Richard Minns. Things he would never say in court. "The way they wanted to kill the girl," he confided, "was the weirdest thing that I ever heard of in my life. Take a person out on a boat and chop 'em into pieces and throw 'em to the fish."

He remembered "all that stuff," Waring told a visitor, when all but Richard Minns were in prison. But he couldn't tell. It would get him killed.

Rick Waring's voice took on a peculiar edge. "I'll tell you one thing about Richard Minns, from my close association. If, for instance, he became irritated with me, I would probably have to kill the first two or three people that came after me to get him to stop."

The karate expert paused for a beat. "He *is* gonna come back one of these days," he said under his breath. "And I don't know what he's gonna do."

EPILOGUE

That was the fear Barbra Piotrowski had been facing every day of her life—that Richard would return, or send someone in his place—since sometime on October 21, 1980, when she realized she was going to survive the four gunshots to her back.

There had been strange occurrences—peculiar, unsettling events suggesting the specter of Richard Minns—even as she lay at the hospital, near death. Hang-ups and bizarre messages on the phone in her hospital room. Weird letters. Threats. When she transferred to a rehabilitation hospital under yet another name, Marvin Zindler appeared one day—by coincidence, he would say—to do an exposé on the hospital. Barbra was so shaken she hid in a back room, quivering.

In a way, her attempted assassins did murder Barbra Piotrowski in the parking lot of the Winchell's Doughnut Shop that Monday afternoon in October 1980. For on that day, Barbra Piotrowski—by that name, at least—ceased to exist. The day she was released from the hospital, Barbra took the name Jennifer Smith—the last alias the hospital staff chose for her—as her own. The new identity never seemed foreign to her. Barbra *felt* like a different person after the shooting—a new person with a new life. The name *Barbra Piotrowski* and all its associations sent a shiver down her spine.

But Barbra had too many other things going on in her life to allow her fear of Dick to overshadow them. The moment she felt one of Nathaniel Ivery's bullets rip through her back and sever her spinal cord, she promised herself she would make her life more meaningful, and she determined that she was going to walk again. Those were the first words

351

she spoke to her father in the intensive care unit, and they were the first thoughts that ran through her brain when she recognized that she was going to survive. In typical Barbra fashion, she set a goal for herself: five years. As she lay in her bed at Hermann Hospital, numb from the chest down, she visualized herself up and walking in the Honolulu Marathon—the race she was training for when she was shot—by 1985. True to her nature, it became an obsession. It was never a question of *if*, she would say, it was a matter of *how*.

The doctors at Hermann grew concerned about her. She was never going to walk again, they advised her. It was impossible. They assigned a psychiatrist to evaluate her. The psychiatric report stated that she had "unrealistic expectations" she would walk. A friend, one of the doctors at Hermann, visited her in her room one day. "Everybody thinks you're crazy," he said kindly. "They're thinking of transferring you to the psychiatric floor because your goals are so unrealistic. You don't know how this sounds to other people. You want to do things that are impossible. You're heading for a crash."

Barbra stared at him. "Why?"

"Because what's gonna happen when you try to do this and you fail?"

Barbra looked at him intently. "Which time? The first? Or the five hundred thousandth?"

Her doctors didn't know Barbra Piotrowski; the girl who didn't know when to give up. *Impossible* was a word she neither understood nor accepted. How could anyone say something was impossible? she would plead. *How do they know?*

While she was in the hospital, Barbra explored the current research in the field of paralysis. Late at night, when no one was around, she would experiment with electrical stimulation. The concept seemed so logical to her: If the reason you're not able to move is because the electrical signal is not getting from your brain to your legs, then why not give that same signal from some outside source? Why not stimulate the muscles directly? Her secret experiments left her with burns and contractures. It was too complex, her doctor friends cautioned her. Electrical stimulation would never be a reality. But Barbra refused to give up hope, in spite of her doctors' continual warnings that in order to go on with the things you have to do, you must first give up hope, otherwise you'll be waiting for the miracle to happen. Barbra wasn't just waiting; she *knew* a miracle was coming, although she knew she'd have to work to make it happen. She could feel it. Other times, she would lie in her hospital room at night, looking out the window at the lights of the city, and wonder if she'd ever live in the world again, or if she was going to be institutionalized forever.

One day, late in the day, after physical therapy, as she was lying in bed, Christopher Cross's song "Sailing" came on the radio. As she lay in bed, exhausted, her fingers suddenly started doing a dance! The dance appeared in her mind and her fingers carried it through. It was so visual, so vivid, she could feel it in her legs. When the song was over, she remembered every step and wrote down the choreography in dance terminology. Later, she asked a friend to do the dance in front of her. She had not missed a single movement.

Barbra was shaken by the experience. Before she was paralyzed, she had always struggled with dance choreography. This had just happened. She was never one to read her horoscope and had no opinion about the supernatural, but, she would tell people, this was not hers. It happened through her. And it continued to happen. It was, she decided, magic.

The night she was released from the rehabilitation hospital in Houston, Barbra was at one of the lowest points in her life. She had no money, no job, and no concept of how to live in the "real world" as a paralyzed person. All she knew is that she wanted to be independent, not to be a burden on her parents anymore. She spent her first night out of the hospital at a Battered Women's Center in a rundown section of Houston and cried until morning. The next day, she went to a friend's apartment.

She called her girlfriend in Las Vegas, boarded a plane, and started an aerobics dance business with the routines she'd been choreographing from her hospital bed—the same business she was planning the day she was shot.

After a year, Barbra Piotrowski—now known as Jennifer Smith—returned to Houston with enough money to buy a condominium in the same complex she was planning to move into when she and Dick broke up. While he was living in parts of the world unknown, dispatching private investigators to locate her, she was working quietly in Houston as a volunteer with the Southwest Wheelchair Association, trying to fill the void in her life with meaningful work.

When one of the wheelchair races her organization was sponsoring needed another contestant, Jennifer Smith filled in. Within a year, she was winning races across the country. Her goal, just as it had been in childhood, when Wes Piotrowski preached the gospel of excellence to her, was to be the best in the world. Jennifer Smith gloried in the competition. By her second year in racing, she was on the front page of *The New York Times* and the cover of *USA Today* with endorsements from the major sports equipment companies. She embraced the publicity. She wanted everyone to know that nothing could stop her.

No matter how many titles or races she won, Jennifer Smith still had a hole in her heart. The night after she raced in the Boston Marathon—the first year wheelchair competitors were officially recognized in the race—she sat in her hotel room, alone, and lonely, with no one to share her victory. Even the losers, she thought poignantly, had somebody. She doubted she would ever be able to love again. The pain was still too great, the loss too enormous.

At other times she was reminded of the danger that still lurked. One night, when she arrived at her River Oaks townhouse, alone, she had an intuition that something was wrong. Horribly wrong. She found a neighbor and returned to the condominium. All the doors and windows were open and a huge, billowing wind swept through the townhouse. Inside, her furniture was rearranged, all the clothes in her closet had been dumped on the floor and her towels were in the middle of the living room. On the walls, the name MINNS had been written in blood. Between the living room and the bedroom, her bottles of nail polish were neatly lined up on the threshold; in the middle was a matchbook with Richard Minns's name scribbled on the back cover. Another wall contained the word PIG.

Jennifer Smith was terrified. For weeks afterward, she slept on the floor in her closet, or under the bed, so a sniper wouldn't be able to shoot her. She refused to take a shower for days, because there was a window in the bathroom. She called on every friend she knew to stay with her at night, so she wouldn't have to be alone.

One day in 1982, she came across an article in a medical journal about a neurophysiologist named Jerrold Petrofsky, who was experimenting with electrical stimulation for people with paralysis at Wright State University in Dayton, Ohio. A few months later, she saw Dr. Petrofsky on *60 Minutes*, demonstrating his technique with a paralyzed research subject who was walking through the use of electrodes attached to her legs and controlled by a computer.

Two months later, she flew to Las Vegas to attend a seminar Jerrold Petrofsky was conducting about his research. She had been calling Wright State every day for weeks, months, trying to get into the program, but there was no space. Jennifer Smith took a seat in the front row of the auditorium. When Dr. Petrofsky opened the floor to questions, she raced up to the stage in her wheelchair and announced, in front of the audience of five hundred, that she was going to work for him without pay. For two years, she had been searching the world for the person who could help her—talking to doctors who prescribed everything from hanging upside down from a tire, to subjecting herself to daily "rubbing," to walking on her hands. She was not going to let this opportunity pass her by.

Early in 1983, she moved to Dayton, Ohio, and began sweeping floors, cleaning electrodes, and sorting slides in Dr. Petrofsky's research lab. At night, when everyone else had gone home, she used the equipment and fantasized about the day she would walk. In 1984, she was selected to carry the torch in the Summer Olympics in Los Angeles, in recognition for her accomplishments as a disabled athlete. By the fall, she was back in Dr. Petrofsky's lab, enrolled in his program. Within days, she was suggesting new designs and proposing changes in his walking system.

The beginning of 1985, Jennifer Smith took her first steps, using Dr. Petrofsky's computerized walking system. It was ten months ahead of her five-year goal. Later in the year, *60 Minutes* returned to Dayton to film another segment on Dr. Petrofsky. At the end of the segment, Jennifer Smith can be seen in the arms of Dr. Petrofsky, dancing radiantly in a flowing gown in her favorite color, white. The close of the year, Jerrold Petrofsky and Jennifer Smith and her family flew to Honolulu together. On December 12, 1985, as cameras for *PM Magazine* and photographers from *People* recorded the event for history, Jennifer Smith walked 6.8 miles in the Honolulu Marathon using Dr. Petrofsky's walking system—the goal she had set for herself in her hospital bed in Hermann five years earlier. The dream everyone told her would never come true.

The only dark cloud on Jennifer Smith's horizon occurred in 1987, when she flew to Houston, as Barbra Piotrowski again, to testify against Dudley Bell. Seeing the man who arranged her near-murder face to face, hearing the details of what was to be her execution, discovering the indifference of the legal system, plummeted her into a depression, followed by a nervous breakdown.

To this day, she has memory lapses. She cannot be alone, in a room or in a car, because she is afraid someone will appear and shoot her.

But her dreams live on. The little girl who dreamed she would grow up, marry a scientist and they would do research together is partners with Dr. Jerrold Petrofsky and conducting research and experiments with him to rebuild paralyzed muscles and make walking a reality for other people who are paralyzed. In her philosophical moments, she reflects on the irony of her life, how everything that happened to her is part of her destiny.

In 1988, Jennifer Smith (now using the name Janni Smith, another security precaution) and Dr. Jerrold Petrofsky opened a rehabilitation research center for people with paralysis in Irvine, California, with Janni Smith as its president. A second clinic opened in Pennsylvania in 1990, another is scheduled to be constructed in New Zealand, and several more are planned, one in Italy and perhaps one in Houston. The clinics, Janni Smith notes with irony, are a paralyzed person's version of a President's-First Lady health club.

In March 1990, Janni Smith was named one of the Ten Outstanding Young Americans by the United States Jaycees, in a televised ceremony in Oklahoma City. In November 1990 she was presented an award as Outstanding Young Person of the World in Medicine by the International Jaycees at a banquet in Puerto Rico. Her dream now is to build a huge rehabilitation ranch for paralyzed children, far out in the country, with animals of all descriptions.

Richard Minns's most recent residence is a Marriott Hotel in London, where he comes and goes with his live-in girlfriend. At Christmas of 1988, she gave birth to Richard Minns's third son. Although his doctor claims he is confined to bed with post-concussion syndrome, two police officers from Houston have seen him every summer since 1984 at Lakeway in Austin, behind the wheel of his boat, the *SPA II*, pulling skiers on marathon water-skiing sessions, for hours on end. His friend Bob Delmonteque says he has ballooned up to two hundred pounds, and that he lives in a constant state of paranoia that he will be arrested any day. He thinks and talks about Barbra Piotrowski, insiders report, all the time.

POSTSCRIPT

In February 1991, Judge Bill Elliott and a jury of twelve Houstonians heard Richard Minns's appeal of Barbra Piotrowski's $28.6 million default judgment against him. As in the previous eight years, Richard Minns was not present. The man who doctors swore was too ill to leave his bedroom was now claiming, through his son, lawyer, and once avowed enemy Mike Minns, that he had joined the Israeli army two weeks earlier.

Mike Minns immediately ripped into Janni. "She destroyed him," he snarled, pointing at her in the courtroom. His "daddy," Mike told the jury, was "destitute." Richard Minns's only income, Mike swore, was from drawing cartoons for European newspapers and magazines. "He has no money," Mike said pitiably. "He can get a pension from Israel, and that's primarily what he lives on. I wouldn't be his lawyer if he had ten thousand dollars."

What Mike Minns did *not* tell the jury was that, two months earlier, Richard Minns had spent nearly that sum of money to retain the services of Houston private investigator Bobby Newman, for the fourth time in ten years, to do yet another "check" on Barbra Piotrowski in preparation for the trial. Richard Minns's call to Newman was placed from Switzerland, where, he told the detective, he owns a house on the lake in Lausanne.

Throughout the four-day trial, Mike Minns continued to attack Janni. Her injuries, he scoffed, were "minor" and "exaggerated." Whatever spinal-cord damage she "may" have could have been caused by "breast implants" or "venereal disease." She was, and is, he had witnesses tell the judge, a drug user, with "numerous and frequent sexual partners." "Look under every rock," he warned. She was "pulling a scam" to extort money from his daddy and the government. Dr. Petrofsky, Mike Minns told the judge, is a "phony" and a "liar," whose medical work is a "hoax." Janni Smith sat in the courtroom in horrified silence: It was, she winced, like listening to Richard all over again.

When the verdict was announced on February 28, 1991, Janni Smith cried tears of joy: The jury ordered Richard Minns to pay her $6 million in past damages, $12 million in future damages, and $14 million in punitive damages for causing her injuries on October 20, 1980, plus interest—a total of nearly $60 million—one of the largest judgments in U.S. history. Mike Minns immediately called a press conference. The judge, the trial, and the jury, he fumed, were "un-American." Richard Minns, as usual, got on the phone from an office in Geneva. "I'm so bitter," he ranted to a reporter from the *Houston Post*. "I'm so goddamn bitter."

Janni Smith ignored him. For the first time in ten long years—since she first voiced her fears about Richard Minns to the Houston police—she felt vindicated. Finally, she rejoiced, the world believed her.

If you would like to help Janni Smith fulfill her dream and bring the benefits of her work with Dr. Jerrold Petrofsky to paralyzed children, or if you are interested in their miraculous research, please write or call:

The Petrofsky Center for Rehabilitation and Research
(Children's Fund)
13765 Alton Parkway, Suite E
Irvine, CA 92718
(714) 855–4837

AUTHOR'S NOTE

As of this writing, nearly a year and a half after her stunning judgement against Richard Minns, Janni Smith has not collected a penny. Richard Minns long ago liquidated or secreted his U.S. assets.

While his attorney/son Mike was telling a Houston judge and jury his father was in the Israeli army, penniless, Richard Minns was in fact luxuriously ensconced in a $600,000 condominium called Shangri-La on Paradise Island in the Bahamas, using the nom de guerre Richard O'Toole and calling himself an international tax lawyer. His business stationery featured a "family crest" of the O'Tooles—he was a cousin, he told Bahamians who hired him as a legal consultant, of the actor Peter O'Toole. Mike Minns—calling himself Mike O'Toole—visited his father several times in the Bahamas, where Richard Minns introduced him as an "internationally famous lawyer and bestselling author."

During his two-year interlude in the Bahamas, Minns/O'Toole lived with Elizabeth Gables, the thirtyish blonde Houstonian who bore his fifth child on Christmas in 1988. He referred to her as his wife, although she would leave the island for periods of time, during which Richard had, according to the islanders, numerous affairs. Contrary to his sworn statements, his son Mike's courtroom pronouncements and the affidavits of his physicians that he is bedridden, Richard Minns is in fabulous physical condition. His daily routine in the Bahamas consisted of heated tennis matches at the Ocean Club, marathon waterskiing sessions, and several hour work-outs at the Crystal Palace gym with a personal trainer named Dale. He has been involved in several altercations with residents, including an American,

360

John Sitomer, who claims Minns/O'Toole defrauded him on a real estate transaction, then attempted to have him thrown in a Bahamian prison on a bogus charge, and finally tried to run over him with his car. More recently, Sitomer says, he has learned of several plots initiated by Minns in the Bahamas to burn down Sitomer's businesses, remove him from the country, and/or have him killed. "He would do anything he could get somebody to do for him," Sitomer says bitterly.

In his final months on Paradise Island, Minns romanced a young Bahamian masseuse. He was unhappily married, he told the girl, loved no one but her, planned to get a divorce and make her his wife. When Janni Smith heard the story, she shuddered. It was, she observed eerily, déjà vu.

In July of 1991, this author appeared on the "Larry King Show." During the broadcast, Minns's residence in the Bahamas was discussed. The next day, Richard Minns fled the island for his private apartment at the Grosvenor House Hotel in London. Since then, he has been on the run, living, presumably, in different countries under different aliases.

His last words to his Bahamian girlfriend are, Janni Smith hopes, prophetic. "If they put me in prison," he entreated, "will you come visit me?"

On October 1, 1991, Dudley Bell was released from prison after serving only four years for solicitation of capital murder. Although required by law to receive notice of his pending release by the parole board, Judge Mary Bacon, who presided over Bell's trial, got no notification. "Now I have one more reason to look over my shoulder when I go home at night," she says ruefully.

Within several months of his release, Bell attended the wake of the wife of an old Houston chum. He drove up, his friends noticed, in a new luxury car, bragging about a $3 million "inheritance" his niece received and "gave" to him. "We all know that's bullshit," his childhood friend and fellow P.I. Bobby Newman says with disgust. Bob Delmonteque agrees. Shortly after Bell was released from prison, Delmonteque says, the detective phoned him wanting to know where Delmonteque's "old buddy" Richard Minns was. "I told you he'd go straight to Dick for his money as soon as he got out," Delmonteque cackled. "That money didn't come from any inheritance!"

As for Janni Smith, she has fulfilled her childhood dream. On November 30, 1991, in a small ceremony on a cliff overlooking the Pacific Ocean in Laguna Niguel, California, the once-little girl who fantasized that she would marry a scientist and they would perform research together that would change the world walked down the aisle to wed Dr. Jerrold Petrofsky, the man who invented her computerized walking system.

At the close of the ceremony, as live white doves were released into the California sky, she presented her father with a single white rose. Wes Piotrowski's sad Polish eyes welled with tears. His little girl, his first-born, his favorite, whom he had christened with the Polish name Jannike Petrofska thirty-nine years earlier was now, by this twist of fate, Jannike Petrofsky once more.

She had, at last, come full circle.

Suzanne Finstad
July 1992